THE WAY ACCORDING TO LUKE

THE WAY ACCORDING TO LUKE

Hearing the Whole Story of Luke-Acts

Paul Borgman

WILLIAM B. EERDMANS PUBLISHING COMPANY
GRAND RAPIDS, MICHIGAN / CAMBRIDGE, U.K.

Wm. B. Eerdmans Publishing Co.

255 Jefferson Ave. S.E., Grand Rapids, Michigan 49503 /
P.O. Box 163, Cambridge CB3 9PU U.K.

Printed in the United States of America

11 10 09 08 07 06   7 6 5 4 3 2 1

Library of Congress Cataloging-in-Publication Data

Borgman, Paul Carlton, 1940-
The way according to Luke: hearing the whole story of Luke-Acts /
Paul Borgman.
p.   cm.
ISBN-10: 0-8028-2936-8 / ISBN-13: 978-0-8028-2936-8 (pbk.: alk. paper)
1. Bible. N.T. Luke — Criticism, interpretation, etc.
2. Bible. N.T. Acts — Criticism, interpretation, etc.
I. Title.

BS2589.B67   2006

226.4'06 — dc22

2005033760

www.eerdmans.com

Contents

CONTENTS

Contents

Preface

Luke-Acts is among the greatest of ancient literary works. Though Luke's gospel and Acts are generally recognized as accomplished narratives by religious and nonreligious readers alike, much of their genius goes unappreciated — with meaning obscured — for two basic reasons: we read the two volumes separately, and we read silently something meant to be heard. Luke's two-volume story has roots in an oral storytelling world. In this study, I will explain major repetitive techniques of this masterpiece in order to reveal its narrative power and meaning. This is a reader's guide, not only for fellow scholars but for their students as well, and for any layperson serious about the literature of the Bible. Volumes about Luke's gospel and about Acts abound: what is distinctive about my literary analysis can be found by way of brief observations concerning the book's title, *The Way according to Luke: Hearing the Whole Story of Luke-Acts.*

1. *The Whole Story of **Luke-Acts**:* Only rarely, in early canonical lists, do we find the single story of Luke-Acts placed together (in an Eastern list: John, Matthew, Mark, and Luke-Acts). Clearly a unified literary whole, Luke-Acts became separated because of how well Acts seemed to function, in the finally agreed upon "New Testament," as a bridge between Matthew-Mark-Luke-John and the epistles. The canonical expediency of separating Acts from Luke's gospel has led to glaring misunderstandings about each, while robbing Luke-Acts of its unified and compelling vision.

2. *The Whole **Story**:* The historical and theological goals of Luke are embedded in a story. This narrative is quite unlike modern history or the-

ology. In order to get at the text's meaning, I use literary tools of exploration appropriate to what Luke has produced: a work of literary genius.

3. *The **Whole** Story:* I will uncover the dominant literary features governing the story's plot, character, and action. These features yield Luke's "Big Picture," in the light of which all textual details find their meaning.

4. ***Hearing*** *the Whole Story:* We can approximate the experience of a pre-literate audience by paying close attention to the story's sophisticated system of echoes. Whether it was originally read or heard, Luke's story reveals its roots in the techniques of oral storytelling. "Hearing-clues" are arranged in major patterns that take us through the narrative. By focusing on these systems of echoes — common in all ancient literature — my readers will engage, as did original listeners, in a constant circling-backward even while reading forward. I provide modern readers with the special "tuning" that would have been a common facility for a listening audience. Especially for the major and central section of Luke's gospel and for the speech-clusters of Acts, "hearing-charts" will be provided.

5. *The **Way** according to Luke:* The whole story, in a nutshell, is an unfolding of *God's Way,* a quite unnatural and counterintuitive way of living taught and demonstrated, in the gospel, by Jesus. Precisely this Way, in Acts, is taught and demonstrated by redeemed Israel, in the name of Jesus. "The Way of God" (Luke 20:21) represents a distillation and reinterpretation of Scripture (the Hebrew Bible) and is synonymous with *the Way of salvation, the kingdom of God,* and *the Way of peace.* To enter the kingdom — to participate in salvation — one needs to understand the Way and do it. Such careful listening and arduous doing are impossible without (1) the grace of an empowering Spirit sent by the risen Jesus and (2) God's forgiveness. The latter depends on a God whose mercy it is always to forgive those who repent — who turn from natural, intuitive, but wrong ways toward God's Way.

6. *The Way **according** to Luke:* Whoever "Luke" was — scholars are not sure — the writer takes pains in his opening remarks to suggest that, in the light of other existing versions of the Jesus-story (Mark's, Matthew's, Paul's, and perhaps John's), he feels obliged to offer his own account. He it is, we hear, who offers "authentic knowledge" (Luke 1:4). According to Luke, God's ultimate purpose for this earth is crystallized in events surrounding Jesus, most especially the redemption of Israel dramatized in Acts. According to Luke, the divine purposes will be fulfilled in a "universal restoration," a global *shalom* whose ancient roots are to be found in God's ancient promise to Abraham of blessing for all families (Acts 3:21, 25).

The two-volume story written by Luke and rehearsed by an expert storyteller/reader would have been heard (or read) by its original audience as a whole and unified drama. I hope to replicate this experience by focusing on the dominant patterns of repetition that inform the story's theme, character, and action, thus honoring the ultimate goal of Luke himself as expressed in the opening words of his two-volume masterpiece:

Many writers have undertaken to draw up an account of the events that have happened among us, following the traditions handed down to us by the original eyewitnesses and servants of the Gospel. And so I in my turn, . . . as one who has gone over the whole course of these events in detail, have decided to write a connected narrative for you, so as to give you authentic knowledge about the matters of which you have been informed. (Luke 1:1-4, New English Bible)

Acknowledgments

For the attentive reading of my students over more than two decades I am very thankful: their insights and even their critique of my writing have been invaluable.

For the careful thought given to my book-in-progress by fellow scholars I am deeply grateful: the results of conversation-like dialogue with Joel B. Green, David Moessner, Charles Talbert, and Robert Tannehill were both clarifying and encouraging.

For reader-editor Sara Sullivan, special thanks, and most especially for Meghan Good, whose scrutiny through multiple drafts was unflagging and always on target.

For the helpful collegiality and always cogent comments of Ted Hildebrandt, Steven Hunt, Elaine Phillips, and especially Harold Heie, thank you, my friends.

What We Miss in Luke's
Two-Part Story, and Why

Up through the first century of the common era, we can find no greater literary work than Luke-Acts. In terms of action adventure, the Homeric epics and Virgil's *Aeneid* excel. But in all of ancient western literature, the overall literary genius of Luke's two-part story covering the events surrounding Jesus and Israel is rivaled only by two of its literary ancestors, the biblical narrative of Genesis and that of David in 1 and 2 Samuel. Our exploration will prove the point, but more importantly will bring to light meaning that is embedded in the drama and easily glossed over or even misunderstood and misappropriated.

We miss the drama and meaning of this story told by Luke in large measure because we read it. Luke's original audience[1] was mostly preliterate though highly skilled in listening. The text was written not so much for the private reader as for the public auditor — a text more like a dramatic script than anything resembling a modern narrative in print (more on this, in a moment).

Luke's drama centers on the status and role of both Jesus and Israel, with Jesus center-stage in volume one and Israel center-stage in volume two. The stakes of this drama are high, extending backward in time to the

---

1. I use "Luke" to designate the traditionally ascribed author of both *Luke* and *The Acts of the Apostles*. When I say anything like "according to the author" or "Luke's original audience," I am referring only to the empirical evidence of the text of Luke, not to any intuited and unprovable insight into the author's intention and the specific people for whom he wrote. About such issues as authorship and "actual" audience there is much scholarly debate.

world's creation and Adam, "son of God," while looking forward into the immediate future for "the universal restoration of all things."[2]

Brilliance within Luke's two-part narrative has been recognized: striking parables (the good Samaritan, the prodigal son); compelling real-life vignettes (Jesus calling Zacchaeus down from a tree in order to stay at the "sinner's" home); and highly unconventional forays of Rabbi Jesus (an against-the-religious-rules visit to the home of two women for the purposes of teaching Torah). Those readers who go back, and back, begin picking up on further narrative sophistications: the dramatically paralleled descents of God's Spirit on Jesus early in the gospel and then again on Jewish believers early in Acts; the choreographed teachings of Jesus in the gospel's middle section; the interestingly paralleled experiences and speeches (seven each!) of Peter and Paul in Acts — and the parallel between Jesus and Israelites in volume two, especially Stephen, Peter, and Paul. But for many readers, Luke and/or Acts (they must be understood in light of each other — or not understood at all) do not add up to a coherent and compelling narrative.

Luke-Acts is religiously important for some, yes, though the meaning remains hidden for the most part because the drama is not grasped. Luke embedded his meaning in the drama. And the drama was meant for ears. This study intends to capitalize, always, on ear-clues, on the techniques of repetition and interlocking patterns that force the audience to be circling backward (by way of echoes) even while moving forward.

I offer a single-volume guide that approaches Luke's two-part story on its own terms, as a narrative whose meaning comes from an extraordinary web of interconnections among brilliant musical-like strands: sayings, parables, extended poetic teaching, event. All of Luke's narrative parts lead to and flow out of a centering vision — a sense of the world and God's dealing with it that is implicit in all aspects of the story. For secular and religious readers alike, the narrative will come alive as the superior drama that it is. For the religiously inclined, I repeat an observation already made: Luke's "theology" as intended for his audience is nothing less, and can be nothing more, than the web of meanings embedded within his narrative. As would seem obvious, narrative meaning is impossible to grasp without narrative analysis, which I will provide. Our task is at once elementary, arduous — and exhilarating.

Why did Luke write yet another version of Jesus and the events surrounding him? The author himself claims that, having examined care-

---

2. Lk 3:38; Acts 3:21. Throughout, the New Revised Standard Version is used unless otherwise indicated.

fully the interpretations of other writers like Mark, Matthew, and Paul,[3] he has deemed it necessary to write his own version of the story. And here is the reason: "So that you may know the truth" — can be utterly sure — "concerning the things about which you have been instructed."[4]

Concerning what *things*, exactly? The bulk of the instruction that Luke recounts from the lips of Jesus occurs in the carefully orchestrated middle section of the gospel (9:51–19:44). At the beginning of a momentous journey to Jerusalem we hear an essential message of peace;[5] the journey comes full circle with Jesus breaking into tears: "If you, even you," Jesus sobs, "had only recognized on this day *the things that make for peace!*"[6]

God is quoted directly only twice, once to some disciples: "Listen to Jesus!" is the divine directive.[7] Only in such true listening — hearing and obeying the word from God as taught by Jesus — is there to be any salvation, any kingdom experience of peace. Proper listening characterizes all believers in Acts, those "who belonged to the Way" — the "Way of salvation."[8] What followers of Jesus in Acts believe and rehearse as the word of God taught by Jesus is not a random or even organized list of rules, but

---

3. So important is Paul's thinking in what Luke wants to distinguish as his own carefully considered perspective that he places himself, rather awkwardly, within the story as a traveling companion to Paul. Luke is willing to commit a literary indiscretion in order to insist on his familiarity — first-hand — with Paul's interpretations of salvation. Late in Acts, Luke switches in certain "we" passages from a somewhat distant third-person point of view ("Martha was distracted by her many tasks" [Lk 10:40]) to a more intimate point of view emphasizing that Luke is right there, with Paul, who, he tells us, for example, "met us in Assos [and] we took him on board" (Acts 20:14). There are thirty-seven "we" or "us" passages in Acts, beginning with 20:6, 7, and 8. *I know Paul's thinking first-hand,* Luke is telling us. Whether an early or late date for Luke's gospel and Acts, virtually all scholars agree that Luke wrote some years after the major epistles by Paul and the gospels of Mark and Matthew (or a source common to both Matthew and Luke). Most scholarship is agreed on placing the date of Luke's writing somewhere in the 90s (with Paul in the late 40s & early 50s; Mark a bit earlier). John Wenham argues for a much earlier date for Luke's two volumes (62 C.E. for Acts; Luke's gospel, early 50s), though agreeing that Luke followed Matthew (early 40s); Mark (mid-40s); and Paul (mid- to late 40s; early 50s), in *Redating Matthew, Mark & Luke: A Fresh Assault on the Synoptic Problem* (London: Hodder & Stoughton, 1991). For the relationship between Luke's gospel and John's gospel (with Luke following John), see Mark A. Matson, *In Dialogue with Another Gospel? The Influence of the Fourth Gospel on the Passion Narrative of the Gospel of Luke* (Atlanta: Society of Biblical Literature, 2001).

4. Lk 1:4.

5. Lk 10:3-6; we will find nine or ten principles of peace (not rules) on this journey, each repeated once in ring-like reversals — a *chiasm*.

6. 19:42.

7. Lk 9:35.

8. Acts 9:2; 18:25, 26; 19:9, 23; 24:14, 22 ("Way of salvation," Acts 16:17).

rather an organically interwoven set of principles that unfold dramatically, suggesting not so much a religious club run by certain beliefs and rules but a journey suggesting a "Way."

In Acts, Luke shows Peter recounting the one significant word from Moses regarding Messiah: He whom God will raise up, *listen to whatever he tells you!*[9] And Luke demands that his audience listen carefully, that it may be utterly certain about the Way of salvation and blessing at the heart of God's desire for the entire world. The challenges of listening well are presented by the text as quite formidable. But the modern reader has special problems that prevent even the most elementary getting-to-hear. I suggest a few reasons:

I. We readers miss meaning because we *read* the text: "The normal method of reading [gospels and other ancient literature] was reading aloud," as Birger Gerhardsson points out; the audience had finely tuned skills of listening and memory.[10] In such an oral culture, as Walter J. Ong observes, "thought come[s] into being in heavily rhythmic, balanced patterns, in repetitions or antitheses. . . . Serious thought is intertwined with memory systems"[11] — in patterns of what I call hearing clues.

II. We read piece-meal: Ancient literatures like Luke's narrative were usually heard in their entirety, in one sitting. Furthermore, they "were not intended to be read and heard with half one's mind or to be skimmed through, but were to be read and listened to, time and time again, with attention and reflection."[12] For the religiously oriented reader, close attention to the text yields the additional value of clarity about this particular scripture and its unique revelatory power within a canon that features distinct though complementary views.

---

9. Acts 3:22.

10. Birger Gerhardsson, *Memory and Manuscript: Oral Tradition and Written Transmission in Rabbinic Judaism and Early Christianity,* trans. Eric J. Sharpe (Lund: Gleerup, & Copenhagen: Ejnar Munksgaard, 1961), pp. 163-64. This reading aloud was animated and highly inflected, as Gerhardsson points out — a one-person story performance complete with dramatic pause and appropriate gesticulation.

11. Walter J. Ong, quoting Havelock (1963), in *Orality and Literacy* (New York: Methuen, 1988), p. 34. We haven't quite understood, as Ong points out: "Verbal memory skill is understandably a valued asset in oral cultures. But the way verbal memory works in oral art forms is quite different from what literates in the past commonly imagined. In a literate culture, verbatim memorization is commonly done from a text, to which the memorizer returns as often as necessary to perfect and test verbatim mastery" (p. 57).

12. Gerhardsson, *Memory and Manuscript*, p. 64.

III. We are strongly predisposed: Whether religious or non-religious, our accumulated perceptions or vague impressions get unwittingly projected into Luke's particular story.

IV. The text often appears choppy: Even with our predispositions kept in view — and as much as possible, in tow — Luke's storytelling technique can appear rough, as if one sequence bumps into the next one with no discernible transition: for example, "Just then a lawyer stood up to test Jesus" (and a tale about a good Samaritan) followed by "Now as they went on their way" (toward the home of two sisters).[13] We miss the connection between the lawyer and Martha, and between the Samaritan and Mary. Narrative time-markers work more as thematic connectors than chronological indicators. We easily get the impression, reinforced in traditional biblical commentaries, of text-chunks placed together without much narrative rhyme or reason.

V. Scholarly and liturgical practices typically reinforce this sense of a bits-and-pieces narrative: a bit of text for the homily this week with another piece the next. Here a chunk for exegesis in a typical commentary, and here another. Failure to be consistent in tracing interconnections and discovering context results in loss of story meaning and leads to an arbitrary and subjective wrenching of the text for our own purposes — however innocent and well intended.

We embark on our exploration of this text by entering the realm of story, not sermon — of narrative art, not theological treatise. We must give ourselves to the dictates of narrative. That is, our exploration must be dictated by how the text presents itself, as narrative.

By now it is commonly accepted among scholars that Luke "chose to write history because this was the most serviceable vehicle for the expression of his theology, and his theology must be gathered from the overall way he handled his history."[14] But as Stephen Moore nicely points out, a narrative such as Luke's two-part story did not begin with a theological system to be worked out in story terms, though the selection and organization of material are clearly guided by a narrative vision of God's char-

13. Lk 10:25; 10:38; increasingly, as we will see, commentaries on Luke's gospel and Acts display a particular literary sensibility, a capacity to capture and articulate the connections among pericopes.

14. Eric Franklin, *Christ the Lord: A Study in the Purpose and Theology of Luke-Acts* (Philadelphia: Westminster, 1975), pp. 3-4.

acter and the role of Jesus in the ongoing interplay between divine and human.[15] Most ancient history was written not to present a system of thought but to be "truly profitable to the reader,"[16] and Luke's text is no different except that his intended profit — "instruction" he calls it[17] — is of a religious nature.

Unlike most commentaries and studies, though with their help,[18] I provide a close reading of this two-part story on its own narrative terms, with careful attention to its patterns of hearing clues. I proceed, hope-fully, with the kind of "rigor that narrative criticism [of the gospels] de-mands but has yet to realize."[19] I conclude this introduction, now, with a

15. "Redaction and composition critics, then, attempt to recover the theology of the evangelist; to do so they paradoxically recast that narrative theology in a systemic and topi-cal form alien to it. But narrative criticism, with its imported dictum of the inseparability of form and content, implies a rather different understanding. An evangelist's theology or thought — which we define minimally as a socially shared system of theocentric convic-tions as reformulated rhetorically by the evangelist — is not expressed in narrative. Narra-tive is not its vehicle of instrument; it is narrative thought through and through. The media-tion of a set of events centered on Jesus of Nazareth by emphasis of certain details and repression of others, by plotting, characterization, manipulation of point of view, deforma-tion of chronological sequence, stylistic nuance — the rendering of this enigmatic set of events as structured, coherent narrative is the evangelist's thought and that of his immedi-ate tradition. This is what it means to say that it is narrative thought." "The Place of Gospel Theology in a Story-Centered Gospel Criticism" in his *Literary Criticism and the Gospels: The Theoretical Challenge* (New Haven: Yale University Press, 1989), pp. 61-62.

16. Dionysius of Halicarnassus, *Roman Antiquities* 1.1.3; cf. Josephus, *Antiquities of the Jews* 1.3; other material in Avenarius, *Lukians Schrift*, quoted by Jacob Jervell in Ben Witherington III, ed., *History, Literature, and Society in the Book of Acts* (New York: Cambridge University Press, 1996), p. 115. "Luke's history is useful in a completely different manner from what the historians in antiquity ever considered," Jervell goes on. " 'Profitable' is not the word; we should say 'fateful.' Luke's aim as historian has nothing to do with political or even moral benefits as defined by the historians." Luke's narrative is "salvation history, and so the benefit of history for Luke is of strictly religious character" (pp. 115-16).

17. Both at the beginning of his gospel (1:4) and of Acts (1:2); in the letter, Luke repre-sents Jesus "giving instructions through the Holy Spirit."

18. There has been a very helpful sea change among biblical scholars toward grasping the whole story, and its parts, in context. The greatest initial push for this wonderful break-through came over two decades ago from Robert Alter's studies of narratives from Jewish scripture, *The Art of Biblical Narrative* (New York: Basic Books, 1981). As we will see, the work of Robert Tannehill and Charles Talbert on Luke and Acts reflects the literary sensibil-ities of Alter, as do many other works including even commentaries — among others — like those on Luke's gospel by Joel B. Green and David L. Tiede.

19. Stephen D. Moore, *Literary Criticism and the Gospels: The Theoretical Challenge* (New Haven: Yale University Press, 1989), p. 61.

bird's-eye look at the story Luke tells and the orally based patterns of ear-clues upon which the plot, character, and theme depend.

Brief Overview of Luke's Story

In pursuing Luke's story, we will try to become an ideal audience, one that hears rather than simply reads. That is, we will explore the patterns of repetition that not only allow us but force us to approach the story through circular pattern — circling backward, jumping ahead — rather than in the more customary straight-ahead linear reading. In the brief overview of Luke's story that follows, I indicate the patterns covered in my successive chapters.

As in any great narrative, Luke's two-volume story establishes plot, character, and theme expectations very early in the story. Proper listening is all, as suggested in the gospel's initial drama. A maiden listens well to God's news of an unusual birth while a priest, hearing the same sort of news, does not respond well. Promise, conflict, and resolve are embedded in the paralleled dramatic situation. Mary is encouraged for listening well and responding with a promise to obey, while the priest, Zechariah, is punished for his very poor listening.[20] The echoing parallels at the very beginning of Luke's story are about the births of John and Jesus but just as much about the significant similarity and crucial difference in the ways a religious professional and then a maiden listen to a word from God (Chapter 1).

Word from God: this is what Jesus has come to teach, the word of God reinterpreted, a word that must be heard and done if there is to be salvation and its *shalom.* The unusual narrative phenomenon of twelve clustered poems allows the text to pinpoint what the word of God is that Jesus will be teaching. A main theme emerging from the twelve poems early in the gospel is this: God favors those who favor God by listening to and obeying the word taught by Jesus, serving God's purposes of bringing blessing to others (Chapters 2 and 3). It is the good news.

But for any follower of the Way, this good news is both disruptive and demanding, as the first nine chapters of the gospel reveal. (1) Eleven instances of disease and social displacement are overcome, but in the context of difficult struggle with demonic activity. (2) "A sword will pierce your own soul," a prophet tells the mother of Jesus, and we see it happen

---

20. We take up the Mary-Zechariah contrast in Chapter 1.

twice to Mary. (3) John the Baptist and his dire end are paralleled in the experiences of Jesus, present and anticipated. (4) In the crucial chapter leading up to the journey to Jerusalem (Luke 9), we find a five-beat escalation of darkness and failure on the disciples' part, and a greatly agitated Jesus: "How much longer must I be with you, and bear with you?" Jesus exclaims.[21] This good news is simple (hear the word and do it), but apparently complex as well (Chapter 4).

How much longer, indeed! Jesus sets his face for Jerusalem, since it is soon time for him to depart, to leave earth.[22] So much teaching needed, so little time. With exquisite craft, the author collects and orchestrates the major teachings of Jesus about this new Way. Nine themes are paralleled, repeated — but in reverse order! Ancients were very familiar with *chiasmus* (*chiasm*; ring-composition). Instead of serial parallelism (1-2-3 echoed by 1*-2*-3*), we find a reversed parallelism (1-2-3, then 3*-2*-1*) that creates a ring effect, complete with a "bull's-eye" at the center.

Many scholars have noted this chiasm for "the journey section," also referred to as the "teaching section" or "central section"; no one to my knowledge has explored the full dimension of the chiasm's dynamic, or the extent to which it proves central for the perspective of Luke's entire two-volume story.[23] I offer a chart as visual compensation for us readers (see p. 9). This chart suggests, as well, the nine chapters of Part II of my study.

For an ancient storyteller, one of the distinct advantages of such a repetition device, beyond the memory help (for both speaker and listener), is the matter of narrative emphasis: the material is framed by the outermost ring (first and last item), while moving inward to the center of the circle, the "heart" of meaning — a "bull's-eye." At the center of this journey is a hub of meaning for the two-part story: strive to enter God's kingdom, not the human kingdom represented by Jerusalem. The frame announces — and echoes — the story's focus on a kingdom of peace.

Within this journey we find another kind of repetition, quite subtle but extremely important and compelling. From one section to the next we find a thematic concern brought up, and then repeated but in another

---

21. Lk 9:41.

22. Lk 9:51.

23. The story as a whole, incidentally, has a geographic chiasm as well: the gospel moves from outside the city of Jerusalem into the actual city, while Acts parallels the movement in reversed fashion: from Jerusalem where thousands upon thousands of Jews from around the world are saved, the drama moves beyond Jerusalem to Rome and "the ends of the earth" (Acts 1:8).

guise, or with an attending issue that hadn't been treated adequately. Often it feels like a buried question that was waiting to be asked — which the audience may not "get" until the actual asking of the echoing sequence. For example: we move from a tale told by Jesus — to an anxious lawyer — about a Samaritan who *does the word of God* to a visit from Jesus to the home of an anxious sister whose *doing* is inappropriate while the younger sister *listens to the word of God* and is praised. Among the other linkages between these two successive narrative units, we find here a composite portrait of the one who inherits eternal life (one who is "saved") by *hearing* God's word (Mary), and *doing* it (the Samaritan). The portrait is complete with a probing look at what prevents such eternal life: the anxiety of self-justification and status-preservation exhibited first by a male lawyer, then by a female hostess. I call this *spiraling repetition*, since it develops like a dialectical movement, a "spiraling" in which something from the prior passage is qualified or expanded by what follows. The buried questions or possibilities of the first sequence come to the surface in the next one.

Jesus concludes his teaching, and enters Jerusalem. All havoc breaks loose. Confrontation between Jesus and the traditional leadership of Israel comes to a head (Chapter 14); Jesus speaks directly and passionately to his followers about the disruption and confrontation awaiting both him and them (Chapter 15). We have seen the easily recognized repetition of "motif" in section one, with the disruption of the good news coming at the audience like a staccato drumbeat. As is the case for the first two sections of Luke's gospel, the last depends on a living rehearsal of the challenge "Strive to enter God's kingdom": we have heard this at the precise center-point of the gospel, and Jesus himself strives mightily, in the gospel's third and last section, with those rejecting him and the Way he has been teaching.[24]

The repeated question in this ultimate confrontation, and in the striving of Jesus, is that of authority: whose version of God's word is to be followed and accepted, that of Jesus and the appointed Twelve, or of Israel's current religious leaders (Chapter 14)? All the prior conflict between the new "Leader" of Israel[25] and these old-guard leaders is repeated and comes to a head, here at the end of the gospel volume. This struggle between Israel's old-guard leadership and the new leadership under Jesus, in the name of Jesus, will constitute much of the drama in Acts.

Those who are choosing the Way are urged by Jesus to remember the salient features of what he has already explained about the need for striving. Even those Israelites who have chosen the Way fade, a fading that includes disappearance and outright desertion; the striving of disciples to enter God's kingdom once again leads to failure, but on a grander dramatic scale. Judas, who had been striving for such salvation along with the other eleven disciples, fails beyond recovery. As "Savior" and "Leader," Jesus sets the standard for kingdom life, and challenges his followers to do the same, to bear the same ridicule and hauling-before-councils and even death (Chapter 15). "A disciple is not above the teacher," Jesus has said, "but everyone who is fully qualified will be like the teacher" (an idea dramatized fully in Acts).[26] Among the very last words of Jesus to his followers is an emphasis on salvation that they are

---

24. Lk 13:23-30; explored in Chapter 13.
25. Acts 5:31.
26. Acts 5:31; Lk 6:40.

to proclaim and demonstrate in his absence, a mandate about which Acts reveals the believers' complete faithfulness. The emphasis is to be on (1) God's raising Jesus from death (establishing authority as Teacher, Israel's new "Leader"); (2) repentance — a catch-word that embraces the turning-around from ordinary striving to the counterintuitive demands of God's Way; and (3) a waiting upon the empowerment necessary for salvation, the Holy Spirit.[27]

Luke's prefatory word to Theophilus at the beginning of volume two, Acts, parallels the preface to volume one, the gospel. We will discover early in Acts at least four distinct "hinges" — repetitions that function as reminders that Acts cannot be understood without volume one, and that the gospel volume cannot be understood without Acts. The four hinges are these: paralleled last-words speeches by Jesus; paralleled prefaces with echoing features; paralleled departure scenes; and an echoed insistence on *twelve* new leaders for a delivered Israel (Chapter 16). Throughout Acts we will be hearing signal words or phrases often repeated: *believe, kingdom,* the *Way,* Jesus as *Lord, repentance,* and *resurrection.* Hearing-and-obeying-the-word-of-God-as-taught-by-Jesus is summarized in Acts with the single word *repentance.*

The action of Acts is oriented around nineteen speeches, most of them in clear patterns determined by audience. Peter and Paul, whose experiences are consistently paralleled, deliver seven speeches each. The action at the beginning of Acts revolves around three major speeches by Peter, all of them addressed to fellow-Israelites (Acts 2:14-36; 3:12-26; 4:8-12; covered in Chapter 17).

Early in Luke's story, in his gospel, we found an indication of the major plot conflict of Acts, in the prophetic utterance of the godly Simeon. "This child," says Simeon, holding the infant Jesus, "is destined for the falling and the rising of many in Israel."[28] Thousands upon thousands accept their Messiah following these three major speeches of Peter to fellow-Jews; a notable few refuse.

Twice in Acts all twelve rulers of Israel speak, literally, in one voice, first to God and then to the old-guard leadership of Israel. Together with Stephen's very long speech, these three consecutive speeches constitute model speeches from which all the speeches of Acts take their narrative cues (4:23-30; 5:29-32; 6:15–7:60; covered in Chapter 18). Here is the full gospel on full review. The forward motion of the action, as al-

27. Lk 24:45-49.
28. Lk 2:34.

ways in Acts, is oriented around — and gains its meaning — from such speeches.

Two recurring themes occur in the three speeches concerning Gentiles, delivered by Peter: God's presence through the Holy Spirit, and the inclusivity of God (10:34-43; 11:4-17; 15:7-11). Peter and the twelve who constitute Israel's new leadership must themselves repent regarding the Gentiles, a strategic dramatic development in these three speeches and their respective narrative contexts. Redeemed Israel reaches out, as part of their salvation, to all peoples. Non-Jewish believers become, as James D. G. Gunn observes, "an extension of Israel."[29] Essential to Luke's centering vision is this inclusion of non-Jews into the *ekklēsia*, the assembly/community (not "church").[30]

Paul's first and last speeches — a "frame" for his seven speeches — are addressed primarily to Israel (13:16-41; 28:25-28; covered in Chapter 20). In Paul's first speech, we find a major statement of "the gospel according to Paul" as represented by Luke. This major speech concludes with a warning to those of Israel resisting their Messiah; Paul's last speech is all warning. In each, there is an echo back to Simeon's word early in volume one, that there would be many "rising in Israel" but "many falling" also. Paul's warning is to the falling, those who stand to be "rooted out of the people," as Peter puts it.[31]

The authority of Jesus as teacher of God's word is at stake throughout Acts, and before the Athenians it is no different. Salvation hinges on hearing and doing this word. Paul captures the point in his only speech directed to a non-Jewish audience:

> [God] commands all people everywhere to *repent*, because he has fixed a day on which he will have the world judged in *righteousness* by a man whom he has appointed, and of this he has given assurance to all by raising him from the dead.[32]

---

29. James D. G. Dunn, *The Acts of the Apostles* (Valley Forge, Pa.: Trinity Press International, 1996), p. xx. Covenant fulfillment is intimated at the very beginning of the story, in the respective poems of Mary and Zechariah, and stated explicitly by Peter in Acts 3:25, echoing Gen 12:3. Prophetess Anna speaks about the child Jesus "to all who were looking for the redemption of Jerusalem" (Lk 2:38); "Jerusalem" functions metonymically for "Israel," as witness the context of Simeon's words, along with the first two poems, respectively, by Mary and Zechariah.

30. *Ekklēsia* is mistranslated "church" in Acts: *ekklēsia* in Acts 19, for example, is a pagan assembly — hardly the "church"! (vv. 32, 39, 41).

31. Acts 3:23.

32. Acts 17:30-31, emphasis mine.

According to Paul and the witnesses of Acts, Jesus will judge all peoples (including Israel) on the basis of a daily turning-away from wrongdoing toward right-doing — that is, on the basis of *righteousness*. Jesus has been authorized as teacher of righteousness by God's "raising him from the dead."[33] In the narrative companion to this speech, we find Paul reviewing for believers the two gospel essentials of repentance and resurrection, but with elaboration on the cost of continuing repentance for believers. With two disparate audiences placed side by narrative side — Athenian skeptics and Ephesian believers — we get to hear the full range and disclosure of Paul's gospel message (according to Luke): a salvation based on one's righteousness. Such right acting is dependent on hearing the word and doing it — a continuing repentance — and on God's continuing mercy both in forgiving those who repent and in supplying God's own empowering Spirit (Acts 17:22-31; 20:18-35; Chapter 21).[34] Luke's gospel and Acts conclude similarly insofar as Jesus and Paul are in a life-and-death struggle with Israel's old-guard leadership. Paul, late hero of redeemed Israel, has three speeches in his defense.

In his three other speeches Paul establishes what he understands as the fundamental nature of the charges against him, namely, that he is proclaiming to Israel a hope in the resurrection (Acts 22:1-22; 24:11-21; 26:1-23; Chapter 22). In these last three major speeches of Acts, Luke confirms what is central to his version of the Jesus story: (1) salvation is grounded in the *resurrection*, which has established the authority of Jesus to be the "light" of revelation; and (2) *repentance* activates this salvation, a repentance requiring the "light" Jesus brings to the Law and prophets, summarized in Acts by the term "the Way."

In our last chapter before the Conclusion, we explore the narrative logic of glaring discrepancy in detail among the three accounts of Paul's transforming experience on the road to Damascus: the "light" changes,

---

33. 17:29-31.

34. Paul's account of salvation, as we will see, insists on right-doing for each Israelite as it is for all non-Jews; it is a righteousness provided not by the death of Jesus as a covering for sin, but by the sovereign generosity of God, based on *repentance*, an obedience to the divine word as taught by the appointed Messiah and an obedience empowered by God's own Spirit. Rather than an escape from the personal consequences of sin, the cross of Jesus in Luke-Acts is presented as an invitation and challenge to bear — in the name of Jesus — the consequences of others' sin, including the visited wrongs of dishonor, ridicule, legal battles and jailing, flogging, and even murder. "Repent," says Paul to these Greeks — because God has appointed a man who "will have the world judged in righteousness." This right doing, based on good hearing, is "the Way" taught by Jesus to which all believers in Acts testify (Lk 13:23-24; Lk 8:19-21; 20:21; Acts 9:2; 16:17; 24:14).

while the heavenly "voice" is heard by others in one account, not heard in the next, and becomes intimately directed to Paul in the third (9:1-19; 22:4-16; 26:9-18; Chapter 23). Why such variations on a repeated theme and motif? Part of the answer is that the entire two-part narrative builds toward the last major speech of Paul, which contains the third account of his turning-around experience. The story begun in Luke's gospel is coming full circle here at the end of Acts.

Wherein is the dramatic conflict and resolve for Luke-Acts? The "peace on earth"[35] announced by angels early in the gospel and inaugurated by Jesus is a perfecting of the communal well-being celebrated by ancient Israel[36] but hotly contested by the contemporary religious leadership of Israel. They are threatened at two levels. First, the Way is so challenging. Not only must traditional outcasts, prisoners, and diseased within Israel become released and restored members of the community,[37] but, as we find in the last part of Acts, "servant Israel" must actually solicit non-Jews to join them in this inclusive reality known as God's kingdom! Second, the status and power of their leadership are threatened. They are peevish, then jealous, and finally murderous. But still Paul speaks with Jewish leadership throughout Acts and up through its very last verses — some repenting, some not.

Even though removed in time and cultural "space," it is not difficult for a modern audience to understand the clash between these two fundamentally different ways, God's Way of radical love (of enemy, for example) and the normal way, the ordinary path of self-interest and clan loyalty. Here is the central drama of Luke's two-part story.

With a full complement of narrative techniques culled from his oral culture, Luke has created a whole and unified drama of extraordinary genius and persuasiveness. Without recognizing the "how" of this particular narrative genius, we miss the story's particular "what."[38] I hope to

35. Lk 2:14.

36. Perhaps the most moving celebration of such *shalom* is that provided by King David, at the height of his rule, for the entire multitude of Israel. Included in this token feast of communal well-being are the individual food-treats offered by the king to each of his happy subjects, both male and female: "a cake of bread, a portion of meat, and a cake of raisins" (2 Samuel 6:17–19).

37. See the initial and programmatic words of Jesus about how he understands the meaning of his salvation role, as assigned and empowered by God, Lk 4:18-19.

38. Marianne Palmer-Bonz says something similar, in *The Past as Legacy: Luke-Acts and Ancient Epic* (Minneapolis: Fortress, 2000). But finding parallels with other ancient litera-

provide the deepest pleasure of any great narrative, which is simultaneously profit, the inner journey of being stretched beyond our own familiar worlds.[39]

---

ture, as she tries to do, can be misleading, as in this example: "above all, Luke appears to have been inspired by Virgil in his presentation of the church as the natural and, indeed, the only legitimate successor to ancient Israel" (p. 192). In fact, as I have suggested, there is no such thing as a "church" that replaces faithful Israel, which *is ekklēsia*. Charles Talbert knows how to make sense of the particular narrative, but errs in too-easy an overview: "So when one recognizes that the narrative of Luke-Acts is a working out of the divine plan, one must ask: what aim is the author pursuing against this background? The obvious answer is that in the Third Gospel it is Christology (explicitly stated in Acts 1:1); in Acts, ecclesiology." *Reading Acts: A Literary and Theological Commentary on the Acts of the Apostles* (New York: Crossroad, 1997), pp. 3-4.

39. An ideal: trying to read a text "objectively" (a bad word for many critics). As a literary critic, C. S. Lewis was among the best, and his *Experiment in Criticism* (Cambridge: Cambridge University Press, 1961) remains as one of the great and lucid testaments to the viability of the "objective" ideal in reading a text, recognizing and taking into consideration the realities of hermeneutical circling.

PART I

The Way: Narrative Preparations

Luke 1:1–9:50

Chapter 1

Story in a Nutshell: A Girl versus a Priest, and the Matter of Proper Listening

Luke begins his story with a striking contrast between a young girl and an older priest. After hearing word of unexpected and unnatural birth, each asks the same visiting angel a question with nearly the same words, though on closer inspection the respective questions reveal one subtle difference that suggests entirely opposing motives. The priest is punished, the young girl praised. Luke launches his story by providing a glimpse of the whole story to follow, brilliantly expanded in the respective poems of maiden and priest.

The Priest and the Girl: A Mini-Drama That Tells the Whole Story

To both the experienced priest Zechariah and the very young Mary, a word comes directly by way of God's angelic messenger and proves shocking to each.[1] Against all odds and natural law there will be a baby born: to the post-menopausal wife of the priest and to the unmarried girl, a virgin. In each case, the miracle baby will become great. Zechariah, elderly and respected religious professional, responds in an ordinary manner, and is punished; Mary, a young girl without social standing or privilege, responds well and is honored.

1. Whenever I cite what any character says, or how characters respond (shock for both Mary and Zechariah, for example), it should be understood that I am referring to the author's representation of the same — not the historical facts. This is not a denial of the historicity, but a reminder that we are dealing with a narrative representation selected and ordered by an author.

A crucial note for the two-part story ahead is being sounded early, and will echo with interesting variations throughout the entire story, culminating in the very last scene of Acts. Much depends on listening well to the word from God, especially as taught by Jesus.

The angel appears first to the elderly priest, who is performing religious duties in the Jerusalem Temple, and then to the young maiden, presumably in her home, up north in a small town of Galilee. God's messenger Gabriel speaks in poetry (a matter we will explore shortly). The parallels in these two poems are remarkable, as are the respective responses of Zechariah, then Mary.

Poem-Message, Gabriel to Priest	Poem-Message, Gabriel to Maiden
Do not be afraid, Zechariah, for your prayer has been heard,	*Do not be afraid,* Mary, for you have found favor with God.
and your wife Elizabeth *will bear you a son,*	And now, *you will . . . bear a son,*
and *you will name him John.*	*and you will name him Jesus.*
You will have joy and gladness, and many will rejoice at his birth,	
for *he will be great* in the sight of the Lord.	*He will be great,* and will be called the Son of the Most High,
He must never drink wine or strong drink; even before his birth he will be filled with the Holy Spirit. He will turn many of the people of Israel to the Lord their God. With the spirit and power of Elijah he will go before him, to turn the hearts of parents to their children, and the disobedient to the wisdom of the righteous, to make ready a people prepared for the Lord. (1:13-17)	and the Lord God will give to him the throne of his ancestor David. He will reign over the house of Jacob forever, and of his kingdom there will be no end. (1:30-33)

To both Zechariah and Mary the angel says *do not be afraid.* Zechariah's wife and Mary *will bear a son.* Each is instructed, *you will name him* (respectively, *John* and *Jesus*). Each of these sons *will be great*. The parallels will be developed in the prose action ahead, but the immediate rhetorical effect is a lead-in to the remarkable similarity but significant difference in the responses of the two who hear the surprising news of miraculous birth:

> Zechariah said to the angel, "How will I know that is so?
> For I am an old man, and my wife is getting on in years." (1:18)

> Mary said to the angel, "How can this be,
> since I am a virgin?" (1:34)

In case we have missed the profound difference between these responses, which appear so much the same, the text insists on a reexamination insofar as the angel punishes the priest but praises the maiden. *"Because* you did not believe my words," Gabriel exclaims to the priest, "you will become mute, unable to speak, until the day these things occur."[2] But to Mary's question comes a breathtaking answer:

> The Holy Spirit will come upon you,
> and the power of the Most High will overshadow you;
> therefore the child to be born will be holy;
> he will be called Son of God. (1:35)

Why does Mary receive such a positive response while Zechariah suffers critique and negative consequence? What is the difference in their respective questions? The text forces the audience into the drama in search of an answer, as will be the case throughout this story (as in any great narrative): by posing questions without explicit commentary from the story's narrator the audience must participate in completing the actual sense of the drama.

How Such a Great Matter in Such a Small Difference?

We listen again to the questions:

- Zechariah: "How will I know that this is so?". . since I am old.
- Mary: "How can this be?" . . . . since I am a virgin?

---

2. 1:19-20.

21

How will I know?: The priest wants proof.
How can this be?: The maiden seeks explanation.

Zechariah will receive no further evidence than the spectacular presence of God's angel standing before him and his subsequent muteness for wishing a sign. On the other hand, Mary receives the information she wonders about. How will it happen? How can this be? "The Holy Spirit will come upon you, / and the power of the Most High will overshadow you."

A careless audience might have thought that God simply favors Mary and frowns on the priest . . . because God is God and does the inexplicable. We might have thought, wrongly, that Luke's vision is of a God whose sovereignty includes the mysterious and unfathomable — as illustrated by these paralleled events. But the angel's answer to Mary indicates something different. Gabriel not only answers Mary's "how" question, but does so graciously. It will happen, answers Gabriel, through the presence of God's own Spirit. The drama of salvation and deliverance in Acts, volume two, hinges on the answer given to Mary: starting with Jesus in the gospel and continuing in a much more comprehensive way in volume two, the Holy Spirit "comes upon" those who choose God's Way; there can be no salvation without this Spirit, since doing the word taught by Jesus is otherwise "impossible for mortals."[3]

What Gabriel has heard in Mary's question, apparently, is what the careful listener can detect: an acceptance of the human impossibility accompanied with profound perplexity over the means of accomplishment — along with willingness to be partner to that accomplishment. The question is not about further assurance, as in the priest's question, *How will I know?* Rather, in a state of wonder and acceptance, Mary's *how* presumes her knowledge that virgins do not conceive. She does not ask for certifiable data in order to reassure herself, as does the priest. Mary asks about process, not proof.

In place of "how will this thing come to be?" Zechariah asks, "how can I be sure?" Though he is an experienced and devout priest, the old man nonetheless seeks something as a sign that will vindicate his presumed trust of God's word. Perhaps he does not want to prove himself a fool in accepting and making public such preposterous news, even though it is the thing for which he and his wife have been praying. The angel answers the priest's wrong-headed question by giving verbal ex-

---

3. 18:27; an answer by Jesus to the question "who can be saved?" — given the unthinkable demands of the Way leading to salvation (18:24-26).

pression to the angelic vision that terrified Zechariah in the first place. You want a sign? "I am Gabriel. I stand in the presence of God."[4] That is a stark answer. Here is another way to understand the angel's response: *What more do you need than my sudden glorious and angelic presence, in this otherwise isolated and holy space?* And why should this announcement create such doubt and fear for the priest, since the God of Zechariah's scriptures has frequently been in the business of opening barren wombs?[5] The audience is being prepared for the critical divide between hearing well and not hearing well.

Zechariah's "how-can-I-know" is an anxious clutching; Mary's "how-will-it-happen" is faithful risk. Gabriel's news to Mary of miraculous birth would be even more preposterous than the same news to Zechariah: conception without human intercourse trumps post-menstrual conception, though both are clearly impossible at a merely human level. In addition, Mary's pregnancy will be shameful, since she has not consummated her betrothal. Nonetheless, her wonder-filled question indicates an assumption and essential attitude that receives expression: "Here I am, the servant of the Lord," says Mary; "let it be with me according to your word."[6] God gains the service of Mary, but temporarily loses the service of the now-mute Zechariah.[7] This is the kind of "orderly account" Luke provides, proceeding often in balanced pairs and parallels whose similarities and differences create layered meanings. The "pairs" are very often female-male.

Hearing and Doing the Word of God: Salvation in a Nutshell

"According to your word": the drama of Luke's two-volume story, as I have indicated, will depend on hearing the word well, and doing what the word suggests. Such intent listening involves furrowing one's brow, apparently, and pondering:

4. 1:19.

5. Most notably, there is Abraham's wife Sarah, Jacob's wife Rachel, and Elkanah's wife Hannah.

6. 1:38.

7. Zechariah cannot join with other priests in offering the people God's benediction — that which would have been expected for a priest coming from the temple's holy of holies back out to the people. See Leon Morris, *The Gospel According to St. Luke: An Introduction and Commentary* (Downers Grove, Ill.: InterVarsity, 1974), pp. 78-79.

— Hearing the word from God delivered by Gabriel,
  • "[Mary] was much perplexed by his words and *pondered* what sort of greeting this might be";
— Hearing the word from God delivered by angels, via shepherds,
  • "Mary treasured all these words and *pondered* them in her heart."[8]

To ponder is to allow words to interrupt the flow of normal thought and life. Hearing God's word will be no simple thing for Mary, whose close attention to what Gabriel and the shepherds report requires neither closure nor further assurance. For Mary, as for all good listeners to come, it is a matter of willingness and pondering, of openness and mulling over. In declaring herself servant to the word from God, Mary becomes for Luke an ideal character, a portrait of the truly godly person.

"Listen to him!" God will say to Peter, James, and John, in one of only two direct quotations of God.[9] How one listens to the word of God as taught by Jesus is primary for this story. Speaking the word of God will be the major role of Israel's Messiah, the child of Mary who will be named *Jesus*. Listening to and embracing the Way of God[10] that Jesus teaches will be the requirement for Israel's salvation (thousands upon thousands upon thousands within Israel will be saved; Israel will be redeemed[11]). Hearing and speaking, so crucial within this two-volume narrative and in the story-telling world of Luke, generally, are problematic for religious professionals like Zechariah the priest, whose function, ironically, is to speak God's word to the people after hearing what God has told him. Zechariah hears but does not listen: he becomes mute. Mary hears — and listens, as indicated by her acquiescent response: she is honored with eloquent speech, poeticizing in what has come to be known as "The Magnificat."[12] Unlike most religious professionals in this story, Zechariah recovers, and bursts forth into a comparable poem of great promise to Israel.

As we will see, Mary is far from perfect in her response to her son Jesus. His words will disturb her; the twelve-year-old son elicits an expressively agitated response from his mother.[13] Mary is not presented as a

8. Lk 1:29; 2:19.
9. Lk 9:35; the other occasion is God's speaking to Jesus during prayer, "You are my Son, the Beloved; with you I am well pleased" (3:22).
10. Lk 20:21; Acts 24:14.
11. Acts 2:41; 4:4; 22:20; we explore this drama of Israel's being saved in Part IV.
12. Lk 1:46-55; we look at this in a moment.
13. 2:48; 8:20-21.

person perfect in knowledge and faith, but rather as someone open to a journey of surprising and even soul-piercing reality.[14] "Be it done unto me" is, for Luke, the undertaking of a process that requires precisely what Mary demonstrates: a willingness to say *whatever this word implies, I am ready to search its demands and be a servant to the unusual.* Mary's engaged response to God's word is perhaps Luke's most repeated idea of the entire two-volume story: blessed are those who hear the word of God and do it.[15] Such blessing, in Luke's view, is nothing short of salvation itself.

In a striking narrative move, Luke clusters twelve poems closely together in the opening chapters of his story.[16] The first two are spoken by Gabriel, respectively, to Zechariah and Mary. There follow in quick succession the poems, respectively, by Mary and Zechariah, then one by angels, another by a godly man ready to die, and finally two poems from Isaiah — one describing John and the other recited by Jesus. Each of these eight poems explored in the following chapter repeats primary features of the story to follow, as we might expect from scriptural precedent.[17]

14. 2:35.

15. 8:21.

16. Gabriel's poem, to Zechariah (#1, 1:16-17); Gabriel's poem, to Mary (#2, 1:32-33); Mary's poem (#3, 1:46-55); Zechariah's poem (#4, 1:67-79); The angels' poem, to shepherds (#5, 2:14); Simeon's poem (#6, 2:29-32); Isaiah's poem, for John (#7, 3:4-5); Isaiah's poem, borrowed by Jesus (#8, 4:18-19); Jesus' poem ("Poem on the Plain") (#9, 6:20-49); poem #10 (7:27); poem #11 (7:32); poem #12 (8:10).

17. Perhaps the most conspicuous example is found in the most masterful of all narratives in the Jewish scriptures, namely, the story of King David. Not only does this narrative begin with a preparatory poem by Hannah, mother of Samuel, but it concludes with back-to-back poems by David that echo in obvious detail the thematic "platform" of Hannah's initial poem 1 Samuel 2:1-10; 2 Samuel 22:2-51 & 23:1-7. These last two poems appear at the center of the narrative's concluding ring-composition (2 Samuel 21–24; Saul's sin [21:1-14] and David's sin [24:1-25] are the outer "ring"; David's loyal warriors provide an inner "ring" [21:15-22 & 23:8-39]; the center-most "ring" is the two poems).

Chapter 2

Story Distilled: The First Eight
of Twelve Preparatory Poems

Twelve clustered poems[1] orient the early action of the narrative. The distillation of the two-volume story's major themes through poetry provides perspective to the numerous healings of the gospel's first section, eleven of them specified. The poems proclaim a "good news" — not only about the deliverance of Israel but also about its role as "servant Israel" to the world of non-Jews, including enemies. This poetic distillation of God's word proves fundamental to the developing action of the entire narrative ahead. The blessing brought by Jesus to Israel, and then by Israel to the world, in Acts, is characterized by the one word "peace." Such salvation is for those whom God favors. But whom does God favor, and why? The first eight poems go a long way in establishing the story's focus.

The story begins, as we have seen, with the contrasted response to God's word of a religious professional and a presumably untutored girl. *Listen!* is the point. *Listen to Jesus!* becomes the major challenge for those within Luke's story. And the text demands no less of its audience. In the first nine chapters, our listening is sharpened by an unusually high concentration of both poetry and healing scenes. From Gabriel's two poems, respectively, to Zechariah and Mary, up through the angels' briefest of poems and the first public words of Jesus — a poem borrowed from Isaiah — we find the kernel of all that is to follow in the story. When Jesus re-

1. Gabriel's poem, to Zechariah (#1, 1:16-17); Gabriel's poem, to Mary (#2, 1:32-33); Mary's poem (#3, 1:46-55); Zechariah's poem (#4, 1:67-79); the angels' poem, to shepherds (#5, 2:14); Simeon's poem (#6, 2:29-32); Isaiah's poem, for John (#7, 3:4-5); Isaiah's poem, borrowed by Jesus (#8, 4:18-19); Jesus' poem ("Poem on the Plain") (#9, 6:20-49); poem #10 (7:27); poem #11 (7:32); poem #12 (8:10). I do not count the devil's use of biblical poetry in 4:10-12.

cites his poem about bringing the good news (poem eight), he immediately goes on to enact that good news in a significant healing, the first of a flurry of healings recorded in the early chapters.

About three of the earliest poems, Stephen Farris comments, "It seems reasonable to suppose that [Luke] placed these poems at the head of his work because they contain themes which would reappear later in his writings. They are the overture which sets out certain motifs which will recur in the body of the composition."[2] This shrewd comment is to be faulted only in its omission of the entire cluster of twelve poems that function to announce the interrelated themes of the story to follow.

Narrative-embedded poetry would not have been new to Luke's audience. For example, in 1 and 2 Samuel, the beginning and ending of David's story are highlighted by single poems: Hannah, mother of Samuel, speaks programmatic words that are echoed later in the lyrical reflections of David.[3] The role of poetry in biblical narrative is to pinpoint and summarize the action.

But how would the preliterate audience recognize a poem by ear, without seeing it indented on a page? What distinguishes all twelve preparatory poems from their prose context is a characteristic that is true for all poetry: the balanced line. Individual lines of a poem are always intentional; that is, each is determined by the author rather than arbitrarily by the running out of space on a page. Modern translations of the Bible indicate poetry — *this-is-a-poem* — by indenting the intentional lines, emphasizing the inherent integrity of each line as it plays off the following line.[4] Readers familiar with biblical poetry — in the Psalms, for example — will easily recognize the poems within Luke's narrative as poems:

2. Poems within the first two chapters: Mary's, Zechariah's, Simeon's; Farris neglects mention of the two poems by Gabriel (many translations do not indicate these as poetry). Stephen Farris, *The Hymns of Luke's Infancy Narratives: Their Origin, Meaning, and Significance* (Sheffield, U.K.: JSOT Press, 1985), p. 151; the choice of the symphonic metaphor is apt, since the text was intended to be heard, as I have suggested in my introduction. Seven of the initial poems focus especially on the Way: Mary's poem, 1:46-55; Zechariah's poem, 1:67-79; the angels' poem to shepherds, 2:14; Simeon's poem, 2:29-32; John's poem, from Isaiah, 3:4-5; Jesus' poem, from Isaiah, 4:18-19; and the greatest of these, Jesus' poem on the plain — a "mini-version" of the Way, 6:20-49.

3. 1 Samuel 2:1-10; 2 Samuel 22:2-51 and 23:1-7.

4. The ancient biblical scrolls, of course, had no indented lines signifying a poem, a fact that further highlights the intentional nature of poetry's balanced line: an audience easily hears the repetition in word-sense from one line to the next, usually lines that parallel each other.

they share the same essential parallelism and balance of line as do all biblical poetry.[5]

A convenient example of this intentional-line phenomenon of all poetry is the brief two-line poem sung by the angels to shepherds. Here, succinctly, is what lies at the heart of Luke's narrative vision:

"Glory to God in the highest heaven,
    and on earth peace among those whom he favors!" (2:14; poem #5)[6]

A prior word from an angel has told the shepherds about "good news of great joy," nothing less than "a Savior who is the Messiah, the Lord."[7] The "good news" is characterized in the poem as *peace* — the one-word summary in this story of what salvation's good news actually looks like. Israel's *Messiah, the Lord,* is a *Savior* bringing salvation's *peace.*

This is the peace known, in the Scripture of Jesus, as *shalom,* a communal well-being that characterizes the very nature of God. An ancient altar of one of Israel's judges is named *The-Lord-Is-Peace.*[8] Similarly, the angels' brief poem of the good news alludes to *shalom* as describing God's very character by linking God's heavenly glory to earthly peace.

For Jews like Jesus, *shalom* is a "term primarily [used] for interpersonal or social relations where it comes very close to meaning 'justice.'"[9] *Shalom*-justice is the whole of a preparatory poem spoken by Jesus (the eighth of twelve). In his first recorded words as an adult in public life, Jesus claims that

the Spirit of the Lord is upon me, because he has anointed me
    to bring good news to the poor.
He has sent me
    to proclaim release to the captives
    and recovery of sight to the blind,
    to let the oppressed go free,
    to proclaim the year of the Lord's favor. (4:18-19; poem #8)

---

5. See Robert Alter's helpful summary of biblical poetry, "The Dynamics of Parallelism," in his *The Art of Biblical Poetry* (New York: Basic Books, 1985), pp. 3-26.

6. "Peace for those he favours" (New Jerusalem Bible); "peace to all in whom he delights" (Revised English Bible); "peace to men on whom his favor rests" (New International Version).

7. 2:9-11.

8. Gideon, a judge; Judges 6:24.

9. *The Anchor Bible Dictionary,* vol. 5, ed. David Noel Freedman (New York: Doubleday, 1992), p. 207.

This "good news" is *shalom*-justice for the disenfranchised, the one out-side of any communal well-being. Here is an elaboration of the angels' definitive word for salvation, a peace-among, a profound harmony among certain people favored by God: the poor, the captive, the blind, the oppressed. As we will see, the subsequent preparatory poems elaborate on just such *shalom*.[10] Precisely here does the text offer a tell-and-show, the first example of good news being brought: Jesus wrestles, successfully, with an unclean spirit.[11] Oppression and disease, in this story, are the Evil One's doing. Right here, in the synagogue, is a spirit of the Unclean One, and Jesus casts it out; the man is released, and re-stored to community. The struggle for "universal restoration"[12] in this story is an earthly one played out within a cosmic battle between God and Satan.

Such *shalom*-justice is a gift that brings with it responsibility. The preceding poem, referring to John the Baptist, suggests that those favored by God must make the Lord's way straight. Only with a responsibility termed *repentance* will the divine mercy of forgiveness be experienced. "[John] went into all the region around the Jordan, proclaiming a baptism of repentance for the forgiveness of sins, as it is written in the book of the words of the prophet Isaiah,

> The voice of one crying out in the wilderness,
> 'Prepare the way of the Lord,
> make his paths straight.
> Every valley shall be filled,
> and every mountain and hill shall be made low,
> and the crooked shall be made straight,
> and the rough ways made smooth;
> and all flesh shall see the salvation of God.'"
>
> (3:3-6; poem #7; see Isaiah 40:3-5; also Malachi 3:1)

---

10. "Peace" (*eirēnē*, in the Greek) is used four times by Matthew (10:13, twice; 10:34, twice), once by Mark (5:34), six times by John (14:27, twice; 16:33; 20:19; 20:21; 20:26), and twenty-one times by Luke (fourteen in the gospel, seven in Acts). As we have seen in the prior poems, Mary cites herself and Israel as servants to God's intentions; Zechariah refers to God's "servant David," and to the possibility of Israel serving God "without fear" on the way to peace; the shepherds serve God by going to the barn with good news; Simeon can be dismissed in peace, as God's servant, as one who understands the covenant fulfillment ("light to the Gentiles") as that which brings "glory to your people Israel."

11. 4:33-37.

12. Acts 3:21.

"John said to the crowds that came out to be baptized by him, 'You brood of vipers! Who warned you to flee from the wrath to come? Bear fruits worthy of repentance.'"[13]

The mood of Isaiah's poem, quoted by John, is imperative: you do this, Israel, and thus-and-so will happen. *Israel* must prepare the Lord's way by making paths straight. How can Israel, or anyone, do that? How do mere mortals "make [God's] paths straight"? "Repentance" is John's answer, an action-word that, for Luke, defines the daily texture of preparing and going God's Way. "Repentance" is the single word that covers the entire dynamic of obtaining salvation in Luke's gospel and Acts. Repentance, daily, leads to God's forgiveness. Along with resurrection, repentance is what the apostles must bear witness to, in Acts.[14] John, indeed, prepares "the way of the Lord." Those listening to John are told, "bear fruits worthy of repentance" — the fruits of *shalom*-justice, giving up a coat if you have two and your neighbor none, distributing food if you have plenty and your neighbor none.[15] The opposite of the justice lying at the heart of repentance and forgiveness are the "crooked ways" of tax-collectors seeking salary supplements by cheating taxpayers, of soldiers unhappy with their pay and extorting money from helpless victims.[16] As in the prior poems, God favors the straight path and those who have worked to make it straight — those who are lowly servants of God, preparing "the Way of the Lord."

Another of Isaiah's poems, as our author no doubt knew, speaks of the organic relationship between peace and justice:

> The way of peace they do not know,
> and there is no justice in their paths.
> Their roads they have made crooked;
> no one who walks in them knows peace. (Isaiah 59:8)

"All flesh shall see the salvation of God," John concludes, a picture of *shalom*-justice at the heart of Isaiah's vision — and of Luke's.[17] The "crooked ways" to be corrected, for John, are precisely the no-justice/no-peace paths referred to by Isaiah.

Immediately preceding the angels' poem proclaiming peace, *shalom-*

13. Lk 3:7.
14. 24:46-49.
15. 3:11.
16. 3:12-14.
17. 3:6.

justice, Zechariah has uttered a magnificent poem about Israel's deliverance through "a mighty Savior," a poem that culminates with the purpose of this salvation: "to guide our feet into the Way of peace."[18] This "Way" of peace will become a signal word in volume two, Acts, for what Jesus taught and demonstrated, a "Way" to which thousands of Jewish followers of Messiah belong. "Those who belonged to the Way" constitute, in Acts, a delivered Israel.[19]

The angels have offered a two-line summary of good news that encompasses not only what salvation looks like, but *for whom* such salvation is intended, and *by whom*. The story's central character, God, intends peace on earth. This, apparently, is God's glory: to find peace among those on earth whom God favors. The parallelism of these two lines — a balancing of one line with another that distinguishes all poetry everywhere and at all times — evidences an exquisite balancing that yields connection and meaning:

1 Glory to God
   2 in the highest heaven,
   2' and on earth
1' peace among those whom he favors.

What is happening in heaven ("glory to God") is connected with what happens on earth ("peace among those whom God favors"). That is, God's glory is connected to — expressed in? — earthly peace. Such *shalom*, presumably, brings glory to God. "Glorifying God and recovering human wholeness," as Charles Talbert understands the implicit vision of Luke's narrative, "are not mutually exclusive: they are an indissoluble whole."[20]

Peace "remains"[21] *among those whom God favors*. But whom does God favor? Preceding this poem by the angels we have heard four poems, each of which alludes to Israel and its fortunes — its imminent good fortune. Those whom God favors, then, are Israelites. But the answer turns out to be *no*, along with *yes*. Among the surprise reversals that mark Luke's two-volume narrative, the answer about which Israel-

---

18. Lk 1:79.
19. Acts 9:2.
20. Charles H. Talbert, *Reading Luke: A Literary and Theological Commentary on the Third Gospel* (New York: Crossroad, 1982), p. 34.
21. Joseph A. Fitzmyer, *The Gospel According to Luke I-IX*, The Anchor Bible (Garden City, N.Y.: Doubleday, 1981), p. 391.

ites God favors — and what deliverance actually means — are key. Messiah will bring the peace of God's favor only to those Israelites who serve God. Only to *servant* Israel, those who love God by serving purposes made clear by Messiah, will God show the favor, the blessing, of *shalom*.

Gabriel tells Zechariah, in the story's first poem, that his son "will turn many of the sons to the Lord their God"; and he (John) will "turn the hearts of the fathers to the children, and the disobedient to the wisdom of the just."[22] Many will turn; many will repent and become obedient to God's word, "the wisdom of the just." But not all Israel. In his second poem, Gabriel announces to Mary that the reign of her child will be "over the house of Jacob forever, and of his kingdom there will be no end."[23] But not all within "the house of Jacob" will become citizens of "his kingdom." In the sixth poem, immediately following the angels' poem to the shepherds, we hear a poem by the elderly and godly Simeon:

"Master, now you are dismissing your servant in peace,
    according to your word;
for my eyes have seen your salvation,
    which you have prepared in the presence of all peoples,
a light for revelation to the Gentiles
    and for glory to your people Israel." (2:29-32)

As foretold by the prophet Isaiah, God will be favoring Gentiles with a salvation that is "a light for revelation," a light that will be brought to these non-Jews by delivered Israel,[24] "servant Israel" as Mary calls them

---

22. 1:16-17, RSV; the NRSV obscures with prose what the RSV renders properly as a poem.

23. 1:33.

24. As should be obvious already, Luke relies heavily on the Jewish scriptures. From Genesis and Exodus through the prophet Isaiah, Israel's glory is connected with its service as "covenant" bearer and "light" bringer to the world's nations, the Gentiles:

> I am the LORD,
> I have called you [Israel] in righteousness,
> I have taken you by the hand and kept you;
> I have given you as a covenant to the people,
> *a light to the nations* . . . (Is 42:6)
> And God said to me,
> "You are my *servant, Israel*,
> in whom I will be glorified. . . .
> It is too light a thing that you should be my servant

32

in her poem (the fourth of twelve).[25] Such will be "for glory to [God's] people Israel." But not all Israel.

Such, presumably, will be both shocking and unacceptable for many Israelites within the story Luke tells. Simeon follows up his poem with a word that describes most of the action of Acts: "This child [Jesus] is destined for the falling and the rising of many in Israel."[26] God's favor of salvation's *shalom* is to be "for the rising of many in Israel" as Gentiles are brought this blessing by saved Israel, but such divine favor is to be withheld from the many who are "falling . . . in Israel." In fact, these will not remain Israel at all: they will be, as Peter declares in Acts, "utterly rooted out of the people."[27]

God's glory in highest heaven is connected with the favor of *shalom* on earth, as the angels have sung to shepherds. We might assume, along with I. Howard Marshall, that the selection of these despised Jewish shepherds[28] indicates "God's free choice of those whom he wills to favour and save."[29] Or does it? Is this a God whose majesty and sovereignty will be measured by mystery, by an arbitrary exercise of power? The angel has offered a challenge to these shepherds: "This will be a sign for you: you will find a child wrapped in bands of cloth and lying in a manger."[30] Will they leave their flocks to see the infant, based on this word from God's messengers? Will they risk their livelihood? Will they go into a town from whose perspective they are outsiders? And if they manage to express well enough the word of this "good news," who would trust these rough-hewn field-hands? The shepherds, in fact, go "with haste," making "known what had been told them about this child; and all who heard it were amazed at what the shepherds told them." Everyone is stunned, shocked, amazed, "but Mary treasured all these words and pondered them in her heart."[31] God's peace comes, as the angels say

---

to raise up the tribes of Jacob
and to restore the survivors of Israel;
I will give you as *a light to the nations,*
that my salvation may reach to the end of the earth." (Is 49:3, 6; emphasis mine)

25. 1:54.
26. 2:34.
27. 3:23.
28. Shepherds in this day and culture were considered low-life.
29. I. Howard Marshall, *Commentary on Luke,* New International Greek Testament Commentary (Grand Rapids: Eerdmans, 1979), p. 112.
30. 2:12.
31. 2:15-19.

in their poem, "among those whom [God] favors." The shepherds must return to their positions in the fields, literally outside "society." But they have been included in a conspicuous communal event, though in a barn; they have held their audience captive by the words they have uttered. They have experienced a special favoring by God, a favoring inextricably linked with their proper hearing — and doing — of the angelic word.

The prior two poems, respectively by Mary and Zechariah, point to just such an answer: those are favored who fear God by serving God without being afraid. Poem three, by Mary, speaks of both herself and Israel as servants to God's purposes: to such comes God's favor.

> "My soul magnifies the Lord,
> and my spirit rejoices in God my Savior,
> **for he has looked with favor on the lowliness of *his* servant.**
> *Surely, from now on all generations will call me blessed;*
> *for the Mighty One has done great things for me,*
> *and holy is his name.*
> **His mercy is for those who fear him** *from generation to generation.*
> *He has shown strength with his arm;*
> *he has scattered the proud in the thoughts of their hearts.*
> *He has brought down the powerful from their thrones,*
> *and lifted up the lowly;*
> *he has filled the hungry with good things,*
> *and sent the rich away empty.*
> **He has helped his servant Israel, in remembrance of his mercy,**
> *according to the promise he made to our ancestors,*
> *to Abraham and to his descendants forever."* (1:46-55; emphases mine)

God looks with favor, but not on all: "His mercy is for those who fear him." God looks with favor on Mary, because Mary in her "lowliness" fears God and is servant to God's purposes. God helps Israel, but not all Israel; God remembers divine mercy for those who constitute *servant* Israel. God favors with salvation's *shalom* those who are not "proud in the thoughts of their hearts"; those who are proud, God brings down. There is nothing arbitrary or mysterious here regarding those whom God favors.

Because she fears God in serving the divine purposes — "according to [God's] word" — Mary is favored by God, whose "mercy is for those who fear him."[32] Here we have a blueprint for the narrative dynamic be-

32. 1:38, 50.

34

tween divine and human will. As suggested, God is the story's central character, whose intentions toward Israel — and through Israel toward all peoples — are being reaffirmed in all of these early poems.[33] Such divine intention, however, is an interplay between human and divine choice, "a dialogue between God and a recalcitrant humanity, rather than God's monologue."[34] This is the scriptural vision implicit in Luke's work, a dynamic of divine and human will cooperating toward blessing.[35] Mary has heard God's part of the conversation well, and has responded well. God's favor is connected with human response. Mary is servant; Israel is servant; even Jesus is God's "holy servant," one on whom God looks with special favor.[36]

Zechariah's poem overlaps thematically with Mary's, as we might expect, with the repeated theme that only *servant* Israel will be favored, along with the favoring of God of such a people. Delivered Israel are the favored "rising many" within Israel who allow their feet to be guided into the Way, a Way of *shalom*.

> "Blessed be the Lord God of Israel,
> for **he has looked favorably on his people and redeemed them.**
> He has raised up a mighty savior for us in the house of his
>   servant David,
> as he spoke through the mouth of his holy prophets from of old,
> that we would be saved from our enemies
> and from the hand of all who hate us.
> Thus he has shown the mercy promised to our ancestors,
> and has remembered his holy covenant,
> the oath that he swore to our ancestor Abraham,
> **to grant us that we, being rescued from the hands of our enemies,**
> **might serve him without fear, in holiness and righteousness**
>   **before him all our days.**
>   And you, child, will be called the prophet of the Most High;

33. As we will discover, both the "method and message in Luke-Acts" are a narrative "centering on God." So Robert L. Brawley entitles his work: *Centering on God: Method and Message in Luke-Acts* (Louisville: Westminster/John Knox, 1990).

34. Robert C Tannehill, *The Narrative Unity of Luke-Acts: A Literary Interpretation*, vol. 1 (Philadelphia: Fortress, 1986), p. 2.

35. For example: "[God] will not forgive your transgressions or your sins," says Joshua to the people, unless you "revere the Lord, and serve him in sincerity and in faithfulness." Furthermore, "if you forsake the Lord and serve foreign gods, then he will turn and do you harm, and consume you, after having done you good" (Joshua 24:19, 14, 20).

36. Acts 4:27, 30; Lk 2:52.

for you will go before the Lord to prepare his ways,
to give knowledge of salvation to his people
by the forgiveness of their sins.
By the tender mercy of our God,
the dawn from on high will break upon us,
to give light to those who sit in darkness and in the shadow
    of death,
to guide our feet into the way of peace."

(1:68-79; emphases mine)

Zechariah begins his poem by pointing out that God's favor is shown to Israel as "the house of his *servant* David," recalling God's promise to father Abraham that they "might *serve* [God] without fear." That is, God's favor (*charis*, grace) is extended to those who serve God's purposes, a theme that Mary's poem has anticipated. By the end of the priest's poem, God's mercy is specified as light for those in darkness, and as a guide for walking "into the Way of peace." As the story unfolds, it is clear that this peace is something quite different from a peace that is merely kept in the face of hostile enemies. This is a *shalom* that must be made, not kept — not merely an absence of conflict but a pursuit of "things that *make for* peace."[37]

Zechariah's summary term, "peace," has several aspects articulated within the poem itself: "saved from our enemies"; "rescued from the hands of our enemies"; "the forgiveness of sins"; "light to those who sit in darkness." Each of these aspects will be explored by Luke in the story ahead. For each there will be a reciprocity between divine initiative and human response: divine rescue in synch with human service to God; forgiveness from God in response to human turning from self-protecting, self-promoting ways; God's light seen when one is ready to be responsive to that light.

The idea of serving God's purposes — working toward "the Way of peace" — appears not only in the poem's frame but in its middle section as well. Here is a key to what both Zechariah and Mary mean by "Savior" and "salvation," by "servant" and "service." God has shown mercy (as Savior) by remembering the agreement between God and God's people:

that we, being rescued from the hands of our enemies [salvation],
might *serve* [God] without fear.

---

37. Words of Jesus (Lk 19:42; emphasis mine).

And how is God's purpose served? Zechariah's poem ends with an answer: feet will be guided "into the Way of peace."[38] Here is the *shalom* of which the angels sing to shepherds, a "universal restoration" of Edenic harmonies, as Peter will say in Acts.[39] Such blessing marks "the Way of salvation" that is established early and throughout Acts by "those who belonged to the Way."[40] This is the "kingdom" of which Gabriel sings to Mary, a Way of repentance. This is "the Way of peace" with which Gabriel concludes his poem to Zechariah, a Way made possible through the teaching, example, and sending of the Holy Spirit by Jesus.

Those experiencing God's mercy serve God's purposes of peace, in holiness and right-living *"before him* all our days."[41] This language parallels God's words to Abraham, "Walk *before me,"* and "be blameless," righteous, "and I will make a covenant with you."[42] Zechariah refers to God's remembering "his holy covenant" established with "ancestor Abraham," a covenant which, in scripture, was established as a mutual responsibility between the two parties: "As for you, [Abraham], you shall keep my covenant."[43] For listeners accustomed to the Jewish scriptures, the poems by Mary and Zechariah would have sounded the familiar note of God's self-imposed need for human participation in carrying out the divine purposes.[44]

Mary concluded her poem with mention of God's covenant with Abraham. Fundamental to all the promises to Abraham is this, that Abraham would be a blessing "to all peoples."[45] The importance of Israel and

---

38. 1:79.

39. Acts 3:21.

40. Acts 16:17; 9:2; see 2:41-47 and then the inclusiveness of healing performed by this community, Acts 3:1-10.

41. Lk 1:75.

42. Gen 17:1-2.

43. Gen 17:9.

44. At the climactic end of Abraham's story, for example, God addresses Abraham through an angel, in a poem:

> *Because* you have done this, and not withheld your son, your only son,
>   I will indeed bless you
> And by your offspring shall all the nations of the earth gain blessing . . .
>   *Because* you have obeyed my voice.
> (Gen 22:16-18, trans. Robert Alter; emphasis mine)

The entire story of Abraham builds toward this scene. The framing words "because you have . . ." suggest the distance Abraham has traveled toward being a servant to God's purposes.

45. Gen 12:3; 22:15-18.

its ancestors, for Luke, is focused on this dominant theme within the Abraham narrative, that Israel become a "blessing to all peoples." Mary's "servant Israel" is echoed by Zechariah's "servant David."[46] In the original Greek, "David" appears before "servant" and "Israel" before "servant." This makes "servant" stronger than a modifier: it is an appositive — a term paralleled with the very name of the person or nation, a defining essence of that person or nation. Salvation, in these poems, is connected with being-the-servant. Redemption and responsibility are intertwined. Even Jesus, the "mighty savior" raised up "in the house of his servant David," will be an unusual king from David's kingly line. "I am among you," Jesus will say to his disciples at a strategic point in the story, "as one who serves," and this is reaffirmed in volume two, where Jesus is referred to as God's "holy servant."[47]

It appears that Mary is "picked out" — favored — because of her fundamental orientation as servant. Will Israel become such a servant, as Mary hopefully suggests in her reference to "servant Israel"? The story ahead works with this question and its answer all the way through to the very ending of Acts.[48] In Zechariah's poem, being rescued is tied to serving God. But how the rescue works, and who the enemies are, will be part of the story's coming reversals and surprises, a glimpse of which we have seen already in the contrast between girl and priest. With great care, Luke will provide a lengthy conclusion to his story, in Acts, where the reality of surprising rescue from the hands of enemies occurs over and over, with explicit use of the word "rescue."[49] The circumstances of this rescue of God's people are symbolized in the experiences of Paul, a representative figure for all of the followers featured in Acts. Such literal rescues from identifiable enemies and even from natural elements pale, however, when compared to God's deliverance of a Stephen, who loves his enemies even as they stone him to death (asking God's forgiveness for them): Stephen sees Jesus standing, exalted in heaven and awaiting Stephen's arrival.[50] That is, the deliverance from enemies through loving them — serving

46. 1:54; 1:69.

47. Lk 22:27; Acts 4:27, 30.

48. The answer will be *yes;* Israel by the thousands upon thousands (though not all within Israel) have turned to God and become "servant Israel" to the world; Israel has indeed been "helped," delivered from her enemies by learning to love them; or, like Stephen, become impervious, "his face . . . like the face of an angel" in the immediate context of looming death at the hands of enemies (Acts 6:15; 7:59-60).

49. Acts 26:17.

50. Acts 7:56-60.

them, not necessarily liking them — is a much more radical vision, played out in Acts, than any literal and oftentimes temporary rescue.[51]

Such rescue is exemplified by Mary and by Mary's literary ancestor, Hannah (Mary's poem has over a dozen allusions to Scripture[52]). Mary's lines of praise closely parallel the poem by Hannah, the prophet Samuel's mother, and places Mary within a line of mothers that yield their sons to God's service of bearing God's word.[53] Rescue, for both mothers, involves relinquishment of what is dearest. Mary's rescue will include, as Simeon declares to Mary, "a sword [that] will pierce your own soul."[54] Mary and Hannah are examples of "servant Israel,"[55] Jews who embrace God's purposes and thereby elicit divine "favor" (*charis*, grace). Righteous Simeon, also, is an example of "servant Israel": "Master, now you

---

51. To be explored in a further chapter of this book, the rescue is from enemies associated with Satan's kingdom (Acts 26:18). The Roman empire is not the enemy of Paul (representative of all Jews following the Way), but, surprisingly, the benefactor — God's agent of literal rescue! (as chronicled in the concluding "act" of Acts, which in one grand dramatic motion begins with a journey to Jerusalem evolving into a journey to Rome, Acts 19:21 to the end, in Rome, 28:31).

52. 1:46-55; a reminder that "Scripture" will always refer to what Mary and everyone else in Luke's audience would have recognized as the Bible: the Jewish scriptures. Timothy Luke Johnson refers to Mary's poem as a "speech" (p. 43), and points out that half of the first eight chapters of Acts are speeches, a "narrative device" for interpreting the story. Whether "poem" or "speech," what is clear is Luke's reliance on such specialized language in the preparatory material of each volume, his gospel and Acts. In fact, the speeches continue in Acts, though not in as concentrated a fashion, as we will see. The nineteen speeches by believers orient and explain the action of Acts. *Gospel of Luke*, in *Sacra Pagina*, vol. 3, ed. Daniel J. Harrington (Collegeville, Minn.: Liturgical Press, 1991), pp. 13-14, 43.

53. Another mother with a peculiar story regarding conception, Hannah gives miraculous birth to a great word-bearer from God. She praises God with a magnificent poem that begins,

> "My heart exults in the Lord;
> my strength is exalted in my God." (1 Sam 2:1)

"The Lord" is "*my* God," says Hannah; Mary's "Lord" is "God *my* Savior." The salvation to be taught by Jesus will be both communal and personal; the Most High who rules a kingdom on earth is also *my* Savior. The middle portions of each woman's poem continue the echoing: each has an emphasis on the reversals characterizing God's kind of kingdom wherein can be found an unusual justice. The justice begins with the reversal of favor and fortune for this woman and that, this social outsider and that. Who was Hannah to be singled out by God? And who is Mary to be so blessed and favored? Why, in fact, has Israel as a people been favored, this people whom God "has helped"? Luke will answer these questions, whether or not the audience has been sufficiently alert to ask them.

54. 2:35.

55. Lk 1:54.

are dismissing your servant in peace," he has begun his poem; as *servant*, his "eyes have seen [God's] salvation."

The two initial poems by human participants, Mary and Zechariah, elaborate what Gabriel has already poeticized about, and what the angels, the godly Simeon, and Jesus himself will reaffirm:

- God favors those Israelites who are lowly, able to listen to words from God and serve God's stated purposes — like God's servant Simeon; Mary, a young soon-to-be-pregnant girl without a husband; despised field-hand shepherds.
- Israel is favored with salvation — is shown mercy and help — to the extent that it turns to God, away from "disobedience" and toward "the wisdom of the righteous," serving God's purposes as "servant Israel."[56]
- The experience of divine favor is the experience of salvation's rescue and peace, *shalom*.

What has Jesus to do with God's divine intention to bring the blessing of *shalom?* Luke's Jesus, as we learn early in volume one, is "Son of the Most High" and descended from Adam, "Son of God."[57] As such, his teaching of God's word about "the things that make for peace" is authoritative, the last and definitive clarification of Scripture. Listening to Jesus is half the story on obtaining salvation; the other half involves what Jesus accomplished in volume two, the pouring out of God's Spirit who enables those listening to obey. Mary's pondering, as we saw in the last chapter, is an attentiveness that allows words to interrupt the flow of normal thought and life. Mary's care with what is being said anticipates God's urging some disciples *to listen!* — listen to what Jesus says; in Acts, we hear an echo, from Peter quoting Moses: "Listen to whatever he [Messiah] tells you!"[58] Such listening necessitates doing, as we will see in the ninth poem, the greatest of the twelve preparatory poems.

The last four of twelve preparatory poems summarize and extend. Jesus the poet is featured. As teacher, Jesus brings a salvation that is "a light for revelation to

---

56. 1:54.

57. Gabriel's words to Mary (about the child to be born), Lk 1:32; genealogy of Jesus — traced through Joseph! — presumably in order to end up with "Adam, Son of God," 3:38.

58. Lk 9:35; Acts 3:22.

Gentiles" — a light brought by a delivered Israel and redounding to their glory, a glory that fulfills their ancient covenant with God.[59] By those who hear and obey this word, salvation's <u>shalom</u> will be experienced — as Jesus himself makes clear in the longest, most brilliant, and most programmatic of Luke's preparatory poems — often referred to as the "Sermon on the Plain."

59. Gen 12:3; Acts 3:25.

Chapter 3

Story Distilled — and Elaborated:
The Last Four Poems

Between the first and second poems spoken by Jesus (numbers 8 and 9 out of the 12) we find five healings and two summaries of healing activity: his poetic word about the good news is a word that Jesus does. The second poem recited by Jesus (#9 overall) is the longest of the twelve clustered poems, and the most important. Thereafter we find six more healings, eleven in all up to the journey to Jerusalem that comprises the gospel's middle section. We focus in this chapter on the last four poems.

God favors the poor with good news, as we have just seen in the first poem and in the first healing by Jesus.[1] The "poor" to whom the good news is offered include a wide range of characters in the story to follow: anyone marginalized from community,[2] like the shepherds, like the women Mary and Elizabeth, like the wrong-doing tax collectors and the Roman soldiers chasing after John; those who are diseased and wracked by demonic activity; foreigners, "heretics," and children.

Now is a time of "the Lord's favor." God's favor is specified by reference to the Jubilee Year, a special time of release and restoration for slaves and debtors, and a returning of land to its original occupants.[3] But is the story insisting on the good fortune of those whose luck has been bad?

---

1. Poem #8, 4:18-19. (See previous chapter.)

2. The good news is a reversal, as Joel B. Green sees, "for those of low status, for those excluded according to normal canons of status honor in the Mediterranean world." In Luke's vision, the poor who are favored by God with good news are those whose low status can be a combination of factors, "including education, gender, family heritage, religious purity, vocation, economics" (*The Gospel of Luke* [Grand Rapids: Eerdmans, 1997], p. 211).

3. Lev 25; Is 61:2.

Conversely, for the rich and comfortable: Will fortune's wheel be turning?[4] But we have already seen persons in good communal standing on whom God's favor rests — like the ultimately responsive priest Zechariah; the devout Simeon; and the prophetess Anna, who praised God for the infant Jesus and spoke "to all who were looking for the redemption of Jerusalem" (2:38).[5] These in blessed circumstances do not thereby forfeit being favored by God, giving way to God's exclusive concern for the poor, the outcasts, and imprisoned. God's favoring, in this story, is always a grace-for-now. One can be healed of demonic oppression, for example, but ultimately end up worse off because of the failure in responding to God's continuing word; no one, however "favored," can continue in God's grace, according to Luke, without listening and trusting, without obedience.[6]

Among whom, then, does the favor of God's peace "remain"?[7] The answer is given, definitively, in the next poem, number nine — by Jesus. Listening to such demanding teaching and obeying it, as we hear now, is what it means to love God and serve God's purposes. Only then does anyone gain God's continuing favor. Such counterintuitive principles for living are referred to later in the narrative as a *striving* required for entrance to God's kingdom; this central aspect of the story's vision remains the same through the last words of Acts.[8] What this striving is all about is distilled in the longest of the preparatory poems,[9] Jesus' "poem on the plain" (6:20-49).[10] The

---

4. The unfolding story suggests something quite different: those who have blessing are responsible for bringing it to others — or losing all. And those considered "losers" by society will be found by God, but only if they choose to be found; further, they will remain in God's favor only if they serve God's purposes in reciprocating by "finding" others who are lost — those who suffer dispossessed or disordered lives because of being among the "poor," the diseased and hungry, or the one cast out from society because of gender or foreign status.

5. The number of godly folk who would have listened seriously to a woman prophet might have been small; in any case, that Anna had any status as a woman, beyond the production of children, would have been the exception proving the rule concerning the outcast station of women in that culture.

6. 11:14, 24-28.

7. Lk 2:14; see p. 31 n. 21 on the word *remain*.

8. Lk 13:24-30; no salvation, for Luke, is gained without striving; those who do not participate in what salvation's light reveals are banned from God's presence (13:24-27).

9. Translations generally ignore the extended poetry of this "sermon"; as will be evident in what lies ahead, the poem is distinguished as such by remarkably balanced lines — with the possible exception of the concluding parable about a wise man and a foolish man.

10. Matthew's somewhat paralleled "sermon on the mount" (5:3–7:27) appears, in a

striving is not about getting-in, about gaining salvation. Rather, as Jesus has been demonstrating, the striving is on behalf of others, their healing and release. After his poem about bringing good news to the poor, Jesus does so in terms of healing: an unclean spirit is cast out of a beleaguered man;[11] a woman's fever is cured.[12] Next, a summary: "As the sun was setting, all those who had any who were sick with various kinds of diseases brought them to him; and he laid his hands on each of them and cured them. Demons also came out of many, shouting, 'You are the Son of God.'"[13] A leper's skin is healed;[14] a paralytic walks;[15] someone with a withered hand has the limb straightened.[16] Then, immediately preceding the second poem by Jesus, another summary: "They [crowds] had come to hear him and to be healed of their diseases; and those who were troubled with unclean spirits were cured. And all in the crowd were trying to touch him, for power came out from him and healed all of them."[17]

Like Moses, Jesus has gone up a mountain for conversation with God before returning to the people with word from God on how to be saved, on how to enter God's kingdom. Unlike Moses, Jesus has gone up with those he has been teaching, and after prayer with God, Jesus singles out from among his closest associates twelve disciples.[18] They must teach and do what Jesus teaches and does. They come down the mountain to the people, and Jesus now shines his light on the Mosaic Law, with some twists and implications that might have surprised Moses himself.[19] After the summary of his bringing the good news to all, after the healings, we find Jesus looking not at the crowd but at his dis-

---

greatly abbreviated version, in Luke's gospel. I call it the "poem on the plain" because it is a poem (as I will demonstrate) and it was spoken on a plain, not a mountain.

11. 4:33-37.
12. 4:38-39.
13. 4:40-41.
14. 5:12-14.
15. 5:17-26.
16. 6:6-11.
17. 6:18-19.
18. 6:12-19.

19. 6:20-49; in Mark's gospel, Jesus ascends the mountain to appoint the twelve disciples but with no ensuing "sermon" (3:7-19), while in Matthew's gospel, Jesus goes up the mountain with no special appointment but with a delivery of the "sermon on the mount" — which has much of the same material as Luke's version — to the disciples, alone (4:23–7:29). Luke's distinctiveness helps to alert the careful listener to the more precise Mosaic parallel and the purpose of the parallel, an emphasis on the new "word" of God — a reinterpreted Law — for the people, to be delivered by Jesus but also by the disciples (Acts) whom Luke shows descending the mountain with Jesus.

ciples.[20] This word is for them, and a difficult and unusual word it is. To remain in God's favor is to serve God in this fashion: rejoice when you are excluded and reviled (section one); love your enemies (middle and key section) — what good is it to love those who like you, whom you like? Last section, look to your own inner darkness, not that of others — and listen!

Poem 9, First Section (6:20-26)

The first section represents a complete reversal of what would have been considered in Luke's day, if not our own, quite "normal":

"Blessed are you who are poor,
   for yours is the kingdom of God.
Blessed are you who are hungry now,
   for you will be filled.
Blessed are you who weep now,
   for you will laugh.
Blessed are you when people hate you, and when they exclude you,
   revile you, and defame you on account of the Son of Man.
     Rejoice in that day and leap for joy,
      for surely your reward is great in heaven;
     for that is what their ancestors did to the prophets.

But woe to you who are rich,
   for you have received your consolation.
Woe to you who are full now,
   for you will be hungry.
Woe to you who are laughing now,
   for you will mourn and weep.
Woe to you when all speak well of you,
   for that is what their ancestors did to the false prophets."

We have come full poetic circle: Mary's poetic vision of this upside-down reality is echoed here in the longest and most significant preparatory poems, with extraordinary increase in the challenge of what constitutes salvation. Mary's "lifting up of the lowly" and her "rich [sent] away empty" are represented in rather stark detail. Normal ways of living lead

---

20. 6:20.

to woe, while the counterintuitive Way of God brings blessing. For Luke's day especially,[21] this is all rather upside down, counter to common notions of honor and loyalty. For example:

> "Blessed are you when people hate you, and when they exclude you,
>   for that is what their ancestors did to the prophets.
> . . . .
> Woe to you when all speak well of you,
>   for that is what their ancestors did to the false prophets."

Jesus offers blessing to the lowly and hungry, as does Mary, but he goes further: blessings come to those who are spoken of poorly by ordinary persons.[22]

Jesus then pronounces woe, not just on Mary's proud and rich, but on those who are honored in society. "When all speak well of you," says Jesus, *you can be sure something is dreadfully wrong.*[23] When honored by all, who would expect woe? To approach the question from the opposite angle: Who would volunteer for the certain dishonor associated with going God's Way? But perhaps these questions were more appropriate for the original audience of Luke's story than for the modern reader two thousand years later.[24] For the original audience familiar with Jewish scriptures, the reversal in blessings and woes should not have been all that surprising, the text implies. After all, one need only remember the public reviling of true prophets and compare that with the public favor enjoyed by false prophets.

Perhaps the question is emerging, for Luke's audience: If this is what God's favor looks like, who would want it? In any case, Luke's audience has been disabused of the possible notion, from the prior poem recited by Jesus, that being poor is good luck because of the favor one gains from God. *Woe to you when all speak well of you!* In ordinary life, as represented in this story, being spoken well of is desirable, sought after — and wrong. *Blessed are you when people hate you, and when they exclude you!* Again, who ordinarily wants this kind of "blessing," a reviling that excludes, amounting to no less than being hated? Within the story, Jesus has to

21. That is, governed by implacable family and clan systems of reciprocal favor and protection.

22. 6:20-23.

23. 6:26.

24. I will be repeating this distinction between the original audience and a modern audience throughout, since it helps in understanding the text in its original context. But I find Luke's vision, for myself, quite universal and very compelling — if quite disturbing.

plead with his followers to be heard on this matter. Such teaching looms very large, especially in the gospel's third and concluding section.

Poem 9, Middle Section (6:27-38)

After the echoing and extension of Mary's unconventional idea of justice, Luke provides another echo in the poem's middle section:[25] those whom God blesses must become a blessing, must be agents of God's favor, God's *shalom*-justice. Here are the things that make for the kind of peace with which Zechariah concluded his poem — the same "things that make for peace" referred to by Jesus at the end of his journey.[26] I have highlighted the pivotal words of a refrain that hold this section of the poem together. The first lines of the respective stanzas state the point succinctly:

Heart of Poem, Stanza 1, "Love your enemies."

Heart of Poem, Stanza 2, "If you love those who love you, what credit is that to you?"

Heart of Poem, Stanza 3, "Love your enemies."

Stanza 1

> *"Love your enemies,*
> do good to those who hate you,
> bless those who curse you,
> pray for those who abuse you.
> If anyone strikes you on the cheek, offer the other also;
> and from anyone who takes away your coat do not withhold
>> even your shirt.
> Give to everyone who begs from you;
> and if anyone takes away your goods, do not ask for them again.
> Do to others as you would have them do to you." (6:27-31)

This is a "love" that fleshes out — perhaps unexpectedly for its audience — what the covenant with Abraham always had as its ultimate purpose: that "all the clans of the earth through you shall be blessed," that "all the nations of the earth will be blessed through your seed because you have

---

25. Whether sections #2 and #3 qualify as "poetry" is arguable, and can be determined by the reader; translations honor only section #1 as a poem. The entire monologue is "of a piece," displaying an integrity of theme and movement and — I will argue — balanced line.

26. 19:42.

listened to my voice."[27] Israel will be delivered from its enemies — within and outside of Israel — by loving them, by bringing to all who threaten them the good news of God's Way.

Luke's poem moves on to explore the difficult but basic psychology of this upside-down love, this matter of serving in love those whom you dislike and have a right to fear.

Stanza 2

"If you love those who love you, what credit is that to you?
For even sinners love those who love them.
If you do good to those who do good to you,
    what credit is that to you?
For even sinners do the same.
If you lend to those from whom you hope to receive,
    what credit is that to you?
Even sinners lend to sinners, to receive as much again." (6:32-34)

For Luke, God's Way is the Mosaic Law — love God and your neighbor — interpreted by Jesus. Salvation's blessing and God's favor are available for all, but reserved for those who go the arduous way of love. The poem's middle section circles back to the summary, "Love your enemies."

Stanza 3

"But love your enemies, do good, and lend, expecting nothing in return.
    Your reward will be great,
    and you will be children of the Most High;
    for he is kind to the ungrateful and the wicked.
    Be merciful, just as your Father is merciful.
    Do not judge, and you will not be judged;
    do not condemn, and you will not be condemned.
    Forgive, and you will be forgiven;
    give, and it will be given to you;
    A good measure,
    pressed down, shaken together, running over,
    will be put into your lap;
    for the measure you give
    will be the measure you get back." (6:35-38)

27. Gen 12:3; 22:18; trans. Robert Alter, *Genesis: Translation and Commentary* (New York: W. W. Norton, 1966).

The "love" being called for encompasses all whom the audience thinks of as "ungrateful" or even "wicked." As God is, so you be also: "Be merciful, just as your Father is merciful."

Because this word from God goes against the grain, it is all the more important to listen carefully to what the teacher is saying. And so we begin the third and last section of the poem.[28] To whose teaching will you listen? By what authority will you trust this teaching? In the gospel's concluding section these questions will define the drama of conflict within Israel.

Poem 9, Concluding Section (6:39-49)

"Can a blind person guide a blind person?
Will not both fall into a pit?
A disciple is not above the teacher,
but everyone who is fully qualified will be like the teacher." (6:39-40)

Jesus needs good students, because "everyone who is fully qualified will be like the teacher." This remarkable claim for those who respond well to his teaching hints at the significant role of God's servants, of "servant Israel" as dramatized in Acts.

Becoming like the teacher is impossible without the utmost in self-scrutiny — as opposed to the very normal tendency of scrutinizing others. To ensure blessing and prevent woe, be advised about two essentially opposed ways of going about business in life: to be judging others as worse than you, or to be judging yourself as better for others:

Why do you see the speck in your neighbor's eye,
but do not notice the log in your own eye?
Or how can you say to your neighbor,
    'Friend, let me take out the speck in your eye,'
    when you yourself do not see the log in your own eye?

---

28. As I have indicated, whether the preceding love section qualifies as "poetry" is arguable, though the balanced line and continuing thematic emphasis are clear. Charles Talbert argues, at the very least, that what I call a poem (6:20-49) is a single unit with three parts. See Charles H. Talbert, *Reading Luke: A Literary and Theological Commentary on the Third Gospel* (New York: Crossroad, 1982), pp. 69ff. As illustrated, the lines of both sections #2 and #3 "fall" naturally into the intentional line, the balanced and echoing line of poetry. It is important to keep in mind the single distinguishing feature that sets poetry off from prose: the "intentional line," the balanced play between lines that in some way echo each other and can therefore be set by author's arrangement (as I have done), rather than by the dictates of a margin.

You hypocrite,
    first take the log out of your own eye,
    and then you will see clearly to take the speck out of your
        neighbor's eye." (6:41-42)

According to Luke, you yourself are the only one whose disposition toward God you can fix. Toward the other, your neighbor, you can only and
always prove neighborly, by proclaiming good news, teaching and healing and forgiving, as God forgives you.

With an eye trained on yourself, then, the truth becomes obvious. Think
of a tree bearing good fruit versus a tree bearing rotten fruit. The tree is you:

"No good tree bears bad fruit,
nor again does a bad tree bear good fruit;
    for each tree is known by its own fruit.
Figs are not gathered from thorns,
nor are grapes picked from a bramble bush.
The good person out of the good treasure of the heart
        produces good,
and the evil person out of evil treasure produces evil;
    for it is out of the abundance of the heart that the mouth speaks."
                                                    (6:43-45)

Darkness of motive produces evil. Luke encourages his audience to look
at the kind of fruit one bears in order to determine "the abundance of
[your] heart." Persons in Luke's audience, apparently, confused piety
with goodness.

The poem's conclusion is climactic. It not only repeats the story "in a
nutshell" from the Mary-Zechariah contrast, but it also homes in on the
core of what daily repentance requires, of what being "saved" demands:

"Why do you call me 'Lord, Lord,'
and do not do what I tell you?
I will show you what someone is like who comes to me,
hears my words, and acts on them.
That one is like a man building a house,
who dug deeply and laid the foundation on rock;
when a flood arose, the river burst against that house
but could not shake it, because it had been well built.
But the one who hears and does not act
is like a man who built a house on the ground without a foundation.

When the river burst against it, immediately it fell,
and great was the ruin of that house." (6:46-49)

Hear the word and do it — and enjoy a life that is eternal, not shaken. But "the one who hears and does not act" is going to self-destruct, and all his holdings with him.

"What must I do to inherit eternal life?" is a question that gets repeated on the journey to Jerusalem.[29] The answers Jesus gives in each case have this in common: yes, there is something to do to inherit eternal life. Do the word of God that you are hearing. Nowhere is that word summarized more succinctly than in this poem on the plain, and nowhere more clearly in the poem than at its center with the word about love. The word of God is about the practice of an uncommon love through a difficult relinquishment of normal self-directed concerns.

What we hear in this grand poem by Jesus is not an offer of escape from the real world, but a challenge to enter the world in all its pain and suffering. The poem is bracketed by that real world and by Jesus' healing compassion for it. The poem is spoken after several instances of healing, and now, right afterwards, Jesus is seen healing the slave of a Roman centurion who has been good to the Jews[30] and raising to life a widow's dead son.[31] In response to John's messengers wondering if Jesus is "the One who is to come," Jesus responds by pointing to his healings.[32]

In addition to the nine major poems that we have explored, there are three more poems, each of which in a very brief way summarizes key aspects of the prior nine poems while indicating response to what Jesus is teaching.

In the first, Jesus is musing about John, having answered the messengers about his being the One anointed by God, indeed, as attested by his bringing good news to the poor. In this brief poem, Jesus repeats the borrowing of the narrator earlier, from Malachi:

See, I am sending my messenger ahead of you,
who will prepare your way before you. (7:27; Mal 3:1)

This echoing about John's preparing the Way reinforces the developing motif and expectations surrounding "the Way," most perfectly expressed

29. 10:21-42; 18:15-30.
30. 7:2-10.
31. 7:12-15.
32. 7:18-23.

in the long poem on the plain by Jesus. But much awaits in the carefully ordered teaching of the gospel's dramatic centerpiece, the journey to Jerusalem — a teaching that is referred to even by Jesus' enemies as "the Way of God."[33]

The second to last poem, also very brief, indicates negative response to this Way from those who are "falling" within Israel. The poem, borrowed from popular folklore, describes poor listeners as petulant children who are "sitting in the marketplace and calling to one another,

'We played the flute for you,
    and you did not dance;
we wailed,
    and you did not weep'" (7:32)

The meaning seems to be something like this: *we played for you, Jesus, but you didn't dance to our tune;* on the other hand, *when we wailed our own particular sorrow, you did not commiserate with us.*

Or, the "we" could be Jesus and his followers calling out to the ordinary and wicked generation for communal celebration or sorrow, and being rebuffed. In either case, the response of Jesus relates to the wrong-headedness of normal ways. John, Jesus points out, "has come eating no bread and drinking no wine, and you say, 'He has a demon': the Son of Man, has come eating and drinking, and you say, 'Look, a glutton and a drunkard, a friend of tax collectors and sinners!'"[34] The opposition here — the Jewish leadership — wants it both ways. Those who follow normal ways of rejoicing and regret are clearly on a different page from the one who follows God's Way as "a friend of tax collectors and sinners." This old-guard response will soon erupt into murderous jealousy and rage. The new "Leader" of Israel[35] and its old leaders turn out to be on opposite pages of a songbook.

But you Israelites on the Way, says Jesus a narrative moment later, are different. You are the right sort of children, remaining open to "secrets of the kingdom of God,"[36] whereas to this recalcitrant generation of traditional religionists, I must speak in parables, so that

"looking they may not perceive,
and listening they may not understand." (8:10; Is 6:9)

33. Lk 20:21.
34. 7:33-34.
35. Acts 5:31.
36. 8:9-10; see 10:21-24.

This last of the twelve preparatory poems will be echoed at the very end of the story, in words borrowed from Isaiah by Paul concerning those Jews who refuse to repent: "You will indeed listen, but never understand. . . . For this people's heart has grown dull, and their ears are hard of hearing, and they have shut their eyes so that they might not look [or] listen with their ears. . . ."[37]

The Twelve Poems: A Brief Summary

God favors those within Israel who serve God's purposes by reaching out with healing to the poor. God's favor rests on Mary's "servant Israel," though there will be many falling away from Israel, as Simeon had foreseen. God's purposes are summarized by the one-word term *peace* — a *shalom*-justice that is all-inclusive, of outsiders, diseased, oppressed, prisoners, and enemies. Blessed are those Israelites (the primary audience of Jesus) "who, when they hear the word, hold it fast in an honest and good heart, and bear fruit with patient endurance" [38] That word is based on Scripture, and distills the essence of its good news: release and restoration through the radical living-out of the Law — by loving your enemy, for example.

Luke's listening audience has been prepared for the teaching of this Way by these twelve interrelated poems and the interspersed healings: here, if there is to be blessing, is the importance of proper response to the word of God as taught by Jesus. *Preparing the way:* John prepares the way of Jesus. Luke is preparing his audience for the Way, orchestrated as a literal journey to Jerusalem and more importantly a thematic journey toward the heart of God's kingdom. In the middle section of volume one, the "teaching section," we find a description of a kingdom that begins in earnest at the start of volume two, a kingdom of which "there will be no end."[39]

But there is one more word in preparing the way, a dark word, a word about disruption and even death. The good news is not easy news for those remaining in God's favor, as we will find in our exploration of remaining motifs in the first nine chapters. Even healing, an expression of the good news, suggests turmoil and striving.

---

37. Acts 28:26-28; Is 6:9-10.
38. 8:15.
39. Lk 1:33.

Chapter 4

A Motif of Darkness and Disruption

Luke 1:1–9:50

The "good news" has its very dark and disruptive aspects, which the first nine preparatory chapters emphasize as distinct motifs. When a diseased and disordered creation is made whole, there is a struggle against the Evil One. When religious rules are threatened by a higher ordering of godly wholeness, there is a struggle. When ordinary religious and/or political rulers are threatened by what is truly right, there is a struggle — in John the Baptist's case, and in hints about Jesus — to the death. When well-meaning followers succeed and then fail, the failure is emphasized by a staccato-like repetition; Jesus himself becomes greatly exasperated. When a mother's son as good as Jesus follows perfectly the Way of God, ordinary mothers like Mary can become greatly agitated with that son, and can be curtly refused by the son himself. When this Son of God goes God's Way perfectly, God's great opponent, Satan, comes with temptations of a lifetime. The preparatory chapters orchestrate carefully these motifs of darkness and disruption inherent in the good news.

I. The Struggle for Wholeness and Order, Against Satan: The Healings

We have caught glimpses of the clustered healings of these preparatory chapters, all eleven instances[1] coming after the first poem by Jesus. As in the case of the eleventh and last healing — of a convulsing child — so it is

1. 4:33-37; 4:38-39; 4:40-41 (summary); 5:12-14; 5:17-26; 6:6-11; 6:18-19 (summary); 7:2-10; 7:12-15; 8:1-3 (summary of women healed — who are followers, providers); 8:26-39; 8:41-42, 49-56; 8:43-48; 9:38-42.

54

with the very first healing: the struggle is against no less than the Power of Darkness, the devil and his demons. Immediately after announcing his anointing as one "to bring good news to the poor" and then being nearly killed,[2] Jesus goes to another town where a demon-possessed man confronts Jesus. "Let us alone!" scream the inhabiting demons. "What have you to do with us, Jesus of Nazareth? Have you come to destroy us?"[3] The answer is *yes*, and a struggle it will be. "In attacking this one unclean spirit," as Joel B. Green notes, "the Spirit-empowered Jesus has initiated a ministry of 'release' constituting an onslaught against all the forces of evil."[4] The Holy One battles the Unholy One, just as followers will, in Acts.

Jesus conquers even the evil of death, raising the widow's son; Peter and Paul each do the same, claiming victory over the worst that Satan can do. Just as Jesus *rebukes* the unclean spirit, so in the next scene "he stood over [Simon's mother-in-law] and *rebuked* the fever, and it left her."[5] Both the man and the woman are unclean, unwhole, and in each case, there is a departing of the evil.[6] (As is frequently the case, starting with Zechariah and Mary, Luke pairs male and female.) Jesus is God's "holy servant"[7] who is opposed to the unholy spirit of disorder and disease. Such is the understanding of Jesus regarding his special anointing by God.[8]

From the start of biblically recorded time, God's purposes are steadfast, a desire for blessing and order against curse and disorder.[9] God con-

---

2. 4:18-30.

3. 4:34.

4. Joel B. Green, *The Gospel of Luke* (Grand Rapids: Eerdmans, 1997), p. 223.

5. 4:39; "release" is featured in the first poem and first public words of Jesus: "release to captives" and to the oppressed; "recovery of sight to the blind" (4:18).

6. Notes Joel B. Green, "As Jesus 'rebuked' the demon . . . so he 'rebukes' this fever; just as the demon 'went out' of the man, so the fever 'departs' this woman" (*The Gospel of Luke*, p. 225).

7. Acts 4:27, 30.

8. See the prior chapter, poem #8, 4:18-19.

9. "When God began to create heaven and earth
   and the earth then was welter and waste
   and darkness over the deep
   and God's breath hovering over the waters,
   God said, 'Let there be light.'

   . . . .

   . . . then the Lord God fashioned the human,
   and blew into his nostrils the breath of life." (Gen 1:1; 2:7; trans. Robert Alter,
   Genesis: Translation and Commentary [New York: W. W. Norton, 1966]).

As I suggest elsewhere, Luke may be relying on the common knowledge of his audience regarding this original ordering out of disorder, through God's powerful words.

fronted the primal elements of great disorder with powerful words, and with the "hovering" of the divine spirit and the "touch" of his breath. Perhaps the audience is being reminded, in the reordering powers of Jesus and then of the disciples, that God's word, properly understood and applied with rigorous focus, has the efficacy of God's "standing over" disorder, that only God breathes life into the human creature from "dust of the ground," *ha'adam* from *'adamah*.[10] It is from this effort that God rested, on the seventh day. Jesus restores order from disorder similarly, with strong words and touch.

The effort required by healing is not just an overcoming of cosmic disorder, but of human fabrication — religious scruple! No religious rule or ritual should stand in the way of such restoration to order. Jesus strives against the strong forces of his religion, touching an unclean leper and thus violating the religious law by becoming "unclean" himself.[11] Then he himself is touched — by a bleeding woman; such touching brings release for the woman but ritual uncleanness for Jesus. With another woman, the feverish mother-in-law of Simon, Jesus "stood over her" before rebuking the disorder. Later, on the journey, he will twice heal on the holy day and come under religious scrutiny.[12]

Five sequences of human healing are preceded by disturbances or potential loss within a context of tumultuous or possibly threatening nature: a cliff from which a person can be thrown to her death; a sea whose absence of fish threatens physical sustenance and livelihood; a flood and bursting river; howling winds and a sea that threatens to sink a boat and all its passengers; and, finally, a human-consuming cloud that terrifies three disciples.[13] All of this havoc is dealt with or spoken about by Jesus.

---

10. Gen 2:7; just prior to the temptations of Jesus, we have had his ancestry. It is traced from Jesus son of Joseph ("as was thought," 3:23) back through Abraham and Noah to "Adam, son of God" (3:23-38). (Matthew's genealogy for Jesus begins with Abraham, in keeping with Matthew's more programmatic focus on Israel; Luke has a wider-angle lens that consistently brings into view both Israel and the Gentiles — that is, Jews and non-Jews of the earth.) Perhaps Luke is reminding the good listener of the first parents and their Creator-God — and of their descent into the chaos of normal choosing. They each succumbed to the temptation to advance their "standing" — to become like the gods, the everlasting human argument about greatness. Such power-moves — and Luke shows them to be extremely subtle at times — begin with Eve and then Adam, and are chronicled in every major story of the Jewish scriptures. These were the biblical stories so familiar to Jesus, and to Luke.

11. Green, *The Gospel of Luke*, p. 237.

12. 13:10-17; 14:1-6.

13. 4:29-30; 5:4-11; 6:48-49; 8:22-25; 9:34-35.

In Luke's story there is something new — good news — going on in dimensions that are cosmic, communal, and individual. At the heart of Luke's story, as mentioned, is nothing less than the "universal restoration" in Acts — the restitution of the blessing intended by God for the original creation.[14]

Agents of God speak order into the disarray — agents like Jesus, the disciples, or even the Jewish exorcists who do not follow Jesus.[15] In several cases restoration comes partially through the effort and faithfulness of friends working together against great odds.[16] Twice the restoration to wholeness is actually resisted by the person, who is dominated by inhabiting evil spirits.[17] Such healing cannot be accomplished without a willingness of healers to pay attention to others at the expense of their own status and comfort. Social barriers must be ignored, the stigma of disease must be overlooked, religious rules suspended. Foreigners are to be included, along with social and religious outcasts — as we might have expected from the early poetry's emphasis on good news for Israel and then for all-the-rest, the non-Jews of the world.

II. The Struggle Within Family:
The Three-Part Darkness of Mother Mary
(2:35; 2:41-51; 8:19-21)

Three times we find Mary at the center of a storm, a struggle centered around the very son whose birth she willingly embraced as servant to God's purposes.

(1) Pierced Soul

Holding an eight-day-old Jesus in the temple, Simeon praises God, in the sixth poem, for this "light for revelation to the Gentiles" and this "glory to your people Israel."[18] But then this godly prophet turns his attention to Mary with very disturbing words:

14. Acts 3:21.
15. Lk 11:19.
16. 4:38-39; 5:17-26; 7:2-10; 8:41-42 and 49-56; 9:38-42.
17. 4:33-37; 8:26-39.
18. Lk 2:29-32.

"This child is destined for the falling and the rising of many in Israel, and to be a sign that will be opposed so that the inner thoughts of many will be revealed — and a sword will pierce your own soul, too." (2:34-35)

Simeon suggests that the news Jesus brings will not be good for everyone. While many in Israel will be rising, many will fall. Inner thoughts will be revealed — not a very pleasant prospect for anyone. And finally, Mary herself will suffer a pierced soul. How will Mary's soul be pierced? Luke does not make his audience wait long for the answer.

(2) An Angered and Agitated Mother

A few verses removed from the soul-piercing reference, we find Mary and Joseph traveling to Jerusalem to celebrate Passover with their twelve-year-old son.[19] Festivities over, the entourage heads home, to tiny Nazareth. They have been on the road a long day's journey, but "the boy Jesus stayed behind in Jerusalem, [and] his parents did not know it."[20] Having finally discovered that the lad is missing, the entire caravan turns back — a second day's journey. They search in the busy city for an additional three days. Five days, and there is no trace of the child. When finally located, the boy seems not the least bit concerned about his parents' obvious frustration. He is listening to teachers, at the temple, and putting questions to them. There has been no expressed concern from the twelve-year-old about the whereabouts of his parents or any of the accompanying adults.

His mother has a question for the young Jesus. It expresses exasperation, at the very least. "Child, why have you treated us like this?" she asks. "Look, your father and I have been searching for you in great anxiety."[21]

"Why were you searching for me?" the child retorts.

Is this response casual? Insolent? Disingenuous? Jesus appears in this instance to be "a precocious but apparently inconsiderate child."[22] How are we to understand the boy's extraordinary question, after these several days of no-contact with family, friends, and fellow-travelers?

---

19. 2:41-51.
20. 2:43.
21. 2:48.
22. "Jesus looks like something less than the son one dreams of." Sharon Ringe, *Luke* (Louisville: Westminster/John Knox, 1995), p. 47.

Young Jesus is not through: "Did you not know I must be in my Father's house?"

The reader has already been informed that "Dad" is not the biological father of Jesus. How does Joseph respond, then, to his son's implicit question, Did you not know that my "real" father has claims on me that supersede any you might have? Did you not know, even when traveling back home and realizing that I was not with you — didn't you understand that my home is *here*, not with you? That "I must be in my Father's house"?

Joseph and Mary have heard marvelous things said about their son from shepherds, who report their heavenly message, and from the venerable Simeon and Anna. Mary, in fact, has been addressed by an angel concerning the greatness of her child-to-be. And yet: "They did not understand what he said to them."[23] Nor, presumably, could Joseph and Mary determine the tone in which the stark responses from their twelve-year-old were offered. There appears to be a "puzzle as to why Jesus' calling as Son of God should require him to cause pain to his human parents."[24] The story goes on to reveal the answer, not only for Jesus but for all others he calls.

There will be difficult talk about family in Luke's two-volume story. And yet, before John's birth it was told Zechariah that his son would "turn the hearts of parents to their children" (1:17). Something wrong would be righted: with the coming of God's good news and subsequent repentance of those willing to change, parents would pay a different kind of attention to their children than was normal in that time and place.[25] But the toll of this good news on ordinary family loyalty will be great.

Just before and just after this episode of family discomfort, we are told that the twelve-year-old is growing in wisdom.[26] Is this what God's wisdom looks like? In that day, such behavior would have been even more outlandish than in modern cultures.[27] The picture of a seemingly haughty and inconsiderate youngster is framed emphati-

23. 2:50.

24. Robert C. Tannehill, *Luke*, Abingdon New Testament Commentaries (Nashville: Abingdon, 1996), p. 77.

25. See Robert Tannehill's helpful summary of conventional scholarly insight into the role and plight of children in the culture of Jesus' day (*Luke*, p. 165).

26. 2:40, 52.

27. "Jesus' treatment of his parents would probably be more disturbing in ancient Mediterranean society than in our own" (Tannehill, *Luke*, p. 76).

cally by this same boy's growing wisdom and God's growing pleasure with the boy.

Something of the same distancing and seeming arrogance occurs a little later in the narrative; Jesus is now fully grown.

(3) A Mother Curtly Rebuffed by the Adult Son, Jesus

The infant Jesus, held by Simeon, will become *a sword [that] will pierce your own soul, too;* the young boy Jesus responds to a clearly and understandably frenzied mother with a retort; the adult Jesus responds to his mother with apparent rudeness.

After recording seven healings by Jesus, Luke shows the adult Jesus teaching in a crowded house. "His mother and his brothers came to him, but they could not reach him because of the crowd." Jesus is then told, "Your mother and brothers are standing outside and want to see you."[28] But Jesus apparently refuses to see them, turning to those he is teaching with what for Luke are cornerstone words: "My mother and my brothers are those who hear the word of God and put it into practice."[29]

The response of the adult Jesus to his family would have sounded even more dismissive and jarring to Luke's audience than the seemingly rude questions posed by the twelve-year-old Jesus to his frantic parents. Here, he refuses to leave the house, even for a moment: *tell my mother and brothers that, on the basis of an un-normal and counterintuitive standard, I have other mothers and other family members who take precedence over any mere parochial consideration of blood-tie.*[30]

"Listen," Jesus had just said, "anyone who has ears to hear!" — and then he goes on to tell a story about hearing the good word and doing the goodness of that word, and of how the normal "cares of life" — family concerns included? — can get in the way.[31] Perhaps the family of Jesus was

---

28. 8:19-20.

29. 8:21.

30. On the journey's Way, beginning at 9:51, the theme of family will come up again, in closely paralleled episodes. Once again, traditional family values like loyalty and honor, characteristic of the normal way, will prove to be in opposition to the building blocks of community under God's reign.

31. 8:14; in the parable, a sower goes out to sow. The seed, which is the word of God's Way being taught by Jesus, can fall on the well-worn paths (ordinary people going everyday ways) and get trampled underfoot and taken up by birds — snatched away by Satan. Or it is like seed falling on rocky soil, easy prey to wilting in conditions of no soil or mois-

seeking him out of normal concern, traditional family "care." Perhaps they wished in some way to protect him against public dishonor — which Jesus incurs often. Such dishonor, after all, would reflect on the family. We don't know, but the textual fact is that theirs is a family concern rebuffed by Jesus.

Mary had the extraordinary good sense, early in the story, to ponder.[32] Something was to unfold, and she wondered deeply about the import, the implications. She hears that her soul will be pierced; her twelve-year-old son proves disruptive, causing great agitation and responding with what normally would be considered haughtiness; her adult son reduces his mother and brothers to the status of anybodys: those who would be his "mother," brothers, and sisters must join in a greater family, citizens of a kingdom where all that counts is hearing and doing God's word.[33] No longer is there parochial privileging of Mother, of Brother, of Sister. Here is a piercing of a mother's soul.

III. The Struggle for What Is Right:
The Early Death of the Good Ones, John and Jesus

The lives of John and Jesus have been intertwined in carefully ordered parallels since before birth.[34] As an adult, John teaches salvation, repen-

---

ture. With this seed-and-soil example, there are joyful belief and the enjoyment of God's favor — but "they believe only for a while and in a time of testing fall away." Then a third category of response, subtler, more complicated: this seed falls on weed-infested ground, but grows quite well. There is more than merely an initial joy of salvation and belief. But, finally, alas, after good growth, the seeds "are choked by the cares and riches and pleasures of life" (8:14).

32. Mary "was perplexed by [the angel's] words and pondered what sort of greeting this might be," and, later, treasured the shepherds' words "and pondered them in her heart" (1:29; 2:19).

33. This "hearing and doing of God's word" is at the heart of Luke's story. In the sower tale, the seed — the word from God — thrives only in the soil of an "honest and good heart" (8:5-15). Both Matthew and Mark use this parable, but Luke alone describes the good listeners as those with "an honest and good heart." Unlike Mark, whose gospel focuses on the increasing failure of the disciples to hear well and produce any kind of harvest, Luke pays special attention to those hearers whose soil is good enough to be cultivated toward bearing fruit in the end. Luke sees that cultivation process as the teaching of Jesus, most especially on the journey to Jerusalem. Here it is that the listener is provided with Way principles — ways of thinking, not rules prohibiting thought.

34. There are the announcements for their respective births by the same angel, which we saw in Chapter 1. The mother of Jesus recites a marvelous poem, as does the father of John. Each poem regarding respective offspring contains echoes between them. There occur

tance, and the forgiveness of sin.[35] Jesus will do the same, though in much elaborated fashion.

John's father, Zechariah the priest, has seen that his infant son "will be called prophet of the Most High," called upon to "go before the Lord to prepare his ways." John will prepare by giving "knowledge of salvation . . . by the forgiveness of their sins." The prepared-for one, the Messiah, will then "guide our feet into the way of peace."[36] And yet, in giving the good news of forgiveness, John himself faces darkness.

Herod the ruler hasn't liked the conditions for forgiveness and salvation. John's call to righteousness is resisted by Herod, since he is a doer of "evil things"; he solves the problem of this affront "by shutting up John in prison."[37] John prepares the Way for Jesus and is quickly gone, in twenty narrative verses. He then reappears in the text, at a point just before a momentous and ominous journey by Jesus to Jerusalem. John is still in prison, and finds himself in some doubt, or at least confusion, about the events surrounding Jesus, and about Jesus himself. Is he the Messiah? What exactly is Jesus up to? He sends messengers to inquire. Tell John, responds Jesus to the messengers, about all these healings that I am doing: that the poor are hearing the good news. And add this: that "blessed is anyone who takes no offense at me."[38]

Why these words, "Blessed is anyone who takes no offense at me"? Surely John might have had second thoughts, at the very least. He had been offering the good news of salvation and forgiveness of sins, and he had seen genuine repentance and had granted forgiveness for the people's sins. Why would God allow Herod to shut off such a public ministry so soon? John might very well take offense at Jesus, God's Messiah, on whose account he was suffering. "Blessed is anyone who takes no offense at me," Jesus wants John to hear.

---

parallel accounts of each miraculous birth. We are given separate accounts of the circumcision rites for each, at eight days. Even the summaries of their human maturation process share precisely the same formula of expression:

- "The child grew and became strong," we hear about John (1:80);
- "The child grew and became strong," we hear about Jesus (2:40).

John's growing strong is in "spirit," while the growing strong of Jesus is in "wisdom." Jesus will receive nothing less than God's own spirit, but is distinguished here by a twist of difference: Jesus grows in wisdom — the teacher, seer, wisdom-sayer.

35. 1:76-77.
36. 1:76-77, 79.
37. 3:19-20.
38. 7:18-23.

A bit later we hear the last of John. He has already been beheaded, the ultimate disruption — the loss of one's life — that all followers of the Way must be willing to face if they are to be saved.[39] This third and last notice is after-the-fact, a simple word concerning Herod's confusion about whether this Jesus could be John risen from the dead, since "John I beheaded."[40] What then awaits this Jesus, Luke's audience might well wonder, this Jesus who is so closely paralleled with John within Luke's text that even Herod confuses the two?

Asked if he is the expected Messiah, John has answered in the negative, citing one who will come after him, and is much greater: "I baptize you with water; . . . he will baptize you with the Holy Spirit and fire."[41] The distinction between John and Jesus is not in the offer of repentance and forgiveness of sins, but in the baptisms. Luke sets up this difference between baptisms with great care:

> Now when all the people were baptized and when Jesus also had been baptized and was praying, the heaven was opened, and the Holy Spirit descended upon him in bodily form like a dove. And a voice came from heaven, "You are my Son, the Beloved; with you I am well pleased." (3:21-22)

Jesus "*had been* baptized": John leaves the narrative stage even before the audience gets to see Jesus baptized (unlike the account in Matthew, which flows from John's baptizing Jesus to the Holy Spirit's descent as a dove).[42] The absence of John from the account of the baptism of Jesus and the discontinuity of Jesus' baptism itself from the Holy Spirit's descent accentuate a narrative purpose: the descent of the Holy Spirit is most closely associated with prayer. "[Jesus] was praying" when the Holy Spirit descends on him.[43] This linkage between prayer and help from God — the Holy Spirit — will prove critical in the story ahead: salvation's grace in this two-volume story comes in two phases, the gift of God's word as taught by Jesus, Messiah, and the gift of God's Spirit, made pos-

39. 9:9.
40. 9:9.
41. 3:16.
42. Lk 3:21-23; Mt 3:13-17.
43. Jesus "had [already] been baptized," and in the present "was praying" when the Spirit's descent occurs — a detail that is echoed at the beginning of volume two, when, similarly, the followers of God's Way are praying and the Holy Spirit descends on them (Acts 1:14; 2:1-4). There is to be a new coupling, for anyone: prayer and Holy Spirit; conversation with God, and God's empowerment.

sible by Jesus, "Leader" of Israel, "Savior" of Israel.[44] It is the special function of the Holy Spirit, in this two-volume story, to provide the empowerment and help necessary in the struggle for salvation. Entering the kingdom, salvation, is difficult because of the darkness inherent as "cost" for those bearing good news.

The *fire* connected with the baptism of Jesus further distinguishes this "dying-and-rising" from John's baptism. Jesus will baptize "with the Holy Spirit and *fire.*" On the one hand, the fire is associated with the Holy Spirit, an enabling Spirit who has descended on Jesus and will descend on disciples as "tongues as of *fire.*"[45] On the other hand, the burning-away fire comes in part from "the linkage of baptism with the use of water to cleanse a person in Jewish thought," a cleansing of sins that requires, for John and Jesus and the later apostles (as represented by Luke), a rigorous journey of repentance. Such a journey of repentance is filled with a suffering that can lead to death.[46]

The paralleled baptisms of John and Jesus represent the reality of repentance, a death to all normal ways of living in favor of life according to God's kingdom, God's Way. The striving required by such repentance is made possible through a Spirit that will be sent by the departed Jesus, which explains the significance of John's distinction between his baptism and that of Jesus. But the "stress" that Jesus experiences in such baptism is a very loud echo of what John has experienced. "I came to bring fire to the earth," Jesus will say, ominously, "and how I wish it were already kindled! I have a baptism with which to be baptized, and what *stress* I am under until it is completed."[47] Fire, baptism, *stress:* these necessarily accompany the striving required for salvation, as the narrative ahead will show. Among such fire and baptismal death is associated the division within families: "father against son, and son against father; mother against daughter and daughter against mother."[48] The baptism of fire is a significant twist of difference in the paralleled baptisms of John and Jesus. John had alluded to the worthless part of lives, "chaff,"

44. Acts 5:31; from the beginning to the end of this two-volume story, the baptism associated with repentance leading to the forgiveness of sins will remain the same from John's baptism through Acts, but with the added empowerment to obey the teaching of Jesus and so be "saved" (Lk 13:23-24, for example).

45. Acts 2:3.

46. Green, *The Gospel of Luke,* p. 164. That repentance is a requirement for forgiveness is clear from the text here; it is also a gift from God, as Acts makes clear (5:31; 11:18).

47. Lk 12:49-50.

48. 12:53.

which Jesus "will burn with unquenchable fire."[49] Jesus will be featured, especially by Paul in the second half of Acts, as Judge — the one who is designated by God as being in charge of the "unquenchable fire" for chaff.

Later in this preparatory section, Jesus is shown trying rather unsuccessfully to explain his own upcoming death to uncomprehending disciples at the narrative point where we have just had a flashback to the beheading of John.[50] With narrative near-simultaneity, we hear of two deaths, John's past beheading and Jesus' future murder. Jesus says that he "must undergo great suffering, and be rejected by the elders, chief priests, and scribes, and be killed, and *on the third day be raised*."[51] John's death will be paralleled by the death of Jesus with one extraordinary difference: God will raise Jesus from the dead.

Why does the purely good arouse such fury as leads to death? Why do these good ones, John and Jesus, die young? The story seeks to lay bare the underlying causes. After overcoming his initial struggle with Satan, Jesus faces his hometown neighbors who wish to kill him after hearing what he has to say.[52] At the heart of their wrath is Jesus' refusal to privilege their parochial desire. "Do here also in your hometown the things that we have heard you did at Capernaum," his neighbors insist.[53] Clutching after clan interests, Jesus responds, has been anticipated by the prophets: Elijah ignored the famine in his homeland and went to help a foreigner, and a woman! Elijah's understudy Elisha, Jesus goes on, did the same thing, ignoring local lepers to heal a leprous Syrian.[54] Enraged at this challenging word from Jesus, the townspeople "led him to the brow of the hill . . . so that they might hurl him off the cliff."[55]

Why not give the people a sign that you can be trusted, the devil has suggested to Jesus, that your word is indeed *not* heretical, that your attention to healing those outside the neighborhood and clan is indeed what God wants? But the only "sign" to be offered, as it turns out in this story, is God's endorsement of the authoritative teaching of Jesus by raising him from suffering and death — though even then, the person of

---

49. 3:17.

50. John's prior beheading referred to, 9:9; first prophecy of Jesus' death, 9:22; second, 9:44.

51. 9:9, 22.

52. 4:16-30.

53. 4:23.

54. 4:25-27.

55. 4:29.

normal ways will not "be convinced even if someone rises from the dead."[56] The parochial interests of hometown and even mother, in this story, create genuine and daily areas of struggle for anyone embracing Jesus, his name, and his interpretation of the good news of Scripture.

Later followers of the Way will be subjected to harassments, similarly, once God's Spirit — holy, purely good — comes mightily upon them. Followers in Acts become subject to various forms of human dishonor, harassment, imprisonments, and threats of death.[57] John is beheaded, Jesus crucified, Stephen stoned, and James cut down by sword. Paul journeys toward Jerusalem and then Rome, with the ominous suggestions of Paul's murderous death.

IV. The Direct Struggle with God's Great Opponent, Satan

John has been in the wilderness eating very little and proclaiming a difficult word of preparation for Jesus; Jesus goes into the wilderness, hungry, and is confronted with very real temptations that would allow him a life of ordinary security and comfort. Immediately after the Spirit descends on Jesus, he is led by this same Spirit into a "fiery" sort of confrontation with the Evil Power of the universe, Satan. John has been urging those listening to turn around from the normal ways of using power and privilege.[58] The devil tempts Jesus with something of the same, and uses biblical poetry to prove the legitimacy of his satanic appeals. (Jesus is portrayed in this story as consistently opposing such use of scripture that fastens on rule-bound detail while missing the essential truths.)[59] The words Jesus uses from Jewish scriptures — and Satan's twisted use of the same — indicate the need for such an interpreter of Torah and the prophets as Jesus.

---

56. 16:31.

57. Luke understands the story of Jesus as on a continuum; as Messiah, Jesus affirms and clarifies the past while making possible the future of a fulfilled covenant with Israel whereby believers can be partners with God toward the accomplishment of God's steadfast purpose, of blessing extended to all peoples through redeemed Israel (Acts 3:25; Genesis 12:3). David is on this continuum, for Luke, as are John and now Jesus and soon — volume two — those who carry on in the physical absence of Jesus.

58. 3:7-14.

59. For obvious reasons, I have not included Satan's poems as among the twelve poems that prepare us for God's Way. Besides, the devil has wrenched these poems from their narrative context!

(1) Satan

Use the magic of your special status with God to feed yourself by turning stone to bread.

Jesus

counters with scripture: *There is more to life than merely focusing one's powers on bread — and the acclaim of an easily impressed public.*

(2) Satan

Use my magical powers to gain for yourself "glory and authority" — what any normal young man on the rise would covet.

Jesus

once again quoting from God's word, *I must worship only God, and serve only God's purposes.*

(3) Satan

Try your magical powers to assure yourself of special standing with God; twisting Scripture, he implores, *throw yourself down and get a short-cut verification of significance from the highest possible source.*

Jesus

once again quoting words from God, *one does not relate to God in such a "testing" manner.*[60]

All three temptations represent the constant pull toward self-aggrandizement and self-promotion by way of the spectacular. This is the great pull toward the ordinary and perfectly normal, a shunning of service to God's purposes and blessing by taking care of oneself and becoming, if possible, someone great, like a god. Such is the primal and very first temptation offered humankind, in Eden's garden.[61] To resist is difficult. Alone in the wilderness, Jesus defeats the devil, and chooses to serve God's purposes. Alone in a garden toward the end of his life, Luke will show Jesus once again facing a time of trial like this one. The testing is sufficiently serious and severe as to bring Jesus into a state of anguish.[62]

---

60. (1) 4:3-4; (2) 4:5-8; (3) 4:9-12; note the "serve" motif, from the poems in the second temptation.

61. Gen 3:5.

62. A longer manuscript version (always suspect, because of the possibility of scribal addition) even suggests that the face of Jesus showed sweat dripping like blood (22:44).

V. Such Good News, Such Possibility of Not-Good: Five Clustered Failures

To complete God's will on earth, Jesus needs the disciples' cooperation. And so Jesus "called the twelve [disciples] together and gave them power and authority over all demons and to cure diseases, and he sent them out to proclaim the kingdom of God."[63] After ten instances of Jesus' bringing the good news of healing by word and by touch, and after some initial success at the same by the disciples,[64] the disciples stumble, badly, in a series of five failures.

Failure #1

Empowered by Jesus with "bringing the good news and curing diseases," the disciples report their success[65] but immediately fail to feed the hungry. "Send the crowd away," they ask Jesus, "to lodge and get provisions. . . . But [Jesus] said to them, 'You get them something to eat.'"[66] The narrative has prepared the audience for the reasonableness of this challenge from Jesus.

Jesus then helps them do the job, with leftovers gathered up in "twelve baskets of broken pieces."[67] Are we to hear in the "twelve" baskets echoes reinforcing the idea of responsibility for the twelve disciples? Just prior, the text has recorded that for just such a mission Jesus has "called the twelve" and that "the twelve came to him" with the suggestion to send the hungry crowd away hungry.[68] In any case, the single-sentence response of Jesus stands out, with the likely emphasis: "*You* give them something to eat."

Failure #2

Almost immediately after the quasi-rebuke about feeding the hungry crowd, Jesus takes Peter, James, and John up a mountain. While praying, Jesus suddenly becomes "dazzling white," in company with Moses and Elijah. The disciples awoke and "saw his glory."[69] Such a vision prompts Peter to blurt out, "Master, it is good for us to be here!" — here, where the

63. 9:1-2.
64. 9:3-6.
65. 9:6, 10.
66. 9:12-13.
67. 9:13-17.
68. 9:1, 12.
69. 9:28-32.

glory is — but "while he was saying this, a cloud came and overshadowed them."[70] An angry cloud? "They were terrified as they entered the cloud," and hear words to the effect, Keep quiet! "This is my Son, my Chosen; listen to him!"[71] Listen to what Jesus has been trying to explain to you about his suffering, and yours. In just a narrative moment, we will see the extent to which these disciples cannot listen, cannot hear, cannot understand.

Peter wanted to make permanent dwellings to stay here at the site of glory; at Gethsemane, the scene of suffering, they all end up fleeing. Framing this glory scene are prophecies by Jesus of the ultimate darkness and disruption of his own suffering.[72] The three representative disciples — who should be the closest to "getting it" — do not understand at all. They want to remain up high, with permanent sweetness and light among the Great Ones. The heart of all five failures is here, a resistance to the underside of glory.

Failure #3

Having healed others, the disciples now fail to heal a child. The distraught father details graphically for an agitated Jesus the situation of his demon-possessed son:

> On the next day, when they had come down from the mountain, a great crowd met him. Just then a man from the crowd shouted, "Teacher, I beg you to look at my son; he is my only child. Suddenly a spirit seizes him, and all at once he shrieks. It convulses him until he foams at the mouth; it mauls him and will scarcely leave him. I begged your disciples to cast it out, but they could not." Jesus answered, "You faithless and perverse generation, how much longer must I be with you and bear with you? Bring your son here." (9:37-41)

For Luke, it is not privileged faith or correct procedure that ensures healing. Rather, it is lack of paying attention — a perversity — that *prevents* healing. The Jewish scriptures speak of Israel as "a perverse generation, children in whom there is no faithfulness" — as those who have ignored "loving the Lord your God" and "walking in his ways."[73] Jesus here accuses the disciples of the same for their failure with the little boy.

---

70. 9:33-34.
71. 9:34-35.
72. 9:21-27; 9:44-45.
73. Deut 32:20; 30:16.

We still do not know why the disciples could not heal this child, though we know, because of the angry response from Jesus, that they should have. Just verses ahead we come to an illumination concerning the cause of what so frustrates Jesus and the cause of the disciples' failure. "How much longer must I be with you?" exclaims Jesus; how much longer must I "bear with you"? With his own leave-taking drawing very close, what can Jesus do with these followers?

Failure #4

Did the disciples experience a failure of nerve, a waning of "belief" in the power entrusted to them? The immediate narrative context suggests otherwise, and leads to yet another kind of failure:

> While he was coming [to the boy], the demon dashed him to the ground in convulsions. But Jesus rebuked the unclean spirit, healed the boy, and gave him back to his father. And all were astounded at the greatness of God. While everyone was amazed at all that he was doing, he said to his disciples, "Let these words sink into your ears: The Son of Man is going to be betrayed into human hands." But they did not understand this saying; its meaning was concealed from them, so that they could not perceive it. And they were afraid to ask him about this saying. An argument arose among them as to which one of them was the greatest. (9:42-46)

The disciples' failure to heal a child immediately precedes their failure to understand the betrayal of their leader — and then an exposure of their true orientations: "which one of them was the greatest."

Perhaps the "meaning was concealed from them so that they could not perceive it" because their perception is hopelessly clouded over by ego-needs. Can it be that *their* leader will be exposed as powerless?[74] Such ignominy would reflect on themselves. Furthermore, we see them actually squabbling among themselves for that very power and standing. Their focus is perfectly normal, a preoccupation with personal status rather than concentrated concern for a little boy's plight. What can *he* do for them? How can this little one advance their agendas for greatness? It is important to keep in mind the low status of children in that culture. Public attention to the needs of a child would have been considered shameful. The

---

74. This cause of incomprehension is noted by C. A. Evans, *Luke*, New International Biblical Commentary (Peabody, Mass.: Hendrickson, 1990), p. 157.

disciples are caught in that cultural net by the very thing that explains the net: normal adult concerns with advancement, honor, status.

The text crescendos here, failure heaped on failure. There have been failure to feed the hungry, the failure of seeking permanence (on the mountain) rather than journey, a failure to heal; and now, a failure to understand that is more a matter of heart than head. "The Son of Man is going to be betrayed into human hands,"[75] and the disciples will covertly share in that betrayal, deserting Jesus.

Failure #5

A final failure within Luke's final preparatory chapter (9) caps the prior four, and sets the stage for the start of the great journey to Jerusalem, which Luke arranges as a special teaching section. The disciples need to listen, as the successive failures just prior to the journey indicate. "Let these words sink into your ears," Jesus has pleaded, just before making it clear that he will "be betrayed into human hands," subject to the "great suffering" and rejection of society's important-ones.[76] The "argument [that] arose among them as to which one of them was the greatest" obviously would drown out that which Jesus had just said should sink into their ears.[77] Through narrative juxtaposition, their deafness is revealed as a condition of the heart, a clutching after precisely that which Jesus is teaching against.

The Teacher engages in a bit of show-and-tell, at the end of which we come to the final failure. He answers pretensions to greatness with a child.

> "Whoever welcomes this child in my name welcomes me, and whoever welcomes me welcomes the one who sent me; for the least among you is the greatest." *John answered, "Master, we saw someone casting out demons in your name, and we tried to stop him, because he does not follow with us."* (9:47-49; emphasis mine)

John answered: this is strange, since it appears a *non sequitur.* What was the question, or problem, that John is supposed to be answering? Does the narrative break down here?

"Whoever welcomes this child in my name," said Jesus, "welcomes me, and whoever welcomes me welcomes the one who sent me; for the

75. 9:44.
76. 9:44, 22.
77. 9:46, 44.

least among you is the greatest." Whereupon "John answered, 'Master, we saw someone casting out demons in your name, and we tried to stop him, because he does not follow with us.'" Within the narrative ordering, what John answers proves precisely to the point of something important being developed in the text's preparatory material: the struggle for followers in following the "Way of peace," a Way of healing, release, and restoration. John's "answer" proves to be a sinister denial of what Jesus is posing as a solution to power-mongering, this welcoming of a child.

"John answered, 'Master, we saw someone casting out demons in your name, and we tried to stop him, because he does not follow with us.'" John "answers" only his own discomfort, his own misgivings, and his own need to justify himself by pointing to someone else "not so good" as he, and they. *What about him, over there? He's not with us!*

"Do not stop him," says Jesus concerning the unknown person who is casting out demons, "for whoever is not against you is for you."[78] John's attention is on an adult who would usurp his "place," while Jesus is insisting on doing God's work, period.

The news was supposed to have been good. Mary had every reason, following Gabriel's poetic word from God, to expect differently from what turned out to be the case, at least within the represented experiences of the early narrative chapters. Zechariah and Elizabeth appear delighted with their infant son, but John grows up only to disappear into the wilderness, then, in short narrative order, into prison and then into the darkness of death, beheaded. Jesus struggles against the forces of Satan, releasing those oppressed by disease and unclean spirits. He is nearly thrown off a cliff by his hometown neighbors, and speaks to his followers of suffering future ridicule, harm, and murder. Through it all the point becomes clear: Jesus pays attention to the least members of society in providing healing, but at the cost of great struggle with those members of society in best standing.

Each of the disciples' five failures indicates the darkness of heart that prevents reception of a good news that promises not only release and restoration[79] but its own grievous sort of darkness, disruption, and even death. The staccato beat of five failures at the end of the gospel's preparatory material underscores the story's insistence that what comes next, the

78. 9:49-50.
79. 4:18-19.

teaching section,[80] is desperately needed; how can Jesus count on these disciples, given such stumbling?

The fivefold failure may also exhibit a ring-composition (more on this in the next chapter). First and last, the failure has to do with *"them out there, or over there"*; second and second-to-last, the problem of failure is exposed as normal self-promotion and security; in the middle "bull's-eye" we have the show-and-tell of a little boy who suffers prolonged agony because of the disciples' failure. What ends up agitating Jesus is arranged in a ring-composition that focuses at the center-point on precisely the thing that frustrates Jesus — the little boy's plight and the failed responsibility of the followers.

1. failure to take responsibility for the Other, a crowd needing food;
   2. wanting glory now, permanently (Peter's suggestion on the mountain of glory);
      3. failure to pay attention to a little boy in need of healing;
   2.' wanting personal greatness and failing to understand the opposing truth;
1.' desire for group greatness at the expense of the Other, that group over there.

"You faithless and perverse generation, how much longer must I be with you and bear with you?" asks Jesus of the disciples; he himself must heal a child the followers were expected to help.[81] Luke's audience, and these disciples and crowd, are ready to hear the Way fully disclosed — and, finally, to have it sink in.[82]

Peter, James, and John had gone up a mountain where Jesus has an important conversation with Moses and Elijah. In the same account of transfiguration recorded by Matthew and Mark, the audience does not know what the three were talking about, but Luke makes this clear: they "were speaking of his departure [*exodus*], which he [Jesus] was about to accomplish at Jerusalem."[83] This leave-taking is crucial for Luke, who is the only gospel writer to even mention the departure of Jesus from earth. The

80. 9:51–19:44.
81. 9:41.
82. 24:32, 45.
83. 9:31.

narrative importance is in the great fact that Jesus is leaving behind those who need to be taught but who are later empowered to live out that teaching, toward salvation. Before they leave the mountain for the more ordinary world below, the disciples hear a voice from heaven. It is God, speaking of Jesus as the Son, the Chosen. There is only one important word, the challenge of the entire two-volume narrative: "listen to him!"[84]

Preparatory themes of this Way have been offered in the gospel's first nine chapters: God favors those who favor the divine purposes of bringing the good news to the poor, anywhere and everywhere; on the way to such strange joy and peace there is disruption. So much hinges, for Luke, on the teaching of Jesus. With the immediate and striking failure of the disciples — a fivefold stumbling — the journey to Jerusalem takes on the kind of importance for which Luke has been preparing his audience. What we view next, in the nine chapters of Part II, is the centerpiece of meaning for Luke's entire two-volume work.

84. 9:35.

PART II

The Way: Principles Taught

Luke 9:51–19:44

Chapter 5

"Peace to This House" and "Things That Make for Peace"

Luke 9:51–10:24; 18:35–19:44

"When the days drew near for him to be taken up, [Jesus] set his face to go to Je-rusalem."[1] The significance of Jesus being taken up is reinforced by an echo at the beginning of volume two: "In the first book," the author reminds us, "I wrote about all that Jesus did and taught from the beginning until the day when he was taken up. . . ."[2] Just before this journey, Jesus had been talking with Elijah and Moses about his being "taken up" — his "exodus," or "departure."[3] The journey serves to indicate the sure destination of Jerusalem as a place of departure — de-parture as the goal of arrival. The journey and its destination are a metaphor of the Way this journey's goal is the kingdom of God. Here is "a Way of salvation"[4] — a journey, rather than a static state of being.

As Jesus travels toward Jerusalem, he teaches. Luke arranges this teaching as principles concerning the Way. Each principle — a theme cluster — is re-peated for emphasis and expansion or even qualification of thought. The geo-graphical itinerary from 9:51 to 19:44 is minimally signified, but the metaphori-

---

1. 9:51; "taken up," or "going up" — "ascension; see Craig A. Evans, *Luke*, New Inter-national Biblical Commentary (Peabody, Mass.: Hendrickson, 1990), p. 160. I. H. Marshall points out that the verb for *taken up* "can be used both of death and of being taken up into heaven." Marshall suggests the possibility that Luke's narrator is playing with both mean-ings: *taken up* can point to Jesus' "death," but "it is hard to resist the impression that there is also an allusion to Jesus being 'taken up' or 'taken back' to God in the ascension, especially in view of the . . . Elijah typology . . . (9:54 . . . ; 9:31)." *The Gospel of Luke*, New International Greek Testament Commentary (Grand Rapids: Eerdmans, 1979), p. 405.

2. Acts 1:1-2.

3. Lk 9:31 NRSV.

4. Acts 16:17.

cal sense of journeying God's Way is strong, achieved through Luke's method of ordering the various interconnecting insights. Here is "the Way of God," which even enemies recognize as such.[5]

The journey of Jesus to Jerusalem ends as it begins, with a focus on peace. In this first chapter of the journey section we will explore the outermost ring — the frame — of what, in effect, is a journey into the meaning of God's kingdom.

A Journey into the Kingdom of God

1a	"Peace to This House"	9:51–10:24
2a	"What Must I Do to Inherit Eternal Life?"	10:25-42
3a	What to Pray For, and How	11:1-13
4a	Not Signs, Not Status, but the Word Heard and Done	11:14-32
5a	Look Inside Yourself, and Do the Word	11:33–12:12
6a	Relinquish Ownership, Possessions	12:13-34
7a	Relinquish Privilege: Use It for God	12:35-48
8a	Relinquish Family and Religious Rules	12:49–13:17
9a	Kingdom	13:18-19
	— Be Saved? Strive to Enter	13:23-30
9b	Jerusalem	13:31-35
8b	Relinquish Family and Religious Rules	14:1-35
7b	Relinquish Privilege: Use It for God	15:1-32
6b	Relinquish Ownership, Possessions	16:1-31
5b	Look Inside Yourself, and Do the Word	17:1-19
4b	Not Signs, Not Status, but the Word Heard and Done	17:20-37
3b	What to Pray For, and How	18:1-14
2b	"What Must I Do to Inherit Eternal Life?"	18:15-34
1b	"The Things That Make for Peace"	18:35–19:44

The urgency of this teaching is underscored by the narrator, as we saw above: "And it happened, when the days of his ascension were being fulfilled, that he set his face to go to Jerusalem."[6] That is, Jesus is departing, leaving behind followers who will be responsible for teaching what he taught,[7] in his name, as recorded in Acts. With departure in view, Jesus is shown preparing his followers for their responsibility in

---

5. Lk 20:21.

6. Lk 9:51, trans. Robert Maddox, *The Purpose of Luke-Acts* (Edinburgh: T. & T. Clark, 1982), p. 46. "Luke prefers to say," as Maddox points out, that "Jesus is going to Jerusalem for the ascension rather than for the crucifixion" (p. 46). We will be exploring the truth of this statement throughout Part II, and on into Acts.

7. Acts 16:17.

bearing the good news of peace. Here is the Way, the kingdom of God "come near to you."[8]

"Peace to this house"[9] we hear as the heart of the first stage of the journey, the first principle. At journey's end, this theme focus is repeated, though now Jesus weeps over that which causes a desolate house[10] — the failure of Jerusalem to recognize and implement "the things that make for peace."[11]

The Opening Frame: "peace to this house" (9:51–10:20)

Besides his twelve disciples, Jesus is sending out "seventy others"[12] with the good news as announced succinctly in the angels' poem to the shepherds;[13] it is "the message of peace" — which does not change in volume two.[14]

> "See, I am sending you out like lambs into the midst of wolves. Carry no purse, no bag, no sandals; and greet no one on the road. Whatever house you enter, first say, 'Peace to this house!' And if anyone is there who shares in peace, your peace will rest on that person; but if not, it will return to you." (10:3-6)

The thirty-five pairs of disciples are to proclaim the good news of *peace.* We noted *peace* as a recurring focus for the preparatory poems — a peace-among, *shalom*-justice.

Such venturing forth on behalf of peace is risky. The seventy disciples are being sent as "lambs into the midst of wolves." Whoever the "wolves" turn out to be (we will soon discover them), the audience recognizes wolves as rapacious and ravenous. Lambs offering peace to wolves would seem a bit unrealistic, as apparently foolish as the commendation by Jesus of childlike adults able to vie successfully, on behalf of God's kingdom, with sophisticated and well-placed adults.[15]

In this story, peace is "established at the grass roots, in the homes and

8. Lk 10:3-9.
9. 10:5.
10. 13:35.
11. 19:42.
12. 10:1; "seventy-two" in other ancient manuscripts; more on this in n. 32.
13. 2:14.
14. Acts 10:36-37, for example.
15. Noted by Sharon Ringe, *Luke* (Louisville: Westminster/John Knox, 1995), pp. 153-54.

towns of common people, not from the top down."[16] But the journey has begun in rather rough fashion, with disciples — "common people" — continuing their judgmentalism and demonstrating a general failure to comprehend the Way. Then three more "grass-roots" sorts of persons state their respective intentions to follow Jesus, but hear harsh rejoinders that state the Way's costly and counterintuitive requirements.

The journey begins with messengers sent out to prepare for a visit by Jesus to a Samaritan village. Luke's audience would recognize this as a precarious beginning, since most Jews looked down on Samaritans for their presumed heretical slippage and racial impurity, while the Samaritans looked down on the "Jerusalem-centered salvation history," the presumed privilege of those Jews centered in Jerusalem and its temple — the only true guardians of Scripture.[17] And so the Samaritans "did not receive [Jesus], because his face was set toward Jerusalem." The messengers are incensed at this inhospitable response to their offer of peaceful meeting. "Lord," they ask, "do you want us to command fire to come down from heaven and consume them?"[18] As a result, Jesus "turned and rebuked them."[19] Determined to reach Jerusalem, Jesus must turn back, if momentarily: he is interrupted by his own followers' continuing judgmentalism. Judgmentalism is *not* a *thing that makes for peace*. The corollary, then, would be true: a thing that makes for peace would be nonjudgmental invitations of peace.

There is a spiraling echo back to the prior sequence, immediately before the announcement of Jesus setting his face for Jerusalem. As we have seen, John was shown worrying that someone over there, not "one of us," was doing God's work. "Do not stop him," Jesus had said; "whoever is not against you is for you."[20] Then, as soon as the journey starts, the same problem occurs again, in different guise: followers wanting to call down judgment on those who are not "one of us" — those who have flat-out refused to offer hospitality. Perhaps they now have cause for such judgmentalism. But no; Jesus stops them. We are not told — for now — exactly why. The messengers are shown assuming that their responsibilities "include the capacity to command fire and dole out judgment."[21] For

16. Sharon Ringe, *Luke*, p. 175.
17. Joel B. Green, *The Gospel of Luke* (Grand Rapids: Eerdmans, 1997), p. 405.
18. 9:53-54.
19. 9:55.
20. 9:50.
21. And that Jesus himself was like Elijah of old who "had called down fire from

Luke, judgmentalism is always wrong because only God's judgment is infallibly right — and appropriate. The Samaritans refuse Jesus' welcome, while the messengers would end any possibility of welcome at all with their lethal vindictiveness.[22] A kingdom of peace requires the extraordinary: hospitality toward "enemies" like the Samaritans, but also, a refusal to write off these same enemies if they prove inhospitable.

> As they were going along the road, someone said to him,
> "I will follow you wherever you go." And Jesus said to him, "Foxes have holes, and birds of the air have nests; but the Son of Man has nowhere to lay his head."
> To another he said, "Follow me." But he said, "Lord, first let me go and bury my father." But Jesus said to him, "Let the dead bury their own dead; but as for you, go and proclaim the kingdom of God."
> Another said, "I will follow you, Lord; but let me first say farewell to those at my home." Jesus said to him, "No one who puts a hand to the plow and looks back is fit for the kingdom of God."[23]

This sequence of relinquishments echoes a foundational vision of Scripture in the initial call to father Abraham. He is challenged in three ways that we find represented here with the three would-be followers: leave your native land, your people, and your father's house.[24] Just as God challenged Abraham to leave his native land, Jesus tells the first would-be traveler that there will be nothing close to a "home" — nothing so good, even, as the foxes who have their holes, and the birds their nests. As God challenged Abraham to leave his kinfolk, so too Jesus refuses a fellow-traveler even the courtesy of a good-bye to kinfolk. As God told Abraham to leave his father's house, Jesus disallows even a father's burial.

In Abraham's case, the journey he began would be without a known geographical destination; would-be followers of Jesus are being called to

---

heaven to consume representatives of Ahaziah, king of Samaria, for his failure to acknowledge the God of Israel (2 Kings 1:1-16)"; see Green, *The Gospel of Luke*, p. 406.

22. 9:51-56.

23. 9:57-58, 59-60, 61-62; the idea of "Let me go and bury my father" is possibly caught in this translation: "Let me look after my old father until he has died and after that I shall be free," reads *Luke's Gospel for Africa Today*, by Ronald Dain and Joe van Diepen (Nairobi, Kenya: Oxford University Press, 1972). Some scholars suggest that the father has not yet died, and that the would-be follower is asking for time to take care of his dying father. See Norval Geldenhuys, for example, *The Gospel of Luke*, in the New International Commentary on the New Testament (Grand Rapids: Eerdmans, 1946, 1988), p. 296.

24. Gen 12:1.

undertake a similar journey, and likewise are just starting out.[25] What is required? As for Abraham, so here the journey of God's Way presents formidable challenges that go to the heart of normal securities and comforts. What Abraham hears from God is echoed rather closely by what the three would-be followers hear from Jesus at the beginning of Luke's journey narrative.[26]

What might strike the modern reader as challenging in Jesus' demands of letting-go would have been absolutely scandalous for Luke's audience, with its code of family loyalties. Jesus' refusal to allow a father's burial, for example, would have seemed a "breach with natural life" of that day.[27] "Burial of the dead was a religious duty," as I. Howard Marshall points out, and burying someone "was a work of love which carried great reward from God both in this life and in the next world."[28] Familiar with the scriptural tradition, Luke's audience would have heard in the refusal for farewells an echo back to Elijah's disciple Elisha, who sought, and received, permission to go home in order to say good-bye to his parents.[29] Although associated with Elijah, Jesus refuses what Elijah allowed.[30] The kingdom of God is at hand in a new way, demanding, as Joel B. Green notes, "the reorganization of former allegiances, with the result that one may be called upon, as in this case, to engage in behavior deemed deviant by normal conventions" — even the conventions of Jewish scriptures.[31]

We never find out whether the three would-be followers leave normal considerations behind in order to journey with Jesus. Luke frequently omits such information, leaving the outcome open. Luke's perspective emphasizes the invitational nature of God: there is divine

---

25. Gen 20:13.

26. Luke consistently exhibits his sweeping and detailed knowledge of the Jewish scriptures (in its Greek version). Most commentaries and many Lukan studies help us see the subtly interwoven passages and narratives of Jewish scriptures, beyond the explicit references to the same that are clear from the gospel itself. In regard to the Abraham story in particular, see especially Nils Dahl, "The Story of Abraham in Luke-Acts." Dahl emphasizes the gospel writer's conversant use of the Abraham story, including an understanding of God's covenant, oath, and promise to Abraham (cf. esp. pp. 140-41). *Studies in Luke-Acts,* ed. Leander Keck and J. Louis Martin (Nashville: Abingdon, 1966), pp. 139-58.

27. C. F. Evans, *Saint Luke* (Philadelphia: Trinity Press International, 1990), p. 441. See also Joel B. Green's excellent comments regarding the Elijah typology (*The Gospel of Luke,* p. 407), and similar observations of I. Howard Marshall, *Commentary on Luke,* p. 411.

28. Marshall, *Commentary on Luke,* p. 411.

29. 1 Kings 19:19-21.

30. 9:60, for example.

31. Green, *The Gospel of Luke,* p. 408.

patience, though not infinite, when it comes to human repentance. Leaving outcomes open also has the rhetorical effect of putting Luke's audience in the role of deciding for themselves what *they* will do.

The journey demonstrates always a spiraling narrative orderliness. Buried in the preceding passages is a question: Why must one choosing God's Way forgo family loyalty, pride of land, and nation? The answer is peace for the outsider. To an expanded group of seventy disciples — a number probably representing all the nations of the world — Jesus gives the essential gospel message: "Peace to this house!"[32] And then he adds, "If anyone is there who shares in peace, your peace will rest on that person; but if not, it will return to you."[33] This is a far cry from the fiery anger of affronted messengers, as just witnessed in the case of disciples rebuffed by a Samaritan village.[34] And let the street-dust of those who rebuff you remain in their streets, says Jesus; wipe it off your feet in protest, not in judgment; advise them — a last invitation! — that "the kingdom of God has come near."[35] But at times it will work: lambs, sent out, will find residence and food among, or in spite of, wolves. If the offered peace is refused, "it will return to you" — though of course such an unusual phenomenon is impossible without the Way-follower's determined will and the empowering presence of God's Spirit.

Normally, to be rebuffed in offering anything good, and especially peace, would lead to hurt and anger, a state of mind conspicuously lacking in peace. But in God's Way, the refused peace "will return to you." This "Way of peace"[36] is counterintuitive from start to finish, and requires

32. 10:1, 5; as many study Bibles point out, Genesis 10 offers a table of nations that is universal in scope (discrepancy between "70" and "72" is rooted in difference between the Masoretic text, which lists seventy nations, and the Septuagint, seventy-two). Another possibility of interpretation is the number of elders appointed by Moses — seventy-two (Numbers 11:16-17).

33. 10:6.

34. 9:54.

35. 10:10-11.

36. Lk 1:79, the very last words in Zechariah's poem (see Part I, Chapter 2). The same phrase and vision are caught by the prophet Isaiah, and are surely recalled by Luke in his representation of John the Baptist as a voice crying in the wilderness about making straight the crooked paths (Lk 3:4-5). Here is Isaiah:

> The *way of peace* they do not know,
>   and there is no justice in their paths.
> Their roads they have made crooked;
>   no one who walks in them knows peace (Is 59:8).

the careful teaching of God's primary word-bearer, Jesus. And that's what the journey to Jerusalem is, essentially: a teaching of the Way.

But what is the end for those who consistently refuse welcome, the message of peace? The buried question spirals forward to its answer in the next sequence: do not be judgmental, because God judges. Local towns with perfectly ordinary Israelites — towns like Capernaum, Chorazin, and Bethsaida — will receive an inevitable return for their ungracious refusal of God's own reign of peace among men and women.[37] Two aspects of such judgment are clear from what Luke has been saying: it will be delayed until it can be delayed no longer, and God will be the determiner of both the delay and the meting out of consequence. And remember this, that "whoever listens to you listens to me, and whoever rejects you rejects me, and whoever rejects me rejects the one who sent me."[38] So do not take things personally when you meet refusals of peace. This statement by Jesus provides a transition from the sureness of God's judgment — the fate of those who refuse the Way — to the sureness of God's joy for those who embrace the Way.

Sent out with the message of peace, and successful in healing — implementing things that make for peace — the disciples return, understandably, extremely excited over their God-given power. But their deep pleasure is misplaced.

"The seventy returned with joy, saying, 'Lord, in your name even the demons submit to us!'"[39] The response of joy-over-power is inappropriate, entirely.[40] This power is nothing to gloat about, since the stakes are so high and the human weakness to relish power is so strong:

> [Jesus] said to them, "I watched Satan fall from heaven like a flash of lightning. See, I have given you authority to tread on snakes and scorpions, and over all the power of the enemy; and nothing will hurt you. Nevertheless, *do not rejoice at this,* that the spirits submit to you, but rejoice that your names are written in heaven." (10:17-20; emphasis mine)

Rejoice rather in this, says Jesus: your identities are held secure in a place that lasts forever. There, "your names are written." Luke undoubtedly

---

37. 10:13-15.

38. 10:16.

39. 10:17.

40. The narrative spiraling never stops, perfectly mirroring the unfolding nature of the journey: the Way develops from insight to further insight.

picks up on the scriptural warning from Genesis against making-a-name-for-yourself.[41] Perhaps confidence in the provision of one's name and significance proves the ultimate source of that extraordinary peace that remains with the person whose offer of peace is refused.

Having clarified that in which to rejoice, Jesus himself now expresses joy on behalf of these followers.

> At that same hour Jesus rejoiced in the Holy Spirit and said, "I thank you, Father, Lord of heaven and earth, because you have hidden these things from the wise and the intelligent and have revealed them to infants." (10:21)

Truths of salvation are hidden from the religious experts, but revealed to the childlike — an unthinkable reversal of expectations in Luke's place and time, if not our own.[42]

"Blessed are the eyes that see what you see!" Jesus continues. "For I tell you that many prophets and kings desired to see what you see, but did not see it, and to hear what you hear, but did not hear it." The reversal between mighty and lowly that appears in Mary's poem is also evidenced here.[43] Perhaps this word about God's reign finds good hearing among the marginal — like shepherds, like women and children — because their lack of social standing makes them more likely to listen about an offered salvation. They have no status, no name — and no prospect for a "name." Those who are Mary's "mighty" — the "prophets and kings," the "wise and intelligent" — share a perfectly normal propensity toward self-interest and self-congratulation. "Just then a lawyer stood up to test Jesus."[44] As we will see in the following chapter, this is a perfect spiraling forward to an example of the un-childlike behavior of the typical wise and intelligent adult.

---

41. People of Babel were faulted for trying to make a name for themselves, whereas Abraham was promised a name by God (Gen 11:4; 12:2). Just as for Abraham, this promise of a name guaranteed by God can come to replace normal fears of losing security, status, and significance: such is the narrative vision being unfolded here.

42. See Darrell Bock, *Luke 9:51–24:53*, volume two of a Luke commentary in the series Baker Exegetical Commentary on the New Testament (Grand Rapids: Baker, 1996), p. 1010.

43. 10:23-24; God "has scattered the proud in the thoughts of their hearts," as Mary put it in her poem, and "has brought down the powerful from their thrones and lifted up the lowly" (1:51-52). Joel Green notices this echoing between the words of Jesus and the poem of Mary. *The Gospel of Luke*, p. 422.

44. 10:25.

"The things that make for peace" include relinquishment of clan securities, family loyalties, personal comfort, and judgmentalism. Finally, at the
beginning of this journey, we come to the issue of identity, of status
through power. Even misplaced joy in possessing God's power can work
against the making of peace, the antidote to which is a profound inner
confidence in God's valuing of your person, your identity and significance: if you "rejoice that your names are written in heaven," there is no
identity issue on earth left for you to be anxious about. Trust in God as
guarantor of the self (one's identity, sense of meaningfulness) alleviates,
if not eliminates, nagging self-doubt and the need to rejoice in one's
power — whatever the source, even God. The imperatives of the narrative unfold as a daunting way.

What makes for peace is letting-go and going-toward, a repentance
first explained by John the Baptist. There is a turning from self-concern
toward the needs of others, toward what we have seen here as the sharing of meals and the curing of disease. Only such a counterintuitive
mindset and daily action provide "peace to this house."[45]

The Closing Frame, an Echo:
"the things that make for peace" (18:31–19:44)

The journey began with the sending out of followers with the message of
peace. The journey itself has focused, as we will see in subsequent chapters, on the teaching of Jesus concerning peace. Now, at journey's end, Jesus breaks into tears at the sight of Jerusalem, with words intended for no
particular audience — a cry from the heart: "If you, even you, had only
recognized on this day the things that make for peace."[46]

Even his followers nearly miss recognizing such things. Just before
this last leg of the journey, Peter is reminding Jesus just how much he and
his friends have given up to receive Jesus and his Way: "Look, we have
left our homes and followed you."[47] Jesus promises his disciples that they
will "get back very much more in this age, and in the age to come, eternal
life," but then goes on to suggest that he himself will suffer what seems to
be the opposite of the "very much more" gotten back.[48] There will be

---

45. 10:5.
46. 19:42.
47. 18:28.
48. 18:30.

mockery, insults, and spit; there will be death — but then resurrection. They do not understand.[49] So we move ahead to a show-and-tell, by Jesus.

Jesus and a crowd approach Jericho, a dozen or so miles from Jerusalem. A blind beggar is crying out, "Jesus, Son of David, have mercy on me!"[50] But "those who were in front" — presumably, those who were receiving Jesus and his teaching well — spoke to the blind beggar "sternly," as adults speak to children: *keep quiet!*[51] Rather than assist in bringing this outcast to Jesus, those who are closest exacerbate the beggar's dilemma by casting him further out of the social circle, beyond status or standing of any sort. Nevertheless, "he shouted even more loudly, 'Son of David, have mercy on me!'"[52] In response, Jesus stops.

Such an interruption is, for Jesus, always the main point — and must be for those who embrace Jesus, who claim his name as do the believers in Acts.

Against the rebuke of his disciples and the crowd, "Jesus stood still." The momentum toward the holy city is stopped. Jesus had "set his face to go to Jerusalem," but here, Jerusalem can wait.[53] Jesus must always be doing the word of God he teaches; otherwise Jerusalem as a geographic goal loses its point. Getting there matters, of course, but how one journeys becomes the kingdom issue, not when, not how fast, and not with what degree of public approval. And so Jesus "ordered the man to be brought to him; and when he came near, he asked him, 'What do you want me to do for you?'"[54]

Jesus has offered the man a voice, a role in what is to happen to him, or not happen. This person without standing in society is asked, in the middle of this community, to express himself. The blind beggar speaks: "Lord, let me see again."[55] Given sight by Jesus, the healed man now finds his own way. He chooses with his new freedom: he "fol-

---

49. 18:31-34.

50. 18:38.

51. 18:39.

52. 18:39; for Luke, mercy is a staple of what everyone asks of God. It is a request for help in one's reorientation of life, and forgiveness, and a plea for restoration, a return to creation harmonies. See Darrell Bock's excellent discussion on "mercy" and this plea for healing (*Luke 9:51–24:53*, p. 1508).

53. 9:51.

54. 18:40-41.

55. 18:41.

lowed [Jesus], glorifying God."[56] This is how one comes to belong to the Way. In brief: the man cries out for mercy, receives it, joins the journeying Jesus, and glorifies God. No longer shunned for his physical liability and beggarly ways, the man can be restored to communal well-being. Here is a thing "that makes for peace."[57]

It is the disciples who have proven themselves blind, unable to recognize "the Way of peace." They are shown to be judgmental of a "little one,"[58] a blind beggar who counts for little in normal societal circles. Just as in the initial theme where the disciples judge the Samaritans as unworthy, here they judge as inconsequential a lowly and needy person who represents the center-point of salvation's good news.[59]

And "[Jesus] entered Jericho and was passing through it."[60] We are about to meet another person who cannot see Jesus, less perhaps because he is too short than because the crowd keeps him apart, as a *persona non grata*. Here is yet another lost one, lacking in status (though wealthy), and refused by Jesus' followers: he becomes, however, the focus of attention for Jesus. Zacchaeus has been figuratively blind — "lost" — and literally too short to see Jesus over the crowd.[61] The blind beggar and Zacchaeus are paralleled in predicament, in negative crowd response, and in the welcoming demeanor shown by Jesus. Whether Zacchaeus earns his money by skimming what he can from his fellow Israelites in taxes collected for Israel's enemy, Rome, or in some other fashion, the point of the story is his outsider's status, a "sinner" in the eyes of the crowd.

But "when Jesus came to the place, he looked up and said to him, 'Zacchaeus, hurry and come down; for I must stay at your house today.'"[62] And the predictable response comes: "All who saw it began to grumble and said, 'He has gone to be the guest of one who is a sinner.'"[63] Jesus demonstrates the Way of God by reversing normal expectations, but so too does Zacchaeus. He "stood there and said to the Lord, 'Look, half of my possessions, Lord, I will give to the poor; and if I have defrauded anyone of anything, I will pay back four times as

56. 18:43.
57. 19:42.
58. 17:2.
59. Lk 4:18-19.
60. 19:1.
61. 19:1-10.
62. 19:5.
63. 19:7.

much.'"[64] Immediately Jesus declares Zacchaeus on salvation's road: "Today salvation has come to this house."[65] Here is the good news of a repentance leading to forgiveness and of a salvation that restores an outsider to community — a vindication of the despised Jew as "a son of Abraham."[66] John the Baptist had said that for repentance — for such turning-around as Zacchaeus chooses — there is the inheritance of citizenship in God's family, a raising up of "children to Abraham."[67] To be a citizen of God's realm, a child of Abraham, is a possibility not to be gained by clan identity, but by hearing the word and by doing it, the only proper response to the good news Jesus is bringing.

Why would Jesus risk dishonor by encouraging familiarity with such a fellow, promoting intimacy in the unthinkable gesture of eating at table with him, in the "sinner's" own home? Zacchaeus has Jesus at his table, to feed him; it is the outsider who brings Jesus in, giving him shelter for the night. It was from a Samaritan, as we see in the following chapter, that a godly and utterly needed assistance was found for someone near death.[68] In the first theme-cluster, at the journey's beginning, the disciples had been taught to expect just this sort of hospitality — to seek it out.[69] But now the crowd, disciples among them, have refused to consider the potential largesse of Zacchaeus, the hospitality of his home, his receptivity to salvation. With such neglect, they stand to be among the "falling" of Israel, the ones who themselves will fail to find salvation by not providing for — paying attention to — an outsider.[70]

Recognized and welcomed by name, Zacchaeus declares an emphatic "as of this moment" repentance, a reorientation of his life that includes a fourfold payback of those defrauded.[71] From blindness of attitude and action, Zacchaeus has moved to the illumination of salvation. His salvation is the beginning of a journey that pays back debt and pays very careful attention to the needs of others. "Lord, I will give to the poor, and if I have

---

64. 19:8.
65. 19:9.
66. 19:9.
67. 3:8.
68. 10:33-37.
69. 10:5-9.
70. 2:34.
71. 19:8; there is debate about how to translate the verbs; I think the future tense captures the intent, though the present tense could more strikingly render the change in this man, as if he were saying, *Lord, I see, I see, I get it. I give to the poor; I give back more than what I have extorted.*

defrauded anyone of anything, I will pay back four times as much."[72] So it was from the story's beginning with John: "Collect no more than the amount prescribed to you," John had said to the tax collectors.[73] To such salvation the followers here, along with the larger crowd, are blind.

Literally and figuratively, Zacchaeus has been an outsider. And he is going to be kept that way if the followers — still flawed, this late in the journey — have their judgmental way. The little rich man and the blind beggar are similar in more ways than their inability to see Jesus. Both are disposed toward discovering what good thing Jesus will do; both have been rebuffed by the crowd of followers, reduced to an outsider status that is reversed by Jesus; both respond to their release and restoration to wholeness with a turning toward Jesus, and with praise.

With these back-to-back episodes about two outsiders wanting to see Jesus, Luke accomplishes a crucial aspect of climax to the journey, the Way. On the one hand, the "lost"; on the other, the presumed "finders," the disciples who are being taught to "recognize the things that make for peace."[74] The brilliance of these balancing scenarios helps to illustrate the contrast between the crowd's faulty following and the true following — the right-doing — of Jesus. What lies behind the blindness of those closest to Jesus, these disciples who refuse the outsiders? These same disciples have left their homes, as Peter had just reminded Jesus — just as in the initial statement of this theme, that to receive Jesus was to leave normal securities behind.[75] But the salvation of this Way is not merely a relinquishment of normal self-interest, but an embrace of God's best interests.[76] Here, in Luke's echoing theme sequence about receiving Jesus, the point of leaving securities becomes clear: look everywhere to find the person who has no coat while you have two; the person who has no food while you have enough; the person who is blind while you can see; the undesirable or enemy whom you most want to remain outside the community — outcasts like the blind beggar and the Jewish Zacchaeus who collects taxes on behalf of the enemy. To receive such as these is to receive Jesus and his words.[77]

Perhaps the disciples fail in their negative responses to both the beggar and to the tax collector due to their covert desire for status and honor.

72. 19:8.
73. 3:13.
74. 19:42.
75. 18:28; 9:57-62.
76. Acts 16:17.
77. When you find such an outsider, pay attention: this is what it takes to be "saved" — the striving required to enter God's kingdom (13:23-24).

Staying overnight at Zacchaeus's will not play well in Jerusalem for Jesus, their leader. They fail, here, because it is so normal not to want associations that bring dishonor. But at the heart of God's reign is precisely this kind of interruption of a journey, and a way of life that is shunned by ordinary persons — at least in this story.

The narrator's transitional language implies a spiraling connection: "As they were listening to this, he went on to tell a parable."[78] The parable will continue from what "they were listening to" with something obviously related. And yet it does not seem so obviously connected. It is a tale that encompasses all of the story's major players and their respective receptions of Jesus and his teaching: from the disciples as those trying to hear and do the word, to the "falling" within Israel as those refusing to hear Jesus.[79]

Imagine a nobleman, says Jesus, who has to leave town, and entrusts his wealth to ten servants. "Do business with these [wages] until I come back," he says. The town's citizens, meanwhile, are reported as hating the nobleman; they want him to stay away. (Jesus has said that he is going away.[80])

After a while, the nobleman returns. Various responses to the nobleman and his purposes are reviewed in the tale. There are three categories of response among the servants and citizens of the town: two servants are found trustworthy, and are given the rule of ten and five cities, respectively, for increasing what the lord had given, tenfold and fivefold.

> "Then the other came, saying, 'Lord, here is your pound. I wrapped it up in a piece of cloth, for I was afraid of you, because you are a harsh man; you take what you did not deposit, and reap what you did not sow.' He said to him, 'I will judge you by your own words, you wicked slave! You knew, did you, that I was a harsh man, taking what I did not deposit and reaping what I did not sow? Why then did you not put my money into the bank? Then when I returned, I could have collected it with interest.' He said to the bystanders, 'Take the pound from him and give it to the one who has ten pounds.' (And they said to him, 'Lord, he has ten pounds!') 'I tell you, to all those who have, more will be given; but from those who have nothing, even what they have will be taken away. But as for these enemies of mine who did not want me to be king over them — bring them here and slaughter them in my presence.'" (19:15-26)

78. 19:11.
79. 2:34; 19:11-27.
80. 9:51.

The three responses to the nobleman cover the gamut of Israel's response to their Messiah, from the "rising" in Israel who gain more responsibility to the "falling" — those Jews who will be "utterly rooted out of the people."[81] The focus of the tale, however, is on how the followers — the "rising" within Israel — fare with their responsibility as "servant Israel."[82] After all, this journey is Luke's manual of salvation's Way.

Immediately preceding this money talk, Zacchaeus — a "rising" Israelite — had promised a striking reorientation with regard to money, in stewardly fashion. Half of all his possessions he would distribute to the poor, with a fourfold payback for those from whom he had skimmed money. Here, the nobleman is pleased with a responsible stewardship that makes much of what is given, but for the master's sake. God's purposes involve blessing for the outsiders, including the poor. Money and possessions are a trust from God, and so the first shrewd investor is given much greater responsibility. Wise handling of money is rewarded with the governance of ten cities, or five cities. The reign of God requires human partners, rulers of cities, blessing-givers to many peoples. God's servants need to hold lightly great sums of money (another theme sequence of the journey) in order to better pay attention to the needs of others. The persons investing wisely are candidates for the responsible rule of government, of cities.

Then there is the flawed follower. Fearful, this servant does nothing with what was given him by the nobleman except to clutch it tightly, as if it were a personal possession, something owned. The nobleman speaks harshly, stripping the servant of all the money and giving it to the faithful rich servants. A great deal of the parable's dramatic energy is focused on this flawed follower, who ultimately strays from God's Way of blessing for others. "From everyone to whom much has been given much will be required," the audience has heard; "and from the one to whom much has been entrusted, even more will be demanded" (12:48). The relinquishment that includes letting go of even one's life, highlighted here in the echo, is not a negative exercise, an ascetic withdrawal for the soul's purification. Rather, such letting-go is for taking-hold, a relinquishment of parochial concerns for the sake of global blessing, of *shalom* — of doing the nobleman's business. The implicit vision of the whole narrative becomes more and more clear.

81. Acts 3:23.
82. Lk 2:34; 1:54.

"After he had said this, he went on ahead, going up to Jerusalem."[83] How has the prior parable about money responsibility prepared us for this shift of focus? What has needed to be said to his followers, the heart of his concern about serving God's purposes, has been summarized in the tale of talents. Jesus is now ready for serving God's purposes in Jerusalem. He sends two disciples to obtain an unridden colt for Jesus, with a message. Messengers had been sent out to a Samaritan village and into other villages at the beginning of the journey, a very low-key start with little fanfare or following of crowds. This time the messengers are sent out in order to inaugurate the entrance of Jesus into Jerusalem. Down from the Mount of Olives and across the Kidron Valley, Jesus rides a procured colt, a lowly beast. A "whole multitude of disciples" greet him. The band of twelve disciples at the beginning of the journey has been expanded to seventy, but now in the echoing theme the disciples have become a "multitude."

They shout out, "Blessed is the king who comes in the name of the Lord." [84] "Glory to God in the highest heaven, and on earth peace among those whom he favors," the angels had sung.[85] This is echoed when the joyful disciples shout, "Peace in heaven, and glory in the highest heaven."[86] The "peace on earth" of the angels' poem is missing from the disciples' praise, and replaced by "peace in heaven." Why is "peace on earth" left out? Where is the "peace" proclaimed by the disciples in the initial frame?[87] We soon find out that in Jerusalem, at least, there is no true peace. The reception of Jesus is mixed, with shouting disciples but stonily resisting leaders.

"Teacher," these Israelites-in-good-standing insist, "order your disciples to stop."[88] These are seriously religious persons, versed in the Jewish scriptures. Do they hear sacrilegious echoes? The ancient psalmist had sung, "Blessed is the one who comes in the name of the Lord"[89] — but does this Jesus presume to accept such a scriptural accolade? The crowd not only welcomes this rabbi who comes "in the name of the Lord," but the rabbi himself sits on the scripturally significant colt, reserved for

83. 19:28.
84. An echo of words that Jesus has already anticipated as appropriate for his arrival, at the journey's center-point; 13:35.
85. 2:14.
86. 19:38.
87. 10:5-6.
88. 19:39.
89. 118:26.

Messiah! An ancient prophet had recorded a similar scenario: "Rejoice . . . Shout aloud, O daughter Jerusalem! Your king comes to you . . . humble and riding on a donkey, on a colt, the foal of a donkey."[90]

In keeping with the willingness of Jesus to insist on such a lowly but royal entrance, the multitude of disciples take off their cloaks. "In Luke's version of the story, no crowds waving palm branches and shouting hosannas greet Jesus as they might greet a general returning victorious from battle, or someone who has come to wage war on their behalf"; instead, "people cushion Jesus' ride with their own clothing, divesting themselves of symbols of their status."[91] So it is that "your king comes to you" — but how strangely. Emphasizing these ancient words, Luke points to the role of Jesus as Messiah, the one anointed to bring a most unusual salvation.[92]

Once again, as in the first theme sequence, the beginning frame, we are shown a contrast between the "infants" and "the wise and intelligent."[93] Here, the lowly disciples cry out their praise while the people of status, the wise and intelligent, offer resisting complaint. Jesus responds to this grousing from Israelite leadership by noting that if this multitude of Israelite disciples did not voice their praise, the very stones — inanimate, infinitely less aware than even the dull-minded disciples — would cry out the truth.[94]

The praise of the crowd is narratively contrasted with the sobs of the one who comes in the name of the Lord. "As he came near and saw the city, [Jesus] wept over it." He has been teaching God's Way of *shalom*, but to overwhelmingly deafened ears.

90. Zech 9:9.

91. Sharon H. Ringe, *Luke* (Louisville: Westminster/John Knox, 1995), p. 240. In John's gospel there is no such placing of removed garments on the road and on the colt; rather, there is a lofting of palm branches (John 12:12-16).

92. As Joseph A. Fitzmyer notes, "For Luke the title [messiah, Christ] used of Jesus designates him as God's anointed agent announcing himself as the bearer of a new form of salvation to mankind and its relation to God's kingdom among them in a new form." In the gospel and Acts there are about two dozen references to Jesus as Messiah, or Christ (the Septuagint translates "mashiah," messiah, as "christos"). Both roots mean "anoint" — common enough for Hebrew kings, as Fitzmyer points out. *The Gospel According to Luke*, Anchor Bible Commentary, vol. 28 (New York: Doubleday, 1981), p. 199.

93. 10:21-22.

94. Unlike the increasingly gloomy view of the disciples in Mark's gospel, Luke concludes his gospel with indications that the disciples are on the road to "getting it" (24:13-27). And Luke's completion to the story (Acts) is entirely focused on the results of understanding who Jesus is and what "Son of Man" means. David Moessner offers an opposing view, insisting on irony, a "hollow ring to [the disciples'] praise." *Lord of the Banquet: The Literary and Theological Significance of the Lukan Travel Narrative* (Minneapolis: Fortress, 1989), p. 172.

"If you, even you, had only *recognized on this day the things that make for peace*! But now they are hidden from your eyes. Indeed, the days will come upon you, when your enemies will set up ramparts around you and surround you, and hem you in on every side. They will crush you to the ground, you and your children within you, and they will not leave within you one stone upon another; because you did not *recognize the time of your visitation from God.*" (emphasis mine, 19:41-44)[95]

Are these things that make for peace hidden from sight through the agency of God or Satan? *No:* "If only you had recognized." Jesus weeps over willed blindness and dullness of ear.[96]

The prophets of Jewish scripture recount Israel's remarkable stiffness of neck and hardness of heart. Acts will show Israel having a second chance, and responding well — with the exception of those who will be rooted out, the old-guard leadership.

"Peace to this house" and "things that make for peace": A Summary of the Two Sequences

Poor response brings its appropriate reward, here at the end of the journey: the enemies against whom you protect yourselves, says Jesus, "will not leave within you one stone upon another."[97] Jesus is acutely aware of a self-destructiveness that precipitates God's judgment.[98] At the journey's beginning we heard God's judgment: "Woe to you, Chorazin!" and to other local Jewish communities; the echo, here, is *woe to you, holy city of Israel.*[99] Unlike the fiery enthusiasm of judgment from the disciples re-

95. There is scholarly debate about whether the fall of Jerusalem and destruction of the temple in 70 C.E. influenced the composition of these verses, or whether references in the Jewish scripture validate the supposition that "the message of Jesus goes back to Jesus himself." See Marshall, *Commentary on Luke,* p. 717.

96. The disciples have heard what the Way requires in terms of ridicule and death for Jesus, but the "meaning was concealed from them, so they could not perceive it" (9:45). As we saw (Part I, Chapter 4), this blindness is no divine mystery involving what God arbitrarily hides from view, nor even a matter of divine "timing," but rather the hardness of heart among disciples vying for their own glory and status.

97. This important note of lament and judgment echoes something at the journey's heart, as we will see (Lk 13:31-35), and anticipates further echoing (21:20-24; 23:27-31).

98. See Fitzmyer for a helpful discussion of the weeping and the self-destructiveness. *The Gospel According to Luke,* pp. 1255-56.

99. 10:13-15.

garding the Samaritans, at the journey's beginning, here there is no relish or gloating in the judgment of Jesus. By contrast, he weeps.

Ignore "the things that make for peace" at the risk of losing that which you seek to maintain. The journey begins with portraits of those receiving or not receiving Jesus and his "Way of peace"; the journey ends similarly, with some responding well and others poorly — as in the talents parable. The primary message of the first sequence — "Peace to this house!" — has been echoed at journey's end by a failure of Israelites to recognize teaching and action "that make for peace." There are, however, some signs of what is to come, a "universal restoration":[100] a blind beggar and a cheating tax collector anticipate the thousands within Israel and the many others who, through Israel, begin their salvation journey on "the Way of peace."[101]

To journey God's Way is to be inheriting eternal life, which requires, as we see next, honest attention to the word of God and a rigorous attention to others in obedience to that word. "How shall I inherit eternal life?" asks a religious person; later, in the echoing sequence, we hear exactly the same question, again from a religious person. The challenging answers are the same in each case.

100. Acts 3:21.

101. The redemption of Israel: thousands (Acts 2:41) and thousands (4:4) and still more thousands (21:20).

Chapter 6

"What Must I Do to Inherit Eternal Life?"

Luke 10:25-42; 18:15-34

"What must I do to inherit eternal life?" The question is asked first by a religious lawyer and then repeated in the echoing sequence by a rich ruler.[1] Jesus treats the question, both times, as a good one.[2] Yes, Jesus responds, there is something you must do to inherit eternal life: hear God's word, and do it. In the first theme sequence, the word is heard well by a younger sister, Mary, and done well by an otherwise despised Samaritan. In the echoing sequence, love of money prohibits a rich ruler from loving God, which not only prevents his own salvation but the prospect of his serving God's purposes of communal shalom. The demands for eternal life — life in God's kingdom, salvation — are so challenging that someone asks, "Then who can be saved?"[3] The response of Jesus indicates the need for God's empowering help.

We know from the opening and closing sequences of the journey that some Israelites appropriate the message of peace, and some do not.[4] Not

---

1. Robert Tannehill, borrowing from Robert Alter (*The Art of Biblical Narrative* [New York: Basic Books: 1981], pp. 47-62) uses "type-scenes" to explain how these two episodes involving the eternal-life question both resemble each other, but differ — the echo providing, as I have suggested, certain variations. Robert Tannehill, *The Narrative Unity of Luke-Acts: A Literary Interpretation,* vol. 1 (Philadelphia: Fortress, 1986), pp. 170-71. What needs to be noted is the consistent use throughout the journey of this echoing device, and the consistently more challenging aspect of the echo itself. Joel B. Green treats this section about the rich ruler and the linkages very nicely; he is aware of how this section about the rich ruler fits into the larger context of the surrounding text. See *The Gospel of Luke* (Grand Rapids: Eerdmans, 1997), pp. 652-53 and 656.

2. 10:25; 18:18.

3. 18:26.

4. We need to remember that Luke's gospel presents Jesus appealing primarily, nearly exclusively, to Israel. The reason for this becomes clear in Acts.

much has been said in this initial stage of the journey about the hidden darkness of those refusing the Way of peace. Simeon has foretold that within Israel, "the inner thoughts of many will be revealed"[5] The narrative time has arrived for an acute probing of motive. In this next leg of the journey, we find normal adult concerns that lead to refusal of Jesus and God's Way. Among these ordinary orientations are anxieties about one's standing in the eyes of others, and about money.

The First Time: "What must I do to inherit eternal life?" (10:25-42)

Jesus has just told his followers they are wrong to rejoice in having God's power over demons. "Do not rejoice at this," Jesus has responded, "but rejoice that your names are written in heaven."[6] Jesus is so delighted at the receptivity of the disciples that he "rejoiced in the Holy Spirit" and gave thanks to God for revealing to "infants" what persons of status have longed to see.[7] "Just then a lawyer stood up to test Jesus."[8]

Will the lawyer prove to be un-childlike? The buried question is articulated indirectly by this following sequence, which zeroes in on the decidedly un-childlike attitude and behavior of two adults, beginning with a religious lawyer. "Just then" is not merely a chronological marker.

The lawyer wants to "test Jesus" (echoes of the devil's "testing"),[9] rather than to obtain a real answer to a question sincerely asked — as most children would do. And so the narrative focus shifts to this adult, one of "the wise and intelligent" from whom, we have just heard, God has "hidden these things." Why would God do something like that? An alert audience finds out.

"'Teacher,' he said to Jesus, 'what must I do to inherit eternal life?'" Jesus affirms the validity of the lawyer's question by responding, "What is written in the law? What do you read there?"[10] *You, an expert of*

5. Lk 2:35.

6. 10:20.

7. 10:21-24.

8. 10:25.

9. The lawyer's testing of Jesus is an echo of the devil's testing, back in the wilderness (4:1-2); such testing will occur again, from an evil generation (11:16, 29). See Tannehill, *The Narrative Unity of Luke-Acts*, vol. 1, p. 179.

10. 10:26.

religious law, know the Way of God. It is in our shared scripture. The law-yer answers appropriately (he knows the answer!): "You shall love the Lord your God with all your heart, and with all your soul, and with all your strength, and with all your mind; and your neighbor as your-self."[11] Yes, Jesus says. "Do this, and you will live."[12] Theng to lawyer is taken aback. "But wanti justify himself, he asked Jesus, 'And who is my neighbor?'"[13]

Here the lawyer's deepest motivations are more fully exposed: want-ing to test Jesus, he now desires "to justify himself." Perhaps the lawyer never really meant to receive an answer, as a child might, to questions about life-that-lasts-forever. He uses the question as a "test": there is something besides an honest answer that the lawyer seeks. He has appar-ently been wanting to "justify himself" — make himself look good — from the very start.

Within this two-volume narrative, such a stance as the lawyer's is consistently exposed as both perfectly normal and completely contrary to God's Way. The lawyer's second question about the identity of "neigh-bor" turns out to be as twisted in its import as is the darkness of motive in the original question about eternal life. Jesus will subvert the lawyer's question about "who is my neighbor?" by turning the question back on the lawyer himself. Jesus tells a fictional tale that helps to answer both the original question about gaining salvation and the follow-up question about who should be considered neighbors.

Someone is traveling out of Jerusalem down to Jericho, the tale be-gins; the person is robbed and stripped of clothing, and beaten. He lies on the side of the road, "half dead."[14] A religious leader passes by, and then another one. Each crosses over to the other side of the road, staying clear of ritual defilement while avoiding possible ambush.[15] To the scene of misfortune comes someone who, from the standpoint of these two reli-gious leaders, is presumed a heretic and societal outcast. This person, a Samaritan, "was moved with pity." He washes the wounds of the injured man with wine and oil and bandages him. Then he places the man on his own animal and brings him to an inn. There, the despised foreigner "took

11. 10:27.

12. 10:28; see 8:21 and 13:23-24; in Acts, we will find a repeated focus on the repentance taught by Jesus.

13. 10:29.

14. 10:30.

15. I. Howard Marshall discusses both possibilities, in *Commentary on Luke*, New Inter-national Greek Testament Commentary (Grand Rapids: Eerdmans, 1979), p. 448.

care of him."[16] The next day, this Samaritan traveler gives money to the innkeeper for continued care of the unfortunate stranger. And more: the innkeeper is told by the Samaritan that he will check back and repay the innkeeper for any further expense in caring for the man.[17]

Jesus concludes by subverting the lawyer's original question, which focused on himself rather than the neighbor: "wanting to justify himself, he asked Jesus, 'And who is my neighbor?'"[18] Jesus turns the question around, as if to say, this is the question you should have asked: *Which of these three do you think was a neighbor?*[19] The lawyer is receptive to the fiction's appeal, and offers the only possible answer, "'The one who showed him mercy.' Jesus said to him, 'Go and do likewise.'"[20] The lawyer apparently would have liked a category in which a person could qualify as *neighbor* — a group in need of the presumably superior lawyer's help. But he is told by Jesus, by way of this subtle and powerful tale, that he must be concerned whether he himself needs help, whether *he* is a true neighbor. That is, rather than ask about the someone out there who might qualify as neighbor-to-be-helped, the lawyer should have asked Jesus, *What can I do, how can I improve, to be truly neighborly?*[21]

Luke's story insists throughout that scrutiny of motive and action should always be self-directed, not other-directed. For example, we have heard in the mightiest of the preparatory poems that one might better observe the log in one's own eye than the speck in another's; the call is to love those one doesn't like, not just those who are nice.[22] Be neighborly toward those who cannot return the favor of your neighborliness, even those who are enemies-down-the-street or across the national border.[23] This lawyer of religion exposes himself, along with other religious leaders, as a "non-neighbor" by wishing to weed out undesirables from the

16. 10:34.

17. 10:35.

18. 10:29.

19. 10:36.

20. 10:36-37.

21. "The question 'Who is my neighbor?' is changed," as Sharon Ringe observes, "into 'Who am I in this relationship of neighboring?'" No person "can simply *have* a neighbor; one must also *be* a neighbor." *Luke* (Louisville: Westminster/John Knox, 1995), p. 160. O. C. Edwards, Jr. makes a similar observation: "Note that Jesus changes the question from 'Whom must I love when I love a neighbor?' to 'What should my love look like when I am truly acting as a neighbor?'" *Luke's Story of Jesus* (Philadelphia: Fortress, 1981), pp. 57-58.

22. 6:41-42.

23. 6:32-36.

category "neighbor."[24] Rather than a proper testing of his own motives, the lawyer has tested Jesus. Rather than concern with *being* good, the lawyer is concerned with *looking* good. As a seriously religious Jew, this man has heard the Scripture, but he has not done it.[25]

The narrative journey spirals forward, from disciples wishing to wipe out the hostile Samaritans to this neighbor on the road, the godly neighbor — a Samaritan! — who comes to the aid of someone falling outside the defined circle of community and ritual cleanness.[26] One problem with judgmentalism, then, is the barrier erected against possible assistance from unexpected and even hated sources. Had the disciples their way, the Samaritans would have been consumed with fire, leaving fewer or no Samaritans to illustrate God's purposes of *shalom*.

The lawyer is left to ponder; perhaps he will be persuaded — and Luke's audience along with him. Almost always Luke leaves open the question of ultimate judgment on any given individual.[27]

Mary's poem, early in the gospel, keeps echoing throughout the story: the proud will be scattered "in the thoughts of their hearts," while the lowly will be "lifted up."[28] In connection with this matter of "thoughts of their hearts," we will be finding numerous echoes as well of what Simeon foresaw, that through the Messiah "the inner thoughts of many will be revealed." Here, the audience has been provided a view of such "inner thoughts" and "thoughts of their hearts," in the lawyer's testing and his anxiously self-justifying psychological needs.[29]

So Jesus has subverted the lawyer's original question about who qualifies as "neighbor." He has had to answer a different question, about who qualifies as "neighborly." His answer, "The one who showed him mercy." The truth is simple and the truth is hard: "Jesus said to [the lawyer], 'Go and do likewise.'"

24. See Darrell Bock, *Luke 9:51–24:53* (Grand Rapids: Baker, 1996), p. 1028.

25. The lawyer may have "read well," as Alan R. Culpepper puts it, but he needs to understand "acting well." *The Gospel of Luke,* New Interpreter's Bible, vol. 9 (Nashville: Abingdon, 1995), p. 228.

26. 9:54.

27. See Joseph A. Fitzmyer's discussion on the ambiguity of the lawyer's response, and fate, in *The Gospel According to Luke,* Anchor Bible, vol. 28a (Garden City, N.Y.: Doubleday, 1985), p. 883. See also Joel Green's excellent comments on the "open-ended" quality of the lawyer-parable sequence, leaving the audience to ponder more closely the question, "How then shall I respond to this question and its answer?" — rather than gloating over the wrong-headedness of the lawyer. Green, *The Gospel of Luke,* p. 432.

28. 1:51-52.

29. 2:35.

Immediately following the punch line to the Samaritan tale, we hear an apparently clumsy transition: "Now as they went on their way, he entered a certain village, where a woman named Martha welcomed him into her home."[30] Who is Martha? Where is this village? When in the journey does this episode unfold? The journey markers — the literal itinerary signals — provide an extremely vague indication of any actual journey. We could easily but wrongly assume that, by modern standards of historical storytelling, the ordering here is rough: a mere bumping-along from one interesting scene to the next. Nothing could be further from the narrative truth, however. Listening carefully, we hear paralleled repetitions between the lawyer and Martha, and between the fictional Samaritan and Martha's younger sister Mary. What emerges is an economically presented view of what it means and what it takes to inherit eternal life.[31] Unless transformation occurs, the lawyer-Martha person will lose out. The Samaritan-Mary person, on the other hand, is inheriting eternal life — or, as the text suggests a little further on, this godly Samaritan-Mary person is entering the kingdom of God's *shalom*.[32]

The dramatic spotlight for this particular journey-stopover is initially on Martha: it is her home, and she does the welcoming. And it is she who has the problem needing scrutiny. Younger sister Mary appears at first almost as a footnote. Like the Samaritan, however, she provides an answer to the episode's major problem.

> [Martha] had a sister named Mary, who sat at the Lord's feet and listened to what he was saying. But Martha was distracted by her many tasks; so she came to him and asked, "Lord, do you not care that my sister has left me to do all the work by myself? Tell her then to help me." But the Lord answered her, "Martha, Martha, you are worried and distracted by many things; there is need of only one thing. Mary has chosen the better part, which will not be taken away from her." (10:39-42)

Luke's audience would have found it difficult to accept the dismissal by Jesus of such hospitality, familiar as they would be with the very high

30. 10:38; the story's frequent segue markers — "just then" and "now it happened" and "the next day" — fill the story, signifying little. The audience must enter in, as with any great narrative. There are the implicit thematic transitions, in Luke's case, the spiraling from one sequence to the next.

31. Among several commentators, Alan Culpepper notes some of the following connections between the lawyer sequence and the Martha-Mary sequence. Culpepper, *The Gospel of Luke* (Nashville: Abingdon, 1995), p. 231.

32. Lk 13:23-30; see Chapter 13.

value placed on hospitality in the Jewish scriptures and many ancient cultures. In addition, Luke's Jewish audience[33] would find improbable this scene of a rabbi visiting and teaching two women.

The point, then, becomes all the more dramatic: Martha's worry and distraction as hostess are entirely "normal." And this isn't good, as the narrative goes. Martha's problem is in her motivations and psychic clutter. She is "worried and distracted by many things."[34] There is an echo here back to the lawyer, who has been preoccupied in his testing of Jesus and his anxious justification of himself. With both Martha and the lawyer the audience can see "forms of self-justification or self-concern."[35] They are both distracted by the desire to give a pleasing account of themselves before others. Both the lawyer and Martha presume a superior position relative to Jesus: "Martha presumes to tell Jesus what he should do; Mary lets Jesus tell her what she should do."[36]

Martha is being directed by Jesus to learn from her younger sister. "Mary's posture expresses zeal to learn," a scenario most Jewish teachers would have opposed, since "women for the most part were excluded from training in Torah."[37] Mary "sat at the Lord's feet and listened," a "bold action in leaving her expected role of serving dinner in order to listen to Jesus; . . . Mary, if she is really listening to Jesus, cannot remain a passive listener."[38] We have seen this already, in the preparatory chapters of the gospel: there is hearing, and there is listening. The mother of Jesus and Zechariah the priest both heard a message from God: the mother of Jesus listened; the priest did not.

Martha's problem with her sister Mary reflects on the elder sister's poor state of spirit. "Martha's speech is centered in 'me-talk,'" as Joel B. Green observes [39] The lawyer, as we saw, was similarly me-obsessed. This juxtaposition of the lawyer with Martha illustrates, among other things,

---

33. In spite of research, the precise make-up of the various audiences of the canonical gospels remains fuzzy. Certainly Luke would have in mind something of a mixed audience; given his emphasis on Israel's becoming saved and fulfilling its covenant with God — themes running through the entirety of Acts — I would argue that the author has in mind his Jewish audience as well as any God-fearing outsiders.

34. 10:41, an echo of 10:40.

35. David L. Tiede, *Luke*, Augsburg Commentary on the New Testament (Minneapolis: Augsburg, 1988), p. 210.

36. Culpepper, *The Gospel of Luke*, p. 232.

37. Marshall, *Commentary on Luke*, p. 452.

38. Robert C. Tannehill, *Luke*, Abingdon New Testament Commentaries (Nashville: Abingdon, 1996), p. 186.

39. Green, *The Gospel of Luke*, p. 437.

that within this story women can do as well or as poorly as men. Women, too, are lost and need finding. Women, too, can become least in order to be great. They too, like the mother of Jesus, are among the lowly who can be "raised high" — outstripping, on occasion, presumably superior male counterparts like the priest Zechariah. (Such a Western and modern commonplace notion concerning women was anything but common for the original audience of this text.) As already suggested, that this rabbi visits the home of two sisters and actually sits down to teach them Torah and the words of God would have seemed scandalous in actuality and in its retelling.

"Martha, Martha, you are worried and distracted by many things." The follow-up "Martha" indicates invitation. This is not an exclamatory and condemning "Martha!" Jesus points to Mary's good listening in the spirit of gentle correction. To help the lawyer, Jesus had drawn attention to a fictional doer of good rather than pointing a finger in the lawyer's face, accusingly. Through story-telling, Jesus allows the lawyer a space of time and luxury of psychic distance in which to entertain the fictional possibility of a better world for himself. Jesus expresses his real concern for the frenetic older sister with a quiet "Martha, Martha." The audience is able to understand, through the back-to-back portrayals of the lawyer and Martha, how anxious distraction can surface in human lives and how such fear can be overcome on the journey toward salvation.

In order to be inheriting eternal life — the question driving this theme sequence — one must listen to the word of God and do it. The fictional Samaritan and the real-life Mary are a composite picture of the one who gains salvation.[40] Each is fulfilling Torah by expressing an interpretation and distillation of the Law: the Samaritan shows love for his neighbor; Mary, her love for God. The lawyer's cure is to be found in the person of an outsider, a "heretical" Samaritan, who does what the Law actually teaches. Martha's cure is demonstrated by her younger sister's listening — a completely focused child — to amazing words of true and eternal life.

And so the answer to the lawyer's good question emerges from hear-

---

40. As stated, the lawyer's deeply seated problem is paralleled with Martha's, while the Samaritan's following of God's Way is echoed by Mary's. There are other echoes as well. Zechariah took a wrong turn by seeking something external for validation of the angel's surprising news — a sign whereby he could be sure; likewise, Martha falters by attaching too much importance to the "many things" (10:41). Just as Mary the mother of Jesus is open to the word she hears from Gabriel (1:38) and ponders special words from the news-bearing shepherds (2:19), so, too, Mary the sister of Martha treasures words worth hearing.

ing the entire narrative sequence. "What must I do to inherit eternal life?" is answered by what the Samaritan and Mary do. Such an "eternal life" has a particular face to show the world: the restored well-being of the beaten fellow on the side of the road, left for dead. Paying attention to God's word as Mary does is to pay attention, like the Samaritan, to "the things that make for peace." The journey moves forward.[41]

The Echo: "What must I do to inherit eternal life?" (18:15-34)

Later in the journey, the precise question about inheriting eternal life is asked again, under similar circumstances and with a similar answer — but with a more challenging response by Jesus. Just before the lawyer had asked his question about eternal life, Jesus was rejoicing about the truths available to "infants" but not to normal adults — the wise and intelligent, the powerful and rich.[42] The echoing of this question about inheriting eternal life is prefaced in the same way, here, with reference once again to children and God's truths.

> People were bringing even infants to him that he might touch them; and when the disciples saw it, they sternly ordered them not to do it. But Jesus called for them and said, "Let the little children come to me, and do not stop them; for it is to such as these that the kingdom of God belongs. Truly I tell you, whoever does not receive the kingdom of God as a little child will never enter it." A certain ruler asked him, "Good Teacher, what must I do to inherit eternal life?" (18:15-18)

There are two challenges here: embrace children into your lives, and continue being like children: "Whoever does not receive the kingdom of God as a little child will never enter it."

In moving once again from considerations about children to considerations of what motivates ordinary adults, the audience hears a reinforcement of an instructive contrast: normal adults have concerns that ex-

---

41. And where are we, geographically, on this journey? How long have Jesus and his followers been traveling? The answers are quite vague, and unimportant: somewhere in Galilee, somewhere in the vicinity of Samaria . . . some days or weeks or months after setting out. What are not at all vague are the intricately spiraling echoes of the advancing insights.

42. 10:21.

clude children, or the need to be childlike. There is a great irony in the disciples having been praised for being like children in the first sequence, and now, in the echoing sequence, refusing children. Again: children were of such little social standing in Luke's day that a person would incur disgrace for paying much attention to them, particularly in public: they were among "the expendables."[43] Protecting Jesus from having to deal with children would have been a common and even commendable response. "When the disciples saw [children being brought], they *sternly* ordered them not to do it." Jesus counters:

> "Whoever does not receive the kingdom of God as a little child will never enter it." A certain ruler asked him, "Good Teacher, what must I do to inherit eternal life?" (18:17-18)

There is none of the lawyer's testing, no apparent need to justify himself in front of others. The ruler's dilemma appears all the more formidable.

Why does the ruler address Jesus as *Good* Teacher? "Why do you call me good?" Jesus asks, with disapproval; "no one is good but God alone."[44] Flattery of anyone presumed great might disguise a spirit of seeking special considerations or a spirit of complacency, as in "you and I are *in the know*."[45] Though we can't be sure of this interpretation, the retort from Jesus fits the larger story's perspective: there is no inner circle of privileged persons, no hierarchies of honor. There is only this new idea of God's kingdom, a community of *shalom* ruled by God.

Jesus probes deeper. Yes, he says, you know the essential Law: "You shall not commit adultery; You shall not murder; You shall not bear false witness; Honor your father and mother."[46] The ruler answers that he has kept this love-of-neighbor portion of the Law, an observation Jesus does

---

43. "Children lacked power and status . . . the counsel of the wise regarded chatting with children a waste of time" (Tannehill, *Luke,* p. 165). And as Joel Green points out, except for their future worth as laborers and heirs, children in this time and place had little intrinsic value; infanticide and child abandonment were widespread (*The Gospel of Luke,* pp. 650-51).

44. 18:19.

45. "Jesus takes offense, [since] in addressing him as 'Good Teacher' the ruler is engaged in a word game deeply rooted in concerns with status. According to this linguistic system, one commendation deserves another." Green, *The Gospel of Luke,* p. 655. But note Darrell Bock, who suggests that the response of Jesus, that no one is good except the Father, is a reminder that "being good is not sufficient" (Bock, *Luke 9:51–24:53,* p. 1478). This idea strikes me as foreign to the immediate context, in which the goodness of Jesus is assumed to be sufficient, as is that of the Samaritan, whose godly goodness is held up as commendable.

46. 18:20.

not directly contest.[47] "There is still one thing lacking," Jesus responds: "sell all that you own and distribute the money to the poor." The ruler "became sad; for he was very rich."[48]

In rehearsing the Law, Jesus left out the first four commandments about loving God. This glaring omission highlights for an alert audience the ruler's problem: his treasure is something other than God. What is missing from the Law's recital is missing from the ruler's life. The rich man's impeccable religious outlook and comportment are compromised by a fundamental orientation toward something other than God and God's purposes of blessing for all peoples. "You cannot serve God and wealth," Jesus has said.[49]

Except for honoring one's parents, that portion of the Law focusing on a love of neighbor is prohibition: do not kill, do not bear false witness, do not commit adultery. Such observance will not guarantee what Jesus insists upon regarding the Law: pro-active love of neighbor recognizes and implements "the things that make for peace."[50] To love all peoples is to serve God — and "you cannot serve God and wealth." Take, for example, the illustration used by Jesus in the prior sequence, where the lawyer wonders who might qualify for his neighborly attention. Jesus speaks of a Samaritan who we presume keeps the commandments: *not* to beat and rob his neighbor, *nor* speak ill behind his back, *nor* covet his goods. But the point goes far beyond the negative cast of the commandments to the fulfilling of the Law's essence, to love in a pro-active way toward all peoples. With tenacity and at an expense of both time and money, the godly Samaritan tended to someone who had been pummeled. Such echoing between the paralleled scenes reinforces the point about the ruler's failure to love God above his wealth: the Way's neighborliness requires a love of God that plays out in an unnormal fashion. For the wealthy ruler, letting-go of his number one preoccupation is neither "an ascetic ideal" nor a "simple renunciation"; it leans into the world, addressing the world's injustice through "the disposition of one's material goods . . . for the sake of the poor."[51]

We do not know the outcome of the conversation between Jesus and the rich ruler. At stake, however, is an "eternal life" to be realized "in this age" as well as in the age to come.[52] "How hard it is for those who have

47. 18:21.
48. 18:22-23.
49. 16:13.
50. 19:42.
51. Green, *The Gospel of Luke*, p. 656.
52. 18:30.

wealth to enter the kingdom of God!" Jesus exclaims; "indeed, it is easier for a camel to go through the eye of a needle than for someone who is rich to enter the kingdom of God."[53]

"Those who heard it" are stunned by the un-normal nature of such relinquishment: "Then who can be saved?" they ask — a key question for the gospel, given the demands of repentance.[54] "What is impossible for mortals is possible for God," Jesus responds, anticipating the coming empowerment of God's Spirit in Acts.[55] Being "saved," for Luke, requires God's grace, the empowering Holy Spirit.[56]

"Look," Peter responds to Jesus after this question of who can be saved: "we have left our homes and followed you."[57] *Good,* Jesus says: no one who relinquishes "wife or brothers or parents or children" will fail to "get back very much more in this age, and in the age to come eternal life."[58] But there is still further relinquishment with which Peter must reckon, represented in the following verses. One who serves God rather than wealth or even family must, like Jesus, be willing to face the inevitable dishonor and even death. This is the third time we have heard a "passion prophecy";[59] here, Jesus is calling attention to what the disciples find

53. 18:24-25.

54. 18:26.

55. Such empowerment is already anticipated by the citing of the Holy Spirit as God's greatest possible gift for those who ask in prayer (11:13).

56. 18:27; 13:23-30; how God interacts on the human scene will be demonstrated in the next theme sequence, on prayer: God wants to give the Holy Spirit for enabling (11:13), and mercy to those who cry out for it (18:13). The follower of God's Way is portrayed in the entire two-volume story as one desiring to hear well and do well but finding it all quite difficult, if not impossible. In fact, this is what the life and death and resurrection and ascension and exaltation of Jesus will come to mean: the authority of one appointed by God to teach the Way, and the one who, in leaving, is able to send the Holy Spirit.

57. 18:28.

58. 18:29-30.

59. Whereas Luke separates the third passion prophecy from the first two (just before the journey), Mark's gospel has all three in syncopated order, a hinge-point for his story in chapters 8, 9, and 10 that defines the precipitous decline of the disciples. Mark's rhetorical strategy is more "alarmist," warning his audience that what has happened once to these who were closest to Jesus could happen to them. In fact, at one point the author jumps into the text with flags waving ("Let the reader understand!" [13:14]). By the end of Mark's story (16:8a), the disciples have completely and most abysmally failed. They are those among whom the seed fell but, lacking root, "endure only for a while; then, when trouble or persecution arises on account of the word, immediately fall away" (Mk 4:17); or, those overtaken by "the cares of this world" — which for Mark include most strikingly status and name, as for Luke — and such cares "choke the word, and it yields nothing" (Mk 4:19). Luke's portrait of the disciples is not any kinder than Mark's, but it is more extended, precisely to reveal the positive impact

unimaginable, that the Son of Man "will be mocked and insulted and spat upon."[60] Such public disapproval can become more and more physical in its harm, extending even to flogging and the possibility of being killed.[61] Do Peter and the disciples comprehend what is required to "inherit eternal life"? They too must bear a cross, daily.[62] Jesus is God's "holy servant" — an "anointed agent"[63] for the purposes of teaching and demonstrating God's Way — and sending the empowering Spirit. In Acts, the disciples ultimately will prove to be such agents.

The rich ruler, for all his goodness, served money more than God. For him, relinquishing wealth would have been especially difficult. For the disciples, relinquishing social honor and privilege, and even their physical safety, proves unthinkable, for now. They fail to comprehend such letting-go. "They understood nothing about all these things; in fact, what he said was hidden from them, and they did not grasp what was said."[64] What is hidden is what they themselves refuse to see (see the concluding section of Chapter 4).

"What must I do to inherit eternal life?"
Summary of the Two Sequences

Martha's sister Mary and the good Samaritan of the first sequence answer the question: to inherit God's life, listen to God's word and act al-

---

of the primary role of the Messiah to teach the Way. And so Luke delays the last prophecy until late in the journey, and though the disciples still do not understand, they receive more teaching, more intensely, in the gospel's concluding section — where, finally, they are shown comprehending, indeed (Lk 24:32) — ready to bear witness to what Jesus taught, including his own suffering and rising from death (Lk 24:45-49).

60. 18:32.

61. 18:33.

62. 9:23; 14:27; in each of the echoed instances of this "passion prophecy," Luke has followed with indications that disciples must share, literally, in the suffering and death of Jesus (which they will do in Acts). After the first passion prophecy, we find Jesus talking about followers taking up their own cross daily — and the idea that clutching to one's life is to lose it (9:23-25). After the second, Luke follows with an incident of disciples arguing about status, at which Jesus takes a child and says that "the least among all of you is the greatest" (9:48). To become less than least is to suffer death, but making children the priority of one's life, or to become as an outcast child in loss of status and honor, is a sort of daily dying, a taking up of one's cross. Only then will one be ready to die, the text suggests.

63. Acts 4:27 and 30; Joseph A. Fitzmyer uses the term "anointed agent." *The Gospel According to Luke*, p. 199.

64. 18:34.

ways in a neighborly fashion. What prohibits such listening and doing, the second sequence shows, are the obsessions of the heart that prohibit true love of God, a love understood as service to God's loving purposes toward others. Immediately following the rich ruler's disappointment about the answer regarding inheriting eternal life, Jesus goes on — as we saw in Chapter 5 — to demonstrate toward the outcast beggar and tax-collector the radical neighborliness of the Samaritan.

Relinquishment of religious or household status (the lawyer, Martha), or letting go of money and possessions (rich ruler), or of anything that lodges as the heart's truest treasure — all such demands are required not as an ascetic goal for the purification of the soul, but for the serving of God's goal of communal peace and individual wholeness. God's loving purposes toward others have been illustrated in the composite portrait of Mary who listens well and the Samaritan who acts well, and of Jesus who willingly embraces ridicule, dishonor, and even death as a consequence of doing the truly right thing. This doing, as with the Samaritan, must be oriented by that which most perfectly characterizes the author's vision of salvation in Luke-Acts: recognition and implementation of "the things that make for peace."[65]

Such effort to obtain eternal life is impossible, we have just heard. But "what is impossible for mortals is possible for God."[66] And so it is that prayer becomes crucial for those choosing God's Way. Followers need to be in conversation with the Provider, and they need the provision, most critically, of the empowering Spirit. The journey moves on, with continuingly vague space-time transitions that belie the logical thematic connections.

65. 19:42, discussed in Chapter 5.
66. 18:26-27.

Chapter 7

What to Pray for, and How

Luke 11:1-13; 18:1-14

Inheriting eternal life, entering God's kingdom, requires hearing and doing the word of God, as we have just seen. But this is impossible without help from God. And so it is that prayer is a constant refrain throughout Luke's two-volume story. Prayer is viewed as a necessary point of relationship between God and the participation God seeks from those going the Way toward the realization of God's kingdom on earth.[1] Jesus prays often to God, as all followers of the Way are taught to do. In the theme's first statement, we hear that the best gift to pray for is God's empowering Spirit. God's Spirit descends on Jesus while he is praying; God's Spirit descends on the disciples while they are praying.[2] To pray for the Holy Spirit demands, as we discover in the echoing theme, a self-recognition that cries out not only for justice but especially for mercy.[3] In striving to enter God's kingdom, God's mercy is a moment-by-moment requirement — a state of mind and heart.[4] God's empowering Spirit is the supreme manifestation of this mercy.

The First Time: What to Pray for, and How (11:1-13)

Mary has listened to Jesus. Now Jesus listens, in prayer with the Father. And "after he had finished [praying], one of his disciples said to him, 'Lord, teach us to pray, as John taught his disciples.'"[5]

1. 11:2.
2. 3:21-22; Acts 2:3.
3. 18:7, 13.
4. 13:23-24.
5. 11:1.

111

The request may be flawed, however, insofar as this particular disciple wishes to keep up with John's disciples.[6] Whatever the mixture of motives, the disciples are rewarded. We find a paradigm of all prayer.[7]

Father, hallowed be your name.
Your kingdom come.
Give us each day our daily bread.
And forgive us our sins,
for we ourselves forgive everyone indebted to us.
And do not bring us to the time of trial.

(11:2-4; my line arrangement)

The prayer's essence is that God's kingdom would become a reality.[8] So the prayer begins with God, an honoring of God's name. We have just seen the distorting anxiety of a lawyer and the distracting worry of Martha, a fear in both cases that stems from concern for status and recognition, for the honor of a "name."[9] God's kingdom can't come, apparently, without human participants willing to desire above all things the lifting up of God's name, not their own. This hallowing of God's name echoes the first part of ancient Law.[10]

"Your kingdom come," the poem's second line, parallels the first, "hallowed be your name." The reign of God is inextricably linked with the human request for such reign, and is based on a willingness to accept the elevation of God's name over one's own. To reverence God's name, in Luke's two-volume story, never implies an abject elevation of a God who seeks greater and greater distance between divine and mortal. Quite the contrary: to seek the glory of God's name and to seek God's reign on earth prayerfully is to adopt a mind-set that "calls for human partnership

---

6. I. Howard Marshall cites Jeremias, who "suggests that the disciples want a prayer that will be characteristic of their position as a community around Jesus, just as other Jewish groups, including the disciples of John, had their own distinctive prayers." I. Howard Marshall, *Commentary on Luke,* New International Greek Testament Commentary (Grand Rapids: Eerdmans, 1979), p. 456.

7. Matthew has the longer and more familiar version, 6:9-13.

8. The other version, in Matthew's gospel, elaborates where Luke might have assumed his audience's capacity to do so. For example, in Luke's version we find, simply, "Your kingdom come," whereas Matthew adds "your will be done on earth as it is in heaven" (Mt 6:10). Luke may have wished to detail the actual picture of the kingdom, as my text will make clear.

9. 10:29; 10:41.

10. Ex 20:2-7.

in the divine purpose."[11] The two basic portions of the Law, love of God and love of neighbor, are paralleled here in the first two lines of the model prayer: a hallowing of God's name, and a coming to earth of God's community — peace — for all peoples.

The second phase of this little model prayer spells out what the reign of God is to look like: (1) daily bread, survival needs met for all;[12] (2) forgiveness, a mutuality between forgiveness from God and one's forgiveness of others; (3) "the favor of being spared from further testing."[13] God's reign is to be characterized by communal *shalom*, a peace that includes physical well-being, daily bread, and emotional and spiritual well-being, reciprocity between the one forgiving and the one forgiven. Such peace is a difficult peace, and the follower must pray to be spared the worst ("do not bring us to the time of trial").

(1) Ask for Essential Survival Needs

Central to the story's vision, forgiveness is bound up with God's generous provision of daily needs at a physical level — release from hunger, for example. On the matter of hunger, an alert audience hears an echo back to the words of Jesus in suggesting responsibility for giving the crowd its "daily bread."[14]

(2) Ask for Forgiveness, Even as You Are Forgiving

Does God's forgiveness of our sins depend on our forgiveness of what others owe us or of what has been done to our perceived harm? At the very least, it appears that Jesus is saying, as C. F. Evans notes, that "a direct request for forgiveness can be made by those who, as disciples of Jesus, are already in the position of having forgiven others."[15] But there may be a synergy here, a mutual dependence of being-forgiven-by-God and forgiving-others. We may be wrong to read the parallelism here as conditional: *if* you forgive others, *then* you will be forgiven. Perhaps it is more like this: your experience of forgiveness from God will play out as

11. Joel B. Green, *The Gospel of Luke*, New International Commentary on the New Testament (Grand Rapids: Eerdmans, 1997), p. 442.

12. "He has filled the hungry with good things," Mary says, 1:53.

13. Green, *The Gospel of Luke*, p. 444.

14. 9:13.

15. C. F. Evans, *Saint Luke* (Philadelphia: Trinity Press International, 1990), p. 483. See also his extended discussion on the matter.

forgiveness of others, while your forgiveness of others will lead you to the experience of being forgiven by God. In this case, God's forgiveness is a release from sins, the divine largesse in which mortals are challenged to share by forgiving each other. Such release includes the matter of debt, of what is owed: *for we ourselves forgive everyone indebted to us.* Whatever obligations we might think are owed us are to be forgiven.[16] Followers are to do good to their neighbor, "forgiving" any return of the favor. That is, those who go God's Way offer what ordinarily would be considered by the other person a debt to be repaid. But this forgiveness would be the canceling out of that debt, a giving with no thought of return. Such forgiveness of others would have proven a radically topsy-turvy way in that first-century world.[17] God forgives followers as they live out a way of forgiveness.[18]

(3) And Ask to Be Spared

May there be provision of daily bread, communal survival needs; may there be the reality of shared forgiveness. And, finally, may there be "the favor of being spared from further testing." This last petition may put the listener in mind of Satan's testing of Jesus in the wilderness at the start of

16. "Jesus challenges his listeners to be God's people, who refuse the coercive, control-dominated system of relationships characteristic of the wider [normal] world but instead give freely, without expectation of return, [which] is well summarized in the petition in Luke's version of the Lord's Prayer, 'And forgive us our sins, for we ourselves forgive everyone indebted to us' (11:4). In this case, 'debt' must be understood within the framework of patronal friendships. Consequently, Jesus is urging his followers to forgive debts — that is, to treat one another as kin, giving freely, not holding over one another obligations for praise and esteem." Paul J. Achtemeier, Joel B. Green, Marianne Meye Thompson, *Introducing the New Testament: Its Literature and Theology* (Grand Rapids: Eerdmans, 2001), p. 173.

17. Joel B. Green, on the first-century world of tit-for-tat giving (which strikes me as the normal way for all people everywhere): "A form of enslavement was built into the fabric of the Greco-Roman world, a pervasive ethic whereby favors done for others constituted a relationship characterized by a cycle of repayment and debt. . . . The prayer Jesus teaches his followers [particularly the forgiveness clauses] embodies the urgency of giving without expectation of return — that is, of ripping the fabric of the patronage system by treating others as . . . kin rather than as greater or lesser than oneself" (Green, *The Gospel of Luke*, p. 443).

18. This Way is characterized by doing good solely for the doing's sake, for the neighbor's sake and with no thought of material gain or elevated status as a precondition. Such a reign of God — the coming of God's kingdom for which we pray — begins with God's provision for physical needs, our daily bread, even as the Israelites were fed manna in the desert in amounts sufficient for the immediate present.

his public appearances, and again at the Mount of Olives toward the end of his life, when he prays to the Father, "Remove this cup from me." Twice he tells his disciples, "Pray that you may not come into the time of trial."[19] The final temptation — the ultimate "time of trial" — is the lure to forsake God's Way by maintaining life or a "god" such as wealth, at any cost, in the face of threat. A final temptation loomed large enough for Jesus that he requested special consideration from God, an exemption.[20] Jesus embraces the cross by resisting the possibility — "just this once" — of skipping around the challenge of doing and saying the right thing, a thing certain to invite one's own murder. "The answer to this petition" of being spared, as Robert Tannehill points out, "comes not in the form of immunity but as strength to endure and recover."[21]

At the heart of God's reign will be a harmony between neighbor and neighbor, as suggested in the latter part of the Law.[22] God's reign is to be characterized by neighborliness of an un-normal sort, a truly peaceable kingdom. Such neighborly effort requires recognition, as Jesus puts it in his final words of the journey, of "the things that make for peace."[23] To be attentive in kingdom matters requires persistence in prayer, an asking for help. The narrative spirals forward precisely at this point of persistence in prayer.

> "And do not bring us to the time of trial." And he said to them, "Suppose one of you has a friend, and you go to him at midnight and say to him, 'Friend, lend me three loaves of bread; for a friend of mine has arrived, and I have nothing to set before him.' And he answers from within, 'Do not bother me; the door has already been locked, and my children are with me in bed; I cannot get up and give you anything.' I tell you, even though he will not get up and give him anything because he is his friend, at least because of his persistence [shamelessness] he will get up and give him whatever he needs." (11:4-8)

The need for persistence, for shameless repetition, arises not from God's begrudging ways but because of the need for constant reminders of hu-

---

19. 22:40, 42, 46.

20. 22:42.

21. Robert C. Tannehill, *Luke*, Abingdon New Testament Commentaries (Nashville: Abingdon, 1996), pp. 188-89.

22. Ex 20:8-17.

23. 19:42.

man need and God's generosity. These reminders build trust in God's purposes, expressed by the initial perspective — "hallowed be your name," not ours; "your reign prevail," not ours.

But there is more to say about this matter of persistence, a qualification and an elaboration. Persistence is not rote request for a particular thing, a need-of-the-moment; rather, persistence is a moment-by-moment disposition of mind and heart, a dependence on God's empowerment:

> "So I say to you, Ask, and it will be given you; search, and you will find; knock, and the door will be opened for you. For everyone who asks receives, and everyone who searches finds, and for everyone who knocks, the door will be opened. Is there anyone among you who, if your child asks for a fish, will give a snake instead of a fish? Or if the child asks for an egg, will give a scorpion? If you then, who are evil, know how to give good gifts to your children, how much more will the heavenly Father give the Holy Spirit to those who ask him!" (11:9-11)

The best thing for which to pray — key to Luke's vision of salvation — is God's own Spirit, an empowerment for hearing-and-doing the word of God; such hearing and doing are essential for entering the kingdom of God and inheriting eternal life, as we have seen.

"I tell you," Jesus had just said, "even though [the sleeping friend] will not get up and give him anything because he is his friend, at least because of his persistence he will get up and give him whatever he needs" — so "Ask . . . search . . . knock."[24] There is nothing passive about this kind of asking.

But there remains the one thing, the best thing, for which one must always be praying to God. It is on this note that the prayer sequence concludes: if *you* know how to act well, giving some requested bread, "how much more will *the heavenly Father* give the Holy Spirit to those who ask him!"[25] That is, God gives quickly, and fully. The persistence being recommended has to do with the choice of continual praying as followers encounter one situation after another on God's Way.

From the perspective of the story as a whole, God is the central character and the Holy Spirit is God's best gift, a gift which Jesus himself receives and will assist in giving.[26] Disciples are to pray this kingdom into existence by prevailing on God; they are to work this kingdom into existence by for-

24. 11:9.
25. 11:13.
26. 3:22; 3:16.

giving others even as they are forgiven by God. Ultimately, what is impossible for mortals — even the will to forgive or the asking for such intent — is possible with God. Therefore the best gift to expect from God, the best thing to ask for, search for, knock on the door for, is God's own Spirit: persistently, on a daily basis. If daily bread can be supplied, "how much more will the heavenly Father give the Holy Spirit to those who ask him!"

The initial desire for God's name to be honored comes full circle with God honoring supplicants with the best of all gifts, the Holy Spirit. The point of having God's name honored in prayer is to affirm that God alone has purposes on earth worth serving. "So now, O Israel, what does the Lord your God require of you? Only [this], to fear the Lord your God, to walk in all his ways, to love him, to serve the Lord your God with all your heart and with all your soul."[27] Expressed in the scripture of Jesus and Luke, this word of the Law perfectly expresses Luke's perspective, economically illustrated in this prayer sequence. God's giving and forgiving impulses are to be answered by one's love of God, which is service to God's purposes. Through such love of God the name of God is honored. Prayer requires this reminder of whose purposes are to be glorified, whose name is to be honored. But how difficult! And so it is that the best gift for which to ask, the best gift to be given, is the enabling Spirit of God. Acts will play out that to which Luke's first volume points: the coming of God's kingdom through the agency of a Holy Spirit poured out "upon all flesh."[28]

In the echoing sequence to this prayer focus, the demand on human partners toward God's goal of a peaceable kingdom becomes even greater. We hear once again that one must pray persistently. But we find, also, an emphasis on the followers' cry for mercy, for divine assistance. How can there be inheriting of eternal life through hearing and doing the word of God (taught by Jesus) without a continual plea for God's mercy, God's Spirit?

The Echo: What to Pray For, and How (18:1-14)

Just before this echoing theme sequence on prayer, Jesus had concluded some very difficult words about judgment, a warning to "remember Lot's wife" who was turned to salt for looking back on that which she had been

27. Deut 10:12.
28. Acts 2:17.

117

challenged to relinquish.[29] Judgment will come unexpectedly, of course, since someone normal like Lot's wife is not expecting judgment. Of "two women grinding meal together, one will be taken and the other left."[30] Hearing of the sudden and unexpected judgment that befalls the woman grinding meal, the listeners ask, "Where, Lord?"[31] This perfectly ordinary response is very much beside the point. Such judgment is overwhelming, and will happen *to you, perhaps:* to ask about *where* or *when* is a dodge. Seeking the external circumstances of judgment — *where, when, how* — replaces the one needful response to word of judgment: "Me, Lord? To what must I pay attention?" Paying attention to what matters requires prayer. To the question "where" Jesus is shown offering a cryptic reply which serves as an introduction to the second major consideration of prayer on this journey to Jerusalem.

> "Where the corpse is, there the vultures will gather." Then Jesus told them a parable about their need to pray always and not to lose heart. He said, "In a certain city there was a judge who neither feared God nor had respect for people. In that city there was a widow who kept coming to him and saying, 'Grant me justice against my opponent.' For a while he refused; but later he said to himself, 'Though I have no fear of God and no respect for anyone, yet because this widow keeps bothering me, I will grant her justice, so that she may not wear me out by continually coming.'" And the Lord said, "Listen to what the unjust judge says. And will not God grant justice to his chosen ones who cry to him day and night? Will he delay long in helping them? I tell you, he will quickly grant justice to them. And yet, when the Son of Man comes, will he find faith on earth?" (17:37–18:8)

Your interest in *where,* Jesus implies, is foolish and beside the point: when judgment happens, you can check it out by following the route of vultures, settling on the judged, the corpse. What you need to be interested in is how to avoid such judgment for yourselves. So pray.

"Do not bring us to the time of trial" in the earlier prayer sequence is echoed here by preliminary warnings — vultures and corpses, one woman grinder taken and the other left behind: the warning is about the day of judgment when "the Son of Man is revealed."[32]

---

29. 17:32.
30. 17:35.
31. 17:37.
32. 11:4; 17:30; as David L. Tiede notes, in *Luke* (Minneapolis: Augsburg, 1988), p. 304.

In the first sequence, as we have seen, a shamelessly persistent host was asking for bread from his neighbor. Now, a shamelessly persistent widow is asking for justice.

What followers are to pray for does not need persistent repeating: God answers "quickly." Rather, since there is so much about which to pray in fulfilling God's purposes, followers must pray persistently. That is, "pray always." Things happen: "pray always."[33] From ominous possibilities of vultures and corpses, the text has moved to reminders of hope and of God's generosity in providing justice.

Imagine an impossibly wrong-minded judge petitioned by a widow seeking justice. So the tale begins. The man is thoroughly bad: he has no regard for either part of the Law, ignoring God and neglecting his neighbor. To what point, then, is this widow's persistence? What can she hope to gain? She keeps at it. The godless and people-despising judge cannot stand the fuss. "Because this widow keeps bothering me, I will grant her justice, so that she may not wear me out by continually coming." Referred to by the narrator now as "Lord," Jesus offers a majestic moral: God "will quickly grant justice" to those "who cry to him day and night."[34] If someone utterly depraved capitulates and gives something good, how much more readily will a beneficent God respond?

Crying to God "day and night" is not an anxious harping for one thing, but its opposite, a confident faith that recognizes both human need and divine beneficence. "Ask," we have heard, "and it will be given you; search, and you will find; knock, and the door will be opened for you. For everyone who asks receives, and everyone who searches finds, and for everyone who knocks, the door will be opened."[35] Such prayer is not occasional, but daily; not fearful, but full of faith. "When the Son of Man comes, will he find [such] faith on earth?"[36] Persistence, then, is not to be construed as a merely vain repetition each day for the one prized thing that will make all the difference, but rather a continual act of communing with the source of empowerment for every moment and quotidian of need in fulfilling God's purposes — in short, in loving God with our whole selves. Prayer connects one to God's purposes, so keep at it. On behalf of justice, the narrative suggests, there will always be a differing circumstance or person-in-need from day to day.

33. 13:23-24.
34. 18:7-8.
35. 11:9-10.
36. 18:8.

Something more germane to the human condition than even injustice remains, and Luke saves it to last.

> He also told this parable to some who trusted in themselves that they were righteous and regarded others with contempt: "Two men went up to the temple to pray, one a Pharisee and the other a tax collector. The Pharisee, standing by himself, was praying thus, 'God, I thank you that I am not like other people: thieves, rogues, adulterers, or even like this tax collector. I fast twice a week; I give a tenth of all my income.' But the tax collector, standing far off, would not even look up to heaven, but was beating his breast and saying, 'God, be merciful to me, a sinner!' I tell you, this man went down to his home justified rather than the other; for all who exalt themselves will be humbled, but all who humble themselves will be exalted." (18:9-14)

Justice is good, and a good thing for which to ask. But this cry for mercy from the sinner/outsider may be more to the ultimate point of asking, searching, knocking. "Be merciful to me a sinner, God" is a plea that echoes a major focus in the model prayer offered by Jesus, in the first prayer sequence, "Forgive us our sins."[37]

One who prays for such mercy exhibits a great faith, just as one who thanks God for his or her "good standing" — as the Pharisee, above — exhibits merely the self-absorption of monologue. As a foil to what true prayer looks like, we have the religious person's normal sort of prayer in which God is enlisted as a guarantor of one's own good fortune and status. Thank God, this conventional and pious praise begins, that I am so blessed — not like those who are not so blessed, like that obviously destitute person over there, beating his breast.

The socially honored one thanks God for all the blessings of his life, most especially his having escaped a life requiring mercy. But such parading of piety masks a deep complacency that excludes the possibility of need, rendering the request for mercy a moot point. Such prayer of thanksgiving is not directed toward anything except self-congratulation. This religious person's prayer exhibits no-faith, the non-prayer of one who ends up talking to himself about himself. It is normal, and very wrong, in this text, to feel better about oneself by a favorable comparison with at least one other person; such feeling can be masked even to oneself by such piety and prayerfulness as we see here exhibited by the religious person.

37. 11:4; 18:13.

The tax collector, the outsider, understands his need for God. He has done wrong. He would like to do better. He pleads for God's mercy. "I tell you," says Jesus, "this man went down to his home justified." The self-justifying and self-righteous religious leader has returned home entrenched even deeper, presumably, in his vicious complacency.

What to Pray for, and How:
A Summary of the Two Sequences

We have come full circle. The first prayer sequence concluded with a prayer for God's best gift, the Holy Spirit; the second sequence ends with the greatest need that can be presented to God, the need for mercy. God grants mercy, just as God gives the Holy Spirit. Each has to do with ultimate human need and God's greatest provisions.

The ultimate thing to ask for, then, is twofold: mercy (second sequence) recognizes the human situation, always, while the Holy Spirit (first sequence) is God's gift in answer to a petition that must begin with the cry for mercy. One who is inheriting eternal life, on God's Way, must always be crying out for mercy, and for that which ultimately is the only answer to such a cry: God's generous forgiveness and granting of empowerment.

The narrative always emphasizes judging oneself, scrutinizing one's own actions. It is always wrong to look outside oneself for approval and status — or to look beyond oneself at others, judgmentally. Pursuing justice through prayer is connected with the cry for mercy. For Luke, justice requires mercy, and mercy, justice.[38]

Normal attitude and action in Luke's story are always wrong. Self-promotion is normal. God's Way is un-normal. As Jesus puts it, following this prayer for mercy, "all who exalt themselves will be humbled . . . ."[39] The spirit of prayer is connected with overcoming that which opposes God's Way, the making of a name for oneself. Immediately after Jesus' words about the exalted being humbled, Luke goes on with an episode we have seen, about a sincere but dangerously rich ruler.[40] In his own way, the ruler is exalted through riches: perhaps he is unwilling to divest

---

38. Even in altruistic and philanthropic actions, it is normal to feel somewhat superior, at some hidden level, to the "poor person" receiving your attentions.

39. 18:14.

40. 18:1-25.

himself of the elevated status of great wealth. Only through his "disin-heritance" of wealth will he inherit God's life. The rich ruler's question about inheriting eternal life follows logically from the conclusion to the prayer section, the need for God's mercy. Unless he comes to follow God's Way, he will be ultimately humbled. In all his chaste performance of the neighborly portion of the Law, the ruler had failed to reckon with his status *vis-à-vis* God, as one in need of God's mercy.

Similarly, as we have seen, the first prayer sequence flowed logically from the preceding busy-ness and self-exaltation of the anxious lawyer and the fretful Martha. The spirit of prayer is above all a spirit of humil-ity, of the recognition that to let go in order to serve God's loving pur-poses requires gifts from God of both mercy and the Holy Spirit. As audi-ence, we may not have quite grasped the reason why God's Holy Spirit is the best thing to pray for. The parallel sequence answers that question in the growing realization of need.

The need for bread is daily, as is the need for forgiveness and forgiv-ing. Prayer is needed to make things happen, like peace, like the coming of the Holy Spirit, like mercy. And with such comes that which begins all prayer, the concern of God that the kingdom be realized.[41] Prayer occa-sions the descent of God's Spirit on Jesus and the descent of God's Spirit on the disciples.[42] Essential to the Way, to salvation itself, is this matter of prayer. With the lawyer and Martha and the rich ruler, we heard that in-heriting eternal life was a matter of hearing the word of God and doing it — an impossibility in strictly human terms. Thus begins the narrative ex-ploration of prayer. Only then does the impossible become possible: go-ing the Way of God and inheriting salvation.

Luke moves on in the next phase of the journey with scriptural examples of those who listened to God's word as if their lives depended on it. In both the first theme and in its echo, this note is sounded in the context of the need to judge for oneself what is right ("Lord, have mercy on me, a sinner!") rather than trying to judge other persons or scrambling for external signs or magic to bolster one's own standing, of being "right." The failure to assess oneself results in God's certain judgment, a playing out of the destruction inherent in self-protecting choices.

41. 11:2.
42. 3:21-22; Acts 1:8, 14; 2:1-2.

Chapter 8

Neither Signs nor Status:
Hear the Word, Do It

Luke 11:14-32; 17:20-37

We have been hearing that eternal life requires hearing and doing the word of God, and that prayer is intimately connected with this difficult salvation.[1] Luke moves forward in this journey, now, to that which prevents prayer, and how it is that followers must participate in implementing that for which they pray. Ordinary persons are always looking "out there" for signs. In the first sequence, Jonah, Solomon, and a queen from the South represent the only true "sign" — God's word and listening to it; in the echoing theme, we find another series of scriptural notables: Noah, Lot, and Lot's wife. Noah obeys the word of God; his perfectly normal neighbors, not particularly wicked in Luke's telling, conduct themselves in normal fashion, eating, drinking, and living comfortably — but of course they are dreadfully and tragically wrong. Why? We find out. Lot, this sequence goes on, is shown reluctantly obeying God's word even as his wife is ultimately refusing this word by turning back with a longing gaze toward her more normal life back in the city.

As these paralleled sequences make clear, salvation is not available to those who seek a complacent comfort while relying on signs and status for assurance of being in the right.

The First Time: Jonah, Solomon, Queen (11:14-32)

The immediately preceding verses, part of the prayer sequence, conclude with Jesus pointing to the best gift God can give, the Holy Spirit. Immedi-

---

1. Lk 10:21-42; 18:15-30; 11:1-13; 18:1-14.

ately we are presented with an *unholy* spirit, and the ruler of all unholy spirits, Satan:

> "If you . . . know how to give good gifts to your children, how much more will the heavenly Father give the Holy Spirit to those who ask him!" Now he was casting out a demon that was mute; when the demon had gone out, the one who had been mute spoke, and the crowds were amazed. (11:13-14)

In a short narrative moment, we find that seeking after signs to buttress "faith" is of Satan.

Another indication of a narratively forward-moving journey is an illustration of what Jesus had taught about praying for God's kingdom. Jesus is shown helping, now, to usher in that kingdom by healing the mute.[2] We recall that "the seventy" had been sent out on just such a kingdom mission.[3]

Yet another linkage has to do with speech. "He was casting out a demon that was mute," as we just heard, and "the one who was mute spoke." Just prior to notice of this speechless person we heard a lot about speaking:

- "when you pray, *say* . . ."
- "Suppose one of you has a friend, and you go to him at midnight and *say* . . ."
- "So I *say* to you, *ask,* and it will be given you . . ."
- "everyone who *asks* receives . . ."
- "how much more will the heavenly Father give the Holy Spirit to those who *ask* him!"[4]

The person who is mute cannot speak, cannot ask — with voice. One need not vocalize in order to communicate, of course, but in an oral age of mostly illiterate people, a live tongue is significant. Mary's utterance of a magnificent poem is powerful, introducing as we have seen Luke's special attention to hearing and speaking well. Zechariah's becoming mute, as punishment for not listening well, is significant. The demon has made this person's tongue dead. Anyone mute and/or deaf would be especially disadvantaged in such a culture, an outsider to the community of

---

2. 11:2, 14.
3. 10:9.
4. 11:2, 5, 9, 10, 13.

speakers. "The mute man had been kept from sharing in Israel's liturgical life," as Frederick Danker points out. "Now he is able to speak."[5] The good news is about release and restoration: this man is restored to communal well-being. He can pray, with his voice.

The crowd is amazed at this healing of a mute person, but negative responses surface as well. The negativity falls into two distinct species of problem. "Some of them said, 'He casts out demons by Beelzebul, the ruler of demons'"; meanwhile, "others, to test him, kept demanding from him a sign from heaven."[6]

The first negative response — "he casts out demons by Beelzebul" — provides an echo between this unholiest of spirits and the Holy Spirit, the best gift God can give. All restoration and release — the healings and forgiveness that constitute the "good news"[7] — happen in the context of the cosmic struggle between God and Satan, as we have already seen in the case of the initial eleven healings of the gospel.[8] Judas will capitulate to Satan and be utterly lost; Ananias and Sapphira will lie to the Holy Spirit and be utterly lost.[9] As we will see in a moment, this person healed of muteness must move on, resisting Satan and allowing God's Spirit to replace the demon of muteness — or he will be lost. Linking the Holy Spirit and Beelzebul in back-to-back verses is a reminder that the narrative's major character is God, and the main antagonist is Satan, who opposes God and God's purposes of peace on earth. Those who deny the good thing being done by suggesting Beelzebul as a source, the text implies, are in league with Satan. The second negative response — "demanding from him a sign from heaven" — echoes the need for sign-as-proof which began with Zechariah. Looking in this wrong direction is of prime concern in Luke's story, anticipating the focused exploration on this matter of sign-seeking that follows almost immediately.[10]

The suspicion that this good thing is done by the agency of Beelzebul and the seeking of a further sign are both related in their skepticism, their refusal to accept obvious goodness. With a heart and mind tuned to

---

5. Frederick Danker, *Jesus and the New Age: A Commentary on St. Luke's Gospel* (Philadelphia: Fortress, 1988), p. 231. The placement of this healing scene in Matthew's narrative is far different, working toward a different emphasis — a good example among very many of the distinctive marks of Luke's perspective (Mt 9:32-34).

6. 11:14-15; 11:16.

7. 4:18-19.

8. See Chapter 4.

9. Lk 22:3 and Acts 1:18-19; Acts 5:1-11.

10. 1:18; 11:27-29.

God's concerns, Jesus does the right thing, an action that is easily over-looked. Why? Simple good acts on behalf of others, like healing this mute person, indicate kingdom realization, the presence of God. How is it missed? The narrative immediately answers these questions.

Let us look at this with a clear head, says Jesus, in effect; he suggests that only a dark heart can explain the confused thinking. *Can Beelzebul be my source of power?* "Every kingdom divided against itself becomes a desert, and house falls on house; if Satan also is divided against himself, how will his kingdom stand?"[11] The text lines up three if-equations to the point of absurdity, with a final if-challenge:

- *If* a kingdom is divided against itself, how can it stand?
- *If* by Satan the demons of Satan are cast out, where is the unity?
- *If* I work with Beelzebul, by whom do your own exorcists cast demons out?
- "*If* it is by the finger of God that I cast out the demons, then the kingdom of God has come to you."[12]

Jesus poses these *if* propositions as if a child could understand. The fourth "if" is the clincher: "If it is by the finger of God that I cast out the demons, then the kingdom of God has come to you."[13] The climax to this if-logic is God and the obvious activity of God performed by Jesus.

The Beelzebul group seeks to discredit this doer of good: they question the source of his power. The testing group asks for better credentials. Doing a simple good thing, as Jesus has done for this person without capacity to vocalize speech, is not enough for either group. Is there intent to dislodge this doer of good from his position of authority regarding God's Way? This question of authority — and the benefits of aligning oneself with one authority rather than another — will become a dramatically central issue in the last days of Jesus in Jerusalem, and throughout Acts.

The devil has already been linked with the lure of seeking reassurance through external signs. It was Satan who tested Jesus with the lure

11. 11:17, 18.

12. 11:17, 18, 19, 20; "mere" finger of God? The words here may play with the idea of God's activity and power, from the denotation in Jewish scriptures (Ex 8:19; 31:18; Deut 9:10; Ps 8:3), as in, "If I cast out demons with *merely* the finger of God, imagine the coming of God's kingdom when all of God's power is utilized." Or, in the metonymic sense of God's finger: a small part, the finger, is "standing in" for the full power of God's spirit.

13. 11:20.

of signs and of the spectacular: *wouldn't you like to resort to signs of power and of God's care?* asks Satan of Jesus.[14] "The demand for the spectacular is itself evidence of evil nature," suggests C. F. Evans,[15] and is a clear refusal by the crowd of the godly word and good deed in their presence. A desire for signs is wrong; amazement at goodness done here and now is right. How can a good act be anything other than goodness, from God? *Even your own exorcists do such goodness,* says Jesus.[16] And this goodness is not merely a nice thing: it is the real thing, an indication that God's reign has come to you. The whole of God's power is in the finger of God!

For Luke, God's kingdom is about such goodness and blessing being done: release from the various imprisonments that keep human beings from their creation wholeness.[17] God's reign is witnessed, Luke suggests, not in spectacular signs but in small liberations. God is good, and those doing good do God's work. "If I cast out the demons by Beelzebul," Jesus asks, "by whom do your exorcists cast them out? Therefore they will be your judges."[18] As portrayed by Luke, the invitational inclusivity of Jesus becomes a judgment against his accusatory Jewish compatriots. There will be those rising within Israel, and those falling, as Simeon has prophesied, holding the infant Jesus:[19] here, we have Jesus and his fellow Jewish exorcists against the skeptical nay-sayers within Israel. In promoting their own claims to religious truth and societal standing, the established religious leaders are shown throughout the story to be excluding themselves from the circle of God's partners who are actively restoring God's intended creation order.

As evidenced by the eleven healings of the preparatory section,[20] creation reordering is what God's kingdom looks like, that for which we pray. Make no mistake, Jesus says: if such release is effected, and

14. "This is the 'tempting' and 'testing' which the devil himself did to Jesus (4:1-13) and concerning which Jesus has just told his disciples to pray" (11:4). David Tiede, *Luke,* Augsburg Commentary on the New Testament (Minneapolis: Augsburg, 1988), p. 217. Jesus was offered three signs — three external indicators, "props" — whereby he could assure others and himself of God's spectacular care (4:3-13). Pray to avoid a time of such testing, Jesus has just taught his disciples (11:4).

15. *St. Luke* (Philadelphia: Trinity Press International, 1990), p. 488. "To seek a sign from heaven," David Tiede observes, "is to reject the sign [of what Jesus does], and to refuse to hear the word he bears." Tiede, *Luke,* p. 220.

16. 11:19.

17. 4:18-19.

18. 11:19.

19. 2:34.

20. 1:1–9:50; see Part I, Chapter 3.

"the kingdom of God has come to you. When a strong man, fully armed, guards his castle, his property is safe. But when one stronger than he attacks him and overpowers him, he takes away his armor in which he trusted and divides his plunder." (11:20-22)

The "strong man, fully armed" is keeping the peace, guarding his castle. But merely maintaining one's own security, the peace of the fiefdom, is always self-destructive in the long run, since someone stronger, more fully armed eventually comes along and divvies up the spoils. But beyond the pragmatics of doing more than mere peacekeeping is the divine perspective on peacemaking that is mandated by the kingdom of these verses, a kingdom that insists throughout on "things that make for peace."[21] God will be the ultimate "stronger one" who overpowers parochial peace-securing efforts. Judge for yourselves between ways of salvation and ways of destruction, or inherit the whirlwind of judgment, as does this strong man.

The insight develops further: "Whoever is not with me is against me, and whoever does not gather with me scatters."[22] I am doing the obviously right thing, Jesus implies: if you are doing the right thing, you will be with me — otherwise, you are against me and your plunder will be scattered, "divided." An alert audience hears an echo back to the journey's prefatory word: "Whoever is not against you is for you."[23]

1. Whoever is not against you [and me] is with [us].
2. Whoever is not with me is against me.

The two are interesting complements: (1) anyone who isn't against the good that Jesus and his disciples are doing must be with them. From another angle, (2) the same truth: anyone who recognizes the good Jesus is doing and refuses Jesus is necessarily in opposition.[24] Judge for

21. 19:42.
22. 11:23.
23. 9:50.
24. Two perspectives can seem contradictory: (a) "Whoever is not against you is for you" (9:50); (b) "Whoever is not with me is against me" (11:23). The first statement is obviously inclusive, while the second can seem a move toward exclusivity. In the first version, however — "whoever is not against you is for you" — Jesus is correcting John's parochial exclusivity. John was concerned, apparently, that someone down the street doing God's business had no right doing so, since "he does not follow with us" (9:49). No, no, says Jesus: "whoever is not against us is for us." In the echoing statement — "whoever is not with me is against me" — Jesus flips to the other side of the coin. Whoever hears the good I say and sees

yourselves the obvious goodness of the deed and the doer, or be judged yourself.

The sign-seeking crowd and those suspecting Beelzebul behind the works of Jesus — those not with Jesus — have interrupted the healing of the mute. But Jesus is not finished, the narrative implies, and it sustains the momentum by returning to the person who was mute, or to any beneficiary of the good news. Is it enough to be released from disease or demonic oppression? No. If one is to remain in God's favor, the favor must be returned with hearing and doing the word of God.

> "When the unclean spirit has gone out of a person, it wanders through waterless regions looking for a resting place, but not finding any, it says, 'I will return to my house from which I came.' When it comes, it finds it swept and put in order. Then it goes and brings seven other spirits more evil than itself, and they enter and live there; and the last state of that person is worse than the first." (11:24-26)

God's favor, expressed through healing, demands a return of favor — a next step, a "furnishing" of the cleared-out person. But how?

The text answers with what might at first glance seem to be a *non sequitur:* a woman is represented as interrupting Jesus. But within the text, this is no interruption at all but a spiraling forward with a look backward to the question related to the healed person without speech.

> ". . . the last state of that person is worse than the first." While he was saying this, a woman in the crowd raised her voice and said to him, "Blessed is the womb that bore you and the breasts that nursed you!" But he said, "Blessed rather are those who hear the word of God and obey it!" (11:26-28)

Jesus challenges the woman to entertain a "larger" humanity than merely that of motherhood. Embedded in his plea to the woman is a solution, as well, to the person who is mute, namely, to the problem of returning demons. Both the woman and the healed demoniac must take in the word of God and obey it if they are to enter and continue to experience the realm of blessing within God's kingdom — which is to "be saved."[25]

---

the good I do, and fails to get on board, is by that very choice against me. Judge for yourselves between the two realms, or be overcome by someone from the strong/stronger world.

25. 13:23-24, summary verses that zero in on what the blessing of salvation requires.

Implicit in the woman's exclamation, perhaps, is a longing for significance through a son. Jesus rejects the praise and redirects the longing.[26] "Blessed, *rather* . . ." There is something not only better, but different altogether in quality and kind: *you are more than merely the womb and breasts of son-bearing potential. You can become a participant in God's reign.* More fulfilling than being a mother is to hear and do the word of God.

Luke's spiraling narrative technique is perfect: some in the crowd, just prior to this scene, had wanted a spectacular sign to latch onto; this woman seems to admire Jesus as a pathway to the spectacular. What mother would not be proud? *Oh, such a son; oh to have a son like this one!* But Jesus suggests a more significant longing, a larger world of desire: experience the true blessing that comes only from serving God's purposes as taught from the word of God by Jesus. Mary the mother of Jesus will be called "blessed" by generations to come, as she herself understood.[27] But that is precisely the point Jesus is making, which makes the whole scene, this little interlude, so remarkable in its echoing back to Mary's motherhood. Implicitly, Jesus is asking, *Blessed, to be my mother?* "Blessed rather are those who [like my own mother] hear the word of God and obey it."[28] Mary's blessedness, then, is in her willingness to serve God's purposes according to the word she hears.[29] And only such

---

C. F. Evans suggests that exorcisms are not spectacular in themselves, and are meaningful only if evil is replaced by good. Evans, *St. Luke* (Philadelphia: Trinity Press International, 1990), p. 488. That is, "positive possession of, and by, the good is necessary" (p. 494). At the very end of the ninth preparatory poem ("sermon on the plain"), Jesus cited a man who "dug deeply" for an adequate foundation to his house. This is he who "hears my words and acts on them." The echo of this metaphor of one's "house" is heard in the words Jesus addresses to the woman, words that refer back to the dilemma of a cleaned-out but vulnerable "house."

26. Robert Tannehill suggests that the woman's praise "reflects favorably on [Jesus]," though it is also clear that Jesus is calling no one blessed — including himself — who does not hear and do God's word. Robert C. Tannehill, *The Narrative Unity of Luke-Acts: A Literary Interpretation*, vol. 1 (Philadelphia: Fortress, 1986), p. 194.

27. 1:48.

28. To the extent that Mary mother of Jesus is blessed, the divine blessing is not so much in her mothering of Jesus, but in her becoming a member of God's family by hearing and doing the word of God (see Lk 1:38; Acts 1:12-14).

29. 1:38; following Mary's stated intention to respond to God's word as "the servant of the Lord," Elizabeth calls Mary "blessed . . . among women," which is immediately echoed by Mary's magnificent poem in which she claims that God "has looked with favor on the lowliness of his servant" (1:42-48). See Chapter 2.

a posture of willingness as exhibited by Mary will save the demoniac, ultimately.

Earlier, we anticipated a question: What lies behind the skepticism that seeks signs? This narratively buried question is finally uncovered in the illustration of this very normal mother. Here we see greatness-by-association, the ordinary desire of parents to look good by virtue of their children's accomplishments. Jesus is shown condemning this perfectly ordinary pathway to status and "belonging." And at the same time we hear one of the story's most important refrains once again: blessed are those who hear the word and do it. Signs can serve to shore up fragile identities, as we have seen. Zechariah's asking for external proof is a question seeking assurance; the lawyer's insistence on definition (of "neighbor") is a pose seeking self-justification; Martha's frenetic busyness is a posturing that hides anxiety. Look inward, the story insists. Do not cling to externals — like religious proof-signs or privileged wombs — in seeking salvation and true religion.[30]

The text moves from Jesus giving the woman the shorthand version of what provides salvation to that which prevents salvation. "When the crowds were increasing, he began to say, 'This generation is an evil generation; it asks for a sign. . . .'"[31]

The only legitimate sign is no external sign at all, but a word — God's word, spoken by Jonah, by the Son of Man, and by Solomon:

> "For just as Jonah became a sign to the people of Nineveh, so the Son of Man will be to this generation. The queen of the South will rise at the judgment with the people of this generation and condemn them, because she came from the ends of the earth to listen to the wisdom of Solomon, and see, something greater than Solomon is here! The people of Nineveh will rise up at the judgment with this generation and condemn it, because they repented at the proclamation of Jonah, and see, something greater than Jonah is here!" (11:30-32)

This passage recommends that you judge for yourselves on the basis of the word of God as brought by a word-bearer like Jonah. The Ninevites chose well between sign and sign, as the foreign queen chose: rather than external sign, each listened to the word of God.

---

30. In Acts, however, believers will insist on the resurrection as proof of God's authorization of Jesus as ultimate word-bearer.

31. 11:29.

Luke's gospel leaves out what the gospel of Matthew includes: Jonah's three-day stay in the belly of a sea-monster.[32] *That* would constitute a "sign" — the spectacular. From the devil's temptations of Jesus onward, Luke's narrative perspective avoids and in fact condemns the longing for signs and the spectacular.[33] Only God's raising of the Son of Man from death will be stressed by Luke in the category of "spectacular," for reasons that become clear only at the end of the gospel, and in Acts. Here, there is just Jonah speaking words from God. Everything, salvation and the *shalom* God wishes to bring, hinges on hearing and going the Way of God taught by Jesus.[34]

The Ninevites and the queen were foreigners, outsiders, and yet the Jewish scriptures — the Scripture referred to by Jesus — holds them up as recognizing the sign of God's presence, the divine word heard well.[35] And here, listening to Jesus, are fellow Jews, an "evil generation" who seek an outward sign rather than an inward transformation, a "repentance."[36] We have come full circle in this theme cluster, from the initial skeptics and sign-mongers who tested Jesus, through the son-seeking woman, to the sign-seeking of this evil generation.

External signs are tempting, easy to see and grasp after, a security of sorts. The seeing of such signs is opposite to the seeing of God's Way. From Jesus we hear, next: "*See,* something greater than Jonah is here!"[37] — followed by an extended metaphor about *seeing* by way of a light.

> "No one after lighting a lamp puts it in a cellar, but on the lampstand so that those who enter may *see* the light. Your eye is the lamp of your body. If your eye is healthy, your whole body is full of light; but if it is not healthy, your body is full of darkness. Therefore *consider* whether the light in you is not darkness. If then your whole body is full of light, with no part of it in darkness, it will be as full of light as when a lamp gives you light with its rays." (11:33-36; emphasis mine)

On the one hand, simply make sure that the light is placed on the

---

32. Mt 12:40; here and throughout I do not mean to imply that Luke necessarily had Matthew's text before him, or even (as almost all scholars assume) a source common to both himself and Matthew.

33. Lk 4:1-13; see Chapter 4.

34. 20:21.

35. 11:14-23; 11:27-28; 11:29.

36. 11:29; 11:32.

37. 11:32.

lampstand "so that those who enter may see the light." On the other hand, "consider whether the light in you is not darkness."

The narrative connection between light-for-seeing and seeing someone greater than Jonah seemed clear enough.[38] The seeing images get confusing, however: it appears that this light on the lampstand will not help in seeing, after all, since the light by which we see comes from within, not from without. "Consider whether the light in you is not darkness," so that you yourself will be filled with light just as surely as the lamp outside you spreads its rays on you. Lamplight is useless without light already present within the observer! That is, seeing the light in the first place depends on a certain disposition of light within the one who sees.

The enigmatic juncture in any narrative text like this is usually an indication that the puzzling piece is an important clue to the larger picture. We have just come on this journey from a sequence on sign-seeking. Luke now places a sequence having to do with considerations of one's interior, the very opposite of seeking external signs. Do not look at the external trappings, or even the external sources of light: look within.[39] In that time and place, it was assumed that the eyes allowed interior light to go out, permitting sight. This idea works perfectly in this text.[40] The point Jesus makes is clear: "Therefore consider whether the light in you is not darkness."[41]

Look within yourself, this theme sequence is saying: *stop relying on signs to which you can attach your own significance — even such a sign as a fine son that can redound to a mother's glory. Replace the grasping after externals with a*

---

38. One aspect of Luke's ever-present technique of spiraling, in this case, is in the matter of what it takes to truly see. So tight is this spiraling, so deft, that the following lampstand saying can be seen as an exclamation point to the prior sequence (and therefore belonging in my prior chapter), or as a brilliant prefatory note to the following sequence about posing and status. That is, at almost any point in the narrative flow, the audience is experiencing a transition, a segue, an overlap to the spiraling — the circling-back-to-move-forward phenomenon of Luke's artistry.

39. Perhaps, as Joseph Fitzmyer says, this image of lamp, cellar, and lampstand is addressed "to people of Jesus' generation and their sign-seeking." Joseph A. Fitzmyer, *The Gospel According to Luke,* vols. 28 (1981) and 28a (1985) in the Anchor Bible series (New York: Doubleday, 1985), pp. 939-40.

40. "According to a physiology prevalent in Greco-Roman antiquity, the eyes do not function by allowing light to come in but by allowing the body's own light to go out. The eye is the conduit of the source of the light that makes sight possible." Joel B. Green, *The Gospel of Luke* (Grand Rapids: Eerdmans, 1997), p. 465.

41. Lk 11:35.

scrutiny of your interior and with ear tuned to God's word. One's motives are hard to fathom, and the text suggests here and in the following sequence (explored in the following chapter) just how difficult such "seeing" is. "There is no automatic 'inner light' as far as Jesus is concerned."[42] Darkness is dispelled by a willingness to see. "If then your whole body is full of light," Jesus concludes, "with no part of it darkness, it will be as full of light as when a lamp gives you light with its rays."[43]

Earlier Jesus uses precisely this same lamp image — a lit lamp placed on a lampstand — to suggest that one's interior and darkness of motive will be exposed by light. "Then pay attention to how you listen" was the climactic point of that lampstand saying.[44] Pay attention. Listen. Pay attention to *how* you listen. It was "to listen to the wisdom of Solomon" that the queen had traveled long distances, and for the very bad Ninevites it was in their listening to Jonah — truly paying attention — that they were able to repent, and be forgiven.[45] To listen, for Luke, is to be truly receptive, beyond one's cherished or easily assumed notions. The strange twists in both lamp images come to the same conclusion: consider your interior, the light within, your willingness to hear the word.

The Echo: Noah's Neighbors, Lot and Lot's Wife (17:20-37)

The prior instance of this "no-sign" theme featured ancient notables, the Ninevites and Jonah, the queen of the South and Solomon. In this echoing sequence we find Noah and his neighbors, then citizens of Sodom, including Lot and his wife. The essential issue is the same: a seeking after signs linked with a complacency that avoids the difficult word of God. Here leaders want an external sign of the kingdom.

> Once Jesus was asked by the Pharisees when the kingdom of God was coming, and he answered, "The kingdom of God is not coming with things that can be observed; nor will they say, 'Look, here it is!' or 'There it is!' For, in fact, the kingdom of God is among you." Then he said to his disciples, "The days are coming when you will long to see one of the days of the Son of Man, and you will not see it." (17:20-22)

42. Darrell L. Bock, *Proclamation from Prophecy and Pattern: Lucan Old Testament Christology* (Sheffield, U.K.: Sheffield Academic Press, 1987), p. 1101.

43. 11:35-36.

44. 8:16-18.

45. 11:31-32.

The passage warns against looking for things "out there" — the normal disposition, surely — to confirm the existence of a kingdom with signs.

"If it is by the finger of God that I cast out demons," Jesus has said to his skeptics, in the theme's first exploration, "then the kingdom of God *has come to you.*"[46] Here in the echoing sequence, the wording changes: "the kingdom of God *is among you.*"[47] Perhaps "*to* you" suggests invitation, while "*among* you" refers to accomplished or nearly-accomplished fact. God's kingdom is kinetic, not static; expansive, not exclusive. The realm of God's blessing on earth will be described by Jesus as a kingdom with the smallest of beginnings, a tree growing from a mustard seed — so full a growth that "the birds of the air made nests in its branches." The kingdom is present in the seed, in the first flowering, and in the full bloom — like the action of yeast in bread dough, working toward a culmination "until all of [the flour] is leavened."[48]

"Among you" *(entos hymōn)* can also be translated "within you,"[49] or

---

46. 11:20 (emphasis mine).

47. 17:21 (emphasis mine).

48. 13:18-21; the text's audience might hear an echo back to the first theme sequence, where these same Pharisees are advised that "if it is by the finger of God that I cast out demons, then the kingdom of God has come to you." See Sharon Ringe, *Luke* (Louisville: Westminster/John Knox, 1995), p. 222.

49. "The koine Greek term [*entos*], translated 'among' you in the NRSV, occurs elsewhere in the NT only in Matt. 23:26, where it designates the inside of a cup. Its meaning in its present context is debated. Does it mean 'within you' (NIV) — that is, that the kingdom is an inner condition experienced only by the individual believer? . . . Moreover, the pronoun for 'you' [*hymeis*] is plural — a group or collection of individuals? Does it mean 'in the midst of you' — that the kingdom is present among them because Jesus is in their midst? This meaning seems to fit better, but it still does not explain the choice of this unusual term or how the presence of the kingdom in Jesus is to be related to its future manifestation. Other nuances have been proposed: either that the future kingdom has already arrived unobserved or that it is within their grasp if they will only act to seize it." Alan R. Culpepper, *The Gospel of Luke,* New Interpreter's Bible, vol. 9 (Nashville: Abingdon, 1995), pp. 329-30. In addition to the difficulty of choosing the best understanding of 17:21, one must also arrive at some explanation for how Luke understands this assertion to be related to the verses that follow. The next section (17:22-37) is closely linked to vv. 20-21, but it contains admonitions for watchfulness because the Son of Man will come suddenly and unexpectedly. The shift of audience from the Pharisees to the disciples signals the beginning of a new section in v. 22, but the catchword links formed by the repetition of " 'Look there!' or 'Look here!' " in v. 23 (cf. v. 21) and the repetition of verbs for "coming" in vv. 20 and 22 tie this new series of pronouncements to the preceding verses. The structural links may mislead a casual reader, however. Verses 22-37 shift from the theme of the presence of the kingdom in their midst to warnings about the suddenness of the coming of the Son of Man. The coming of the Son of Man, however, is not to be equated with the coming of the kingdom of God. The kingdom is already present.

"within your scope of perception." In fact, Luke pictures God's reign as both "among" and "within." This reign of God transforms individual hearts, as Sharon Ringe notes, but also shapes "institutions and relationships that unite and divide people." In short, the kingdom of God "lies within, among, and surrounding humankind."[50] The reality of God's work being done in their presence escapes these who search for signs "out there" conforming to predetermined systems of thought and expertise.

Jesus turns to the disciples to instruct them on a closely related matter. Given the inward and among-you quality of God's kingdom, the disciples must be on guard against anyone pointing to outward indicators or proof of the Son of Man's coming at this time or that, here or there. Hold in suspicion anyone who says "look there" or "look here!"[51] *All you can know and must know, for now, is this, that difficulty precedes glory and celebration:* "[the Son of Man] must endure much suffering and be rejected by this generation."[52] About such suffering they themselves must be prepared, as we have heard: "If any want to become my followers, let them deny themselves and take up their cross daily and follow me."[53]

Later, Jesus will articulate clearly the suffering of followers that will precede the time of "great distress on the earth,"[54] just as here the text has "the days of the Son of Man" preceded by suffering and rejection. So the quest for or certainty about the *when* and *where* of the future coming of Jesus is an avoidance precisely of Jesus' call to action and endurance. As early as the third chapter of Acts (3:21), we hear that Jesus will not return until the "universal restoration" — the Kingdom — is fulfilled.

Satan's domain is characterized, as we have seen, by a fixation on externals: seeking signs in order to be certain of God,[55] or participation in the religiously spectacular,[56] or assurance of salvation status through

50. Sharon Ringe, *Luke* (Louisville: Westminster/John Knox, 1995), p. 222.

51. 17:23.

52. 17:25.

53. I. H. Marshall notes that there is the "necessity of suffering preceding glory." *Commentary on Luke,* New International Greek Testament Commentary (Grand Rapids: Eerdmans, 1979), p. 661; see also Joel B. Green's discussion on the priority of suffering, in *The Gospel of Luke,* p. 634; and Robert Tannehill's note that there would be the temptation for later followers — Luke's audience — to expect glory without suffering. Robert Tannehill, *Luke* (Nashville: Abingdon, 1996), p. 260.

54. Lk 21:23.

55. *Is it God, or Beelzebul* the critics wonder, falsely (Lk 11:15).

56. Skeptics wish "a sign from heaven" (11:16), an underlying lure behind the temptations offered Jesus by Satan (see Chapter 4).

association with a particular religious clan.[57] God's domain lies in the opposite direction, beginning with an inward scrutiny rather than a search for external sign. God's Way, for Luke, requires a sharing in suffering, not in the spectacular. Public rejection is the fate not only of Jesus, but for all who follow God's Way. Like Jesus, those who claim his name will experience hatred and exclusion and dishonor within normal society.[58]

When the day of the Son of Man comes, Jesus continues, *it will come without esoteric signs to be interpreted by religious experts. It will be obvious to even a child, like lightning that* "flashes and lights up the sky from one side to the other."[59] There is no point, the text suggests, in scouring about for signs before the lightning strikes. When it strikes, it strikes — with no advance warning and with such startling clarity as not to be confusing. Jesus advises his listeners to remember the scenes of judgment from the Jewish scriptures, and thus to scrutinize their own motives, the integrity of desire and action.

Beware the futurists, says Jesus; *beware those who lure you with this sign, or that portion-of-text.* For sign-seekers, the narrative suggests, the only sign will be one of judgment. Remember Noah's neighbors:

> "Just as it was in the days of Noah, so too it will be in the days of the Son of Man. They were eating and drinking, and marrying and being given in marriage, until the day Noah entered the ark, and the flood came and destroyed all of them." (17:26-27)

Instead of citing the spectacular wickedness of Noah's generation — a wickedness that made God temporarily desirous of destroying the entire creation[60] — Luke emphasizes the evil of smug comfort, the complacency of "eating, drinking and marrying."

So too, Luke omits Sodom's spectacular inhospitality and notorious sexual oppression, choosing rather to focus on their humdrum preoccupations, their everyday routines:

---

57. 3:8, where Jesus warns that claiming salvation status through association with the right religious group (through father Abraham) will not suffice.

58. 6:22, a truth played out in Acts.

59. 17:24.

60. Gen 6:5-22; Robert Tannehill suggests the omission as emphasizing the destructiveness of "normal": "Ordinary life is no longer a closed and secure world." Tannehill, *Luke,* 1996), p. 261. Culpepper points to normal activities as the problem: wickedness grows up among everyday concerns. Culpepper, *The Gospel of Luke,* p. 332.

"Likewise, just as it was in the days of Lot: they were eating and drinking, buying and selling, planting and building, but on the day that Lot left Sodom, it rained fire and sulfur from heaven and destroyed all of them — it will be like that on the day that the Son of Man is revealed." (17:28-30)

With its easy assumption of rights and privilege — "eating and drinking, buying and selling, planting and building" — this perfectly normal way of living errs by overlooking the oppression on which it rests, namely, the well-known story of Sodom's rapacious inhospitality toward the wayfarer and stranger.[61] By calling attention to everyday pursuits as suspect, the narrative deftly highlights the thematic concern of looking and going in wrong directions for God's true blessing. Israel can easily fool itself: What possibly can be wrong, ordinary persons well might ask, with "eating and drinking, buying and selling, planting and building"?

Within the two-volume story as a whole we find a drama of ordinary ways pitted against God's Way, with teaching and illustration about just how insidious yet civilized the normal way can be in oppressing others and opposing God's program for blessing in the world. Everyday activities are not inherently evil, but become so when they prove "distractions from the necessity of one's fundamental orientation toward the purpose of God,"[62] a purpose that seeks the blessing of life's good things for those beyond the family and tribal circle.

From subtle forms of self-security and self-promoting comfort to an overt oppression of others the narrative is suggesting that evil is on a spectrum of everyday reality that can appear perfectly fine. Exclusive attention to one's own eating and drinking and marrying precludes a proper attention to the other — the heart of an inclusive neighborliness demanded by God's Way.

As we might expect from Luke's story, the true "sign" of God's word and the wrong signs sought by normal people are exemplified in both female and male exemplars. A queen listens to the word of God from Solomon and is impressed: this is good. Ninevites listen to the word of God as proclaimed by Jonah, and repent: this is good. Noah's neighbors enjoyed the normal amenities of life — eating, drinking, marrying — as did Lot, his wife, and his neighbors: this is bad.[63] Each female character along

---

61. Gen 19:1-26.
62. Culpepper, *The Gospel of Luke*, p. 635.
63. Here is a wise woman, this foreign queen who travels far to hear Solomon's wise

with each male character is faced with the temptation of ordinary living rather than the life in God's kingdom. The text shows no gender preference or bias because the larger narrative perspective is about God's blessing, which supersedes any man's achievement for himself or his family or any woman's womb giving birth, even to Jesus. The alternation of male and female — for better and for worse — is continuous throughout the two-volume story, as here:

> "On that day, anyone on the housetop who has belongings in the house must not come down to take them away; and likewise anyone in the field must not turn back. Remember Lot's wife. *Those who try to make their life secure will lose it, but those who lose their life will keep it.*" (17:31-33, emphasis mine)

The challenge for male and female is the same: hear "the word," the only sign to which you must pay attention.

Jesus has spoken God's word about kingdoms and judgment in the echoed sequence, which we explored in the first half of this chapter. Now, in the echoing sequence, Jesus is shown spelling out God's word about the contrast between looking in the wrong and right directions. Lot's wife is a grim reminder of what Luke is emphasizing about "wrong." She had her community and her life, her dining and drinking and giving of daughters in marriage. Noah's neighbors are portrayed similarly.

Had not Lot's wife simply arranged for whatever security a woman in that day might hope? Yet she is severely faulted. She and her husband must turn their back — and keep it turned! — on an everyday way of life that becomes exposed in its wickedness, its horrendous self-interest at the expense of the outsider, the guest. Sodom is destroyed, along with Gomorrah. Lot's wife stands frozen in her backward-longing gaze. She is loath to leave that to which she had grown accustomed. For Luke, complacency masks a complicity in the world's wrong-doing toward outsiders, toward the diseased and hungry, the shunned woman, the disregarded child.

Judge for yourselves the rightness of God's reign, or you will be judged when you least expect it. "I tell you," Jesus concludes, "on that night there will be

---

words; and here is a foolhardy woman, this wife of Lot who is frozen in her tracks, looking back to homeland, contrary to God's word. In her backward gaze, Lot's wife, the text suggests, was longing for the ordinary pursuits of "eating and drinking, buying and selling, planting and building" (17:27-28).

two in one bed; one will be taken and the other left. There will be two women grinding meal together; one will be taken and the other left."[64] Does the choice seem arbitrary? Ordinary activities are common to all, whether of God's kingdom or Satan's — these two, sleeping in bed for example. One in that bed belongs to God's reign, the other to Satan's domain. On what basis does God distinguish between the two? We have just been told: it is a matter of preoccupation, of attention, of orientation — of fundamental disposition. Looking in wrong directions is a problem being emphasized in the paralleled themes explored in this chapter. Other sequences in the middle section of Luke, the journey, spell out the positive content of a word that must be obeyed.

In a possibly humorous exclamation point to this echoing sequence, Luke includes an extraordinarily obtuse and inappropriate question posed by the disciples. They have heard that God's judgment is sure, though not to be observed as to projected time or place. The disciples ask about it anyway: "*Where*, Lord?"[65] Ironically, the old-guard religious leaders had just asked about the judgment, "*When*, Lord?"[66]

Luke shows Jesus offering a tongue-in-cheek answer to this hopelessly misguided question. To the disciples who want to know *where*, Jesus responds, "Where the corpse is, there the vultures will gather."[67] And to the corollary question of *when*, Jesus points out that only after the fact of death will vultures be seen poking around the corpse. *When* and *where* will be so obvious you need not concern yourselves with the matter now. The fulfillment of God's kingdom will be obvious, and too late for any entering — unless you have made proper choices in advance.[68] "I have set before you life and death, blessings and curses," says God, in the Scripture; "choose life."[69] There is true and false: assess the matter for yourself, that you may live.

64. 17:34-35.
65. 17:37.
66. 17:20.
67. 17:37.
68. See 13:23-30, which we explore a few chapters hence.
69. Deut 30:19; David Moessner points out the many parallels between the journey in Deuteronomy and this journey to Jerusalem. See David Moessner, *Lord of the Banquet: The Literary and Theological Significance of the Lukan Travel Narrative* (Minneapolis: Fortress, 1989). John Drury, much earlier, demonstrated the extensive use of scripture by Luke, and particularly of Deuteronomy. John Drury, *Tradition and Design in Luke's Gospel: A Study in Early Christian Historiography* (London: Darton, Longman and Todd, 1976).

Neither Signs nor Status: Hear the Word, Do It:
A Summary of the Two Sequences

For the sake of standing and status, a mother envies the mother of a great son (first sequence). Better, says Jesus, to hear and do God's word. The religiously serious are attached to reassuring signs of their own salvation and future well-being — attachments that turn out to be marks of the citizen in Satan's kingdom. Better, says Jesus, to do the right thing (first sequence). The kingdom prayed for is opposed to the kingdom of everyday experience. Luke arranges his text to illustrate the deceptive pleasantness of normal ways that oppose God's Way; such ordinary ways, wrong ways, are considered honorable.

Ordinary persons tempt Jesus to prove himself as magic-worker (first sequence), even as they "try to make [their own] life secure" (second sequence).[70] Always we are being reminded that "the things that make for peace" in this kingdom taught by Jesus are the small, good things — Jesus taking care of a person without speech, for example (first sequence). Such a kingdom reality is not observable because ordinary observation looks to something spectacular, a sign of club membership that would guarantee safety and "being right" (first and second sequences). God's Way, however, is a kingdom of doing the right thing, always, a kingdom whose entry requires a rigorous striving.[71] Normal attention to everyday detail — "eating and drinking and marrying" — can mask self-interest, leading to destruction (2nd sequence).[72] The kingdom of God, on the other hand, is not here nor there in that which assures ordinary security and promotion, but among those who hear the word and do it (first and second sequences). The foreign Ninevites and queen from the South did the right thing by turning-around from normal kingdoms to the hearing of God's word (first sequence); Noah's neighbors and Lot's wife did the wrong thing by failing to hear, failing to repent (second sequence).

As we see next on this journey of the Way, one can appear honorable but be filled inside — out of public view — with tainted motive and false deeds. Look within, says Jesus. "Woe!" he says to those most vulnerable to public show, the religious

---

70. 11:16; 17:33.

71. 13:23-24, the heart and goal of the Way that is unfolding for Luke's audience (taken up in the last chapter of this section).

72. 17:27.

leaders, whether Pharisee or disciple. The cure is in true faith, a cast of mind and spirit that does the small good with no thought of applause, notice, or even a "thank you." Only such an un-normal disposition can help usher in the kingdom of God and its peace.

Chapter 9

Look Inside Yourself, and Do the Word

Luke 11:33–12:12; 17:1-19

Stop looking "out there" for signs of your significance, or security: rather, look within at the state of your heart, your motives. Finding solace in signs or in any external source of status — even for a mother to take pride in a son like Jesus — is to miss the living reality of God's kingdom.[1] Luke's represented journey presses the point, now, with a plea for scrutiny that examines interior motives. "Woe!" says Jesus to both the disciples and the old-guard Pharisees, scribes, and lawyers. To both groups of leadership within Israel, the ultimate word is this: "Consider whether the light in you is not darkness."[2] The answer to hypocrisy, in the echoing sequence later in the journey, is a challenging instruction about a difficult integrity between interior and exterior — motives of serving God's purposes in synch with truly good action. Such integrity evidences faith and is best expressed by gratitude. Look within yourself, say these paralleled theme sequences, and live outward from an interior so filled with light as to need no reward of praise or even thanks: live by faith.

The First Time: Look Inside Yourself, and Do the Word (11:33–12:12)

The prior sequence has ended with an emphasis on seeing, looking: "*See, something greater than Jonah is here!*" we heard, followed by a lamp metaphor that included a light put on a lampstand "*so that those who enter may see the light.*"[3] Now we come to the most difficult *seeing* of all, the

1. 11:27-28.
2. 11:35.
3. 11:32; 11:33-36 (see Chapter 8).

call to look inward and see what is there. Such perception is foundational for perceiving the kingdom of God. The scrutinizing gaze must be turned inward rather than "out there" in judgment — as was suggested by the light metaphor itself.[4] We recall the warning against looking "out there" for signs to bolster religious faith,[5] or "out there" at the son or daughter who can bring a parent honor and status.[6]

> While he was speaking [about the lampstand], a Pharisee invited him to dine with him; so he went in and took his place at the table. The Pharisee was amazed to see that he did not first wash before dinner. "Now you Pharisees clean the outside of the cup and of the dish, but inside you are full of greed and wickedness." (11:37-39)

Seeking a good and honorable name takes work, like the cleaning and polishing of dishware by the conscientious host. However normal, such activity disguises self-seeking, "greed and wickedness."

The solution posed by Jesus may seem puzzling: "Give for alms those things that are within; and see, everything will be clean for you."[7] Perhaps this giving of "things that are within" means that if you give to those in need — regardless of family or clan membership — then such "alms" indicate cleanness of interior, a purity of will.[8] Or perhaps this giving of things within means that the only worthwhile giving, regardless of what or how much, is giving that comports perfectly with the pure desire to give. That is, give only because it is the right thing to do, regardless of payback or favorable notice. Both interpretations are borne out by what follows.

Jesus has agreed to dine with his Jewish peers, which leads him to comment rather naturally on matters of dinnerware. Eating together suggested great intimacy in that day. Jesus talks freely and frankly. He offers

---

4. "Therefore consider whether the light in you is not darkness" (11:35).

5. 11:16; Chapter 8.

6. 11:27-28; Chapter 8.

7. 11:41.

8. "Economic sharing was embedded [for Luke's audience] in social relations," as Joel B. Green points out. "To share with someone without expectation of return was to treat [him or her as] family. Conversely, to refuse to share with others was tantamount to relating to them as though they were outside one's community. . . . In such a context, almsgiving cannot be understood according to modern lexicons as 'charity' or 'missionary giving.' Rather, giving to the poor [giving 'alms'] was a signifier of social relations with the poor." Joel B. Green, *New Testament Theology: The Theology of the Gospel of Luke* (Cambridge: Cambridge University Press, 1995), p. 114.

these particular religious leaders, the Pharisees, three separate warnings — Woe! — about showing oneself to the world as a better person than what is indicated at motivational levels within. In addition to the Pharisees, a religious lawyer — another expert on Scripture — is present. He complains, "When you say these things, you insult us too."[9] Jesus responds by going on to pronounce three more warnings, this time on these religious law-guides.

- Religious leaders, woe! You give the religiously prescribed percentage of your goods but "neglect justice and the love of God."[10]
- Religious leaders, woe! "You love to have the seat of honor in the synagogues and to be greeted with respect in the marketplaces."[11]
- Religious leaders, woe! You look fine to the masses, while in reality you are dead and "lying in unmarked graves" which "people walk over . . . without realizing it."[12]
- Scripture experts, woe! You "load people with burdens hard to bear, and you yourselves do not lift a finger to ease them."[13]
- Scripture experts, woe! You are in league with ancestors who killed the prophets; your way of being in the world completes your ancestors' dirty work by building tombs for murdered prophets — covering up the matter.[14]
- Scripture experts, woe! Your knowledge is used as a weapon against the unknowing; you fail to "enter into" the Torah truth with which you have been entrusted.[15]

In all six cases of warning, the problem is a posturing for external effect — normal concern with approval rating, or even recompense — rather than acting out of love for God and neighbor. This is at least one angle on the vice of hypocrisy: a lack of integrity, "a life apparently devoted to God [that hides] a desire for human honors."[16] The temptation toward hypocrisy is greater, apparently, for those entrusted by God with

9. 11:45.
10. 11:42.
11. 11:43.
12. 11:44.
13. 11:46.
14. 11:47-51.
15. 11:52.
16. Robert Tannehill, *The Narrative Unity of Luke-Acts: A Literary Interpretation*, vol. 1 (Philadelphia: Fortress, 1986), p. 199.

the responsibility of leadership within the community. That is, the higher one is located on social and religious scales of importance, the more susceptible one is to a lack of integrity. Conduct that seeks honor and good standing, however admirable it looks in ordinary society, contains a hidden darkness, and will be exposed — as we hear a few verses later: "Nothing is covered up that will not be uncovered, and nothing [is] secret that will not become known."[17]

The disconnect between exterior show and interior darkness is serious. The consistent call of Jesus to listen contrasts with the compulsion of Israel's leaders to silence the prophets by killing them — by shutting up the very possibility of God's word being made clear. Jesus is a prophet in a line of prophets, by his own testimony and by public recognition; like all of them, he will be killed.[18] But he will not be silenced. And here are the ancestors' progeny, a sad line of leadership within Israel lying in wait for Jesus "to catch him in something he *might say*" — rather than to take in what he *is saying*.[19] But how does inner darkness become receptive to light? The warnings of Jesus suggest that these leaders themselves choose darkness. If these leaders are helpless in dealing with their lack of integrity, their hypocrisy, why then would Jesus warn them and ask them and others to "consider whether the light in you is not darkness"?[20] Such self-scrutiny is the beginning of repentance.

The warnings fall on deaf ears, dark hearts. The religious leaders and scriptural experts "began to be very hostile toward him . . . lying in wait for him, to catch him in something he might say."[21] Those who worry about looking good are trying to make Jesus look bad.

Jesus turns to his disciples, warning them also: "Beware of the yeast of the Pharisees."[22] Bad yeast spreads as fast as good yeast; the disciples themselves are at risk. "The Pharisees' hypocrisy shows the disciples what to avoid," as Robert Tannehill notes;[23] the yeast of hypocrisy

---

17. 12:2.

18. 4:24; 13:33; 7:16; 13:34.

19. 11:53-54.

20. 8:18; 11:35.

21. 11:53-54.

22. 12:1.

23. Robert Tannehill, *Luke* (Nashville: Abingdon, 1996), p. 244. In Matthew's gospel version, this whole section of woes is expanded and concerns exclusively the old-guard religious leadership (23:13-39), indicating Matthew's characteristic softening of the disciples' own weakness and susceptibility. Mark presents the harshest view of the disciples'

spreads for anyone entrusted with leadership responsibilities. And consider, Jesus goes on: this darkness that is hidden from public view will be made known throughout the city:

> Meanwhile, when the crowd gathered by the thousands, so that they trampled on one another, he began to speak first to his disciples, "Beware of the yeast of the Pharisees, that is, their hypocrisy. Nothing is covered up that will not be uncovered, and nothing secret that will not become known. Therefore whatever you have said in the dark will be heard in the light, and what you have whispered behind closed doors will be proclaimed from the housetops." (12:1-3)

Darkness within will find its way outward: hypocrisy will not remain forever hidden from public view. "The inner thoughts of many will be exposed," Simeon has warned.[24]

"When the crowd gathered by the thousands, so that they trampled on one another, [Jesus] began to speak first to the disciples."[25] Jesus ignores the surging crowd, so critical are these warnings to the inner circle of leaders-to-be. In fact, the popularity of Jesus, suggested by the flocking masses, is precisely that which warrants the warnings. Doing the right thing, in fact, leads to deadly public reaction: Jesus has just quoted from the Scripture: "I will send them prophets and apostles, some of whom they will kill and persecute."[26] The lethal resistance and suffering that Jesus will face, as prophet, should be an expected outcome for all followers.[27] To do well brings the opposite of what religious leaders and scriptural experts seek. The warning of Jesus occurs as "the crowd gathered by the thousands," a crowd whose size exacerbates the very normal temptation toward public honor and inner darkness: in a word, hypocrisy.

---

hard-heartedness and vulnerability. Luke is somewhere between Matthew and Mark in his portrait of the disciples' strengths and weaknesses. In Matthew's account it is the mother of James and John, for example, who asks Jesus that her two sons have special seats of honor (20:20-21); in Mark they themselves ask (10:35-37); Luke leaves out this most egregious instance of clutching after honor and glory. Whether or not Luke had access to this account (he probably did), the point is that Luke neither elevates nor demotes the disciples in any ultimate way, relative to the old-guard leaders, except as they show willingness to listen.

24. 2:35.

25. 12:1.

26. 11:49.

27. Noted by Joel B. Green, *The Gospel of Luke* (Grand Rapids: Eerdmans, 1997), p. 475.

"I tell you, my friends," Jesus continues, "do not fear those who kill the body, and after that can do nothing more. But I will warn you whom to fear: fear him who, after he has killed, has authority to cast into hell. Yes, I tell you, fear him!"[28] In the end, even one's own physical exterior is expendable. The body can be put to death, but what of that? Rather, fear your spirit being cast into the garbage dump of hell.[29] The warnings prefaced by "Woe" are offered within a perspective that understands the certain consequences of dark interiors and public fakery. But Jesus is addressing these warnings to his disciples, his "friends"; the narrative at this point stresses the collegial relationship that implicates the disciples in the experience of Jesus — throughout the entire two-volume story — for better and for ill.[30] What Jesus is facing, they will face. So do not be afraid, says Jesus; do not wilt "when they bring you before the synagogues, the rulers, and the authorities."[31] Do not prove hypocritical under pressure, when it would be easy to say what your accusers would like to hear. It is one thing to withstand the lure of public acclaim, but quite another to rise above the life-threatening scorn of those in power.

"Fear him who, after he has killed, has authority to cast into hell," Jesus has just said. But on the other hand, "Do not be afraid":

> "Are not five sparrows sold for two pennies? Yet not one of them is forgotten in God's sight. But even the hairs of your head are all counted. Do not be afraid; you are of more value than many sparrows." (12:6-7)

God loves even sparrows. Public honor and status are in reverse proportion to the poor standing in the bird family of sparrows, whose significance before God is good. So fear God, you of low status but so much higher than sparrows: do not be afraid. God's intent is only to give lavishly.[32] Don't be afraid before the various power-brokers of society:

---

28. 12:4-5.

29. 12:5; "hell" is actually "Gehenna," a smouldering garbage dump outside Jerusalem.

30. "All things are common to friends" — an ancient ideal cited here by Green, *The Gospel of Luke,* p. 482.

31. 12:11.

32. 11:13; 18:7-8; to fear God, as Abraham came to learn, is to let go of all normal securities and clutchings through an awe-filled trust in God's generous provision. See Paul Borgman, *Genesis: The Story We Haven't Heard* (Downers Grove, Ill.: InterVarsity, 2001), pp. 96-100.

"And I tell you, everyone who acknowledges me before others, the Son of Man also will acknowledge before the angels of God; but whoever denies me before others will be denied before the angels of God." (12:8-9)

Might the disciples not capitulate to public pressure and deny Jesus?[33] This, too, would be hypocrisy, the "yeast" of the old-guard, the Pharisees and religious lawyers.

Don't worry when speaking out the truth. Though you are faced with the scorn and murderous intent of your audience, Jesus continues, remember this: "the Holy Spirit will teach you at that very hour what you ought to say."[34] But be forewarned that "whoever blasphemes against [God's] Holy Spirit will not be forgiven."[35] God is the center of Luke's story and of Scripture's story. "Everyone who speaks a word against the Son of Man will be forgiven,"[36] but to deny God would be to deny all, and to lose all. Peter will speak against the Son of Man toward the end of Luke's gospel, repeatedly denying Jesus; he will be forgiven. But had he repeatedly blasphemed God or God's own spirit, his denial would have been unforgivable. In fact, it is on the basis of God's Spirit that one need not worry in the first place: "Do not worry about how you are to defend yourselves or what you are to say; for the Holy Spirit will teach you at that very hour what you ought to say."[37]

This theme sequence began with warning: look within the cleaned exterior of a dish for possible darkness, you religious leaders and scriptural experts. Woe! if this darkness is not replaced with light. The sequence ends with the same warnings spelled out — with the comforting promise of God's Spirit — to Israel's replacement leaders, the disciples. Beware, friends, of the "yeast of the Pharisees."[38]

The Echo: Look Inside Yourself, and Do the Word (17:1-19)

The echoing theme begins, as we might have expected, with a "Woe!" — a warning to the future leadership of Israel, the disciples, that is much

33. 12:9-10.
34. 12:12.
35. 12:10.
36. 12:10; though knowing and continuing denial of the Son of Man leads to public denial in heaven — before the angels (12:9).
37. Lk 12:11-12.
38. 11:39; 12:1.

more serious in its consequence than what we have encountered in the first theme sequence — the woes pronounced to the old-guard leadership of Israel. Hypocrisy is shown now to be a more insidious problem than could have been imagined, and integrity a rarer prize.[39]

Jesus had just told a tale about an ignored beggar — a "little one" — who ends up in heaven; a would-be benefactor has failed to do the word of God, dies, and suffers in Hades.[40] "Woe to anyone by whom [occasions for stumbling] come!" Jesus goes on to say, to the disciples: "better for you if a millstone were hung around your neck and you were thrown into the sea than for you to cause one of these little ones to stumble."[41] The good listener's attention is arrested by this clear echoing of the prior six woes, directed at the old-guard leadership of Israel. Again, the woe is addressed to societal leaders, but this time to the new-guard leadership in training, the disciples.

Who are these "little ones" who might stumble, and who or what might be the occasion for such a severe woe, roped around the neck with a millstone and thrown into the sea? From the start, this narrative has emphasized the centrality of just such "little ones" to the story: the diseased, demonically oppressed, imprisoned, hungry — the outsider, the one outside our normal range of concern.[42] In the immediately preceding section, as mentioned above, there is just such "a little one" — a helpless beggar awaiting attention from the rich man. Lazarus is a social outcast whose skin is covered with sores; he is ignored by the rich man, whose superb clothing contrasts with the little one's leprous skin.[43] The beggar is hungry, while the rich man "feasted sumptuously every day."[44] The "cause for stumbling," it appears, is "the injustice and indifference of inhospitality on behalf of those in need."[45] The rich man causes the beggar to stum-

---

39. See Green, *The Gospel of Luke,* p. 611.

40. 16:19-31; we explore this story in the following chapter.

41. 17:1-2.

42. 4:18-19.

43. 16:19-31; 16:19.

44. 16:19.

45. Green, *The Gospel of Luke,* p. 612. Darrell Bock points out that "little ones" are not just children, but a wide range of those on whom the disciples must show compassion. Darrell L. Bock, *Proclamation from Prophecy and Pattern: Lucan Old Testament Christology* (Sheffield, U.K.: Sheffield Academic Press, 1987), p. 1386. In a similar passage, Matthew specifies the little ones as those who "believe in me" (18:6). The effect of Luke's omission of this qualifier, I think, is to open up a wider category of "little ones." Robert Tannehill thinks that "little ones" includes "believers" but suggests the possibility that "the poor who have not yet believed" are included. Tannehill, *Luke,* p. 254.

ble, to remain imprisoned as an outcast from community.[46] In the prior sequence, the old-guard leadership heard "woe" regarding their "neglect of justice."[47]

The warning nature of the opening "Woe!" offered to the disciples initiates a brilliant series of escalating challenges. Warning: be careful how you pay attention to each other, especially when it is difficult to do so.

> "Be on your guard! If another disciple sins, you must rebuke the offender, and if there is repentance, you must forgive. And if the same person sins against you seven times a day, and turns back to you seven times and says, 'I repent,' you must forgive." (17:3-4)

Causing an outsider, a little one, to stumble is a serious offense; so also is lack of care toward your friends, your "brothers and sisters" of the Way.[48]

Go to the one you think has wronged you. Such communal confrontation is the opposite of the judgmentalism consistently warned against. Rather than a covert judgmentalism, go directly to your sister: if she agrees with your assessment, and repents, then you must accept her back into communal intimacy. Continuously, seven times a day — which is to say, always. Hypocrisy is lack of integrity between public posing and behind-the-back whispering; the presence of integrity is the connection between the experience of being wronged and seeking to right the situation. Such integrity involves faith — is the face of faith, as we see next.

The narrative moves on to a request by the apostles: "Lord, increase our faith."[49] We are not told that this request follows immediately in the same scene from what Jesus teaches concerning the rigors of forgiveness.[50] But of course Luke's orderliness has a seamless forward spiraling, always. This matter of forgiving is tangled and extraordinarily difficult: perhaps

---

46. 1:52; 16:24-25; the "little one" and the powerful rich person, as we might expect, find their roles reversed at the end of the tale, just as Mary's poem suggested. The rich man becomes the child, the little one, who calls out to *"Father* Abraham" from his torment. The father answers, *"Child,* remember . . ."

47. 11:42.

48. Green, *The Gospel of Luke,* pp. 612-13: "The NRSV reads 'disciple' for the Lukan term 'brother [and sister],' by which the Evangelist draws attention to kinship that has been severed by sin."

49. 17:5.

50. Matthew's version of this teaching has no such request but rather an illustrative tale about a lord's anger when there is no such forgiveness granted (18:21-35).

such difficult doing requires an extra measure of faith. But the request for *"more* faith" turns out to be specious. "The Lord replied, 'If you had faith the size of a mustard seed, you could say to this mulberry tree, *Be uprooted and planted in the sea,* and it would obey you.'"[51] That is, you have enough faith for the job. Just exercise the faith you have in doing the right thing: add willingness to the existing faith. Consistently good intentions and actions require faith; however slight the faith, the results of faith-full intention and action are far greater than the mere sum of faith and the willingness to serve God's purposes. Five thousand men and their families can be fed from a few loaves and fish, if the community of God's people evidence a tenacious will-to-do-well along with a reliance on God's empowering Spirit.[52] Beyond the will to provide food for the hungry, however, is the will to forgive. In the face of such humiliating business as having to express hurt, then to forgive, and forgive, and forgive, perhaps the disciples desire some sort of miracle-working faith that rides above the fray.

The idea of faith is developed from this point on through the rest of the echoing sequence. What is true faith, and how does it work?

What is normally lacking in ordinary persons posing as religious, Jesus suggests, is not the small quantity of faith, but a lack of will. Perhaps the disciples' desire for *more* faith is a variation of the Pharisee's hypocrisy — "assuming privileges in authority that they do not possess."[53]

The demands for faith and looking within, of the first sequence, grow more challenging in this paralleled theme sequence. And the audience of Jesus narrows. In the theme's first statement, the "woes" are addressed to the old-guard leadership of Israel. Then the disciples are warned of falling prey to the same yeast of hypocrisy as the traditional religious leaders of Israel. Now, in this echoing sequence, we move to the small band of Israel's new leadership, and to a "woe" complete with millstone and drowning. It is the *apostles,* not *disciples,* who have asked for more faith.[54] We are moving from all serious followers, the twelve-plus-seventy disciples, to the inner circle of the twelve, the apostles.

As leadership responsibility increases, so too does the challenge of faith: do not be an occasion for stumbling to the little ones "out there," but beware even more so of the more difficult matter of alienation and

51. 17:6.

52. 9:12-17.

53. David Moessner, *Lord of the Banquet: The Literary and Theological Significance of the Lukan Travel Narrative* (Minneapolis: Fortress, 1989), p. 202.

54. *Apostolos,* apostle, 17:5; disciple, *mathētēs,* 17:1.

lack of confrontation and forgiveness within your own community of friends. Do not be an occasion for alienation among your brothers and sisters of the Way. Don't avoid confrontation, but seek resolve; forgive always.

The narrative moves now to the most demanding self-scrutiny and faithfulness of all: *Do the right thing without regard for notice, perks, or even thanks:*

> "Who among you would say to your slave who has just come in from plowing or tending sheep in the field, 'Come here at once and take your place at the table'? Would you not rather say to him, 'Prepare supper for me, put on your apron and serve me while I eat and drink; later you may eat and drink'? Do you thank the slave for doing what was commanded? You also, when you have done all that you were ordered to do, say, 'We are worthless slaves; we have done only what we ought to have done!'" (17:7-10)

To depend on approval for doing well is to do well for something other than the doing itself — a subtle and deadly hypocrisy. Such action and expectation demonstrate a lack of integrity between the good thing done and a less-than-good motivation. Who is the slave to expect thanks, to desire praise? Even as one does the right thing for another without expectation of thanks, so one does the right thing for the Master of all without doing it for special notice, special privilege, or a chance to boast or be noticed as deserving approval.[55]

"We are worthless slaves" is an admission that eliminates the possibility of boasting, while affirming the importance of the action performed. "If desperate pleas for 'more faith' are excluded on the one side," notes David Tiede, "boasting at obedience is forbidden on the other. . . . The exclusion of boasting is the obverse of the assurance that the power to do the impossible comes from God."[56] What has the just-mentioned request for more faith to do with this present insight? It appears that faith is inextricably linked with doing well. Hearing-and-doing-the-word is, here and elsewhere in the two-volume story, the

---

55. To proffer undue return for services rendered would put the master in a dependent role, as Joel B. Green points out — thanking the slave for rendering a service as if that service could have been refused. *The Gospel of Luke*, p. 614.

56. David L. Tiede, *Luke*, Augsburg Commentary on the New Testament (Minneapolis: Augsburg, 1988), p. 294.

quality of faith. This is the Way's journey, one of faith evidenced by faithfulness, being full-of-faith.

This echoing theme sequence insists on a looking-within that concludes with something within a person best expressing the life of faith, a participation in God's kingdom. The spiraling here between one- and two-verse segments has taken us deeper and deeper into the psyche. Now we learn that faith is not only *not expecting thanks*, but a *giving of thanks*:

> On the way to Jerusalem Jesus was going through the region between Samaria and Galilee. As he entered a village, ten lepers approached him. Keeping their distance, they called out, saying, "Jesus, Master, have mercy on us!" When he saw them, he said to them, "Go and show yourselves to the priests." And as they went, they were made clean. Then one of them, when he saw that he was healed, turned back, praising God with a loud voice. He prostrated himself at Jesus' feet and thanked him. And he was a Samaritan. Then Jesus asked, "Were not ten made clean? But the other nine, where are they? Was none of them found to return and give praise to God except this foreigner?" Then he said to him, "Get up and go on your way; your faith has made you well." (17:11-19)

Faith at its best is the capacity to expect nothing in terms of personal advancement while saying thank you for anything contributing to one's well-being in community. As a cleansed leper, the Samaritan will be restored to community.

"And he was a Samaritan," this person who reverses field to come back with a word of gratitude. Saved until the end of this little story, just before concluding remarks on the story by Jesus, the identity of this person of true faith is presumably shocking to its Jewish audience. This is a foreigner-nearby, with religious views that challenge the claims of the "pure" Israelites, religious cousins to the Samaritans. The leprous Samaritan, released from disease, is brought into the community of faith and becomes an exemplar. The outcast recognizes the blessing of God and goes out of his way to express a word that defines the essence of faith: "thank you." Ah, says Jesus, "your faith has made you well." The others are made well, and yet: "Was none of them found to return and give praise to God except this foreigner?"[57] The wellness of this Samaritan ap-

---

57. Lk 17:18.

parently exceeds the healing of the others, just as his faith is clearly in evidence with his expression of gratitude.

Look Inside Yourself, and Do the Word:
A Summary of the Two Sequences

What began in this repeated sequence of warnings to religious leaders as a serious "woe" — the millstone-assisted drowning — concludes here with a cure for hypocrisy, for the disconnect between public honor and inward darkness. To the extent that one has within a spirit of gratitude, to that extent there is light and not darkness. Such light is a faith that makes one more disposed to giving thanks than expecting thanks, or approval. Such faith allows a life of integrity, a "matching-up" of intention and deed that hypocrisy denies. This is what we heard in the echoed sequence: *Consider whether the light in you is not darkness."*[58]

The first theme sequence featured the old-guard leaders of Israel living a normal life, exemplary and highly respected. Nonetheless, their false way of being in the world neglected justice and love of God's purposes.[59] They were warned to look within themselves. The new religious leaders, in the first sequence, are in danger of the same problem, but in reverse — of failing to stand up in public for a Way to which, in private, they claim allegiance.[60] In the echoing theme, then, this matter of hypocrisy and integrity takes a turn further "inward" as Jesus focuses exclusively on the apostles. Jesus is demonstrating a better Way than the ordinary self-promotion that breeds hypocrisy among the super-religious. The old-guard leaders of Israel and this future new-guard leadership must look within themselves, with the help of Jesus' teaching represented by Luke.

As we will see in the next chapter, the journey moves forward by exploring the difficult specifics of what faith-that-is-action requires. The Way of God is a journey in a very "real world" with everyday concerns like money and possessions. The movement within these paralleled theme sequences once again furthers the challenge in the echoing portion. From giving away all possessions, we move to the more difficult task of keeping possessions — but as stewards toward serving God's purposes of blessing.

58. 11:35.
59. 11:42.
60. 12:8.

Chapter 10

Relinquish Possessions and/or
the Spirit of Possessing

Luke 12:13-34; 16:1-31

The prior sequence on the journey was the paralleled concern that followers look within themselves and focus on doing the word, avoiding hypocrisy. Woe to those who live with dark interiors and external shows of goodness. In the context of these woes, Jesus has told followers not to fear what can happen from the outside, but rather to fear the one who "has authority to cast into hell."[1] The comfort offered is conspicuous, however: "do not fear," we hear; "do not be afraid"; "do not worry."[2] The journey moves now to a man who dies while worrying. He fears the wrong thing: the external state of his holdings rather than the state of his soul. The tale is used by Jesus to recommend a Way that overcomes greed and the worry about possessions. Variations of the do-not-worry assurances, however, carry over from the prior sequence. Jesus concludes by insisting on an unthinkable solution to worry: "Sell your possessions."[3] But the theme's echoing sequence, farther up in the journey, makes the matter much more challenging: do not sell all your possessions but use them, shrewdly, in support of God's purposes. Failure to hold possessions lightly leads to self-destruction and judgment in the long run. Luke's two-volume story is filled with talk about money and possessions, but nowhere more so than in these paralleled sequences.

1. 12:5.
2. 12:4-7, 11.
3. 12:22-32; 12:33.

The First Time: Relinquish Possessions (12:13-34)

The narrative moves from the fear of threats in the external world, to fear for the matter of one's soul. "Do not worry"[4] is followed, now, by that about which ordinary humans worry a great deal.

> Someone in the crowd said to him, "Teacher, tell my brother to divide the family inheritance with me." But he said to him, "Friend, who set me to be a judge or arbitrator over you?" And he said to them, "Take care! Be on your guard against all kinds of greed; for one's life does not consist in the abundance of possessions." (12:13-15)

Ordinary justice, in Luke's day at least, would require a taking care of matters, in court if need be. But this is not so for those choosing God's Way: "Take care! Be on your guard against all kinds of greed."

As we have seen in our prior two chapters, followers are to scrutinize themselves, not others. "Who set me to be a judge or arbitrator over you?" asks Jesus in this present sequence: *you* judge matters and "be on your guard against all kinds of greed." The old-guard religious leaders had just been warned about ignoring an interior that is "full of greed."[5] Greed is linked with concern or worry about even what is yours by right of law — "the family inheritance."

Why worry, Jesus says to the greed-motivated brother, about an "abundance of possessions"?[6] An explanatory tale follows:

> "The land of a rich man produced abundantly. And he thought to himself, 'What should I do, for I have no place to store my crops?' Then he said, 'I will do this: I will pull down my barns and build larger ones, and there I will store all my grain and my goods. I will say to my soul, 'Soul, you have ample goods laid up for many years; relax, eat, drink, be merry.' But God said to him, 'You fool! This very night your life is being demanded of you. And the things you have prepared, whose will they be?' So it is with those who store up treasures for themselves but are not rich toward God." (12:16-21)

In Luke's day, providing insurances for oneself and for one's family toward an uncertain future would have been especially commendable. But

4. 12:11.
5. 11:39.
6. 12:15.

the landholder here wants more than mere abundance, a possible echo of that for which we ask God, daily bread, food sufficient for the present need.[7] The farmer's anxiety about "abundance" and "ample goods" grows out of a preoccupation with his own security and comfort, to "relax, eat, drink, and be merry."[8]

The rich man tears down perfectly good barns, already stuffed with goods. Suddenly dead, the "fool" is asked by God: "the things you have prepared, whose will they be?" The self-absorbed farmer is "selfishly enjoying his riches without thought for his needy neighbors."[9] His abundance sits, stored in bigger and still bigger barns, abundance that could have been distributed to the poor. "Whose will they be," these goods of the suddenly dead everyman? Goods go stale, and a self-absorbed life comes to nothing: "so it is with those who store up treasures for themselves but are not rich toward God."[10] Luke's is a story of reversals: the rich sent away empty, as Mary poetized and Jesus affirms in his major poem.[11] The farmer's lopsided living is exposed as wrong; it can be "righted" only in the divine realm of justice.

What does the text mean, that the farmer was not "rich toward God"? We recall the obsessions of the old-guard religious leaders, whose pretentious tithing was coupled with a lack in their "love of God."[12] A great part of being rich toward God is to pay close attention to what God cares about: the poor and *their* justice. These leaders lacked a love of God; they neglected justice.[13] Work for God's justice, rather than for things typically worried over, like "what you are to eat and what you are to drink."[14] Such preoccupation "acts as a means of security and reflects disregard for God and neighbor."[15] Luke leaves his audience with a sense of disproportion and wastefulness in the rich man's bigger and better-stuffed barns. To be "rich toward God," then, means attending to the priorities of God's kingdom: the poor, the hungry, the diseased, the oppressed — to imple-

7. 11:3; see Chapter 7.

8. 12:19.

9. I. Howard Marshall, *Commentary on Luke*, New International Greek Testament Commentary (Grand Rapids: Eerdmans, 1979), p. 524.

10. 12:21.

11. 1:53; 6:20-25; see Chapters 2 and 3.

12. 11:42.

13. 11:42.

14. 12:29.

15. Charles H. Talbert, *Reading Luke: A Literary and Theological Commentary on the Third Gospel* (New York: Crossroad, 1982), p. 141.

ment on behalf of outsiders "the things that make for peace."[16] This is being "rich toward God."

Immediately the journey turns to repeated injunctions for the disciples: "Do not worry about your life, what you will eat, or about your body, what you will wear."[17] The security in having enough to eat (and drink — in order to be merry) is the farmer's anxious concern. But consider:

> "Life is more than food, and the body more than clothing. Consider the ravens: they neither sow nor reap, they have neither storehouse nor barn, and yet God feeds them. Of how much more value are you than the birds! And can any of you by worrying add a single hour to your span of life? If then you are not able to do so small a thing as that, why do you worry about the rest? Consider the lilies, how they grow: they neither toil nor spin; yet I tell you, even Solomon in all his glory was not clothed like one of these. But if God so clothes the grass of the field, which is alive today and tomorrow is thrown into the oven, how much more will he clothe you — you of little faith!" (12:22-28)

From sparrows a few verses earlier, the text has moved to ravens. Neither species is the most attractive in the kingdom of birds. But "of how much more value are you than the birds!" And think about it: "Can any of you by worrying add a single hour to your span of life? If then you are not able to do so small a thing as that, why do you worry about the rest?"

Worry produces the surplus in the farmer's storehouses — so "do not keep striving for what you are to eat and what you are to drink, and do not keep worrying. For it is the nations of the world that strive after all these things, and your Father knows that you need them."[18] There is a terrible striving, fed by worry, that leads to self-destruction, but there is a good striving — an essential in Luke's Big Picture. Do not worry, do not strive after these externals: "instead, strive for [God's] kingdom."[19]

"Do not be afraid, little flock," the sequence concludes, with words from Jesus: it is God's "good pleasure to give you the kingdom. Sell all your possessions, and give alms."[20] True wealth is that which doesn't fail,

16. 4:18-19; 19:42.
17. 12:22.
18. 12:29-30.
19. 12:23; in the chiastic center of the journey — the heart of the entire gospel — Jesus says that striving is necessary for entry into God's kingdom (13:23-24).
20. 12:32-33.

that does not "wear out" — "an unfailing treasure in heaven," impervious to thieves and moths.[21] Rid yourself of what feeds your fear. But there will be a more challenging solution, as we see in the echoing sequence on the matter of ownership. For both sequences, however, there is a common perspective: "Where your treasure is, there your heart will be also."[22]

The Echo: From "Relinquish Possessions" to Relinquish the Spirit of Possessing (16:1-31)

Just prior to this echoing sequence, back in chapter 15, we were introduced in an oblique manner to the issue of possessions. Three tales stressed responsibility for "things": a small bit of money is lost and needs to be found; one of the flock is missing and needs to be recovered; a son has run off and wasted his inheritance — and needs to be taken back in spite of the lost money.[23] With great narrative logic, the journey moves now to a qualification of what has already been recommended about money and possessions.

In this echoing sequence, we hear again of a rich man, but this rich man — and even his apparently huckstering manager! — are held up for commendation. And we find another man of wealth, with a problem similar to the farmer's of the previous sequence.

The first rich man hears that his manager is squandering property. The point of the story is a challenge to use money well, even though money is itself compromised. The sequence will conclude with an example of how possessions could have been properly used, but were not. In an initial tale, told by Jesus, we have a very strange perspective on the good use of money.

> "There was a rich man who had a manager, and charges were brought to him that this man was squandering his property. So he summoned him and said to him, 'What is this that I hear about you? Give me an accounting, because you cannot be my manager any longer.'" (16:1-2)

Though fired from his post, the manager scrambles for survival, which seems to counter the emphasis of the echoed theme to cease striving after

21. 12:33.
22. 12:34.
23. 15:1-32; to be explored in the following chapter.

mere material well-being.[24] But Luke uses the story to illustrate a more complicated truth about letting go of possessions.

The rich man's manager feels himself caught in a terrible bind. "I am not strong enough to dig," he muses, "and I am ashamed to beg."[25] He becomes mightily resourceful, if a bit dishonest. One by one the manager confronts his master's debtors and discounts their bills in order to collect from them. He is extremely clever, not only in what he is doing but in the way he does it: one person's bill is cut in half; another's is cut only 20 percent. Is there anticipation of what the debtor can bear? And — surprise? — the rich master actually "commended the dishonest manager because he had acted shrewdly."[26]

From the master's point of view, perhaps, the fired manager recouped something rather than nothing. Better that half of the debt be returned than none of it. Perhaps the manager would have received a commission for debt recovered, and he forfeited this commission. What the audience knows for sure is the master's pleasure at recovering what he does, and the master's pleasure with the shady manager. The manager, for his part, has anticipated that these grateful debtors "may welcome me into their homes."[27] What does Luke's text emphasize here about possessions?

The shrewdness of "the children of this age . . . in dealing with their own generation" is applauded, but without endorsement of what the tale's narrator calls the manager's dishonesty.[28] The point seems to be something like what David L. Tiede imagines: "Just think what could happen if people were as clever in pursuing the justice and mercy of the kingdom as they are in looking out for themselves!"[29]

The text moves on, following-up by making the point about being shrewd with possessions: "And I tell you," says Jesus: "make friends for yourself by means of dishonest wealth so that when it is gone, they may welcome you into the eternal homes."[30] Buying friends? Eternal-home insurance? Surely friends are made, not purchased; welcome is nurtured,

---

24. 12:29.
25. 16:3.
26. 16:6-7; 16:8.
27. 16:4.
28. 16:8.
29. David L. Tiede, *Luke,* Augsburg Commentary on the New Testament (Minneapolis: Augsburg, 1988), p. 283.
30. 16:9.

not transacted. The tale, as Jesus is shown using it, is emphasizing something entirely different, that true community — friend greeting friend into the eternal habitation — is gained through the administering of justice and mercy with great shrewdness. Those giving from their stores of money and possessions "will be received into the eternal dwellings" by those *little ones* who were helped on earth. While it is possible to read this purchased welcome "into the eternal dwellings" as ironic,[31] it seems more likely, in context, that the point concerns paying careful attention to others, especially the outsider. Such attention has its ultimate reward, the fruit of justice: "People can guarantee God's . . . eternal hospitality," as Joel B. Green asserts, "by assisting [shrewdly, with great intelligence] the poor in the present."[32]

The assumption of Luke's text, in either case, is that although all wealth is tainted in its trail of ever-changing chicanery, it still can and must be used for God's purposes. And followers of the Way should be clever about it: *do not* sell all your possessions, but use them to create community, friendships, and the prospect of homes whose welcome is forever.[33]

We find out shortly, in this spiraling narrative's own time — just ahead — who these "friends" might be, and what sort of "eternal home" is being talked about.

> If then you have not been faithful with the dishonest wealth,
>   who will entrust to you the true riches?
> If you have not been faithful with what belongs to another,
>   who will give you what is your own? (16:12)[34]

---

31. "If you are impressed by a shrewd fellow like this who wrote the book on how to manage unrighteousness, go ahead. Build up the 'network' of friends who are obligated to you on the basis of the 'mammon of unrighteousness' . . . and see what they can do for you, not when you are fired, but when you are dead! Good luck!" Tiede, *Luke*, p. 283. This minority view is countered by I. Howard Marshall, who points to almsgiving as winning friends, and leading to reception into eternal homes (16:9). Marshall, *Commentary on Luke*, p. 621.

32. Joel B. Green, *New Testament Theology: The Theology of the Gospel of Luke* (Cambridge: Cambridge University Press, 1995), p. 116.

33. It is possible Luke had Jacob's son Joseph in mind, who was a conspicuously shrewd manager of "things" and money — and, as God's perfect servant, was able to provide for his own destitute family, for the nation of Egypt, and indeed for "all the world" (Gen 41:57).

34. The line arrangement is my own — an example of intentional balanced lines, buried poetry in the narrative text.

Possessions and money are to be managed well for God, the only owner — and ultimate giver — of all good things. "Children of light" are being called to exercise faithful administering of "what [ultimately] belongs to another."

If you can prove responsible with mere money — "faithful in a very little" — then you will be "faithful also in much."[35] To be faithful with possessions is to qualify for great social responsibility; we have seen, in the tale of talents, that the person most responsible with money was given ten cities to rule.[36] A person like the overseer of ten cities is full of faith; others, lacking in responsibility, are without faith, faithless. Think of it from the point of view of a slave, Jesus suggests. "No slave can serve two masters," he points out; "for a slave will either hate the one and love the other, or be devoted to the one and despise the other. You cannot serve God and wealth"[37] — though you can serve God through wealth.

The old-guard leaders "who were lovers of money, heard all this, and they ridiculed him."[38] Doesn't God bless materially those who are righteous?[39] Surely money is proof of a righteous life and not the cause of unrighteousness. And so these guardians of the Law ridicule Jesus' views on money.

Jesus responds to the scoffing of these guardians of religious orthodoxy by talking about self-justification, the Law, and even divorce. This apparent diversion from money-talk turns out to be critically linked to the money issue, and to the jeering dismissiveness Jesus experiences. As always, but especially where we might have the most trouble "hearing" it, the journey weaves truths together toward a compelling vision. In the prior paralleled sequences, we heard this as a common thread: "Where your treasure is, there your heart will be also."[40] These old-guard leaders are having their hearts exposed as the journey unfolds.

"God knows your hearts; for what is prized by human beings is an abomination in the sight of God. The law and the prophets were in effect until John came; since then the good news of the kingdom of God is proclaimed, and everyone tries to enter it by force. But it is easier for

35. 16:10.
36. 19:17; see Chapter 5.
37. 16:13.
38. 16:13; 16:14.
39. See, for example, Deut 28:12-13.
40. 12:34; Chapter 9.

heaven and earth to pass away, than for one stroke of a letter in the law to be dropped. Anyone who divorces his wife and marries another commits adultery, and whoever marries a woman divorced from her husband commits adultery." (16:15-18)

The connection between money issues and divorce may not be evident at first glance, or first hearing. What plagues these leaders who ridicule the money-talk is a failure to understand their own culpability with regard to the essential Law and how central is one's handling of possessions to that Law.

The basic problem is described, here, just before the talk of law and prophets. "You [Pharisees] are those who justify yourselves in the sight of others"; you claim to know God, "but God knows your hearts; for what is prized by human beings is an abomination in the sight of God."[41] Then, as an example of "abomination," Jesus points to a violation of one of the ten commandments. From the heart that treasures possessions above all — rather than God above all — flows the darkness of these religious males and their abuse of women, in the form of divorce. In Luke's day, divorce in Jewish circles was the prerogative of husbands only, who would dispatch their wives on the shakiest and most arbitrary of grounds.

"What is prized by human beings is *an abomination* in the sight of God": the word *abomination* indicates idolatry and "immoral financial dealings."[42] Money for these religious leaders has become an idolatrous attachment to a treasure other than God; prizing what human beings ordinarily value, these leaders indulge in all manner of evil, including the actual breaking of a commandment regarding adultery — the result of a husband's wanton disregard for a wife. "You cannot serve God and wealth," we have read, and now we see what happens when the public pose of serving God masks an obsession with possessions: the spouse becomes a disposable commodity.[43]

To treasure justice and the love of God above all else — and to use possessions to foster that treasure — creates disruption, both within one's psyche and within one's ordinary societal circles.[44] Luke's text spirals forward: if

41. 16:15.
42. Is 1:13; 66:3; Deut 25:16; see Joel B. Green's good observations on this and other matters surrounding these verses in which Jesus engages the Pharisees. Joel B. Green, *The Gospel of Luke* (Grand Rapids: Eerdmans, 1997), p. 604.
43. 16:18.
44. 11:42.

to treasure God's kingdom above all else requires a kind of striving, so it is that "everyone is being pressed to enter."[45] The grammar here allows for two readings: (a) "everyone is pressing to enter" and (b) "everyone is [being] pressed to enter." The larger narrative context would seem to recommend (b), that entering the kingdom is not possible without the rigorous demands for repentance being taught by Jesus. In addition, the former sequence about possessions had suggested just such pressing-to-get-in.

"Strive [press] for [God's] kingdom."[46] In the reorientation from normal ways to God's Way, there is, as Luke's preparatory chapters made clear, a soul-piercing violence done to normal expectations and desires — the sword that pierces Mary's soul, for example.[47] One does not enter God's salvation except by force, a striving to overthrow ordinary attitudes and action, and a striving against the opposition of normal folks including one's own family.[48] The response of Jesus to old-guard ridicule regarding money suggests that keeping Torah is a great deal more problematic and strenuous than they might have imagined: *press to get into God's kingdom; strive to enter God's kingdom.*[49]

The old-guard leadership of Israel had "scoffed at him" about money issues, a scoffing that stems, as ridicule usually does, from the discordance between one's comfort zones and an uncomfortable truth.[50] The "pressing" required for entering God's kingdom — or "striving" or "trying to enter by force" — points to the clash between God's reign and Satan's, to the kingdom of God that so radically challenges all normal ways of being in the world. Respected leaders are hearing their prized things referred to as abominations.[51] Jesus first asserts the staying power of the Law (not "one stroke of a letter in the law to be dropped") and then goes on to distill the matter in terms of a Decalogue perspective, the love of God above all else: "You shall love the Lord your God with all your heart, and with all your soul, and with all your might."[52]

45. "Everyone tries to enter [the kingdom] by force," 16:16.

46. 12:31; at the heart of this journey, as we will see, Jesus urges a struggle to gain salvation's entry: "*Strive* to enter through the narrow door," he says (13:23-24).

47. "A sword will pierce your soul," says Simeon to Mary (2:35).

48. 12:51-53; 14:26.

49. Again, 13:23-24.

50. 16:14, NEB; scoffing is a species of fear. To treasure possessions above all else, as with the fretful farmer, is to acquire more in order to stop worry; here, the challenge about such treasuring leads to a further worry. What if it's true? Scoffing and ridicule help disguise such worry from oneself, and are an expression of such worry.

51. 16:15.

52. Deut 6:5.

The text implies an assumption by Jesus that these who ridicule Jesus — each of them male — conveniently ignore the Law, as already pointed out, when it comes to divorcing their wives. *You laugh about my teaching of Torah and money? Let us talk about Torah and marriage.*

The journey moves back to the theme of money and possessions. Actually, the interlude concerning the Law has served to reinforce the narrative emphasis on possessions and money, that they are essential aspects of the Law. Jesus is insisting on this Law, which the old-guard leaders of Israel only pretend to uphold. Avoiding the principle of the Law in favor of derivative rules, these pious traditionalists fix their attention on that which is "prized by human beings" but is actually "an abomination in the sight of God."[53]

The Law is about being radically neighborly, with an attention to wives and to beggars — to matters of justice and peace. Such serving of God's purposes takes money:

> "There was a rich man who was dressed in purple and fine linen and who feasted sumptuously every day. And at his gate lay a poor man named Lazarus, covered with sores, who longed to satisfy his hunger with what fell from the rich man's table; even the dogs would come and lick his sores. The poor man died and was carried away by the angels to be with Abraham. The rich man also died and was buried. In Hades, where he was being tormented, he looked up and saw Abraham far away with Lazarus by his side. He called out, 'Father Abraham, have mercy on me, and send Lazarus to dip the tip of his finger in water and cool my tongue; for I am in agony in these flames.' But Abraham said, 'Child, remember that during your lifetime you received your good things, and Lazarus in like manner evil things; but now he is comforted here, and you are in agony. Besides all this, between you and us a great chasm has been fixed, so that those who might want to pass from here to you cannot do so, and no one can cross from there to us.' He said, 'Then, father, I beg you to send him to my father's house — I have five brothers — that he may warn them, so that they will not also come into this place of torment.' Abraham replied, 'They have Moses and the prophets; they should listen to them.' He said, 'No, father Abraham; but if someone goes to them from the dead, they will repent.' He said to him, 'If they do not listen to Moses and the prophets, neither will they be convinced even if someone rises from the dead.'" (16:19-31)

53. 16:16.

The interlude of ridicule regarding money talk that led to a discussion of divorce and the Law has helped to sharpen, within the text, the essence of Torah, God's Way. Here is a new interpretation of the old scriptures. Here is the essential Law, in a pointed little tale.

Sell all? No. That is the easy way, perhaps necessary for the weak. Rather, rise to this challenge: use your money and possessions for the purposes of God in blessing others. Pay constant and total attention to the care of beggars and all the poor, the "little ones."[54]

This little one, the suffering beggar, needed resources he did not receive. Lazarus is among "the poor" for whom Jesus initially said the good news was intended.[55] The stakes are high in going God's Way: "Make friends for yourselves by means of dishonest wealth so that when it is gone, they may welcome you into eternal homes."[56] To whom does *they* refer? The rich man, in reality, has had no quality of kingdom life on earth and will not be welcomed into an eternal home by, say, a "little one" like Lazarus. The tale about the shrewd manager's using dishonest wealth is linked to the tale of a rich man's failure to use his money well. The rich man could have been shrewd, using his money to help others, like this beggar — who would have been a "friend" welcoming him into the eternal home.

The rich man had been entrusted with much, but he perverted God's intent by providing for his own ease at the expense of the poor. He inherits eternal torment rather than an eternal home. And the barn-building rich

---

54. 17:2; in my previous chapter we saw that "the little ones" who might stumble because of the disciples are very possibly the "lost" — like the beggar in this story and the many outcasts of the larger story told by Luke.

55. 4:18; "The thematic statements designating the poor specify them as outcasts; the narrative shows us that this poverty is not an economic designation, but a designation of spiritual status." Luke Timothy Johnson is defining "poor" very broadly, to include or perhaps to focus on poverty of spirit. I think he underplays the material impoverishment of "the poor" as they appear, for example, in the "solution" of Jesus for the rich man: distribute materially to the poor. But the inclusiveness of the term is indicated, in part, by how often "the poor" appear in tandem with other outcasts needing release. "The tax-collectors could certainly be called 'rich' in economic terms, but though they had money, they did not have acceptance. It is at this level that the thematic statements and the narrative mesh. Because of their outcast status, the sinners and tax-collectors were among the 'poor' to whom the Good News was proclaimed. Because they accepted this prophetic proclamation, they were among the blessed poor to whom the Kingdom belonged." Luke T. Johnson, *The Literary Function of Possessions in Luke-Acts* (Missoula, Mont.: Scholar's Press, 1977), p. 139.

56. 16:9.

man from the first theme sequence also had his life required of him, when he least expected. The climactic revelation, then: *Make friends for your-selves by means of dishonest wealth so that when it is gone, the "little ones" whose restoration into community you aided may welcome you into eternal homes.*

Relinquish Possessions and/or the Spirit of Possessing: A Summary of the Two Sequences

The highest ideal for the followers' response to possessions is in this echoing sequence, an ideal that helps to set up the concluding tale of re-versed fortunes for beggar and rich man: "Use money, tainted as it is"[57] for the blessing of the world's little ones. This is more difficult than the straightforward "sell your possessions and give alms" (and again, "sell all that you own and distribute to the poor").[58] In the end, the spirit of both sequences is the same. Sell all — or, rather than selling all, maintain goods and money as a steward who distributes to beggars at your door, to all little ones. *Sell all, or maintain goods, with no spirit of ownership, or pos-sessing.* The practical playing-out of the "good news" Jesus was commis-sioned to teach is realized in the communal experience of "those who be-longed to the Way," in Acts.[59]

As a partial answer to the lawyer's question about inheriting eternal life, Jesus had told a story of a godly foreigner, a Samaritan, who uses his money — whatever it takes — for the care of a wounded person. Two lo-cal and respected religious leaders had passed by, but the money-spending Samaritan proved his righteousness in the sight of God by us-ing his wealth on behalf of the injured man lying on the road.[60]

Zacchaeus, too, uses wealth for the poor. For the sheer joy of being recognized and "counted in" by Jesus, the transformed Zacchaeus uses half of his tainted money for the poor, and he repays fourfold those whom he has cheated. On this basis Jesus declares, "Today salvation has come to this house."[61] The turn-around that defines repentance is instantaneous. Zacchaeus is "saved," declared righteous in the sight of

---

57. 16:9, NJB.
58. Earlier theme, 12:33; 18:22.
59. Lk 4:18-19; Acts 2:41-47; 9:2.
60. 10:29-37.
61. 19:1-10; 19:9.

God.[62] Zacchaeus becomes a member in good standing in the household of Abraham, with all the responsibility for bringing blessing to others that such communal well-being demands.[63] The transformed tax-man serves God's purposes through good use of money.

Use money, however contaminated by its dishonesty, its long and unsavory history.[64] The parable following the Zacchaeus account, as we have seen,[65] elaborated this idea. Two persons entrusted with about three months' worth of salary — told by the master to "do business[66] with these monies" — produced 1000- and 500-percent returns on the money.[67] The master is pleased. The servant who gave back only the amount entrusted to him, who did not use the money, receives a tongue-lashing; he is deprived even of the amount he was given.[68] This little tale summarizes responses to money and ultimate responsibilities, just before Jesus is to enter Jerusalem. God favors those who favor God, those who are intent on bringing God's blessing and release to the poor, the diseased, the oppressed.[69]

Charles Talbert sums up Luke's perspective on money and posses-

---

62. 19:9.

63. Lk 19:9; Acts 3:25.

64. See 16:9.

65. 19:11-27; explored in Chapter 5.

66. 19:13.

67. 19:13-18.

68. "His lack of imagination in dealing with possessions," as Luke Timothy Johnson observes, "showed him unfit for rule." *The Literary Function of Possessions in Luke-Acts,* p. 169.

69. In two of the most important poems of the preparatory chapters, we find at the heart of these poems reference to those without possessions and without public standing. Servant Mary's poem praised this reversal of "normal":

> "He has brought down the powerful from their thrones,
>   and lifted up the lowly;
> he has filled the hungry with good things,
>   and sent the rich away empty." (Mary, in Lk 1:52-53)

God's "holy servant" Jesus states the good news quite clearly, in similar terms:

> "The Spirit of the Lord is upon me,
>   because he has anointed me
>   to bring good news to the poor.
> He has sent me
>   to proclaim release to the captives and recovery of sight to the blind,
>   to let the oppressed go free,
> to proclaim the year of the Lord's favor." (Lk 4:18-19)

sions nicely: "In Luke-Acts, the purpose of wealth is found in its being shared."[70] Achieving the purposes of God's salvation in the real world takes money, a possibility that is confirmed in Luke's "Part Two," wherein the "acts" of the first apostles are dramatized: money and possessions are pooled for proclamation of the good news and communal well-being.[71] Luke presents Jesus in need of partners to help carry out the reality of such salvation, to give of one's wealth for the beggars at one's gate. If such giving out of stewardly wealth is impossible (2nd sequence), then sell all you have (first sequence). But the real point is to forgo the spirit of ownership in favor of viewing all one's wealth as God's, and using it to bless others (second sequence).

The stages of the journey become increasingly more difficult in their challenges for going God's Way. From relinquishment of possessions we move to relinquishment of privilege and power, with the same ultimate principle for each: use what you "own" and use your God-given privilege for the sake of the world's little ones.

---

70. Charles Talbert, *Reading Luke: A Literary and Theological Commentary on the Third Gospel* (New York: Crossroad, 1982), p. 141.

71. Acts 2:44-47; 4:32-37.

Chapter 11

Relinquish Privilege:
Use It for God's Purposes

Luke 12:35-48; 15:1-32

"Do not be afraid, little flock," Jesus has just said, "for it is your Father's good pleasure to give you the kingdom." And now, spiraling forward, to the disciples: "from everyone to whom much has been given, much will be required."[1] *The kingdom is given to you, not as privilege but as possibility for others: so give. Be responsible, toward serving God and God's purposes of peace. In the theme's echoing sequence, Jesus addresses the old-guard leaders rather than his disciples, but toward the same responsible use of what they have considered privilege and power. The last word of the echo is a word of compassionate invitation to the old-guard leaders: please join God in the work of blessing, and in the pleasure of celebrating recovery of a lost one into God's kingdom of shalom and well-being.*

The First Time: Relinquish Privilege:
Use It for God's Purposes (12:35-48)

One's possessions are best when they are sold, we have just heard.[2] On the other hand, followers must take responsibility for that which has been entrusted to them: goods, and a whole household in fact. The point of God's Way and "the things that make for peace"[3] is not an ascetic denial of goods, but a responsible use of those goods for others. In effect, followers of the Way are slaves to God, put in charge of what in

---

1. 12:48.
2. 12:33-34; Chapter 10.
3. 19:42.

reality is not theirs. One going God's way must be alert, daily, to the Big Picture.

> "Be dressed for action and have your lamps lit; be like those who are waiting for their master to return from the wedding banquet, so that they may open the door for him as soon as he comes and knocks. Blessed are those slaves whom the master finds alert when he comes; truly I tell you, he will fasten his belt and have them sit down to eat, and he will come and serve them. If he comes during the middle of the night, or near dawn, and finds them so, blessed are those slaves." (12:35-38)

The implicit covenant between master and slave, as between God and God's servants, is reciprocal, though not evenly so: the servant provides vital service to the master, while the master — as master — serves the servant.[4] Luke's narrative perspective on the divine-human partnership is exemplified throughout the two-volume story, beginning with Mary and culminating with "holy servant" Jesus and with the communal reality of "servant Israel" (dramatized in Acts).[5]

The servants — followers of the Way — are "waiting," but not passively. Waiting implies action, not the lack of it. "Be dressed for action" is an imperative that parallels the command to the Israelites regarding their celebration of Passover and exodus from Egypt.[6] *Get your lamps lit. Be alert.* Like the master in this metaphoric example, so too Jesus will part company with his followers: once into the tomb, and then again in departing earth. As Acts makes clear, most of the disciples prove themselves equal to the task of active waiting. Some of them have heard and will hear again precisely the same words about waiting: "Be alert." We will hear it again from Paul, in Acts.[7] The believers in volume two are "dressed for action," as this gospel teaching challenges;[8] their active serv-

---

4. Slaves were often entrusted with such responsibility in Luke's day.

5. Acts 4:27-30; Lk 1:54; the relationship between "servant Jesus" and "servant Israel" is introduced most fully in Chapter 16.

6. Ex 12:1-17, especially verse 11.

7. Acts 20:31.

8. Lk 12:37; 21:36; David Tiede points out that this little tale about the absent manager has been taken to refer to "the delay of the parousia," but argues that the immediate context of Luke's two-volume story can suggest an interpretation more in keeping with the experiences of those within the text itself. In the case of the second "leave-taking" of Jesus, of course, Luke can demonstrate the good waiting of characters within the story as completed in Acts, while also addressing the concerns of his own audience about the delay of Jesus'

ing of God's purposes is conspicuous, as the assigned title suggests, *The Acts of the Apostles*. Just as "holy servant" Jesus proclaimed the kingdom and "the year of the Lord's favor,"[9] so too will "servant Israel" further the realization of this kingdom while experiencing the fulfillment of prophecies concerning this year of God's favor and "the last days."[10]

At the conclusion of this admonition to be "dressed for action" we have read, "Blessed are those slaves whom the master finds alert when he comes; truly I tell you, he will fasten his belt and have them sit down to eat, and he will come and serve them." Servants undertake the master's purposes, but this unusual master serves the servants. "I am among you as one who serves," Jesus will say, just before his death.[11]

Luke follows up with a challenge in which the disciples move from their status as servants to that of master — the owner of the house: "But know this: if the owner of the house had known at what hour the thief was coming, he would not have let his house be broken into. You also must be ready, for the Son of Man is coming at an unexpected hour."[12] Whether as servant or owner, followers must use the privilege of their status responsibly, to feed the poor, heal the diseased, release those oppressed by demons and imprisonments, and restore outcasts to community.[13] Either as servant or master, the follower of God's Way must understand that such God-given privilege and the Spirit's power are what bring to fruition "the things that make for peace."[14] In this second example of responsibility, the point is that the owner must be on guard; the disciples, like Jesus in the prior tale, will assume managerial roles. In God's coming reign on earth, the "slave" in reality is a kind of master — but a very different sort of master. As master, then, be on guard against thieves, says Jesus. A thief — any decent thief — strikes when you least expect it. Kingdom work requires vigilance and tenacity of purpose. Inside information about times of parousial delight or apocalyptic disaster is beside the point. The hour a

---

promised return. David L. Tiede, *Luke,* Augsburg Commentary on the New Testament (Minneapolis: Augsburg, 1988), pp. 238-39.

9. Acts 4:27, 30; Lk 4:18-19.

10. Lk 1:54; Acts 2:17, where Peter is explaining the phenomenon that makes "the last days" present tense, the pouring out of the Holy Spirit. We will explore this speech and the redemption of Israel in Part IV (thousands upon thousands upon thousands of Jews are saved, a three-time-mentioned quantitative reminder by Luke of Israel's redemption).

11. 22:27.

12. 12:39-40.

13. Lk 4:18-19.

14. 19:42.

thief may strike is unknown; "the Son of Man," after all, "is coming at an unexpected hour," and not until the "universal restoration" of Edenic harmonies are fulfilled.[15]

"Lord, are you telling this parable for us or for everyone?" asks Peter about this second example of privilege and power.[16] Jesus has been using slave-master talk to urge responsibility for his disciples, so Peter's question seems strange and out of place.[17] Perhaps Peter feels himself and the "little flock" of disciples exempt from the need for this reminder to "be dressed for action." Whether naïve or self-protecting, Peter's question points to the escalating nature of the challenge. Jesus never answers directly. Rather, we find a third fictional variation of the master-slave idea.

Peter's question is implicitly being turned back on him, as if to say: "Who is the kind of person God is pursuing for responsible service? Are you, Peter?"

> "Who then is the faithful and prudent manager whom his master will put in charge of his slaves, to give them their allowance of food at the proper time? Blessed is that slave whom his master will find at work when he arrives. Truly I tell you, he will put that one in charge of all his possessions. But if that slave says to himself, 'My master is delayed in coming,' and if he begins to beat the other slaves, men and women, and to eat and drink and get drunk, the master of that slave will come on a day when he does not expect him and at an hour that he does not know, and will cut him in pieces, and put him with the unfaithful. That slave who knew what his master wanted, but did not prepare himself or do what was wanted, will receive a severe beating. But the one who did not know and did what deserved a beating will receive a light beating. From everyone to whom much has been given, much will be required; and from the one to whom much has been entrusted, even more will be demanded." (12:42-48)

Jesus answers Peter's question about who needs to pay attention with this tale's climactic resolve: "from everyone" who has been given much,

15. 12:39-40; Acts 3:21.
16. 12:41.
17. 12:22, 32; also inappropriate was Peter's suggestion that tents be made to house Moses, Jesus, and Elijah, who are conversing together on the mountain (9:33). Here, Jesus gives no direct response to the question, "for us or for everyone?" — just as Peter's comment on the mountain received no response except the narrator's observation that Peter did not know what he was saying (9:33).

"much more will be demanded." Peter "seems to want to work with a distinction between 'us' (i.e., the disciples) and 'everyone,' but the narrator will allow no such contrast."[18] The only contrast is between those assuming and those abdicating responsibility: the servants have, in fact, been put "in charge of all his [master's] possessions." The "everyone" of Peter's question, then, includes all potential followers represented in the gospel, and then those followers of volume two, and those in Luke's audience — "everyone to whom much has been given."[19]

There is a great deal of bustle and possibility in this third related tale of master-household. The master is absent, and is counting on a slave-manager and other slaves — both men and women. The sense of responsibility increases as the three tales have progressed. Be alert, slaves, we have heard in the first tale: be dressed for action when the master returns. Be alert, master, the second tale advises: thieves come when least expected. And finally, for you slaves: know your responsibility for managing things on behalf of your master; some of you manage things, while other slaves answer to the managing slaves. In either case, avoid excessive eating, drinking, and mismanagement while the master is away. Lack of responsible management leads to destructiveness, affirming the tale's main emphasis: "From everyone to whom much has been given, much will be required; and from the one to whom much has been entrusted, even more will be demanded."

Entrusted with discretionary choices and power in this third tale, slaves who become managers must act responsibly or face the consequences of being cut in pieces and removed from the scene, along "with the unfaithful." This is a serious stewardship. Ignorance of what the master wanted is not entirely excusable: a "light beating" will come the way of anyone in the household not clear about the master's intentions. A "severe beating," however, comes to the one who knew, but "did not prepare."

18. Joel B. Green, *The Gospel of Luke,* New International Commentary on the New Testament (Grand Rapids: Eerdmans, 1997), p. 503.

19. Robert Tannehill notes the faithfulness of leaders represented in Acts — with Paul's farewell address in Ephesus, for example (Acts 20:18-35). Robert C. Tannehill, *The Narrative Unity of Luke-Acts: A Literary Interpretation,* vol. 1 (Philadelphia: Fortress, 1986), p. 250. I. Howard Marshall thinks otherwise, that the answer to Peter's question is not "everyone," but "us," the leadership within the circle of disciples. I. Howard Marshall, *Commentary on Luke,* New International Greek Testament Commentary (Grand Rapids: Eerdmans, 1979), p. 533. This "circle" expands outward, of course, so perhaps the answer to Peter's "us" or "everyone" is yes: both "us" and "everyone."

Beyond the light and heavy beatings is the fate of the manager-slave who has actually subverted what the master wanted by eating and drinking, becoming drunk and beating the other slaves. Both new- and old-guard leaders seem to be implicated here, though it is in the echoing theme, as we see shortly, that the old-guard leaders, the Pharisees, take center stage. All of these religious leaders, old-guard and new, are the ones to whom so much has been entrusted. It is to such persons — both within and outside the text — that this tale is being addressed. Being a follower of Torah and the Way, which Jesus is teaching, carries with it the need for daily vigilance. Whatever suffering of followers is dramatized within the two-volume text — there is plenty of persecution in Acts — such hardship cannot compare to the fate of those entrusted with the Way of God and found to be irresponsible with what they have been given.[20]

Just before these three tales on responsibility, the audience had heard, "Sell your possessions, and give alms."[21] But the more difficult challenge for those entrusted with possessions parallels the final word of this theme sequence while anticipating its echo: *From everyone to whom much has been given, much will be required; and from the one to whom much has been entrusted, even more will be demanded.*[22]

The Echo: Relinquish Privilege: Use It for God's Purposes (15:1-32)

In this echoing sequence, the audience within the story has changed from potential new-guard leadership of Israel, the disciples, to Israel's old-guard leaders. They are the great exemplars of those with privilege, the guardians of Scripture and leaders of Israel. Jesus is shown as genuinely engaged with these Pharisees, around the intimacy of table fellowship. He is invitational. They are exclusivists.

> All the tax collectors and sinners were coming near to listen to him. And the Pharisees and the scribes were grumbling and saying, "This fellow welcomes sinners and eats with them." (15:1-2)

---

20. Acts will feature three followers who fail, and who meet with disastrous and even gory loss: Judas, Ananias, and Sapphira.

21. 12:33.

22. 12:48.

The religious leaders would seem to have a point in their concern that Jesus so freely associates with the wicked. "Let not a man associate with the wicked, not even to bring him to the Law," the Midrash Rabbah reads.[23] And there are injunctions from the Scripture of that day against associating with sinners.[24] But these important religious people have missed the sense and presence of God's kingdom, God's visitation among them for the purposes of peace. Such blindness will cause Jesus to weep.[25] "Let *anyone* with ears to hear, listen." When it comes to "sinners" — societal misfits and outcasts — do the old-guard leaders find the invitation to "anyone" a bit too generous, a bit lacking in moral discrimination? They complain. Jesus is shown in the tales that follow trying to get them to reverse their direction of thought and action. He earnestly solicits their services, as those to whom much has been given.

Those entrusted with privilege and power — as Israel's Torah-keepers and leaders have been — must be the first to recognize the purpose of God is blessing extended to all peoples on earth.[26] "So he told them this parable," after their grumbling about "all peoples":

> "Which one of you, having a hundred sheep and losing one of them, does not leave the ninety-nine in the wilderness and go after the one that is lost until he finds it? When he has found it, he lays it on his shoulders and rejoices. And when he comes home, he calls together his friends and neighbors, saying to them, 'Rejoice with me, for I have found my sheep that was lost.' Just so, I tell you, there will be more joy in heaven over one sinner who repents than over ninety-nine righteous persons who need no repentance." (15:4-7)

The story is not primarily about the "one sinner who repents" but about the person or persons — the shepherd — responsible for bringing about such a joyous thing as a lost outcast restored to God's community. Inclusivity presents occasions for communal joy. "And when he comes home, he calls together his friends and neighbors, saying to them, 'Rejoice with me, for I have found my sheep that was lost.'"

23. Noted by Charles Talbert, relative to this passage. *Reading Luke: A Literary and Theological Commentary on the Third Gospel* (New York: Crossroad, 1982), p. 148. One wonders whether there isn't an implicit difference between a cozy association and a more prophetic sort of relating, as Jesus is shown doing.

24. Prov 1:15; 2:11-15; 4:14; Ps 1; Is 52:11.

25. 19:41.

26. Acts 3:25; Gen 12:3.

To the shepherd entrusted with privilege and power — one hundred sheep — much is expected in the care of all one hundred sheep. We hear an echo of the theme's first statement: "from everyone to whom much has been given [the shepherd, here], much will be required."[27]

Luke shows Jesus trying again, repeating the idea with another story, this one with a female protagonist whose loss, apparently, is quite serious.

> "Or what woman having ten silver coins, if she loses one of them, does not light a lamp, sweep the house, and search carefully until she finds it? When she has found it, she calls together her friends and neighbors, saying, 'Rejoice with me, for I have found the coin that I had lost.' Just so, I tell you, there is joy in the presence of the angels of God over one sinner who repents." (15:8-10)

One coin out of ten would be a grievous loss, proportionately greater than one sheep out of a hundred — an especially difficult loss for a woman in that culture, apparently alone.

Again, the story's focus is not so much on that which is found, but rather on the joy of the community — both earthly and heavenly — in the restoration of that which was lost. "When she has found it, she calls together her friends and neighbors, saying, 'Rejoice with me, for I have found the coin that I had lost.'" Even the angels join in. Entrusted with ten coins, the woman shows responsibility for all ten. The Pharisees and scribes have been entrusted with Torah, and are responsible for proclaiming and living out this word to all Israel — rejoicing when anyone lost, a "little one," is found by God. Given much, these leaders are being asked to use their privilege and power for doing good to "lost" outsiders, and with joy rather than with a patronizing superiority.[28]

By itself, the last tale of a father and two sons is matchless in its economy and power. Primarily, however, this story works as the climactic conclusion to a trio of tales that together echo a theme sounded chapters before, regarding responsibility for that which is given.[29]

27. 12:48.

28. The lawyer interested in inheriting eternal life wanted to know who his neighbor was, so that he could help; Jesus answered, as we saw, by asking the lawyer to consider if, in effect, he himself was neighborly. Such a mindset puts the burden on the person given much, rather than on the one "without much" who might benefit from largesse.

29. Included only in the gospel of Luke, these three tales draw attention to the core of Luke's vision.

"There was a man who had two sons. The younger of them said to his father, 'Father, give me the share of the property that will belong to me.' So he divided his property between them. A few days later the younger son gathered all he had and traveled to a distant country, and there he squandered his property in dissolute living. When he had spent everything, a severe famine took place throughout that country, and he began to be in need. So he went and hired himself out to one of the citizens of that country, who sent him to his fields to feed the pigs. He would gladly have filled himself with the pods that the pigs were eating; and no one gave him anything. But when he came to himself he said, 'How many of my father's hired hands have bread enough and to spare, but here I am dying of hunger! I will get up and go to my father, and I will say to him, "Father, I have sinned against heaven and before you; I am no longer worthy to be called your son; treat me like one of your hired hands." So he set off and went to his father. But while he was still far off, his father saw him and was filled with compassion; he ran and put his arms around him and kissed him. Then the son said to him, 'Father, I have sinned against heaven and before you; I am no longer worthy to be called your son.' But the father said to his slaves, 'Quickly, bring out a robe — the best one — and put it on him; put a ring on his finger and sandals on his feet. And get the fatted calf and kill it, and let us eat and celebrate; for this son of mine was dead and is alive again; he was lost and is found!' And they began to celebrate." (15:11-24)

The loss of a sheep, one of a hundred, can be compensated for through breeding; the loss of one coin out of ten — a loss more grievous to the woman than the one sheep to the shepherd — might be gained back through hard work. But we now come to the irreplaceable loss of a son — from only two sons! The father cannot force the runaway to return, and does not go after him. The one who searches for the lost will not be a hectoring presence, will not — cannot? — force the issue. The son must choose to repent and return home.

What the younger son has done, in the time and place of Luke's audience, would have proven "very irregular and deeply disrespectful, . . . treating his father as if he were dead."[30] Perhaps the father might have appeared as weak, here at the tale's beginning, capitulating foolishly to the unseemly demands of the son. In any case, the boy becomes lost.

---

30. Noted by Sharon Ringe, who is citing laws of the Roman empire of that day. Sharon H. Ringe, *Luke* (Louisville: Westminster/John Knox, 1995), p. 207.

Sheep and coins can't will themselves to be found, but the young man in this story must choose just that, to turn around — to repent — and come home. Whereas the "finding" of the sheep and coin suggests that being-found happens only at the initiative of the one who goes out to look,[31] this third tale rehearses what is true throughout Luke's entire narrative: the responsibility of the one repenting. Repentance is related to the initiative of God, insofar as God forgives sins for those repenting, but the son must change his ways before the "finding" action of the father, including forgiveness, can happen.[32] Salvation, Simeon has poeticized, has "been prepared in the presence of all peoples," but the preparation is only that, a preparation awaiting completion through human response.[33] "All flesh shall see the salvation of God," but seeing is not necessarily believing.[34] Believing begins with a wrenching about-face, a trust in God's forgiveness, daily, and a day-by-day taking up of salvation's cross.

God would favor this poor one, this lost son who became possessed by possessions. But the destitute can choose to remain lost. He cannot expect the father to force him home. Respecting the choice of his son, the father is always on the lookout for the son's repentance, his turn-around. The younger son is like any of Luke's "lost" — the little ones. Toward such it is always like God to forgive, to release, to empower and restore to genuine community. Jesus acts for God, and is asking others to do the same. The father, like the God of Luke's story, cannot force the younger son to return or the elder son to rejoice. The young boy turns around, literally; "he came to himself,"[35] judging himself with careful scrutiny, and perhaps with a shrewdness regarding his impoverished state. He knows what he must say: "Father, I have sinned against heaven and before you; I am no longer worthy to be called your son; treat me like one of your hired hands."[36]

The father, ever on the lookout for the son, but having given full rein to the young man's will, waits. When the son decides to come back, the father sees him from far off, and need wait no longer. He rushes after his son and embraces him joyfully. There will be a banquet thrown, a salvation feast.[37]

31. So Robert Tannehill supposes, based on the first two tales. *The Narrative Unity of Luke-Acts,* vol. 1, p. 238.

32. 3:3, 10-14.

33. 2:30-31.

34. 3:6.

35. 15:17.

36. 15:18-19.

37. A repeated motif, this kingdom banquet feast: most especially at the gospel's center-point, 13:23-30: explored in Chapter 13.

We seem to have come to the end of the story, given the close parallels with the lost sheep and lost coin that were found, and the communal celebration that follows. But this third tale goes on, with a twist that is typical of repetition in this narrative. We come full circle back to old-guard religious leaders to whom Jesus is addressing all three stories. Israel's current leadership is the elder son, the focus of this last tale.

> "Now his elder son was in the field; and when he came and approached the house, he heard music and dancing. He called one of the slaves and asked what was going on. He replied, 'Your brother has come, and your father has killed the fatted calf, because he has got him back safe and sound.' Then he became angry and refused to go in. His father came out and began to plead with him. But he answered his father, 'Listen! For all these years I have been working like a slave for you, and I have never disobeyed your command; yet you have never given me even a young goat so that I might celebrate with my friends. But when this son of yours came back, who has devoured your property with prostitutes, you killed the fatted calf for him!' Then the father said to him, 'Son, you are always with me, and all that is mine is yours. But we had to celebrate and rejoice, because this brother of yours was dead and has come to life; he was lost and has been found.'" (15:25-32)

The various dynamics among the two brothers and their father is complex, but clear. The focus comes to rest, finally, on the difficulty between the father and his older son. The deepest part of the psyche gets probed, here, for both father and son. The tale exposes fundamental orientations and preoccupations, the respective states of their hearts and habits of action.

Something gets tapped in the older brother that is more complex than simple greed or hoarding. Beneath the greed is a grumbling — the grumbling with which we started these three tales. By way of comparison to the father's treatment of his no-good son, the dutiful and good son feels overlooked and undervalued. His rage is eloquent: "'Listen! For all these years I have been working like a slave for you, and I have never disobeyed your command; yet you have never given me even a young goat so that I might celebrate with my friends. But when this son of yours came back, who has devoured your property with prostitutes, you killed the fatted calf for him!" Where does this leave the dutiful one, on the scales of significance, of being appreciated?

What the elder son offers his father appears as perfectly sound and

normal judgment. The complaint makes elemental sense: it is unfair —
out of proportion on any ordinary scale of justice. Is the first son to do
good and receive no reward while the younger son gets a party just because he's returned from a wasted life?[38] From the good-boy's perspective — and from the society's point of view as well — who but a soft-
headed parent wielding arbitrary power would act this way with a son
who has squandered everything, selfishly? No consequences at all for
wasting the inheritance in a shameful manner? "You have never given
me even a young goat so that I might celebrate with my friends," the
older son complains. Not even a goat, while the bad one gets a "fatted
calf." Can the wrong-doer show up with a simple sentence of regret and
receive a full embrace and then — that very night — a banquet?

The God presented by Jesus is like this father, a God who would have
appeared muddle-headed to Israel's religious elite. Justice — certainly
God's justice, a father's justice — requires conditions. So the religious establishment would think. Particularly in Luke's day, such a father would
appear radical and profligate in his response to the wayward younger
son.[39] The elder son's angle of vision would have proven decisive, and
proper. The father's generosity would be a bad precedent, a bad moral
example. Where there is wrong, there must be consequence. In the father's gushing response to the lost son's return, however, there are no
conditions besides the return itself. He sees the son who is still far off,
rushes out, hears one sentence of contrition, and proclaims that all is well
— better than well, as the celebratory preparations indicate. Can such a
father be trusted with the rule of even one family, let alone a whole society, a whole world?

The older and "better" boy expresses estrangement, refusing to acknowledge this lad as his brother: "When this *son of yours* came back," he
grumbles to the father, refusing to say, "my brother." The father has referred to "this brother of yours." The three tales were introduced by the
same sour disposition: "And the Pharisees and the scribes were grumbling, 'This fellow welcomes sinners.'"[40] Behind the sniveling disapproval of the privileged is a devastating parochialism, a stingy me-and-
us versus you-and-them. Having all that is the father's is not good
enough. The "other," especially if that other is disreputable and very
close to you, must have nothing; this is only "fair," a just recompense for

38. 17:10.
39. See Green, *The Gospel of Luke*, p. 583.
40. 15:2.

everything that has been squandered. And yet the father pleads, reasoning gently against the son's self-interested argument about a limited justice. "Son," the father has responded to the begrudging brother, "you are always with me, and all that is mine is yours." Isn't this enough? Don't you know me, having been always with me? All that is mine is yours; can't this generosity be enough to make *you* generous? Have you been given much? Do the good things that make for peace, with a generosity of spirit that pays helpful attention to the outsider.

The prodigal son's restoration to family and community yields instant celebration. The new order of God's Way hinges, apparently, on the more fundamental issue of heart-change, reorientation of behavior, and a new community life based on such repentance. Without a generous and beneficent father, of course, the younger son's return would be weighed on the elder son's scales of justice. The wrong-doer would be, as he himself has said, "like one of your hired hands." At the words "no longer worthy to be called your son," however, the father exclaims with joy, preventing the Law's "sentence" which the younger son was ready to decree upon himself. Yes, the father says: you are my valued son. As for you, my beloved first son, help me celebrate the finding of your brother.

As so often in Luke's story, we don't get to find out about the ill-disposed brother, whose grumbling — the story ahead will show — is both self-destructive and murderous. The next we hear from these elder-brother types — the old-guard leaders — they are ridiculing Jesus for his starry-eyed view of money.[41]

All three tales are intended to instruct the old-guard religious leaders concerning their privilege and responsibility. Within the last parable are three of the narrative's major character-types:

- *The poor — the lost, the little one* (younger son) for whom the good news leads to repentance, release, and restoration;
- *The old-guard leaders* (the older son) who are being invited to proclaim and live out the good news they have, if only they can hear the word of their own Torah, and do it;
- *God* (the boys' father), the central character in Luke's two-volume story: beneficent and generous in terms that would have appeared, in Luke's place and time, as weak, profligate, and irresponsible.[42]

---

41. 16:14; see Chapter 10.
42. Charles Talbert makes a similar point, in *Reading Luke*, p. 150.

Along with these major characters, we are given — as we might have expected — a succinct version of the Way and what Luke's entire story is all about. God cares about the "lost," those who — because of impoverishment, disease, gender, sinfulness, demeaning job, religious heterodoxy — are considered outsiders by normal society and consequently by themselves as well. Those who live by God's word as reinterpreted by Jesus from the Torah will join God as partners in giving much with the much they have been given — as Jesus is doing, proving himself to be God's "holy servant."[43] Jesus is teaching others, inviting others to do the same, to be the same.

Luke places these three stories of invitation to Israel's leaders in a progressively detailed and compelling sequence. The tone here with the old-guard leaders is gentle, magnanimous, sincere — as opposed to the first theme sequence, where the new-guard followers were warned about the possibility of their being cut in pieces and placed with the unfaithful for derelict service.[44] Respected Jewish leaders are being welcomed by Jesus to become partners with the Son of Man in serving God's purposes and pleasure — just as the master's slaves, in the prior sequence, were being asked to be faithful in serving *their* master's purposes, or, a bit later, to model "that slave whom his master will find at work when he arrives."[45] Old-guard leaders have been given much — a premise on which the three tales of invitation rest.

Relinquish Privilege and Use It for God's Purposes: A Summary of the Two Sequences

Salvation takes work, a cooperative venture between God and willing partners. That is the overall point of this repeated theme sequence on privilege, power, and responsibility. A master in the first theme sequence goes off to a wedding banquet with slaves in charge, then comes back for another feast, serving his slaves dinner. In the echoing theme, a father throws a big party for a wayward son who has returned — and seeks to enlist the elder son in the communal celebration. In both the original theme sequence and its echo, there is in-gathering, homecoming, and rejoicing with dinner parties. Luke's portrait of God includes this striking

43. Acts 4:27-30.
44. 12:46.
45. 12:35-38; 12:43.

feature: a generous parent waiting for joy to happen. And it is a joy that seeks company, and rests on the willingness of that company to make the celebration possible.

What is God's will? What are God's intentions in the world? Luke is making the picture clear: look at the master of the household, the shepherd, the woman, and the parent who watches, and waits — a parent who the profligate son knows will take him back. But the joy of salvation takes work, and resources — which the surrounding themes suggest in terms of possessions handled well. This is a new interpretation of the Law, a Way other than privilege and power as ordinarily viewed and acted upon. There will be "power," in Acts; there is privilege in being God's called-out ones from within Israel — saved Israel, *ekklēsia*:[46] power and privilege work within a community whose individuals relinquish self-interest in order to seek the lost and bring them home.

The journey moves further now into the demands that make celebrations possible. There must be greater and more difficult letting go, as the Way unfolds. What is to be relinquished, finally, is usually more treasured than even possessions or money: one's family, one's religious scruples. Bringing good news to the poor, giving much, means a radical willingness to let go of family ties, of religious ties, and even of life itself. Only then will there be the peace of salvation. Only then will there be a grander way of living in the world than the hoarding of what one has been given, or the use of it for self-promoting ends.

46. *Ekklēsia*, as we will see, in no way resembles what we think of today as "church" or "Church"; see Chapter 16 for an introduction on this matter, and on Acts as a drama of Israel's redemption come true.

Chapter 12

Relinquish Family and Religion

Luke 12:49–13:17; 14:1-35

Relinquishing not only possessions but also privilege and power is a demanding principle of the Way, as we have seen. But relinquishing family and religious systems, as we see next, is the greatest challenge of all — with the exception, of course, of a willingness to forgo life itself. Following God's Way will lead to divided families, since ordinary family systems — at least in Luke's day — demanded clan loyalty and codes of honor. To suffer such family strife as a Way-follower is one thing, but even more difficult is what we find in the echoing sequence: the follower must utterly relinquish — hate — family members who maintain normal clan loyalties. Ordinary religious organization comes under the same kind of scrutiny, and the same challenge of relinquishment: twice Jesus goes against the traditional religious understanding by healing on the sabbath. The call to relinquish normal religious rules parallels the challenge to let go of normal family systems. We are close to the heart of the journey, its goal: "strive to enter" the reality of God's kingdom.[1]

The First Time: Relinquish Family and Religion (12:49–13:17)

"From everyone to whom much has been given, much will be required; and from the one to whom much has been entrusted, even more will be demanded. I came to bring fire to the earth, and how I wish it were already kindled! I have a baptism with which to be baptized, and what stress I am under until it is completed!"[2]

---

1. 13:23-24; the chapter following this one explores this chiastic center of the journey.
2. 12:48-50; 12:48 concluded the first theme sequence explored in Chapter 11.

Metaphorically, nothing less than "fire to earth" proves adequate to describe this last stage of the journey, this final principle about going God's Way. Jesus continues,

> "I have a baptism with which to be baptized, and what stress I am under until it is completed! Do you think that I have come to bring peace to the earth? No, I tell you, but rather division. From now on five in one household will be divided, three against two and two against three;
>> they will be divided:
>> father against son
>> and son against father,
>> mother against daughter
>> and daughter against mother,
>> mother-in-law against her daughter-in-law
>> and daughter-in-law against mother-in-law." (12:49-53)

The text moves in the next verses to Jesus' anger at the crowd's knowing about "the appearance of earth and sky" while failing to grasp "the present time — [so] why do you not judge for yourselves what is right?"[3]

The mention of weather forecasters is elaborated with detail that echoes, chiastically, the prior fire and baptism of Jesus, highlighting at the center of narrative attention the matter of family strife:

1. "Fire on the earth I came to bring";
   2. "Baptism I have with which to be baptized";
      3. "Household[s] will be divided."
   2'. "'Rain coming,' you say when you see the cloud rising
       in the west";
1'. "'Scorching heat,' you say when you see the south wind
    blowing."[4]

The outer ring (1 and 1') links fire and scorching heat; then, the waters of baptism (2) connect with rain (2') — which leaves, at the center-point, the heart of what this extreme heat and death-water are all about: family strife because of God's Way. Fire consumes the dross while baptism replicates the death required by true life.[5]

3. 12:54-57.

4. 12:49; 12:50; 12:52; 12:54; 12:55.

5. Among many other commentators who associate the baptism of Jesus and John with symbolic death by water, see Leon Morris in his reflections on Lk 12:49-50. *The Gospel Ac-*

"Do you think that I have come to bring peace to the earth? No, I tell you, but rather division!"[6] John distinguished the baptism of Jesus from his own by reference to fire and the Holy Spirit.[7] Both baptisms — of John and of Jesus — were characterized by calling persons to repentance with the forgiveness that follows. But the repentance spelled out by Jesus requires such baptismal dying and refining fire as to need the enabling power of God's own Spirit — as we will see in Acts.

"Do you think that I've come to bring peace to the earth?" Well, yes, the story's audience might respond: the angels said so, in the story's shortest and very powerful poem: "Glory to God in the highest heaven/ and on earth peace among those whom he favors."[8] But the peace imagined by the ordinary person — the *you* in "do *you* think that I've come to bring peace?" — is not the peace Jesus has in mind when he says, at the end of the journey, "If you, even you [Jerusalem citizens], had only recognized on this day the things that make for peace!"[9] There is peace that is the absence of conflict within clans, and there is peace that is "made" with rigorous attention ("recognition") and implementation, on behalf of all peoples, Jewish or not.[10] To recognize and act on the things that make for peace, apparently, is to suffer the consequence of division in households and clans more interested in *keeping* peace within a parochial setting than *making* it with all peoples in mind.

As we have seen, Jesus himself experienced and initiated family disruption, on behalf of a greater "family circle."[11] At the heart of what dy-

---

cording to Luke: An Introduction and Commentary (Downers Grove, Ill.: InterVarsity, 1974), p. 240. Also, this: "Jesus refers to his death as a baptism and adds, 'how I am constrained until it is accomplished!' (12:50). He sends a message to Herod: 'I cast out demons and perform cures today and tomorrow, and the third day I finish my course' (13:32; he goes on to speak of perishing in Jerusalem)" (pp. 46-47).

6. 12:51.

7. 3:3, 16.

8. 2:14.

9. 19:42.

10. 2:29-32.

11. (1) As a twelve-year-old, Jesus shows little or no concern about the five days of utter havoc experienced by his parents and their entourage. "Child, why have you treated us like this?" the mother asks. "Why were you searching for me?" the boy retorts (2:48-49; Chapter 4). (2) The mother of Jesus and his brothers have come to see him, but at least on this occasion, Jesus "divides" himself from them, son against mother, brother against brothers. He refuses, apparently, to even make his way outside the house to speak with them. To those listening he says, "My mother and my brothers are those who hear the word of God and do it" (8:19-21; Chapter 4). It will happen, finally, that mother Mary and the brothers of Jesus are "reunited" with Jesus, though under entirely new terms and conditions and ex-

ing means, in baptism, and of what fire means, in the burning away of chaff, is the daily and presumably unthinkable relinquishment of family loyalties that privilege the family above the outsider who has no coat and no food.[12] To serve God in such a manner is demonstrated by Jesus within Luke's text. The letting-go required by this salvation, this going of God's Way, can be a literal dying in addition to the daily dying of picking up one's cross on behalf of others.[13] "Baptism I have with which to be baptized," Jesus says.[14] Something lies ahead, beyond the cleansing ritual of baptism that Jesus has already experienced.[15] Jesus is under "stress . . . until it is completed."

"Fire on the earth I came to bring," Jesus also says — an "unquenchable fire," as John explains, that will burn away the "chaff," all that is worthless.[16] Fire will not only clean away, however: it will also create energy and provide empowerment. The gospel has promised, and so it happens: as the Holy Spirit descended on Jesus, this same Spirit descends on followers to initiate the action of Acts. This time the Spirit comes as fire rather than as a dove.[17] The mystery of fire — lethal but also invaluable — is emphasized by Luke as accompanying the in-breaking of God's reign, the kingdom's realization and spread of the "good news." Good news and utter disruption: Luke has prepared us for all this, in his first nine chapters.[18] Whatever peace will be accomplished in the reality of God's kingdom is not an ordinary peace, associated as it is with the fire that Jesus came to bring on earth.[19] Jesus himself does not escape the devastation, as his comment about stress indicates and as the unfolding story will continue to demonstrate: Jesus' suffering and dying are paralleled in the lives of believers, up through the concluding portrait of Paul awaiting certain death in Rome.

---

pectations. When Jesus has died, risen, and ascended, then Mary and the brothers become participating members of the new family of God headed by Jesus (Acts 1:14). "The family now defers to Jesus rather than Jesus revering the family." Robert L. Brawley, *Luke-Acts and the Jews: Conflict, Apology, and the Conciliation* (Atlanta: Scholars Press, 1987), p. 21.

12. 3:17.
13. 9:23; 14:27.
14. 12:50.
15. 3:21.
16. 12:49.
17. Acts 2:3; gospel, 3:22.
18. Chapter 4.
19. 12:49-51.

The baptism and fire, then, are fleshed out as a potential searing loss of family relationship, a loss that allows for a gain: the possibility of "[judging] for yourselves what is right." Within a normal world of family loyalties and clan support, how can one judge independently? A follower of the Way judges "right" in the light of the reinterpretation of Torah being provided by Jesus. Communal well-being is a kingdom reality in which difficult issues are resolved without regard to individual or familial "rights":

> "And why do you not judge for yourselves what is right? Thus, when you go with your accuser before a magistrate, on the way make an effort to settle the case, or you may be dragged before the judge, and the judge hand you over to the officer, and the officer throw you in prison. I tell you, you will never get out until you have paid the very last penny." (12:57-59)

Apart from what one's family thinks, and opposed to normal ideals of family loyalty (and we must remember how dominating family and religious clan-systems were), the individual following God's Way is obligated to discriminate for himself or herself between what is good and what is not good for the greater community. Luke has provided by this point in his story examples of going contrary to normal ways of being in the world,[20] but what we find here is the most daunting of all; only one stage of the Way's journey is more demanding, as we find in the next chapter.

From "judge for yourselves what is right," beyond family claims (implied), the text moves to some people who wonder about a horrible tragedy, with a not-so-subtle judgmentalism. Again, what can appear to be unconnected insights colliding into each other is in narrative reality quite orderly, and compelling.

Some people have told Jesus of a presumably well-known incident, the slaughtering of some Galilean Jews by Pilate, who compounded the horror by mingling blood of those slaughtered in religious sacrifices.[21]

---

20. "Let me first go and bury my father," a would-be follower has responded to Jesus, when invited to follow God's Way. No, says Jesus, "let the dead bury their dead." The time of proclaiming God's Way is now (9:59-60). Peter claimed, as we have seen, that he and his friends had left their homes. Jesus responded, "Truly I tell you, there is no one who has left house or wife or brothers or parents or children, for the sake of the kingdom of God, who will not get back very much more in this age, and in the age to come eternal life" (18:28-30).

21. 13:1.

"Do you think that because these Galileans suffered in this way they were worse sinners than all other Galileans?" Jesus answers his own rhetorical question. "No — but *unless you repent,* you will all perish as they did."[22] Horrible things happen because of human malice. Victims are not guilty, Jesus implies: the point is that each person has normal self-promoting ways that must be repented of — once and for all, and every day.[23] Discernment of the truly right thing begins with self-scrutiny: judge for yourselves what is right.[24] *Unless you repent:* Assess your normal ways in the light of God's Way and turn around, repent![25]

The tendency to deflect scrutiny of oneself takes different forms: threatening a court battle ("[going] with your accuser before a magistrate") or judging the "other" as guilty on the basis of calamitous injury suffered ("Do you think that because these Galileans suffered in this way they were worse sinners than all other Galileans?"). Scrutinizing of the other must yield to a difficult self-scrutiny that leads to change, a turn-around.

Jesus is shown making the case even easier for those wishing to judge the victim as guilty. *"Those eighteen who were killed when the tower of Siloam fell on them — do you think that they were worse offenders than all the others living in Jerusalem? No, I tell you; but unless you repent, you will all perish just as they did" (13:4-5).* You think human malice is problematic, says Jesus; *What do you think about the evil of accidents? Surely this would demonstrate God's presumed judgment against victims of such horror?*

Does God have control in the case of such horrific accidents? Does God know about them ahead of time, and could there have been divine intervention? Does God use such calamity as punishment? From the perspective of the text, these are irrelevant questions, and worse: a distraction from where the attention must always be focused. The narrative point is always other than philosophical/theological musing. "No," says Jesus for a second time: these victims are no more evil than anyone else. The point here, and always, is this: "unless you [all] repent, you will all perish as they did." Typical family securities and religious certainties will

---

22. 13:2-3; emphasis mine.

23. Leon Morris understands the verb form here as implying both a life-orienting decision that "begins" the journey, and also an everyday affair along the journey. Leon Morris, *The Gospel According to St. Luke: An Introduction and Commentary* (Downers Grove, Ill.: InterVarsity Press, 1974), p. 243.

24. 12:57.

25. 13:5.

not suffice to explain why very bad things happen: the only point is *you*, your own disposition to normal but evil ways, your own complicity in what goes horribly wrong. Repentance is a choice an individual makes daily, based on God's word taught by Jesus and not on family expectations and constraints. Everyone must repent, must be helping others, including victims. Not only will family allegiances not help, they will hinder such kingdom effort.

To the extent that a modern audience grasps the intense family loyalties and value systems of Luke's day, it understands the shock to the original audience of these carefully orchestrated words. Luke's orderliness provides an unremitting insistence on relinquishment for the sake of blessing — for others, beyond the normal parochial circles.

From the challenge of repentance and the dire consequences of not doing so, the journey moves in orderly fashion to the possibility of hope. How pressing is this "present time"?[26] Is the lord of the land ruthless and quick to judge, or long-suffering?

> "Unless you repent, you will all perish just as [those in Jerusalem] did." Then he told this parable: "A man had a fig tree planted in his vineyard; and he came looking for fruit on it and found none. So he said to the gardener, 'See here! For three years I have come looking for fruit on this fig tree, and still I find none. Cut it down! Why should it be wasting the soil?' He replied, 'Sir, let it alone for one more year, until I dig around it and put manure on it. If it bears fruit next year, well and good; but if not, you can cut it down.'" (13:5-9)

There is judgment for those failing to interpret the present time, and failing to repent, but there is hope as well, based on a God whose patient beneficence resembles that of the gardener.

Cut-in-pieces will be the fate, we have heard, of unfaithful, unfruitful servants — but the point is in the "will-be," a dire future that can be avoided.[27] There is time to judge yourselves and to judge for yourselves what is right. But not a lot of time. A fruit tree moves ideally toward the "fulfillment" of bearing fruit, just as persons privileged with a hearing of Torah taught by Jesus must finally obey this word of God, by bringing the blessing of good news to the poor.

26. 12:56.
27. 12:46.

The comfort of thinking that God punishes the sinner, either by the hand of an admittedly evil tyrant or "acts of God," is a comfortable way of deflecting responsibility from oneself. Jesus will have none of it, distilling the Law and the tendency toward rules into principles that include but go beyond "commandments" to an entire orientation of life. That word about hope, regarding the fig-tree fruit, is to be remembered as the journey challenges keep escalating.

"Teaching in one of the synagogues on the sabbath," rabbi Jesus offends a respected religious leader by doing the work of healing on this holy day of rest.[28] Tension arises between Jesus and his Jewish compatriots. An un-whole woman becomes the center of the storm. "She was bent over and was quite unable to stand up straight." Jesus speaks healing words, and touches her. She stands up straight and praises God.[29]

The synagogue leader is indignant, with religious tradition solidly behind him: "There are six days on which work ought to be done," he points out — as any observing Jew in Luke's audience would know.[30] The narrator lets his audience know, at this point, that Jesus is no other than "the Lord." Given normal ties to religious institutions, the answer takes on extra weight, precisely when it might most be needed:

> But *the Lord* answered him and said, "You hypocrites! Does not each of you on the sabbath untie his ox or his donkey from the manger, and lead it away to give it water? And ought not this woman, a daughter of Abraham whom Satan bound for eighteen long years, be set free from this bondage on the sabbath day?" (13:15-16; emphasis mine)

Jesus includes all the religious traditionalists in his answer: "You hypocrites!" This specific example of religious scruple is used by Luke to indicate the larger problem, a systemic corruption of the whole religious enterprise. Religious group, family, clan: the more powerful the loyalties, the more insidious the problem — and the more need to "judge for yourself," as Jesus does here. Honor is being unmasked as hypocrisy.

In a prior sabbath healing, "the scribes and Pharisees watched him to see whether he would cure on the sabbath, so that they might find an accusation against him."[31] Jesus wants to know whether it is "lawful to do good or to do harm on the sabbath, to save life or to destroy

28. 13:10-17.
29. 13:11; 13:12-14.
30. 13:14.
31. 6:7.

it."[32] He heals the man's withered hand, and "they were filled with fury and discussed with one another what they might do to Jesus."[33] The good news to the poor, of release from bondage, obeys principle, not rule: Jesus interprets Torah as liberating principle, the religious leaders as restricting rule.

Here is a new community under God's reign that is present "among you," as Jesus has pointed out — the community of true Israel in which the woman released from bondage is restored to the people of God as a "daughter of Abraham."[34] She doesn't praise Jesus, her healer, but God, the power behind and within Jesus: Luke takes every opportunity to emphasize God as the story's central character, the one to whom Jesus is pointing everyone, whose Way Jesus teaches, whose Way Jesus journeys.[35] It is a Way that will bring division within family and religious community because it insists on judging and doing the right thing as guided by God's word, the Torah principle of love.[36]

The Echo: Relinquish Family and Religion (14:1-35)

Just before the echo to this principle of family and religion relinquishment, Jesus has been lamenting the fate of Jerusalem. "How often have I desired to gather your children together as a hen gathers her brood under her wings, and you were not willing!"[37] And so the audience changes to these unwilling children, Israel's leaders — the elite, the social and religious pillars of Jerusalem. Luke presents Jesus as genuinely invitational; though he breaks their religious rules, he communes with them at the table of intimacy.[38] Jesus is having sabbath dinner at the house of a leading Pharisee. The dinner setting couldn't be more cordial, more congenial to the invitational efforts of Jesus, as Luke presents him here.[39] Jesus associ-

---

32. 6:9.

33. 6:11.

34. 13:16.

35. "It is interesting that the woman's gratitude is shown in her praising of *God*, not Jesus." Leon Morris, *The Gospel According to St. Luke*, p. 244.

36. This "Torah principle of love" is most succinctly and powerfully rendered in the ninth poem of the gospel's preparatory section, as we have seen (6:27, 32, 35; see Chapter 3).

37. 13:34.

38. 13:24-28.

39. "To welcome people at the table had become tantamount to extending to them intimacy, solidarity, acceptance; table companions were treated as though they were one's ex-

ated with old-guard religious leaders not only formally, in the synagogues, and casually, along the journey, but intimately, in their homes
and at dinner. But in spite of the comfortable setting, the religious leaders
"were watching [Jesus] closely."[40]

Their sabbath scrutiny is rewarded, apparently: "Just then, in front of
him, there was a man who had dropsy."[41] By now, the proclivity of Jesus
to break important religious rules would have been known, and anticipated. In the prior sequence involving sabbath healing, however, Jesus
went ahead and healed with no preparatory word; acrimonious debate
followed, as we have seen. Something different occurs here, which the
narrative ordering highlights. In place of the possibly impulsive sabbath
healing of the woman, with no conversational context, Jesus is shown on
this particular sabbath day offering a prefatory question. Perhaps the expected outrage can be diffused. "Is it lawful," asks Jesus, "to cure people
on the sabbath, or not?"[42] The leaders remain silent. This a good question,
and no immediate rejoinder may have come to their minds. Indicating his
concern for the Law (is it *lawful*, according to Torah?),[43] Jesus goes ahead
and heals the man, then sends him away.

Once again Jesus turns to his dinner associates. He continues to be
more suggestive than provocative. "If one of you has a child or an ox that
has fallen into a well," Jesus asks, "will you not immediately pull it out
on a sabbath day?"[44] Luke is taking pains in this entire sequence to reveal
the hand of Jesus extended toward those most in a position to help him
with God's work of the kingdom; Luke continues this invitational tone
toward the traditional religious leaders on through chapter 15 and the
three tales of the lost whom Jesus desires these leaders to find.[45] So we
have this hypothetical oxen or child, trapped in a well, and it's the sabbath: *What do you folks suggest can be done?* In the prior sequence, the sabbath healing of the woman was followed by Jesus referring to the water-
ing of oxen on the sabbath.[46] Here the situation is more urgent because of

---

tended family." Joel B. Green, *New Testament Theology: The Theology of the Gospel of Luke*
(Cambridge: Cambridge University Press, 1995), p. 87.

40. 14:1.

41. 14:2.

42. 14:3.

43. 14:2-4.

44. 14:5.

45. As we have seen (Chapter 11).

46. The Mishnah allowed such a practice. See I. Howard Marshall, *Luke: Historian and
Theologian* (Grand Rapids: Zondervan, 1976), p. 558.

the oxen's plight; but the even more excruciating dilemma is that of the child. Current practice among the religious elite allowed for action in such emergencies.[47] Again there is silence from the peers of Jesus: "they could not reply."[48] Rather than trying to put these religious peers on the spot, however, it appears that Jesus is doing everything possible to help them get the point of how he is reinterpreting Torah.

The journey moves on, with great cohesiveness of both motif (dinner, relational intimacy) and insight (the challenge of escalating relinquishments). Still at dinner, Jesus notices that some have tried to position themselves in seats of honor at the dinner table. Luke's audience must make the connection between religion-as-rules — not healing on the sabbath — and this matter of promoting one's own standing before others. Relinquishing such a drive for one's honor — status, name — is, apparently, central to the meaning of relinquishment. Again Jesus is suggestive, imaginative: *Picture a wedding banquet, and then watch yourself choosing a prestigious seat. But wait — now you are being embarrassed by demotion to a lower seat by the host, who has just come into the banquet hall.* "For all who exalt themselves will be humbled, and those who humble themselves will be exalted."[49] The potential demotion here of the honor-obsessed has been heralded from the story's beginning as an aspect of the reversals characterizing God's Way.[50] The normal way of taking up positions of honor is so basic to ordinary life, this gospel suggests, that to resist is to prove disruptive, especially within families and religions that seek to promote their own. That's why division and even hatred result.

Judge for yourselves what is right: respond to sabbath healings in the light of Torah as principle rather than Torah as rule. If you find a problem with Jesus' sabbath healing, the text implies, perhaps you need to look more closely at your motives for clinging to rules: exaltation among your own. At this very dinner table, for example: How do you choose seats for yourselves?

In fact, Jesus goes on, when you think of meals and table fellowship, "do not invite your friends . . . ."[51] Luke's narrative ordering continues its

47. Joel B. Green, *The Gospel of Luke* (Grand Rapids: Eerdmans, 1997), p. 548.
48. 14:5-6.
49. 14:11.
50. In Mary's poem: "God [brings] down the powerful from their thrones, and [lifts] up the lowly" (1:52).
51. 14:12.

brilliantly connective way of upping the ante, of having narrative light il-
lumine further narrative light. Here Jesus is warning not only of the dire
reversal in store for self-promoting leaders, but of the great reversal in
what God requires of relational intimacy in the first place: *do not invite
your friends*. Normal for that day was a practice of "table meals" as a
meeting of similar minds from similar socio-economic classes.

Not your friends? Nor your brothers or your relatives? Nor rich
neighbors? No, says Jesus, don't invite your own kind "in case they may
invite you in return, and you would be repaid"; rather, "invite the poor,
the crippled, the lame, and the blind."[52] We saw this in the first poem by
Jesus: release and restoration to community for captives, the blind, the
imprisoned, and the oppressed.[53] And then, in the next poem, again spoken by Jesus, the presumably unthinkable thought of inviting those who
can't return the favor:

> "If you love those who love you, what credit is that to you?
> For even sinners love those who love them.
> If you do good to those who do good to you,
> what credit is that to you?
> For even sinners do the same.
> If you lend to those from whom you hope to receive,
> what credit is that to you?
> Even sinners lend to sinners, to receive as much again.
> But love your enemies, do good, and lend, expecting nothing
>   in return." (6:32-35)

Here, Jesus repeats: "Invite the poor, the crippled, the lame, and the
blind. And you will be blessed, *because they cannot repay you*."[54] A greater
disruption to the normal state of affairs, in the everyday life of Luke's day
(if not our own), could hardly be imagined.

In this world of odd dinner parties being recommended by Jesus, a third
issue is raised. (Jesus and friends are still at their sabbath dinner scene.)
First issue: don't seek positions of honor; second issue: don't do good
things in expectation of the favor being returned; and now, make sure
you yourself accept an invitation to the right dinner party![55]

---

52. 14:12-13.
53. 4:18.
54. 14:13-14; emphasis mine.
55. 14:7-11; 12-14; 15-24.

This third conversational topic — they are still around the table — gets to the basics of what Jesus is offering: a fundamental choice between God's Way and normal ways. "Blessed is anyone who will eat bread in the kingdom of God!" a dinner guest exclaims; surely this is the ultimate table experience.[56] Again Jesus is imagining a scene, playing it out for his intimates. Someone wants to give a great dinner. Invitations are sent. But regrets are sent back by those already engaged in everyday, legitimate activities: a buyer of land is slated for inspection of that land; a new owner of five oxen must try them out; still another person has just married. Angry, the owner of the house invites "the poor, the crippled, the blind, and the lame" — the very same folks Jesus has just referred to as those who should be wined and dined by his religious associates.[57] But still, after the poor have accepted, there is room at the dinner feast. Beat the bushes; then, says Jesus — "compel people to come in, so that my house may be filled."[58] The blessing must be spread as wide as possible, to all peoples. For those who refused the invitation there will not be even a taste of the dinner.[59] The religious leaders squirm, perhaps: not only do they seek the wrong seats of honor at a perfectly proper party, and not only do they throw the wrong kind of parties: *they don't recognize the kind of feast to which they are being invited!* Jesus is invitational, here, and in the following chapter.

Judge for yourselves about attending this celebration of God's reign — but know that there may be disruption, of land and of livelihood and even of marriage. And so we come back, in this echoing theme sequence, to the truth that one who goes God's Way must go beyond not just the traditional religion but beyond the accepted family system of the day. In the first theme sequence we went from family division to religious disruption; in the echoing sequence the order is reversed, from the challeng-

56. 14:15.
57. 14:16-21; 14:13.
58. 14:23.
59. 14:24; a very similar tale, in Matthew's gospel, highlights in its differences the very invitational tone of Luke at this point of the journey. The servants who go out to get banquet guests are murdered, putting the master into a firestorm kind of frenzy (Mt 22:6-7). One fellow comes ill-dressed, and is cast "into the darkness, where there will be weeping and gnashing of teeth" (Mt 22:13). Luke's version keeps the focus on the unrelenting desire of the master to fill the banquet hall, period. This is in keeping with the solicitous tone of Jesus emphasized by Luke toward the old-guard religious leaders. Jesus is shown as genuinely wanting his Pharisee friends (at this point, anyway) to join with him in sponsoring such banquets for the lost and ill-fed.

ing of religion-as-rules to the questioning of family as priority.[60] Sabbath healing accomplished, the good dinner conversation comes to a close. But the line of thought builds, the challenge now couched in terms of hating one's family members.

"'I tell you, none of those who were invited will taste my dinner.' Now large crowds were traveling with him."[61] What does the crowd want? What they get, from Jesus, is shocking beyond anything they would have heard from him so far:

> [Jesus] turned and said to them, "Whoever comes to me and does not hate father and mother, wife and children, brothers and sisters, yes, and even life itself, cannot be my disciple." (14:25-26)

To be a "disciple" is to follow God's Way; excluded from salvation are any who privilege family over kingdom relationships — to the poor, the outsider, the lame and the blind and the imprisoned.[62]

What have we seen of the family's status? The fictional host of Jesus' dinner tale, just prior, was angry toward those offering excuses not to attend the dinner party, excuses that included the parochial plea of "I can't come; I've just married!" The journey of this Way began long ago with someone wishing to follow Jesus, but pleading time to bury his father. Five chapters later, someone just married is not excused from attending what is being portrayed as kingdom business and kingdom banqueting.[63] Jesus has been the occasion for parental agitation, and in fact dismisses his mother and brothers with no consideration for them at all.[64] But the ante gets upped to its height, here, in a challenge to *hate* family members.

Nowhere is Jesus pictured softening or qualifying "hatred" of family members. There is no *Well, of course what I mean is that by way of comparison to one's love of God, love of family must seem like hatred.* Such interpretation fails to satisfy the sense of the text and its context. First of all, the Greek

---

60. The somewhat arbitrary nature of my chiastic chart is indicated in part by a decision to place family and religious disruption together. They could be separated and the reverse repetition of themes would still hold.

61. 14:24-25.

62. 13:23-30; we will see in the following chapter confirmation of just how demanding it is to enter the kingdom, to be "saved."

63. 9:59; hating one's wife is left out of similar passages in Matthew (10:37) and Mark (10:29). Consistently, Luke seems to emphasize just how un-normal God's Way is.

64. 2:48; 8:19-21; see Chapter 4.

word for "hate" does not connote feeling at all (as in, "I *love* you, my dear"; or, "I *hate* you!"). The language of hatred as for love, in this story, points to intention and will, not emotional state. *To hate* demands a thoughtful action, a formidable choice rather than a visceral reaction based on feeling. The vision being suggested by Luke, as I. Howard Marshall puts it nicely, is "not of psychological hate, but of renunciation"[65] — of "being willing to live without these loved ones, not being so attached to them that their well-being, or even one's own survival, is one's first priority."[66] However such talk comes across to a modern audience — this call to reject family as "first priority" — for Luke's audience it would have been ridiculous and, in fact, seemingly against the Mosaic Law.

As always, the chiastic echo elaborates, extends, or makes more demanding the challenge of the first sequence. In the first theme statement, family division is something that happens to the follower, but here in the echoing sequence, the follower makes such family division happen, by hating. The follower is to go beyond usual human ties, the normal orientation of *my* family's security and well-being privileged above all others. Such letting go is not an emotional state but an act of the will, an utter relinquishment called *hatred*. The point is given an exclamation point by the ultimate — the uttermost — relinquishment: "yes, and even [of] life itself."[67] An orientation to God's Way makes commitment to family and one's own life a lesser priority than meeting the needs of the outsider, even the enemy. Though strange and upside down, such a transformation of fundamental orientations would seem to warrant the radical use of the word *hatred* relative to one's family.

The people in Noah's day, we remember, are not faulted by Jesus for being wicked, but for "eating and drinking, and marrying and being given in marriage."[68] Implicit here is the reciprocal nature of traditional family systems, the taking-care of one's own in terms of "eating and drinking" and giving-in-marriage. Such an ordinary mind-set effectively keeps the outsider outside. Luke's view is consistent as these principles of the Way unfold, building on each other. Jesus is offering a radical renouncing of familiar and familial attitudes that in any way hinder God's Way. This Way, as Jesus is shown making more and more clear, is a generosity of

---

65. I. Howard Marshall, *Luke: Historian and Theologian*, p. 592.
66. Sharon H. Ringe, *Luke* (Louisville: Westminster/John Knox, 1995), p. 201.
67. 14:26.
68. 17:27.

spirit that ignores the possibility of personal gain, including honor within that day's sacrosanct family network and religious clan.[69] Not only does the text refuse to lighten what Jesus is saying about family and religious matters; in fact, the represented journey to the heart of God's kingdom insists at this critical point on the increasing seriousness of the imperative to let go — to go beyond the normal securities of family and religious institution. The narrative will come to a summary statement: to "be saved" requires great effort: "strive to enter through the narrow door" of God's kingdom, salvation's Way.[70]

This very difficult talk from Jesus is followed up by an illustration that points to the need to "first sit down and estimate the cost" before embarking on God's Way.[71] A builder must count the cost of a project in order to avoid ridicule at being unable to finish; a king must consider the strength of his troops before engaging the enemy to avoid the need to sue for peace as the enemy approaches. "So therefore, none of you can become my disciple if you do not give up all your possessions"[72] — in effect, a renunciation of those things that possess *us*, like family, clan, religious scruple. The text never strays from the stringent matter of what it takes to "inherit eternal life," and in fact develops toward the heart of this matter, which we see in the following chapter. Entering God's kingdom takes the greatest of striving.

---

69. Families of Luke's day were rigidly patriarchal, and part of a patronage system that took care of "insiders." (Perhaps we moderns are different. What might Jesus have said on the matter, or said differently, to "developed" nations of the twenty-first century? In the light of contemporary destructive family breakdown, perhaps Jesus would have been talking about "whatever owns us: peer group, media, materialism" — and Luke would have highlighted these sayings in a compelling fashion as he has done for these family views of Jesus.) For Luke's audience there is the abiding concern in the story about loving God by supporting God's best interests toward global blessing, starting with the disenfranchised among neighbors. Such a fundamental alignment with God's reign, this story suggests, puts any audience on alert regarding everyday assumptions about honor and loyalty and patronage. Family and religion are two institutions that in Luke's day, and our own, generate and foster ideals of honor and loyalty and patronage. See Marshall, *Luke: Historian and Theologian*, p. 592 — contra Darrell L. Bock, *Proclamation from Prophecy and Pattern: Lucan Old Testament Christology*, vol. 2 (Sheffield, U.K.: Sheffield Academic Press, 1987), pp. 1284-85.

70. 13:24.

71. 14:28.

72. 14:33.

Relinquish Family and Religion:
A Summary of the Two Sequences

We have come full circle, from family division to hate of family. There must be a willingness to judge for oneself the right thing to do, the right way to go — in spite of what the prevailing religious proscriptions and family loyalties might be insisting upon. *So count on it: families will be divided.* The echo is even harsher: *hate family members insisting on ordinary family systems; relinquish those family bonds that restrict the extension of God's blessing to all peoples.*[73] Jesus has just got through speaking of this principle in different terms: *don't invite those friends and family to your dinner party who are expected to return the favor; rather, invite those who cannot repay you.*[74] This turning upside down of normal priorities is a fleshing out of what in the first sequence was simply called repentance.[75] Here is the one-word summary of proper response to God's word taught by Jesus: repentance. (Repentance will function in Acts as a frequently used word signaling the audience back to the gospel.) The one thing to be gained from the contemplation of God and the problem of evil is one's own role in that evil, or role in solving that evil, as a follower of the Way: *repent, all of you.*[76] Such turning-around is spelled out in the echoing sequence as utter relinquishment of — hating — family. The same principle that applies to family loyalties applies to religious loyalties. In each sequence, Jesus appeals to the higher law of God's kingdom, healing on the sabbath and defying the deeply held religious convictions of his day regarding what constitutes "the holy." Repent, turn around, comes to its greatest pitch of challenge in terms of both family and religion; these parallel thematic sequences immediately frame the heart of the journey, the juxtaposition of kingdoms — God's, and normal — and the need to strive if God's kingdom is to be entered.

And so we arrive at the center of chiasm, the heart of God's kingdom, the journey's true destination. "Strive to enter through the narrow door" of God's kingdom, we hear.[77] *The Way of salvation, of gaining entrance, of inheriting eternal life, is rigorous. And what is the kingdom like? It is true community, shalom-justice — obtained by continual repentance. Repentance is characterized by the need to be always striving.*

73. 14:26.
74. 14:12-14.
75. 13:3-5.
76. 13:1-5.
77. 13:23-24.

Chapter 13

Striving to Enter God's Kingdom — But What of Jerusalem?

Luke 13:18-35

Here at the journey's precise center-point, we find the most succinct expression of Luke's perspective on "the Way of God" — "the Way of salvation" to which believers will belong and according to which they will live and worship.[1] Especially at this center-point of the journey do we find "the truth concerning the things" about which Luke wishes to instruct his audience.[2]

(1)	9:51–10:24	"Things That Make for Peace"	18:35–19:44
(2)	10:25-42	"Inherit Eternal Life"?	18:15-34
(3)	11:1-13	What to Pray For	18:1-14
(4)	11:14-32	Looking in Wrong Directions	17:20-37
(5)	11:33–12:12	Looking Within Yourself	17:1-19
(6)	12:13-34	Ownership	16:1-31
(7)	12:35-48	Privilege	15:1-32
(8)	12:49–13:17	Family/Religion	14:1-35
(9)	13:18-21	**Kingdom/Jerusalem** **"Strive to Enter"** **13:22-30**	13:31-35

The journey to Jerusalem represents actual traveling, but Luke has ordered this narrative primarily as a journey into God's kingdom, the "Way." We have moved, as indicated above on the chart, from "things that make for peace" and the inheriting of "eternal life" up through the

---

1. Lk 20:21; Acts 16:17; Acts 9:2; Acts 24:14.
2. Lk 13:18-35; Lk 1:4.

demands of going God's Way, including relinquishment of judgmentalism, ownership, privilege, family, and religious loyalties. These rigorous demands of repentance are summarized for Israel, here at the heart of the journey, as the need to "strive" for entrance to God's kingdom. The implicit clash between God's kingdom and conventional Jerusalem at the journey's center-point plays out in the gospel's last section,[3] with continuing and escalating action in Acts.

The tension between kingdom and Jerusalem is the innermost ring of the journey's chiastic center. At the center of this innermost ring is both the resolve of this tension (*you* strive to enter God's kingdom) along with consequences for choices made (feasting in God's banquet hall, or lost to the kingdom forever).

The First Time: There Are Kingdoms, and Kingdoms: "What Is the Kingdom of God Like?" (13:18-21)

"He said therefore, 'What is the kingdom of God like? And to what should I compare it?'"[4] The answer to Jesus' question, spoken through a parable, does not fit the normal expectations for kingdoms in Luke's day.

The kingdom is like this, Jesus says, like one mustard seed taken by one person into a garden, and planted. Only later — presumably years later — will "the birds of the air" be able to make "nests in its branches."[5] The kingdom begins small. One of the tiniest of all seeds (1/750th of a gram) is enough. And the kingdom of God is like this, Jesus continues: a pinch of yeast that one woman "hid"[6] in fifty pounds ("three measures") of flour! From the hidden pinch, the woman ends up with fifty pounds of bread-loaves, rather than a fifty-pound sack of flour.[7] Both of these examples, taken from the "lowest" society of that time — a person in the garden, a woman in the kitchen — say the same thing about God's kingdom: its goodness spreads from the lowliest deed of the lowliest person, without grand show, but infectiously. It becomes great through motions and materials that are unassuming. That is, the kingdom of God grows

3. 19:45–24:53.

4. 13:18.

5. 13:19.

6. The NRSV translates the Greek "hid" as "mixed in." See R. Alan Culpepper, *The Gospel of Luke*, The New Interpreter's Bible, vol. 9 (Nashville: Abingdon, 1995), p. 275.

7. 13:20-21.

through small acts demonstrating faithful stewardship, ultimately supplying life's staples and a resting place for all.

Luke has prepared his audience for these metaphors of concrete kingdom deeds. We have just witnessed a generous act of restoration to a palsied woman, a woman "bent over" for eighteen years.[8] The bent woman stands up straight, and the text moves on. "[Jesus] said therefore, 'What is the kingdom of God like?'"[9] The text spirals from an actual kingdom deed to a *therefore* — a generalized picture of the kingdom: it is like a gardener with a tiny mustard seed, a woman with a pinch of yeast. This kingdom salvation flies in the face not only of normal expectations of purpose, but also of process: Jesus had to break the religious "rules" about working on the sabbath. He suffers the scrutiny of fellow Jews who are leading Israel toward another kind of kingdom, toward expectations of an overtly political deliverance.[10] And just after the journey's midpoint, the same healing scenario is repeated. A man imprisoned by a crippling excess of bloated connective tissue is released from his dropsy. Once again a beneficent act on behalf of a societal castoff brings scrutiny from the highest ranks of society, since the healed man's experience of "the good news" occurred on the holy day of rest.[11] The woman's yeast was "hidden"; here, the right action of Jesus is judged as something wrong, hidden from the normal grids of perception and expectation. The farmer's attention is on planting the one tiny seed, just as the attention of Jesus is on the one overlooked member of society — appearing before him on any given day of the week, including the sabbath, and at any hour. From all ordinary perspectives, such mission seems mistaken, beside the main point. In Luke's view, such "interruptions" become the main point.[12] The kingdom is like that.

The Echo: There Are Kingdoms, and Kingdoms: "What is Jerusalem like?" (13:31-35)

Immediately following an extended view of kingdom joy and of those Israelites excluded, the religious leaders — who have reason to be grievously offended by what has just been said — come to Jesus "that very

8. 13:10-13.
9. 13:18.
10. 13:10-17.
11. 4:18-19; 14:1-6.
12. See the stories of a blind beggar and Zacchaeus, second half of Chapter 5.

hour" with news that Herod wants to kill him.[13] What is it that characterizes the heart of Jewish religious life and its leadership — including these
very Pharisees who seem to be warning Jesus?[14]

Jesus responds to the warning by referring to Herod as a fox — wily,
and an example of worthless "low-life."[15] This brushing-aside of the secular
ruler sets up the narrative focus on the real adversaries of Jesus, his own religious peers and fellow Jews. To these Jesus gives a message that begins with
Herod but slips easily into a lament directed at them, the religious leaders.

> "Go tell that fox for me, 'Listen, I am casting out demons and perform-
> ing cures today and tomorrow, and on the third day I finish my work.
> Yet today I must be on my way, because it is impossible for a prophet to
> be killed outside of Jerusalem. Jerusalem, Jerusalem, the city that kills
> the prophets and stones those who are sent to it! How often have I de-
> sired to gather your children together as a hen gathers her brood under
> her wings, and you were not willing! See, your house is left to you.
> And I tell you, you will not see me until the time comes when you say,
> 'Blessed is the one who comes in the name of the Lord.'" (13:32-35)[16]

Unresponsive and murderous Jerusalem lies within the determination of God, which Jesus himself expresses: "I *must* be on my way." This
determination reflects what Jesus has made explicit, that his is a Way suffered by all of God's word-bearers at the hands of Israel's traditional religious establishment.

There is a double sense of such divine determination here, but with
the same essential thrust to each: (1) I *must* go, (2) "because it is *impossible* for a prophet to be killed outside of Jerusalem."[17] These words link-

---

13. 13:31.

14. The Pharisees are less associated with Jerusalem, for Luke, than chief priests and
scribes and of course "temple officers," although of course there are Pharisees in Jerusalem
along with other of the "leadership." For example, "One day, while he was teaching, Pharisees and teachers of the law were sitting nearby (they had come from every village of Galilee and Judea *and from Jerusalem*) . . ." (5:17, emphasis mine).

15. The fox was thought of as not only wily, but dishonorable and worthless as well.
That the fox was also considered a predator and destructive is a possible irony, since Herod
will prove to be fairly impotent in his destructive instincts. Given Jesus by Pilate, Herod
merely mocks Jesus and sends him back to Pilate (23:6-12).

16. In Matthew's gospel, these words appear after Jesus has already arrived in Jerusalem (23:37-39), whereas Luke's positioning of the lament at the journey's center-point, long
before Jerusalem is reached, marks what is absolutely crucial for Luke's perspective, the
clash between the Jerusalem establishment and God's Way.

17. 13:33.

ing the fate of Jesus in Jerusalem directly to that of other prophets — included only by Luke[18] — suggest a death whose meaning is to be understood as the sure fate[19] of all God's word-bearers in confronting normal powers.

For Luke, the death of Jesus takes on meaning through its participation in the inexorable necessity — divinely controlled but humanly motivated — that all of God's word-bearers be murdered in Jerusalem. According to Luke, Jesus himself understands his death in terms of precedent in Israel's history: "it is impossible for a prophet to be killed outside of Jerusalem." By gospel's end, this understanding is declared by Jesus himself as that to which apostles are to bear witness[20] — which they do, as we will see in Acts. This particular perspective is critical within Luke's two-volume narrative insofar as the followers of God's Way in Acts must expect the same suffering and even possible death for bearing God's word as taught by Jesus. They too will bear the consequences of others' sin, not escape them. They too will bear a cross rather than be saved by the cross.[21] Luke's vision throughout emphasizes the grace of God's forgiveness for such radical repenting of all things normal. Jesus becomes part of the long line of prophets in facing death, in Jerusalem; but he is distinguished from all other prophets by both the definitive clarity — the "light"[22] — of his scriptural interpretation and by his being raised from death by God.

In response to this light, Jerusalem kills Jesus. But Jerusalem (or at least part of it) will come to embrace Jesus in the first part of Acts, welcoming "the one who comes in the name of the Lord."[23] Meanwhile, Jesus

18. The direct linkage of the fate of Jesus with that of the prophets ("I must be on my way to Jerusalem, because it is impossible for a prophet to be killed outside of Jerusalem") is missing from Matthew's version — which Matthew places after the entry into Jerusalem, as noted (23:37).

19. 24:26. Mark Reasoner, in "The Theme of Acts: Institutional History or Divine Necessity in History?" claims that "Luke seeks to demonstrate that his story in Luke-Acts is reliable by narrating the particulars in his story as a composite fulfillment of divine necessity." This is an oversimplification of the story. Reasoner goes on, "Luke 2:34 remains programmatic for Acts, since the divine necessity associated with Jesus concerns Israel first: 'This one is appointed for the fall and rise of many in Israel.' This explains why the narrative template of proclamation to Jews and their response is so pervasive in Acts" (6:41). Certainly Luke uses something like a "narrative template," but divine necessity offers both too much and too little of what constitutes that template. *Journal of Biblical Literature* 118, no. 4 (1999): 637.

20. Lk 24:46-47.

21. Our exploration of Acts will help to clarify the meaning, for Luke, of Jesus' death.

22. Lk 1:79, for example, and 2:32.

23. 13:35; it is possible, though not likely, that Luke intends these words to be fulfilled

declares, "I desired to gather your children together as a hen gathers her brood under her wings, and you were not willing." The old-guard leadership — Paul is among the notable exceptions — will remain unwilling. Simeon has looked forward to "the consolation of Israel,"[24] but what shall God do with that portion of the many who are falling within Israel, the chicks who are not willing? They will be "rooted out of the people."[25] Here at the journey's center-point, all is lament concerning Jerusalem — a sorrow that will be echoed, at journey's end, with Jesus weeping over the city and its failure to recognize "the things that make for peace."[26]

Bull's-Eye: A Picture of God's Kingdom Fulfilled, and the Needed Striving for Entrance (13:22-30)

The kingdom of God provides refuge and protection for its citizens, "birds of the air [making] nests in its branches"; in contrast, unfaithful Israel — the murderous aspect of Jerusalem — creates an environment whose children are left unprotected and finally destroyed.[27] "First" in terms of power and covenantal precedence, those who kill the word-bearers will be "last" in experiencing anything like real peace, for themselves and for their children.[28]

God's kingdom is a simple affair of providing lodging for birds and food for the hungry, but such simplicity is not easy to achieve, a point made clear in the scene Luke places at the very heart of the chiasmus. The kingdom is a reality for which one must strive.

"Lord, will only a few be saved?"[29] Jesus answers strangely: "Strive to enter through the narrow door [of the kingdom]."[30] Jesus is not interested in numbers, in "how many or few," but in "how." Specifically, how

---

in the soon-arrival of Jesus in Jerusalem, when a crowd of disciples (not these in 13:35) utter similar words (19:38). What possible other thing God might do for Israel as a nation than what we see played out in Acts, the story leaves purposefully vague — in words, for example, like those ending the journey's center-point: "you will not see me," says Jesus to those refusing him in Jerusalem, "until the time comes when you say, 'Blessed is the one who comes in the name of the Lord'" (13:35).

24. 2:25.
25. Acts 3:23.
26. 19:41-44.
27. 13:19; 13:34; 19:44.
28. 19:42.
29. 13:23.
30. 13:24.

will *you* be saved? A basic aspect of how-to-be-saved is caught in the word "strive," as in "strive to enter" God's kingdom.

God's covenant with Israel, as has always been the case, requires proper response from Israel.[31] And yet, have not the early poems talked of God's promised deliverance of Israel, the "consolation of Israel"?[32] Are some within Israel *not* to be consoled? There must be striving, not complacency based on a presumption of covenantal privilege. The many who are "rising" within Israel, and therefore consoled, rise within a context of reciprocity between God's initiating activity and human striving; those who are "falling" are those who have not "recognized . . . the things that make for peace" and are therefore unrecognized by God.[33]

Those who strive to enter God's kingdom are at a banquet feast, in the kingdom hall. Luke's frequent use of meal scenes to signify a barrier-breaking intimacy comes to a focused point in this kingdom banquet. "Abraham and Isaac and Jacob and all the prophets" and many more from the four corners of the earth will be there at the kingdom feast.[34] From the world's four corners are assembled those who might not have been expected: "some are last who will be first, and some are first who will be last."[35] There are those born into Israel who are lost, forever outside the kingdom precincts — an important truth to keep in mind as we move through the drama of Israel's salvation in Acts. Those Israelites outside God's kingdom are barred because they have gone normal ways, evil ways.[36] Failure to hear and do the word of God's Way, taught by Jesus, leaves some Israelites crying out, "But we ate and drank with you, [Jesus], and you taught us . . . ."[37] The family of God, however, are only those "who hear the word of God and do it."[38] Here at the bull's-eye center of the journey we find resolved the issue of Israel's status: all depends on how individual Israelites choose. We have been led to expect just this, that many would be rising in Israel while many would be falling.[39] Acts

---

31. My book *Genesis: The Story We Haven't Heard* explores this issue throughout, but especially in the narrative concerning Abraham and Sarah; see especially chapters 5 & 6 (Downers Grove, Ill.: InterVarsity, 2001).

32. Lk 2:25.

33. Lk 2:34; 19:42; 13:25, 27.

34. 13:24-29.

35. 13:30.

36. 13:27.

37. 13:25-26.

38. 8:21.

39. 2:34.

follows through on this expectation, with thousands and thousands of Israelites coming to their Messiah,[40] with others being "rooted out of the people."[41]

The "rooted out" Israelites are shocked at their exclusion from God's kingdom. Perfectly normal in their pursuits and religious in their demeanor, these Jews will be exposed as fraudulent, their inner thoughts rank.[42] However unwittingly, what they took for virtue turns out to be vice.

This heart of the journey, this matter of striving for God's kingdom by hearing and doing the word of God, is the heart also of the entire two-volume story. For both a religious lawyer and a rich ruler, Jesus had pointed to the inheritance of eternal life as contingent on doing the good thing, as defined by God's word: strive to love God — which is to serve God's purposes — and strive to love your neighbor.[43] Hearing and doing require great effort, according to Luke's story. Striving for one's own salvation is simultaneously a striving for others, a salvation that is by its very nature communal — a loving-of-God inextricably linked to a loving-of-one's-neighbor.

The rigor of such striving leads to the inevitable question, which we have already seen: "Who then can be saved?"[44] After all, it is all so counterintuitive, so unthinkable — so impossible. But "what is impossible for mortals is possible for God," Jesus has responded, which is why, from Luke's perspective, prayer looms so strategically throughout his story.[45] Through prayer there is a connection with divine purpose and divine empowerment.[46] Salvation is a gift from God — in Luke's perspective — because when one repents and cries out for mercy, God generously forgives; when one prays for strength, the Holy Spirit is given.[47]

---

40. Acts 2:41; 4:4; 21:20.

41. Acts 3:23.

42. Lk 11:39; 2:35.

43. 10:25; 18:18; as we have seen, the lawyer's question was apparently insincere, albeit the right question — which was asked with good intent by the rich ruler, later on. See Chapter 6.

44. 18:26.

45. 18:27; see Chapter 7.

46. Lk 11:13.

47. 11:13; salvation is a gift because it is God's word of a Way that is counterintuitive; it is a gift that requires the further "grace" of God's Spirit — as we will see — for any hope of doing the word that is heard; being-saved is a gift because forgiveness for doing evil is from a generous God. But the gift requires striving. Paying attention to God's word and the other person — outcasts, enemies — is no easy task, as the journey has made clear. Doing the ap-

Prayer becomes false, beside the point, without the striving required by repentance.[48] Without striving, there is no kingdom entrance. Just as Jerusalem and its kind have not recognized its visitation from God and the things that make for peace, God will not recognize them: "I do not know where you come from; . . . go away."[49] A follower must strive *against* the pull of family ties and religious scruples, *against* a spirit of ownership, *against* judgmentalism, and *against* worry over ordinary securities — all the while striving *for* the sake of blessing toward the diseased and imprisoned, the undesirables and communal outcasts.[50]

Heart of the Journey: A Summary

What special thing does Jesus accomplish, for Luke? Primarily, he teaches the word of God and releases the Spirit of God: a word that demands repentance in its doing, and a Spirit to assist in the required striving. In a keynote address for all of Acts, "Peter said to them [Israelites], 'Repent, and be baptized every one of you in the name of Jesus Christ so that your sins may be forgiven; and you will receive the gift of the Holy Spirit.'"[51] John offered repentance and forgiveness of sins with a baptism of water; Jesus offers the same, but with the Holy Spirit for empowerment.[52] And the point never changes. God's purpose in Jesus is to proclaim and demonstrate "the things that make for peace" — as Peter affirms, in Acts: "You know the message [God] sent to the people of Israel, preaching peace by Jesus Christ."[53]

Jesus proclaims and teaches the same striving for salvation and God's kingdom of peace as John before him and, after him, the apostles, Paul, and other Jewish believers in Acts.[54] The one-sentence requirement for entrance into God's kingdom is the same in Acts as in the gospel: repent and be forgiven — impossible, without striving; impossible, without God's enabling Spirit. The difference between Luke's first and second

---

propriate thing in light of that attention is even more difficult. "Strive," says Jesus here, just as he has been saying all along. Pray for God's strength.

48. 18:11-14.

49. 19:42-44; 13:25-27.

50. 4:18-19.

51. Acts 2:38.

52. Lk 3:16.

53. Lk 19:42; Acts 10:36.

54. Jesus: Luke 5:32; 13:3-5; 15:7; 24:47. Apostles and Paul: Acts 2:38; 3:19; 5:31; 8:22; 11:18; 13:24; 17:30; 19:4; 20:21; 26:20.

volume is an empowering Spirit poured out on all willing flesh after Jesus has departed.[55] God's forgiveness comes "in the name of Jesus Messiah" because it is Jesus who has been God's "holy servant" in his teaching and living out of God's Way.[56]

Just as Jesus is servant to Israel, Israel will be servant to all peoples, in the name of Jesus. The angel has announced to Mary that the son she bears "will reign over the house of Jacob [Israel] forever, and of his kingdom there will be no end."[57] For Luke, the spread of the word concerning this kingdom must begin in Jerusalem, the scene not only of Israel's falling but the scene as well of Israel's initial rising.[58]

The drama ahead as Jesus finally reaches Jerusalem is clear: there are would-be murderers among Israel's old-guard leadership. We need to remember that the clash has been brewing for a long time. In trying to explain the kingdom of God to his fellow Israelites, Jesus had been confronted with early and consistent resistance from the representatives of the house of Israel, its leaders. At one point, "the Pharisees and teachers of the law" have come from every surrounding village and most significantly, from Jerusalem, to see what is happening: "Blasphemies!" they declare, witnessing the forgiveness of sin declared by Jesus to a paralytic just healed.[59] "Strange things!" the common Jewish folks burst out.[60] Jerusalem has sent its leadership, and declares Jesus out-of-bound; his kingdom talk is an affront.

We need to remember too that the gospel began with the infant Jesus in Jerusalem, just as the gospel story ends and Acts begins in Jerusalem.[61] This chiastic center-point is central indeed. Just before the journey to Jerusalem, Jesus had been talking about his departure from Jerusalem with Moses and Elijah.[62] Jesus has traveled to Jerusalem, wept over Jerusalem,

55. Lk 3:16; 11:13; Acts 2:17.
56. Acts 2:38; Acts 4:27, 30.
57. 1:33.
58. Lk 24:47; Acts 1:8.
59. 5:17; 5:21.
60. 5:26.
61. At the end of the gospel, we find the disciples continually in the Jerusalem temple in worship of God (24:53). In the gospel beginning, Zechariah is serving in the Jerusalem temple when the angel comes to him; the eight-day-old Jesus is taken by his parents to the temple for purification rites "according to the law of Moses" (which rites and law of Israel are nowhere in the two-volume story repudiated; rather, they are honored as "the law of the Lord" [2:22; 24]); Jesus is lost in Jerusalem and found in its temple (2:41-51); Jesus is taken by the devil to Jerusalem, to its temple (4:9).
62. 9:31.

will be killed in Jerusalem, will appear alive in Jerusalem to all the disciples, will leave from just outside Jerusalem.[63] And all the while, Jesus is teaching the Way of God's kingdom. With fellow Jews at the end of volume two, Paul will be "testifying to the kingdom of God";[64] in the very last verse of the whole story we hear key echoes, that Paul was "proclaiming the kingdom of God and teaching about the Lord Jesus Christ."[65] The gospel's center-point captures this essential dramatic reality of the story as a whole, this dramatic tension between Israel/Jerusalem and the kingdom — and the need for a rigorous repentance characterized as "striving."

This dramatic tension between kingdom and Jerusalem plays out, especially in Acts, within a narrative context of the striving required of Israel for its deliverance, and within a history of God's attempt to bring blessing to Israel. Saved Israel, servant Israel, will fulfill their ancient covenant with God by bringing the blessing of good news to all peoples, to those "nations of the world that strive" — but "after all [the wrong] things."[66] Many Israelites, and non-Jews through the reaching-out of Israel, will learn a proper striving for entrance to God's kingdom. Such a salvation, as Simeon poeticized, would be "for glory to [God's] people Israel" and "a light for revelation to the Gentiles," a redemption that begins in Jerusalem and spreads to the ends of the earth.[67] When the mustard seed has grown to its fullest maturity, when the pinch of yeast has done its hidden work, "people will come from east and west, from north and south" to rest like birds, peacefully, in a tree's welcoming branches.[68] Striving and entrance; forgiveness and banqueting: a kingdom for Israel, salvation for Jerusalem.

---

63. Lk 24:49-50; in Matthew's account, the resurrection appearance occurs in the environs of Jerusalem for the women, but far outside Jerusalem, up on a mountain in Galilee, for the disciples (Mt 28:16-17).

64. Acts 28:17-23.

65. 28:31; at the center of salvation is "the Lord Jesus Christ" (28:31), about whom Paul is teaching. For Paul and Stephen and the apostles, Jesus has been shown to be the Christ, Messiah, and Lord, by being raised from the dead by God. To believe in Jesus as Lord Christ, then, in Acts, is to embrace the Way Jesus taught, recounted in the gospel. It is this Way that fleshes out the kingdom that God is bringing to Israel. To hear and do the word of this Way is to be delivered — to "be saved" — from one's enemies and their pernicious ways (Lk 21: 12-19), but also from one's own normal but evil ways.

66. Lk 12:30; Acts 3:25.

67. 2:30-32.

68. 13:19, 29.

The journey has reached its true goal, the kingdom of God. This concludes the Way taught by Jesus. He will now be shown striving, in the gospel's third and concluding section,[69] against the resistant leadership within Israel, in Jerusalem. And he will be giving last instructions to his disciples about the striving they must face, a drama that fills the action of Acts.

69. 9:45–24:53; we will explore this portion in Part III, immediately ahead.

PART III

The Way Demonstrated

Luke 19:5–24:53

Chapter 14

Jesus Strives against Israel's Old-Guard Leadership

Luke 19:45–24:53

In this last section of Luke's gospel, the Jewish people finally capitulate — if only momentarily — to their traditional religious leaders. All of this will change, in Acts, but for now the old-guard is successful in asserting their status as "first" while Jesus suffers as "last," ridiculed and killed (his resurrection remains a private affair, for now — among only the closest of friends). The authority of Jesus as teacher of God's word, within Israel, appears undermined; he strives to the death. But at the center-point of the gospel we were reminded not only that the kingdom requires such striving but also that "some are last who will be first, and some are first who will be last.[1]

The initial drama of Luke's passion story is located entirely within the temple. Here we find a two-chapter narrative section that is framed by repeated emphases on the primary role of Jesus in Luke's salvation history and the primary response of the old leadership. Immediately after Jesus begins teaching in the temple, "[the old-guard leaders] did not find anything they could do" to Jesus because the people were "spellbound" by the rabbi's teaching. When Jesus finishes this teaching and leaves the temple, we get to the psychological heart of what matters to the old-guard authority: "they were afraid of the people." Their care is not for Torah or the people. Their concern, rather, is a favorable reaction from those they lead. Their status is threatened.

---

1. 13:24, 30.

When Entering the Temple (19:47-48)	*While Leaving the Temple* (21:37-38; 22:2)
"Every day he was teaching in the temple."	"Every day he was teaching in the temple."
"The chief priests, the scribes, and the leaders of the people kept looking for a way to kill him";	"All the people would get up early in the morning to listen to him in the temple. . . . The chief priests and the scribes were looking for a way to put Jesus to death,"
"but they did not find anything they could do, for all the people were spellbound by what they heard."	"for they were afraid of the people."

At the end of his journey, immediately after weeping over Jerusalem's failure to recognize "the things that make for peace" and "the time of [their] visitation from God," Jesus enters the city, and its temple. "Every day he was teaching in the temple. The chief priests, the scribes, and the leaders of the people kept looking for a way to kill him."[2] They could not "find anything they could do," however, because "all the people were spellbound by what they heard."[3]

While it is unclear what exactly it is these leaders fear from the people,[4] the irony is clear: these "leaders of the people" fear the very people they wish to lead. As the entire story to this point has been suggesting,

2. 19:47.

3. 19:48.

4. Perhaps they are afraid that the people would physically prevent such outrage, or afraid of how the people might react to their putting Jesus to death. Or, more simply — as the sentence suggests — they wanted to kill Jesus *because* (for) they were afraid of the people. As prior references to their desire for currying favor would suggest, they are apparently afraid of losing power over the people. Nowhere in the story, nor here, do we find a suggestion that (a) the leaders are afraid of a mass uprising if they kill Jesus, or (b) that the people's fascination with Jesus will lead to some sort of revolution that would jeopardize their cozy relationship with Rome. Rather, as we have seen, (c) the leaders parade before the people while attacking Jesus, the people's apparent favorite, a situation indicating the power struggle — the popularity-contest mentality — felt by the leaders. See Joel B. Green, who alludes to the two latter possibilities, (b) and (c), in *The Gospel of Luke*, The New International Commentary on the New Testament (Grand Rapids: Eerdmans, 1997), p. 753.

the leaders' opposition to Jesus has been related to a fear of loss: their public standing with the people is threatened. This fear manifests itself as jealousy regarding Jesus and a usurpation of their power, which Acts makes clear.[5] What Jesus has to strive against in this temple scene, and later before the Jewish council and in the council-inspired appearance before Roman authorities, is oriented around this vying for power. "The leaders of the people" seek to assert their authority over the people, and so they challenge the authority of Jesus.

After Israel's leadership attacks the authority of Jesus in the temple, we will see Jesus, still in the temple, teaching his followers about their own coming trials and inherited positions of authority. The traditional authorities then come back onto the dramatic stage, arresting Jesus and bringing him to trial. Their question will be the same: Whose authority, Jesus? Finally, Jesus will be impugned as unrighteous, a plague to the house of Israel and a public nuisance for Rome. As the Jewish scriptures have foretold, Jesus will be murdered — but he will also be raised from suffering and death in a definitive answer to the authority question.

I. Authority against Authority: In the Temple

Before he begins his temple teaching, Jesus has cleared the temple of its merchandising predators. In front of these and everyone in the temple, and on the basis of their mutually shared scripture, Jesus cites the temple's proper function as a "house of prayer," not of commerce.[6] "By what authority are you doing these things?" the chief priest, scribes, and elders protest.[7] Jesus responds with a question: What of John's authority? Did his salvation "come from heaven, or was it of human origin?"[8] They understand the trap: if John's revered authority is questioned, then the people will be after them, but if they declare John's authority to be based in heaven, then Jesus will answer, "Why did you not believe him?"[9]

---

5. Acts 4:17; 13:45; 17:5; even the ancient authorities, the "patriarchs," sought to kill Joseph — the one accompanied by God — because they were "jealous of Joseph" (Acts 7:9).

6. 19:45-46; see Isaiah 56:7; Jeremiah 7:11.

7. 20:2.

8. 20:4.

9. 20:5-6; the teaching of Jesus, as I have been suggesting, is an extension of John's, centering on the same repentance from normal self-aggrandizement and the same forgiveness of such sin. Again: the distinct difference between what John and Jesus offer will come later, with a "baptism" from Jesus that provides empowerment for doing the word of God.

We do not know about John's authority, the leaders answer. And so Jesus refuses to answer them about his own authority.[10] Jesus does not let the leaders slip away without a strong warning, however. His response to verbal attacks does not stop with his artful dodging of the question: he goes on the counter-offensive, implicitly asserting the very authority for himself about which he has declined to comment.

"A man planted a vineyard, and leased it to tenants, and went to another country for a long time."[11] This vineyard owner, Jesus continues, sends back three slaves — one at a time, for appropriate return of proceeds from the vineyard. The tenants, however, send each slave away with beatings and wounds, and nothing for the owner. The landholder resorts to sending his "beloved son," thinking that surely there will be respect for the authority vested in the person of his son. But the son is killed by the tenants — who are then destroyed, in turn, by the owner. "Heaven forbid!" exclaim the leaders, apparently feeling incriminated. "But [Jesus] looked at them and said, what then does this [scripture] text mean?"[12] The "looked at them" note is a gesture an oral audience would recognize as decisive from a good storyteller, a bringing-it-home intensity for this or that person in the audience. (In a narrative moment, Jesus will be shown looking, simply looking, at Peter — who breaks into sobs.)[13] It is at this point, then, that Jesus subtly but powerfully claims his own authority while implicating the leaders' disastrous rejection of the same. Here is the scripture about whose meaning Jesus begs interpretation, looking at them intently: "The stone that the builders rejected has become the cornerstone. Everyone who falls on that stone will be broken to pieces, and it will crush anyone on whom it falls."[14] *Rejecting me is to invite destruction: mine is the authority. I am the cornerstone of whatever house Israel hopes to have.*

The authority issue continues in the following scene, with the presiding "leaders of the people" acknowledging something special about Jesus. The scene provides a succinct summary of what is going on here in the temple between Jesus and his opposition. "Teacher," begin the leaders' spies, "we know that you are right in what you say and teach, and you show deference to no one, but teach the way of God in accordance with truth."[15] All

10. 20:7-8.
11. 20:9.
12. 20:17.
13. 22:61-62.
14. 20:17-18; see Psalm 118:22-23 and Isaiah 8:14-15.
15. 20:21.

that we have seen of Jesus on the journey to Jerusalem is here affirmed, and most notably that he teaches "the Way of God" with authority — "in accordance with the truth."

But they will press the authority question further, by dragging in the question of Rome. Surely Jesus will fail their clever question. "Is it lawful for us to pay taxes to the emperor, or not?" Jesus answers by pointing to the paradox in which a follower of God's Way must live, with split allegiances to two authorities, only one of which can demand ultimate loyalty. "Whose head and whose title does [this coin] bear?" asks Jesus. "The emperor's," they answer. "Give to the emperor the things that are the emperor's, [but] to God the things that are God's." At the point of hopeless conflict, as we will see in Acts, God's demands must always trump those of any earthly authority. "And they were not able in the presence of the people to trap [Jesus]," who had just a moment ago successfully "trapped" the bosses of these spies, with a fictional tale.[16]

The authority-attack mounts. Some Sadducees, who don't believe in resurrection, try to expose Jesus by posing a nonsense question about legalities of marriage in heaven, a question Jesus sidesteps by proving the resurrection from their own scripture.[17] Again Luke accomplishes two important things in one scene: (1) the possibility of resurrection is asserted because Jesus' resurrection will be God's answer in establishing his authority as teacher; (2) the Sadducees' opposition to Jesus appears more foolish than they could have ever dreamed of making Jesus look. "Some of the scribes" — who also believed in the resurrection — respond, in front of the Sadducees, "Teacher, you have spoken well." All of these leaders, scribe and Sadducee, seem defeated, or at least deflated: "they no longer dared to ask him another question."[18]

The leaders fade from the temple scene, only to reappear soon with sinister maneuvering toward a more tangible entrapment of Jesus. Meanwhile, "he said to them [the people and disciples], 'How can they say that the Messiah is David's son?'" With an interpretation of a passage from the Psalms, Jesus shows that the Messiah of scripture cannot be merely the son of David, but "Lord" — God — as well (20:41-44). That Jesus

16. 20:20-26.

17. 20:27-38. They ask about who would be married to whom "in the resurrection," posing a hypothetical situation in which seven childless brothers succeed each other in death, each having had the same wife.

18. 20:40.

thinks of himself as God's anointed one, the Messiah, is clear from the start of the story, in spite of there being no explicit acknowledgment on his part.[19] Attack and counterattack: Luke is establishing a clarity about Jesus' use of native wit along with his profound grasp of Scripture, capacities of Jesus and of later followers that will be among the many parallels between the gospel and Acts. Still within the temple, Jesus teaches the disciples and all other listeners. We return to this in a moment.

II. Authority against Authority: Trial and Murder

After the temple section, and further teaching of the disciples, Luke takes up the second phase of attack by Israel's old-guard leadership, a more frontal attack. Presuming the guilt of Jesus, the religious authorities come to arrest their fellow Israelite, who has been praying with his small band of followers about "the time of trial." We hear an echo back to the wilderness testing by Satan, a testing that carries with it a connotation of demonic activity and "the power of darkness."[20] We should recall that "when the devil had finished every test, he departed from [Jesus] until an opportune time."[21] Here, Satan has already "entered into Judas," and Judas now leads a crowd of authorities to Jesus.[22] The final assault is under way.

Anticipating a signal of intimacy from the betrayer, Jesus asks a question that exposes both ultimate hypocrisy (a theme of Luke's) and ultimate authority: "Judas, is it with a kiss that you are betraying the Son of Man?"[23] This self-reference to the authoritative role of "Son of Man"[24] echoes the question of authority, in the temple. What plays out

19. 4:17-19.
20. 22:40, 46; 22:53.
21. 4:13.
22. 22:3.
23. 22:48; "[Judas] approached Jesus to kiss him," at which point Jesus asks his question. Matthew and Mark have Judas clearly kissing Jesus — and do not have Jesus' self-referral as "Son of Man." Luke is intent on the authority question, and on the capacity of the authoritative "Son of Man" to anticipate matters even in so minute an instance as an intended kiss of betrayal.

24. Scholars are not sure what this self-reference means, other than its obvious insistence on the son's humanity, and some sort of authority — as suggested, perhaps, by a reference from the scripture:

> As I watched in the night visions,
>   I saw one like a human being [son of man]

in Jesus' final striving against these leaders is a particular form of innocence that is simultaneously the righteousness of Isaiah's suffering servant, an ideal Luke draws on.[25] This servant of God suffers "a perversion of justice" as the innocent one, "the righteous one."[26] Innocence and righteousness can be apparent or real, a public face or a genuine disposition. Judas comes with a kiss, a pretend-token of regard that mimics innocence. In service of Satan, the wicked community of unrighteous authority, and his own greedy self-serving, Judas turns back from having turned around toward God's Way of true innocence and righteousness.

The possibilities of authority and power are on full display. One of the followers swings his sword against the high priest's slave, but catches only an ear: "No more of this!" exclaims Jesus, who then heals the ear of his enemy.[27] Only Luke of the four gospel writers mentions the power of healing at this point. The reattached ear provides a pointed contrast in power and authority between God's Way and ordinary ways. Far from sentimentalizing the picture, or making it more melodramatic, the effect of this reattached ear brings into the foreground the very essence of what Luke has been trying to establish as the Way taught by Jesus: do good for others, even to enemies — and without thanks.

"This is your hour," Jesus says to the religious authorities, "and the power of darkness."[28] With Satan himself in league with the desires of jealous leaders, these authorities possess real power, indeed. They are able to effect the death of Jesus, Son of Man. Jesus dies because of a

---

          coming with the clouds of heaven.
       And he came to the Ancient One [God]
          and was presented before him.
    To him [the son of man] was given dominion
         and glory and kingship,
       that all peoples, nations, and languages
         should serve him.
       His dominion is an everlasting dominion
         that shall not pass away,
       and his kingship is one
         that shall never be destroyed. (Daniel 7:13-14)

25. Explicitly, in the reading by an African diplomat of scripture, explained by Philip — the passage from Isaiah remarkably leaves out any reference to Isaiah's note on this suffering as a covering for sins (Acts 8:32–33, referring to Isaiah 53:7-8).

26. Is 53:8, 11.

27. 22:51.

28. 22:51, 53.

power struggle whose origins and scope Luke sees as cosmic: God and followers of the Way against Satan, the powers of this world, and ordinary folk engaging in normal behaviors when the chips are down. For Luke, the most important fact and perspective regarding the death of Jesus — its "meaning" — is in this: he was killed, as word-bearers before him.[29]

Power dealing with power, authority with authority: those in charge of Jesus for the evening blindfold and taunt him, "heaping many other insults on him."[30] At their council the next morning, the religious authorities say, "If you are the Messiah, tell us."[31] Jesus, stating their refusal to believe and unwillingness to answer *his* questions,[32] refers to himself once again as the "Son of Man," who "will be seated at the right hand of the power of God."[33] Power. Authority. Asked if he is, then, "the Son of God," Jesus replies, "You say that I am."[34] That is, they have explicitly acknowledged an awareness of what the good listener already knows to be the case.[35]

Questions regarding authority crescendo as the assembly of religious leaders take Jesus to Pilate, Roman procurator of Judea. They suggest that Jesus is usurping the authority of Rome and subverting the Jewish nation by recommending not paying tax to Rome.[36] This, in spite of what they have just heard Jesus say concerning the appropriateness of paying the tax.[37] And another authority issue: Jesus claims to be Messiah, they say, the king of the Jews (he hasn't explicitly made either claim); and "he stirs up the people by teaching throughout Judea from Galilee where he began . . . ."[38] To Pilate's question, "Are you the king of the Jews?" Jesus answers as he had the religious leaders: "You say so."[39] Pilate claims to find no basis for "an accusation against this man," and refers Jesus to

29. Jesus will be distinguished from the prophets as the word-bearer, Messiah, by God's raising him from the dead.

30. 22:65.

31. 22:67.

32. The authority question regarding John the Baptist, for example (20:3-8).

33. 22:69.

34. 22:70.

35. 1:35; 9:35.

36. 23:2.

37. 20:25.

38. 23:5; Galilee was considered a hotbed of revolutionary activities against the established authorities.

39. 23:3.

Herod, since Jesus began in Galilee and Herod is the Roman tetrarch of Galilee.[40]

Herod is happy, since he "was hoping to see him perform some sign" — just as Herod's curiosity had already been roused concerning Jesus.[41] In a chillingly cavalier manner, Herod had mused, "John I beheaded; but who is this about whom I hear such things?"[42] The detail regarding such normalcy is deft: authority loves to witness exhibitions of power. As we have seen in the journey to Jerusalem, such hankering after signs — of magic-as-power — is a very bad thing.[43] Jesus doesn't answer any of Herod's frivolous self-entertaining foolishness, and so Herod sends him back to Pilate in a mock-royal robe.[44] Meanwhile, the Jewish leaders had "stood by, vehemently accusing [Jesus]."[45]

"That same day Herod and Pilate became friends with each other; before this they had been enemies."[46] The political powers unite in their common problem: what to do with this Jewish nuisance? The two political leaders representing Rome face the ire of Israel's religious leaders, for whom they are responsible.

Pilate cooperates with the leaders as little the second time as the first, but finally these leaders of Israel succeed by winning over "the people." The narrative has not prepared us for this shocking turn of events, since we have just seen Jesus favored by the people while feared by the traditional leadership because of this public favor. The story acknowledges this corporate failure, while rushing on to note public remorse and, at the very beginning of Acts, a wholesale repentance by thousands upon thousands in Israel. For this disastrous moment, the leaders cajole the Jewish people, and together they refuse Pilate's desire to release Jesus. The Roman procurator has a mob scene on his hands. But Jesus is innocent, Pilate insists: "I have examined him in your presence and have not found this man guilty of any of your charges against him."[47] The people and leaders clamor, "Away with this fellow! . . . Crucify, crucify him!"[48] They

---

40. 23:6-7; the "Herod" who is king of Judea, in 1:5, is the father of this Herod, tetrarch of Galilee (3:1).

41. 23:8.

42. 9:9.

43. 11:16, 29; echo, 17:20-21. See Chapter 9.

44. 23:11.

45. 23:10.

46. 23:12.

47. 23:14.

48. 23:18-21.

go so far as demanding Jesus' death in exchange for the release of an insurrectionist and murderer; Pilate finally agrees.[49] Jesus is led to his execution.

Where, now, are the people of Israel in the plan of God? Where, now, are Israel's salvation and deliverance, testified to in the gospel's early poems? For the briefest of moments Luke allows the Jewish populace to side with the wrong authority, though signs of recovery by the people are almost immediate. Israel *will* be delivered![50]

Among "the people" of Israel some women follow Jesus to the death-site "beating their breasts and wailing for him."[51] A bit later, "the crowds who had gathered there for the [crucifixion] spectacle . . . returned home, beating their breasts."[52] Some among Israel come to their godly senses very soon.

As Jesus hangs from the cross, the nature of beneficent authority is clearly highlighted. The question of authority and loyalty is encapsulated in a scene of two criminals on either side of the dying Jesus. It is a divide that carries over into Acts, with thousands of Israelites becoming redeemed while others fall. As here, the issue that gets played out in Acts is a power struggle involving the embrace of Jesus as Israel's final authority and bearer of God's word.

Among the taunts uttered by the leaders and echoed by the soldiers is the jeering and "temptation" proffered by one of the criminals:

- "He saved others; let him save himself if he is the Messiah of God, his chosen one!"[53] (Leaders)
- "If you are the King of the Jews, save yourself!"[54] (Soldiers)
- "Are you not the Messiah? Save yourself and us!"[55] (Criminal)

The pattern of similar taunts goes to the heart of what Luke has been emphasizing about God's Way, about Jesus, and about striving for salvation that followers also must learn. Interwoven with the taunt is a temptation

49. 23:24-25.
50. There is great scholarly confusion on this issue, which I address in my chapters on Acts, and in the Conclusion.
51. 23:27.
52. 23:48.
53. 23:35.
54. 23:36-37.
55. 23:39.

that reflects the heart of all trial, of that which Jesus has been telling his disciples to pray to avoid:[56]

> Now at the end, hanging on the cross, his life ebbing away, the same question [put to him by Satan in the wilderness] is raised again: "Will you use the divine power with which you are endowed for self-preservation?" The final attachment in this world to which one is tempted to cling in an idolatrous way is life itself, mere continuance of physical existence: *"If you are the Christ, the king, save yourself."*[57]

The community's religious and political/military powers have aligned themselves with society's criminal element, Barabbas, and ultimately with Satan, succumbing to the normal uses of power and authority.

There are two ways to live life, Luke is hammering home: one leads to salvation, the other, to destruction. Only Luke among the gospel writers fully draws out the cross scene with Jesus and the criminals. After the one "kept deriding [Jesus]" with taunts and challenges to save himself, and them, his fellow criminal offers a sharp rebuke, based on what he assumes is the obvious innocence of Jesus.[58] "Do you not fear God?" asks the second criminal; "we indeed have been condemned justly, for we are getting what we deserve for our deeds, but this man has done nothing wrong."[59] The second criminal then turns to the Righteous One: "Jesus, remember me when you come into your kingdom" — and is granted his request.[60] This criminal is promised the garden of Paradise[61] because:

- he fears God,
- he recognizes his wrong-doing,
- he asks for mercy.

Since John the Baptist, this has been the path of salvation. It will not change in Acts, except for the empowering Spirit.

---

56. 11:4; 22:40, 46.

57. Charles H. Talbert, *Reading Luke: A Literary and Theological Commentary on the Third Gospel* (New York: Crossroad, 1982), p. 220.

58. 23:39-41.

59. 23:40-41.

60. 23:42-43.

61. Perfect garden, possibly a holding-place of the righteous dead.

The Striving of Jesus: A Summary

Jesus dies, in part, because he offends mightily those in positions of power by teaching and going the Way of God. The meaningfulness of Jesus' death lies in this, that as "last" — dying an ignominious death, as a criminal — Jesus becomes "first." Again, we are the center of the gospel, its heart — the center-point of the journey: *strive*, we are told, for "some are last who will be first, and some are first who will be last."[62] Jesus strives to the death, which is not the journey's end after all. Jesus is moving on. He will be vindicated in resurrection, attested by God as Israel's authoritative teacher of righteousness.

It is one of the presumed oppressors, a Roman, who initially penetrates to the truth about Jesus on the question of innocence. Whereas in two other gospels a Roman centurion declares that "Truly this man was the Son of God,"[63] Luke's Roman centurion exclaims that "certainly this man was innocent."[64] Luke's perspective demands a different emphasis at this point. Innocence and true righteousness characterize a new kind of authority in a new kind of communal experience — the kingdom of God coming to earth. This righteousness[65] is positioned by Luke as a last and definitive word on the dying of Jesus. All that has preceded this word has built up to the "answer," given by the centurion.

After all the legal posturing by both religious and civil authorities — with no verdict of guilty — Jesus has been put to death, as will be the case for other followers of the Way. For Jesus and for other followers, however, the journey of God's Way does not end in death. A fundamental reversal of the many reversals in this story is the exaltation of Jesus as "first," after he has had to suffer as "last." And so we have heard at the gospel's center-point: "Some are last who will be first, and some are first who will be last."[66] As for Jesus, so for others who would strive to follow God's Way, in Acts.

The reversal of first-and-last is not merely a happy-ever-after ending to the story of Jesus, however. What is at stake for this grand rever-

---

62. 13:24, 30; see Chapter 13.

63. Matthew 27:54; Mark 15:39; Matthew has no "man" in the sentence.

64. 23:47.

65. Immediately following, we find "a good and righteous man named Joseph" preparing the body of Jesus before placing it in a tomb (23:50-53). Matthew and Mark both note this Joseph and his actions, but without the telling description of him as "a good and righteous man" (Mt 27:57-60; Mk 15:43-46).

66. 13:30; Chapter 13.

sal is the question of authority. Who bears God's word? Who will emerge with the "authorized" version of Torah? Who will receive God's imprimatur, the divine seal of approval — and how can characters within the story, and in Luke's audience, decades after Jesus has departed, be able to tell for sure? These are among the questions raised by this entire last section of the gospel and answered in Acts, Luke's concluding volume to his story. At the gospel's center-point we saw the implicit tension between the kingdom-authority as proclaimed by Jesus and a Jerusalem-authority distinguished by leaders who have always killed the word-bearer.[67]

The question of authority has serious consequences, since it is about whose version of God's word should be listened to, and done — toward the matter of being saved, or not, of being among the many in Israel "rising" or "falling."[68] Whose teaching will be embraced, and on what grounds?

For Luke, salvation is grounded in the resurrection, the stamp of divine approval on Jesus as Israel's Messiah. Jesus is departing, however, and leaving behind followers who need to get it straight about the Way they will proclaim and teach. In his gospel's last section, Luke provides a telescoped version of what Jesus has been teaching the disciples all along. The Way requires striving. The striving proves altogether too difficult for one follower, while all the disciples — led by Peter — betray Jesus, if only for a time. They must learn about why Jesus must die, as this suffering and death is what they themselves are being called to. By the end of the gospel, we see that they understand — an understanding that is embodied by action in Luke's volume two, the book of Acts.

---

67. 13:18-20; 13:31-35.
68. 13:23-30; 2:34.

Chapter 15

You Must Strive:
Jesus Challenges Followers

Luke 19:45–24:53

The confrontations between Jesus and religious leaders in the temple are harsher than anything encountered on the journey to Jerusalem. Before his death, Jesus offers his disciples final words. They, too, will have to strive mightily in the face of the same kind of opposition. Luke channels all of the conversation about "last days" into one simple point made by Jesus: "Be on guard" and "be alert." The personal stakes are high — a salvation that allows them to "stand before the Son of Man."[1] Only "by your endurance," Jesus adds, "will you gain your souls."[2] In a last meal together, Jesus points to the difficult end of his own striving and the need of disciples to share the same. On a mountain, Jesus explains that such "time of trial" cannot be successfully endured without the gift of God's strength. Then, after his resurrection, he offers a last-words speech that outlines the two things to which they must bear witness. All of this we see played out in Acts — but not until the disciples have received the promised empowerment, by the Holy Spirit for whom they are to wait, in Jerusalem.

In the gospel's last section, 19:45–24:53, Luke has a double focus. We have just seen the first: final confrontations with Israel's traditional leadership that leads to their murder of Jesus. The second focus is on the new leadership that will rule over Israel, a story that will be continued in Acts. Jesus is shown highlighting the idea of *striving* — which the disciples fail to do. They choose to disassociate themselves from their teacher's impending death. They must learn — and they do learn, in

---

1. 21:34-36.
2. 21:12-19.

Acts — to reverse this kind of ordinary choosing, this thoroughly normal clutching to life. They must un-choose such normalcy; they must repent. Stephen and James shed their blood (recounted in Acts) as a consequence of such radical repenting. Jesus is shown emphasizing the challenge of such striving to his disciples in three successive settings, in each of which the details of challenge escalate: (1) the temple, where he teaches about future catastrophe (the old-guard leadership has drifted away from the temple by this point); (2) at a final meal with only his closest followers; (3) finally, in the most intimate of settings, praying together on a mountain (just before the traditional leadership break in and arrest him).

Three Teachings on Striving

(1) Temple Teaching: "Last Days" and Striving

Only Luke's account locates the teaching about the "last days"[3] in the temple. Mark's gospel and especially Matthew's situate much more of Jesus' teaching after the entry of Jesus into Jerusalem than does Luke, but they set less of that teaching in the temple. Luke's focus on Jerusalem and its temple — and "being saved" — will be extremely important in volume two.

The leaders have faded from the temple scene, but the followers and "all the people" remain in the temple to hear alarming words about difficult days ahead, words that indicate that "the kingdom of God is near."[4] "When some were speaking about the temple, how it was adorned with beautiful stones and gifts dedicated to God," Jesus responds by turning everyone's attention to the near future, beginning with the destruction of this very temple.[5] The days are coming when none of these temple stones will be left standing, Jesus says. The temple will be razed and synagogues will turn hostile to fellow Jews who follow the Way, but "my words," Je-

---

3. Luke's gospel downplays both the signs and the timetable of these "last days" compared to other gospel accounts. In fact, in this temple teaching, there is no reference to any such term as "last days." The closest is "days of vengeance" (21:22).

4. 21:31; see 20:45 for "all the people" — an indication of just how important "the people" are in this story, since they have been at least implicitly contrasted, for the better, with their religious leaders.

5. 21:5-6.

sus adds, "will not pass away."[6] And Israel — the faithful, servant Israel — will be saved.

Not only will the temple be destroyed: there will be "wars and insurrections" and natural disasters as well. "But the end will not follow immediately."[7] Luke leaves the issue of the last days — the precise answer to when and where — relatively vague and open-ended.[8] The point of the end-times horror, however, is as clear as the details about "last days" are vague: pray for strength, in order to "stand before the Son of Man" (a phrase not found in the accounts by Matthew or Mark):

> "*Be on guard* so that your hearts are not weighed down with dissipation and drunkenness and the worries of this life, and that day catch you unexpectedly, like a trap. For it will come upon all who live on the face of the whole earth. Be alert at all times, praying that you may have the strength to escape all these things that will take place, and *to stand before the Son of Man*." (21:34-36, emphasis mine)[9]

As we saw on the journey to Jerusalem, the ordinary "worries of this life," echoed here, can "catch you unexpectedly, like a trap." These "worries" include not only survival needs, but status-needs as well. The answer to such seductive anxiety is to "be alert," and to pray. Pray, because there is no salvation without God's help. In Acts, Luke continues this emphasis on prayer, but stresses the "answer" to such prayer: grace[10] and power from God, through the Holy Spirit sent by the resurrected and glorified Jesus.

---

6. 21:6, 12; 21:33.

7. 21:9.

8. This was the case on the journey to Jerusalem, with its emphasis on not paying attention to externals, to "signs." Such purposeful ambiguity fits the story's general insistence that it's not externals that are needed — signs of the times, final determinations of "consolation" — as much as thoroughgoing interior renewal, and the translation of a right attitude into a doing of the right thing. Commentators take differing views of the extent to which there is a delayed parousia in Luke's account, compared to other New Testament writers like Mark and Paul who often seem to presume an early return of Jesus. In Acts 3:20-21 we will hear that Jesus won't return until the fulfillment of "the universal restoration."

9. Mark 4:19 mentions "the cares of this world," in the context of a sower parable; Mark has the plea for alertness, though not the consequence of standing before the Son of Man.

10. "Grace" (*charis*, translated "favor" in Luke's gospel but "grace" in Acts) is usually linked with the "power" unleashed by the Holy Spirit given by God. See Acts 4:33; 6:8; 14:3. Having established the linkage between grace and power in these verses, Luke can expect the audience to continue such an understanding when Paul mentions "grace" (never in connection with a sacrificial atonement): Acts 18:27; 20:24; 20:32.

The disturbances of these troubling times, then, are an occasion for endurance, not for prognostications; for guarding one's own heart, not for guiding others into esoteric truths.[11] Such difficult times require prayer for one's strength, not pointing to magic "escape" possibilities. Prayer, as we saw in the repeated theme on the journey, is essential, not peripheral.[12]

What Luke thinks is most important about the "last days" talk is indicated in the shift from far-off to near-at-hand, from international chaos to personal persecution.[13] What lies immediately ahead for these followers is what the text emphasizes: the predicted suffering of the followers — which parallels the already-predicted persecution of Jesus that we have just heard about in the story of the vineyard owner's son, who was murdered.[14] It is important for the followers — and Luke's audience — to gain a clear view of the persecution and murder of Jesus in order to better consider the meaning of their own persecution and possible martyrdom. "They will arrest you and persecute you," Jesus warns; "they will hand you over to synagogues and prisons, and you will be brought before kings and governors because of my name" — all of which comes true for Jesus in the gospel and for other followers in Acts.[15]

The teaching of Jesus about the last days, in Luke's account, comes down to one important point: the need to endure, to be alert, to keep striving. The culmination of the end times, when people "will see the Son of Man coming in a cloud with power and great glory," is not something to be discovered by religious specialists and spiritual leaders: the "signs" of utter havoc, as underscored in the journey, will be obvious enough for all people to see.[16] Rather, it is "by endurance you will gain your souls."[17]

11. 21:19; 21:34-36.

12. 11:1-13; 18:1-14. See Chapter 7.

13. 21:9-11, shifting to 21:12-19.

14. 21:12-19; 20:9-16; the audience has heard of such suffering before the arrival of Jesus in Jerusalem (9:21-22; 9:44-45; 18:31-33).

15. 21:12. How salvation plays itself out in this scenario of suffering is chronicled in Acts: it will take, indeed, the endurance Jesus here urges. It will always be the case, for Luke, that participants in the work of God's kingdom will have to be striving for entry to that kingdom, as volume one insists. That is, they will have to reorient their lives toward the blessing of others by letting go of self-promoting attitudes and actions — a daily carrying of their cross (9:23; 14:27).

16. 21:27; 21:25.

17. 21:19. There are variations on the theme: "Be alert at all times, praying that you may have the strength to escape all these things that will take place, and to *stand before the Son of Man*" (21:36); for entrance to the kingdom, "*Strive to enter*" (journey, 13:24); for

After telling the rich ruler that he must sell all in order to gain eternal life, Jesus adds this: "There is no one who has left house or wife or brothers or parents or children, for the sake of the kingdom of God, who will not get back very much more in this age, and in the age to come, eternal life."[18] That is, relinquish all, and "get back . . . eternal life."[19] Endure so that you may gain your souls; ask for strength that you may strive — and stand before the Son of Man. Luke's focus on the "last days" is brilliantly clear, and gathers into itself what Jesus has already taught about the Way.

(2) *Meal Teaching: Striving to the Death*

Striving has a cosmic context. No less than the devil is behind the "worries of this life," the ordinary ways of self-protection and self-promotion. "Satan entered into Judas" is a somber note that helps Luke make the transition from Jesus teaching in the temple to Jesus eating his last meal with his students, his disciples.[20] Stymied to this point in seeking the death of Jesus, the Jerusalem leaders, it turns out, have powerful allies both in Satan and in Judas.[21]

The meal is Passover, a celebration of the deliverance of Israel from suffering and oppression — God's accomplishment, through Moses. This is what Jesus has been describing as God's goal: a spread of the kingdom's "good news," a deliverance from various imprisonments and the oppression of disease.[22] The meal here anticipates a deliverance to be accomplished by Jesus.[23] Luke emphasizes the eagerness of Jesus to eat this meal which commemorates suffering and deliverance past and present: "I have eagerly desired ['desired with great desiring'] to eat this Passover with you before I suffer; for I tell you, I will not eat it until it is fulfilled in the kingdom of God."[24]

More than the other gospel writers, Luke emphasizes the parallels between Moses and Jesus: essentially, each serves God in delivering

---

"eternal life," "*Do this, and you will live*" (journey, 10:28); for "eternal life," "*Sell all that you own* . . ." (journey, 18:22).

18. 18:30.
19. 18:29-30.
20. 22:3.
21. 22:2.
22. 4:18-19.
23. 22:15.
24. 22:15-16.

God's people, and each is involved with a significant departure.[25] The Passover meal means deliverance, but departure as well — all wrapped up in a new *exodus*. Like the old exit from Egypt, the new exodus is both a departure (Jesus departs for his Father) and a deliverance of the people. Like the deliverer Moses, then, who suffered much, Jesus is delivering God's people, acting as God's servant who suffers much.[26]

The Passover meal traditionally had various cups of wine with specific meanings for each cup, along with the unleavened bread. In continuity with Israel's past history, which we have come to expect in this story, Luke's account shows Jesus sharing the exodus/deliverance celebration with followers who will take center stage — as leaders of the twelve tribes of Israel! — for whatever new thing God is accomplishing through Jesus the Messiah:[27]

> Then he took a cup, and after giving thanks he said, "Take this and divide it among yourselves; for I tell you that from now on I will not drink of the fruit of the vine until the kingdom of God comes." Then he took a loaf of bread, and when he had given thanks, he broke it and gave it to them, saying, "This is my body. But see, the one who betrays me is with me, and his hand is on the table. For the Son of Man is going as it has been determined, but woe to that one by whom he is betrayed!" (22:17-22)[28]

25. See the speech of Stephen, and especially Acts 7:37: "This is the Moses who said to the Israelites, 'God will raise up a prophet for you from your own people as he raised me up.'" This connection is thoroughly explored by scholars David Moessner (*Lord of the Banquet: The Literary and Theological Significance of the Lukan Travel Narrative* [Minneapolis: Fortress, 1989; paperback edition, Harrisburg, Pa.: Trinity Press International, 1998]) and John Drury (*Tradition and Design in Luke's Gospel: A Study in Early Christian Historiography* [London: Darton, Longman and Todd, 1976]). They document the parallels between Moses and Jesus, including the echoing of themes between the journey of Jesus to Jerusalem and the journey of the Israelites, under Moses, in the wilderness.

26. Acts 4:27, 30.

27. 22:30.

28. There is also a longer manuscript version that includes these words (after "This is my body"): "'. . . *which is given for you. Do this in remembrance of me.' And he did the same with the cup after supper, saying, 'This cup that is poured out for you is the new covenant in my blood'*" (22:19b-20). Luke's exact words regarding the meal are subject for much scholarly debate, since there is manuscript evidence for two differing versions. These are key words around which the earliest liturgy of the church was based. Scribes who were making their copies of Luke's earliest version, whatever that might have been, would want to add (or subtract), based on their well-intentioned desire to bring Luke's version into closer conformity with this or that other account. There was no "Bible" consisting of gospels and epistles, of course,

It is a difficult cup, so bitter that Jesus will ask his Father to have it removed.[29] On the other hand, this cup is a gathering together of Passover's four cups, which "in effect, [offers] 'toasts' to God"[30] and to God's power of deliverance — "when the kingdom of God comes," as Jesus promises here.

"Divide [the cup] among yourselves": the deliverance of Israel[31] is to be provided through servants who share the suffering of their Teacher. They do, as Acts will demonstrate.

After the cup, Jesus took the bread of Passover and "broke it, and gave it to them." Followers are "renewed as one body through participation in the one loaf, which is the body of Christ, [signifying] the incorporation of the disciples into the 'person' of Jesus. . . . In Jewish thought, that would involve what he does or is about to do."[32] Such participation in what Jesus "does or is about to do" is what the story has been suggesting, especially in the journey to Jerusalem. Such a view

---

so copyists relying on oral tradition and the existing manuscript copies would see themselves as clarifying rather than tampering. The integrity of the two-volume story as a unified whole, which bypasses a sacrifice-for-sins view, suggests, I think, the authenticity of the shorter version, which recent study supports. See, for example, Mark A. Matson, *In Dialogue with Another Gospel? The Influence of the Fourth Gospel on the Passion Narrative of the Gospel of Luke* (Atlanta: Society of Biblical Literature, 2001), pp. 182-83. See also, Bart Ehrman, *The Orthodox Corruption of Scripture* (New York: Oxford University Press, 1993), p. 200.

In a very careful examination of the longer version, Charles Talbert notes that even here the blood and the bread "should not be understood in terms of an atoning sacrifice." He concludes, "Since the dominant thrust of Luke's understanding of Jesus' death is that of martyrdom, it seems preferable to understand the language here [in the longer version] in those terms as well." *Reading Luke: A Literary and Theological Commentary on the Third Gospel* (New York: Crossroad, 1982), p. 209. An even more obvious linkage of blood and covenant are the two instances of Abrahamic covenant: cutting open of animals' flesh and the cutting of circumcision (Gen 15:12-20; 17:2-21). Furthermore, as C. K. Barrett points out, any "shedding of blood [in Acts 20:28] does not (or at least not necessarily) imply the idea of sacrifice [for sins]. Stephen shed his blood (22:20), but his death was not a sacrifice." *The Acts of the Apostles,* vol. 2, International Critical Commentary (Edinburgh: T. & T. Clark, 1998), p. 977.

29. I think the gospel's consistent pattern of echoing suggests at least a strong parallel between Passover cup and the cup of suffering in the prayer of Jesus.

30. Luke Timothy Johnson, *The Gospel of Luke* (Collegeville, Minn.: The Liturgical Press, 1991), p. 342.

31. Luke keeps the gospel focus on Jews and the Torah and the temple; only in Acts, as I have suggested, does he allow the "bottom-line" of the Abrahamic covenant to appear explicitly, that God's purpose in choosing Abraham and the people of Israel is their role in bringing blessing to all peoples of the earth (Acts 3:25).

32. C. F. Evans, *Saint Luke* (Philadelphia: Trinity Press International, 1990), p. 789.

of the meaning role of Jesus' death is in complete harmony with Luke's larger perspective. Luke holds that what is special about Jesus — his salvation role — is his teaching of the Way, as in this scene, and empowerment to go this Way through the Spirit.[33] Jesus "broke" the loaf, as his body will be broken. As Messiah, Jesus is the great deliverer and servant of God, with "servant Israel" led by the twelve, the new rulers of Israel.[34] These twelve apostles must break the bread and divide it among themselves, literally — and on behalf of others. This is part of the good news they will spread, as we have seen in an actual feeding of hungry persons. "What was left over [from the feeding] was gathered up, *twelve* baskets of *broken* pieces."[35] On that occasion, the disciples had wanted to send the crowd away, hungry. The twelve must learn to offer their broken selves for the life of the world, which we see them doing in Acts. Jesus had responded to what he perceived as a failure to divide the responsibility, and the bread, for distribution: "*You* give them something to eat," he had said.[36] The same empowering Spirit from God that descended on Jesus will descend on followers of the Way to enable their own striving to bring blessing to others, after Jesus has departed.[37]

This request by Jesus to share in his sufferings — to strive to the death — is so demanding as to help cause a traitorous refusal to pursue this "Way of salvation" any further. "But see, the one who betrays me . . . his hand is on the table." Intimacy with Jesus and following the Way for a time are no guarantee against failure. "Lord," some will say who are excluded from the kingdom, "we ate and drank with you!"[38] At the heart of the gospel and its journey, this grim reversal of expectations is echoed in the experience of Judas.

---

33. Among others, Mark A. Matson understands the logic of the shorter manuscript version (see n. 28 above): "Although the external attestation is strongly in favor of the longer text of Luke's Lord's Supper, internal probabilities make it almost certain that the short text is, in fact, original. The extremely close similarity of the variant text to Paul's language, the dissimilarity of the theology of atonement found in those verses to Luke's theology, the probability that the interpolation of these verses served both to harmonize the text to other accounts of the Lord's Supper as well as to aid in anti-docetic arguments, and the absence of any reasonable explanation why the long text might have been deleted all argue convincingly for the short text" (*In Dialogue with Another Gospel?* p. 184).

34. Lk 1:54; Acts 4:27, 30.

35. 9:17, emphasis mine.

36. 9:12-13.

37. 3:22; Acts 2:2-4.

38. 13:25-26.

The Passover meal anticipates the forthcoming trials of Jesus and the need of followers to participate in such trial as Judas faces. Judas chose to strive, but finally Judas reneges. Like Judas, the other eleven apostles will also fail Jesus, at least for a time. Satan has entered Judas, and seeks the same with the other eleven gathered here. Luke provides a staccato beat of failure and betrayal: Judas' outright betrayal; the arguing about being "first" by the remaining eleven; Peter's outright denial of Jesus.[39]

The guilt of Judas is difficult for a modern mind to comprehend, since the act of betrayal has a cosmic, communal, and personal basis:

- Cosmic: "Then Satan entered into Judas";[40]
- Cosmic: "For the Son of Man is going as it has been determined . . .";[41]
- Communal: "[The religious leaders] were greatly pleased and agreed to give him money";[42]
- Individual: ". . . but woe to that one by whom he is betrayed!"[43]

The words of Jesus regarding Judas, however, are clear about the consequence of choice: "woe to that one by whom he is betrayed."[44] The culpability of Judas plays itself out against the backdrop of communal support from respected leaders and the supernatural assistance of Satan — and of course, within the ultimate sovereignty of God. The divine will works out in terms of human struggle, suffering, and choice.[45]

Judas "was numbered among us," Peter will say in the second volume, and had been "allotted his share in this ministry."[46] At the very be-

---

39. 22:3; 22:31.

40. 22:3.

41. 22:22.

42. 22:5.

43. 22:22; in considering the turning-back of Judas from the Way, God's determination rules — though Satan's determination is also powerful. In the end, however, "woe to that one by whom [the Son of Man] is betrayed." Judas acts wrongly, and is held accountable. The woes and the blessings pronounced by Jesus in the great poem of the preparatory material (6:20-26) are viewed as consequences of human choice, not as calculations by a God who determines those to be blessed or not. The complexity of guilt of this one specific player on God's earthly stage reflects Luke's concern with "the whole story," the cosmic and earthly circles that encompass a history of God-and-the-world, circles that overlap and affect each other. In other words, the present stakes for choosing to go this way or that way are high — as they always have been from the time of earliest human life.

44. 22:22.

45. 22:22.

46. Acts 1:17.

ginning of the journey, Jesus had cautioned, "No one who puts a hand to the plow and looks back is fit for the kingdom of God."[47]

Immediately the text balances the upcoming betrayal by Judas with a present betrayal by the rest of the disciples — which the other gospel accounts do not do. The disciples are shown by Luke as going back to normal ways, like Judas, rather than following God's Way. And the timing couldn't be worse. They are disputing among themselves about "which one of them was to be regarded as the greatest."[48] *All* hands are on the table, and all will fail Jesus. Worry about status, however subtly disguised even from oneself, has been uttered in precisely these words already.[49] This is ordinary pettiness, words about one-upmanship that reflect "worries of this life."[50] The deadly jostling among friends (to say nothing of how they might respond to enemies) goes to the heart of all self-destructiveness and communal ill. It betrays, for Luke, the thrust of God's Way, and a trust in the one teaching it.

But failure gives Jesus another key teaching opportunity, in Luke's account. One must strive not only against the drive to secure status and significance but against a more insidious version of the same, the desire to be viewed as virtuous. Those in normal authority, says Jesus, like to be called "benefactor," and desire to be the only ones observed in a position of offering benefaction, blessing. "But not so with you; rather the greatest among you must become like the youngest, and the leader like one who serves. . . . *I* am among you as one who serves."[51] This is a repetition of what we heard just before the journey to Jerusalem.[52] Serve without notice; love without return.[53]

The last will become first; the first, last.[54] But it doesn't seem to work out in real life — in the lived experience, here, of the disciples. Jesus con-

---

47. 9:62. Having striven with Jesus on God's Way, having been chosen by Jesus as a special partner to this Way, having participated in the spread of the kingdom's good news of salvation, having participated in salvation itself, Judas turns his back on Jesus. As we will see in Acts, Judas is lost to the kingdom, to salvation. He is one who has striven, hand on the plow — but looked back, returning to normal ways, of money obsession at the very least. And so he is among those who "will not be able" to enter the kingdom, though he will say, I "ate and drank with you, and you taught [me] in our streets" (13:25-26).

48. 22:24.

49. 9:46.

50. 21:34.

51. 22:25-27, emphasis mine.

52. 9:48.

53. 6:32-36; 17:7-10.

54. 13:30.

cludes the meal with a word about what's waiting "out there," trying to alert his followers about the extraordinary struggle ahead of them. "The one who has no sword must sell his cloak and buy one."[55] Ill-clad, next-to-naked swordsmen? The dull-minded followers miss the hyperbole about readiness; "Here are two swords," they exclaim.[56] Jesus responds curtly, "it is enough" — as in, "enough of this!"[57] Meal over. How will they make it, if they still think swords will help their striving? The answer comes immediately. They must pray for strength.

(3) Mountain, Prayer Time: Strength for Striving

The temple teaching has focused on endurance and alertness in the troubling days ahead, while the meal teaching has emphasized the striving of Jesus himself in the immediate future (22:15), and the need for followers to "partake" in this striving.[58] Now Jesus "went out, as was his custom, to the Mount of Olives."[59] It is a mountain of prayer. The disciples have followed.

"Father, if you are willing, remove this cup from me," Jesus prays.[60] This is the time of "cup" for Jesus, a cup of suffering that is the worst possible, a willingness to suffer certain death.[61] "Yet not my will," Jesus adds,

55. 22:36.
56. "Failing to grasp the point [be on guard during the difficult days ahead], the disciples take Jesus' words literally" (Talbert, *Reading Luke*, p. 211). But see Robert Tannehill, who suggests that Jesus is referring to literal swords, which the disciples would need if they fail to act in faithful courage; they stand in danger, at the very least, of becoming part of the "lawless" among whom Jesus has said he must be counted, in fulfillment of Scripture (22:37). *The Narrative Unity of Luke-Acts: A Literary Interpretation*, vol. 1 (Philadelphia: Fortress, 1986), p. 267.
57. 22:38.
58. 22:17.
59. 22:39.
60. 22:42.
61. "Thus says your Sovereign, the LORD, your God who pleads the cause of his people: See, I have taken from your hand the cup of staggering" (Is 51:22). There is in scripture the cup of God's wrath and on the other hand the cup of salvation; this cup appears to be both. Luke Timothy Johnson comments, "Although the 'cup' *(poterion)* in the OT could mean a sharing in consolation (Jer. 16:7), its overwhelming use is in reference to 'God's wrath' coming on humans as a punishment for sin (LXX Ps. 74:8; Isa. 51:17, 22; Hab. 2:16; Jer. 25:15, 17, 28; 51:7; Lam. 4:21; Ezek. 23:31-33). Still another level of symbolism is suggested by LXX Ps. 115:14: 'I will lift the cup of salvation and call on the name of the Lord,' which continues in the next verse, 'precious in the eyes of the Lord is the death of his saints' (Ps. 115:15)." *The*

"but yours be done."[62] The "cup" here is an apparent echo back to the cup Jesus has just asked his disciples to divide among themselves.[63] "Take up your cross," Jesus has said; "follow me."[64] Anticipating the present and future struggle of the disciples in sharing such a cup, Jesus frames his own prayer with admonition to his followers about the absolute necessity to avail themselves of God's power and grace — without which there is no salvation.[65] The journey teaching on prayer has been rehearsed and demonstrated, at this eleventh hour:

- "Pray that you may not come into the time of trial."[66]
  - "Father, if you are willing, remove this cup from me."[67]
- "Pray that you may not come into the time of trial."[68]

This miniature chiasm emphasizes the parallel between the cup that Jesus must bear and the cup the disciples will have to bear. "Those who cannot understand the divine purpose behind Jesus' rejection and death cannot understand rejection and death as part of God's purpose in their own lives."[69] After praying, Jesus comes back and finds the disciples sleeping, and he repeats to them the urgency of their praying. They falter in their striving, in prayer, by sleeping.

Jesus finishes praying and the followers finish sleeping, and Judas betrays Jesus. Immediately "one of [the disciples] struck the slave of the high priest and cut off his right ear."[70] That which tempts Jesus at both of his great trials, early and late in his public life, is that which tempts the disciples. It all adds up to the same thing: use of power for personal ends.

Gospel of Luke (Collegeville, Minn.: The Liturgical Press, 1991), p. 339. But nowhere in Luke-Acts is there any hint of God's wrath placed on Jesus. Suffering because of others' wrong-doing certainly is the case — a cup of suffering

62. 22:42.

63. 22:17.

64. 9:23.

65. As I have noted, Luke links "power" and "grace" in Acts, through the Holy Spirit, as part of God's key role in salvation, along with God's anointing of Jesus (4:18) and sending him the divine Spirit (3:22) so that the Way of God would be clearly proclaimed for all desiring salvation: hear this word from the Messiah, from "my Son, the Beloved" (3:22), and do it (11:28) — and be saved.

66. 22:40.

67. 22:42.

68. 22:46.

69. Tannehill, *The Narrative Unity of Luke-Acts*, p. 262.

70. 22:50.

Sleeping rather than praying has led to no-strength, and failure, a betrayal of the Way. "No more of this!" Jesus exclaims.[71]

Overcoming the temptation of ordinary power and the subtle lures of status is daunting and humanly impossible. God's empowerment — "grace," as Acts has it — is needed. Needed, because Satan, who we have heard seeks to "sift" the followers, influences even such a stalwart as Peter.[72] Unlike the other gospel writers, Luke keeps all the material concerning Peter's denial in one developing drama, from start to finish.

There is acute public pressure on Peter, who represents the best of what the apostles can offer. Unlike the others, he is shown to be in some physical proximity to Jesus, who has been led away into the custody of religious authorities. "He is a Galilean," says someone in the courtyard, near Peter. The observation has ominous overtones, since Jesus came from Galilee, a place of presumed revolutionary fervor.[73] This is not a time to volunteer one's close association with Jesus, the Galilean. Peter denies knowing him, three times. On the third betrayal a rooster crows, as Jesus predicted. What happens next is only in Luke's version: "the Lord turned and looked at Peter."[74] There is something extraordinary in the speech of Jesus, and also in his gaze. "The sound of the rooster may confirm Jesus' standing as a prophet, but Peter's memory is jogged not by the rooster but by the Lord's actions: turning and looking at Peter."[75]

Memory, and remorse. Like King David, whose heart God loved, Peter needs only a clear indication of his wrong-doing to feel stricken, to feel remorse and to act on it with repentance.[76] Going God's Way, as we see here, requires a repeated cry for mercy, a plunge into the shadowy depths of one's own wrong-doing — that is, "remorse." Only such painful review can lead to repentance. But of course Peter has been repenting all along, up to and including this point: he has been learning the great turn-around of God's Way, though this particular time of remorse is huge. "Repentance [for Luke] is both a once-for-all event that shapes the whole subsequent course of the life and a day-by-day affair," Leon Morris suggests about

71. 22:51.

72. 22:31.

73. 22:59; as already mentioned, Galilee was thought to be a seedbed for political rebels.

74. 22:61.

75. Joel B. Green, *The Gospel of Luke* (Grand Rapids: Eerdmans, 1997), p. 788.

76. Of course we can't be sure Luke has David in mind at this point, though surely this feature which most distinguishes David from Saul in earning God's favor would be known by Luke.

Luke's vision of the matter.[77] We can only add that such a "once-for-all event" happens at least three times for Peter in this story: when he first turns from his fishing nets to follow Jesus; here, at this time of "eureka" and remorse; and in Acts, when he turns around most strikingly in regard to the Gentiles.[78] Striving is everyday, and includes a bearing of the cross that recognizes the need for God's mercy and God's forgiveness.

Peter's turning-around is as assured as the turning-away by Judas. Jesus has promised to pray for Peter, that "when once you have *turned back*, [you will] strengthen your brothers."[79] Willingness to turn back to God's Way, to be last (and an associate of the last, the soon-to-be-crucified one), will lead to Peter's being "first" in volume two. He will be the first great proclaimer of the good news after Jesus leaves. But for now, at the "time of trial," there is this sifting by Satan of all the followers. Their striving falters. For Judas, the end of striving will be a very sad end indeed, as the beginning of Acts makes clear.

Resurrection and Departure:
The Disciples Understand All Scripture

With both success and failure, the disciples in Luke's story have yet to fully comprehend all that Jesus has taught. There has been a lack of sufficient faith caused by self-absorption. But they have stood by Jesus in his trials, and are commended by Jesus for doing so.[80] After God raises Jesus from death, however, the Scripture Jesus has been teaching all along becomes an open book for the disciples.[81] In the very last verse of the gospel, we hear that they "worshiped [Jesus], and returned to Jerusalem with great joy; and they were continually in the temple blessing God."[82] What has God done? What has been accomplished in the death of Jesus, and in the overturning of this death?

During the days after the death of Jesus, two dejected followers are walking from Jerusalem to a little village seven miles away. A stranger ap-

77. Leon Morris, *Luke* (Grand Rapids: Eerdmans, 1974), p. 243.
78. Within Acts 10–15, a large dramatic portion of the narrative is devoted to Peter's repentance regarding non-Jews (covered in Chapter 19).
79. 22:32; emphasis mine.
80. Lk 22:28.
81. 24:32, 44-47.
82. Last verse, Lk 24:53.

pears, and walks alongside them. Luke's audience is told what the two companions don't recognize, that the stranger is Jesus. "What are you discussing with each other while you walk along?" asks the third party.

The answer is one of astonishment: "Are you the only stranger in Jerusalem who does not know the things that have taken place there in these days?"[83]

"What things?" asks the stranger.[84]

And so Jesus is informed of the bare facts concerning himself — that some women had reported an empty tomb — it's been three days since the death of Jesus — and that this Jesus was "a prophet mighty in deed and word before God and all the people."[85] And then the source of dejection, a longing not met: "We had hoped," the two say, "that he was the one to redeem Israel."[86]

What these two and much of Israel had been expecting and hoping for is a redemption quite other than what God was actually making available to them through Jesus. Israel, as these two have been hoping, is indeed on the verge of being saved. Acts, the second volume soon to follow, is the story of that salvation, a redemption that fulfills Israel's God-scripted destiny for "servant Israel" to be freed from its own self-aggrandizing ways and to be a blessing for others; freed, also, from its enemies through the counterintuitive measure of loving them.[87]

How much of all this that Jesus taught is in the foreground of thought for these two anonymous travelers to Emmaus is not revealed. But Luke's account does show Jesus — the stranger — taking away the blinders:

> Then he said to them, "Oh, how foolish you are, and how slow of heart to believe all that the prophets have declared! Was it not necessary that the Messiah should suffer these things and then enter into his glory?" Then beginning with Moses and all the prophets, he interpreted to them the things about himself in all the scriptures. (24:25-27)

After "opening the scriptures," Jesus is shown doing the same for his apostles, a few verses later: he "opened their minds to understand the scriptures" about the Messiah.[88] Luke has shown Jesus teaching from

83. 24:18.
84. 24:19.
85. 24:19.
86. Lk 24:21.
87. Lk 1:54; 6:35; Acts 3:25; Gen 12:3.
88. 24:45.

Scripture about his death and resurrection — but not being understood on the matter by the disciples, who seem unable to comprehend the coming ridicule and ignominy to be undergone by their Teacher and Leader.[89] Raised from death, Jesus is shown solving the hidden piece of the puzzle regarding his death and its significance for salvation: Scripture itself told that the Messiah would have to suffer and be killed but then be raised from the dead. For Luke, it is the resurrection from murderous death that is the ground of salvation.

As a brief last-words speech by Jesus makes clear, the main aspect to be understood about the opened Scripture is its testimony to the efficacy of repentance in bringing God's forgiveness, the importance of the resurrection in attesting to the authority of the One who taught such repentance, and the impossibility of such a journey without the Holy Spirit.[90]

Key signal words in Acts, referring the audience always back to Luke's gospel, are emphasized by Jesus in a last-words speech, in the gospel, before departure:

(a) *repentance* "proclaimed [by faithful Israel] in his name to all nations,"
(b) which is verified by the *resurrection*;
(c) a clothing "with power from on high" by the *Holy Spirit*.[91]

Israel's new leadership will be found faithful in their witness to this outline of salvation, of how to gain entrance to God's kingdom. They will be shown sit[ting] on thrones judging the twelve tribes of Israel."[92] But such

---

89. 9:21-22, 44-45; 13:31-35; 18:31-34.

90. Lk 24:46-49.

91. Lk 24:46-49.

92. The meaning of "judge" has more to do with leadership than with mere "sentencing" — as in the vocation of rulings handed down by the judges of Israel. See Green, *The Gospel of Luke* p. 770. Such rule is "an exercise of authority that Luke . . . will show [and I will demonstrate] being fulfilled in the apostolic ministry of the Jerusalem Church (Acts 1–6)," and more specifically, in having the apostles stand at the middle of the community of possessions and wait on tables (Acts 4:32-37; 6:1-2) (Luke Timothy Johnson, *The Gospel of Luke*, p. 349).

One might argue that such salvific authority is entirely "eschatological," reserved for its fullest realization in the days when the kingdom comes entirely, and the "consolation of Israel" is complete. One would need to reckon with consistent warning by Jesus and later the apostles that those who don't strive properly are excluded from the kingdom promised Israel. Robert Tannehill thinks Luke to be suggesting that Israel will be saved as a nation (the particularity of "twelve tribes") in the parousia; see *The Narrative Unity of Luke-Acts*, p. 270. I think that Luke wants to leave the question of Israel's salvation as a nation, at the end of time,

service to Israel won't come easily: evildoers will try to persecute, evildoers who include "parents and brothers, . . . relatives and friends [who] will put some of you to death."[93]

The third and last section of Luke's gospel has rehearsed the teaching of Jesus in both the words of Jesus to his opposition and to his followers, and in his demonstration of the ultimate stage of going God's Way, the relinquishment of life itself. This teaching is demonstrated as authoritative through God's raising Messiah from death.

Acts, as we see next in Part IV, depends on Luke's gospel for its meaning. Jesus taught God's Way, based on Scripture.[94] "According to the Way," Paul says before Jewish and Roman rulers, "I worship the God of our ancestors."[95] Believers in Acts will rehearse what Jesus taught of this Way. What changes, in Acts, is the sending of the Holy Spirit and the deliverance of Israel — the fulfillment of the ancient covenant between God and Israel (though some within Israel are on their way to being rooted out of the people). Salvation is completed with the sending of God's empowering Spirit, who provides a cohesive thread in the longest speech in Acts, the dramatically pivotal speech by Stephen. The rift within the house of Israel is made clear as a result of this speech; the destiny of delivered Israel in serving all peoples of the world — the move beyond Jerusalem — begins with the murder of faithful Israelite Stephen. Though Peter initiates this ministry of Israel to non-Israel, it is Paul who will carry the mission forward, after Stephen's death. Still, Paul ministers primarily to Israel, though always many Gentiles are added to those within Israel who "belonged to the Way."[96] In seven speeches, Paul addresses an exclusively non-Jewish audience only once: his concern is Israel. In the playing out of this concern, and in the harsh reality of what Paul suffers, Luke is able to play out the truth of what Simeon saw — and so crucial is this plot line that it bears repeating once again — that there would be many rising and many falling within Israel,[97] and that, indeed, Israel would experience its redemption by the thousands and thousands and thousands.[98]

---

fairly open. The extraordinary amount of debate on this question might indicate such purposeful ambiguity and lack of treatment in the story. What is certain is the rule as judges over Israel by the twelve apostles, and the need in-the-present for those within Israel to choose well, or suffer the consequence of exclusion from the kingdom — a desolate house.

93. 21:16; there must be utter relinquishment of family loyalty, we have heard on the journey, a severe loosening of family ties, referred to as "hatred" of one's family members (14:26).

94. Lk 20:21 makes this point explicitly.

95. Acts 24:14.

96. Acts 9:2.

97. Lk 2:34.

98. Three separate references in Acts to saved Israelites: 2:41; 4:4; 21:20.

PART IV

The Way Spreads

Chapter 16

Luke's Gospel in Early Acts:
The Hinge-Points

Acts 1:1-26; Luke 24:1-53

Volume two of Luke's narrative, Acts, dramatizes the spread of God's word as taught and demonstrated by Jesus (recorded in the gospel by Luke). This inter-pretive reality of Scripture came to be known as "the Way," a "Way" to which Jewish believers belonged[1] and a "Way" that they faithfully rehearsed in their mission to Israel, and then beyond, as redeemed Israel, to non-Jews. Peter's first speech, echoing Jesus' words, establishes the key role "the twelve" play in ruling delivered Israel. Early in Acts we also find code-words, or signal-words, requir-ing for their meaning a recollection of all that Jesus taught and did: "repen-tance," "resurrection," "Holy Spirit," and "kingdom of God." We also find spe-cific "hinge-points," suggesting the strategic interdependence of Acts and the gospel: a preface, a last-words speech and departure of Jesus, and a descent of the Spirit, all paralleling the same in Luke's gospel. These early chapters establish the expectation that nothing "theological" will be added in Acts to the Way of salvation taught by Jesus, as recorded in Luke's first volume, his gospel.

Paralleled Last Words from Jesus (Luke 24:46-49; Acts 1:7-8)

Toward the end of the gospel, Jesus tells his followers exactly what he wants them to rehearse in their telling of the good news. Having "opened their minds to understand the scripture" concerning his role in salvation, Jesus offers a last-words speech:

---

1. Acts 9:2.

"You are [to be] witnesses to these things. *Thus it is written that the Messiah is to suffer and to rise from the dead on the third day, and repentance and forgiveness of sins are to be proclaimed in his name to all nations.* Beginning from Jerusalem, you are witnesses of these things. And see, I am sending you what my Father promised; so stay here in the city until you have been clothed with power from on high." (Lk 24:46-49)

Early in Acts, the echoing last-words speech by Jesus repeats the idea of witness and underscores what Acts will emphasize regarding the kingdom: the coming of God's empowering Spirit.

"It is not for you to know the times or periods that the Father has set by his own authority. You will receive power when the Holy Spirit has come upon you; and you will be my witnesses in Jerusalem, in all Judea and Samaria, and to the ends of the earth." (Acts 1:8)

In the first of these speeches, Jesus provides an outline of all that believers will teach about salvation and the meaning of his own role in procuring it. In both, salvation and its proclamation are shown to be impossible without the empowering Spirit.[2] The outline of all that believers testify to, then, looks like this:

1. Repentance and Forgiveness (Luke 24:47)

The forgiveness resulting from daily repentance,[3] as we have seen in Luke's gospel, is at the core of striving to enter God's kingdom of salvation.[4] The principles of repentance, the turning-around from normal ways, are not explained in Acts. What we find are brief summaries, like this: it is God's purpose, Peter says to all Israel, "to bless you by turning each of you from your wicked ways."[5] Turning to God's purposes is necessary, *"so that"* — as Peter is also to say — "your sins may be wiped

2. Lk 18:26-27; 11:13. The import of the Holy Spirit will become clear as we explore the unfolding drama of Acts.

3. Repentance, as the gospel has made clear, is "both a once-for-all event that shapes the whole subsequent course of the life and a day-by-day affair that keeps putting sin away." Regarding the repetition of "unless you repent" in Lk 13:3, 5, Leon Morris then elaborates on "the urgency of repenting by pointing out Luke's use of a present imperative (with continuous force) in verse 3 and an aorist (of a single decisive action) here." *Luke* (Grand Rapids: Eerdmans, 1974), p. 243.

4. Lk 13:23-24.

5. Acts 3:26.

out."[6] This turning-around way of living, repentance, has to be recalled from especially Luke 9:51–19:44, the teaching section. The audience of the text is told that believers proclaim and teach repentance, but for a full explanation the author expects us to recall the extensive teaching of Jesus on the matter.

2. Resurrection (Luke 24:46)

Luke-Acts insists on resurrection as the ground of salvation: the question of authority regarding the teaching of Jesus has been resolved by God's raising Messiah from death, as Scripture foretold. The question of authority, as we have seen, is central to the conflict bringing death to Jesus. "As [Jesus] was teaching the people in the temple and telling the good news, the chief priests and the scribes came with the elders and said to him, 'Tell us, by what authority are you doing these things? Who is it who gave you this authority?'"[7] In Acts, we find the believers emphasizing the answer as "God": the authority of Jesus as Israel's new leader has been established by God, who raised Messiah from death.[8] Salvation, for Luke, is gained and the kingdom entered only by hearing and doing the *authorized* version of Scripture as taught by Jesus, Israel's new leader.[9]

3. The Holy Spirit (Luke 24:49; Acts 1:8)

The matter of being "clothed with power from on high" in the gospel's last-words speech is echoed by the promise in the last-words speech of

6. Acts 3:19; 28:24, emphasis mine; see Deut 30:1-6.

7. Lk 20:2.

8. In each of Peter's three sermons to unbelieving Jews the resurrection is prominent (2:14-36; 3:12-26; 4:7-12), as it is in his sermon to the non-Jewish centurion, Cornelius (10:34-43). In each of these speeches, forgiveness is based on the resurrection and tied to repentance — or, in the case of Cornelius, to belief "in [Jesus]" (10:43). Stephen is able to declare to unbelieving leaders among the Jews about to kill him that he sees the "Son of Man standing at the right hand of God" (7:55). And Paul, privileged with an encounter with the risen Jesus — though not an eyewitness of the actual resurrection — manages to emphasize explicitly the resurrection of Jesus as the ground of salvation in three out of his five speeches to nonbelievers (13:15-41; 17:22-31; 26:2-23). In the other two of these five speeches to nonbelievers, Paul offers (1) evidence of the resurrection insofar as Jesus has appeared to him (22:1-21) and (2) a "hope in God" grounded in "the resurrection of the dead [for which] I am on trial before you today" (24:15, 21).

9. Acts 5:31. Recall the entire teaching section of Luke's gospel, so carefully arranged (9:51–19:44), and its emphatic distillation in 13:23-30.

early Acts: "you will receive power when the Holy Spirit has come upon you." Being so clothed allows for salvation — for "continu[ing] in the faith," as Paul is to put it.[10] What Acts adds most essentially to Luke's gospel regarding the Way is this emphasis on the need for the Holy Spirit.[11]

That for which Jesus asks faithful witness in paralleled last-words speeches is realized in Acts: forgiveness of sins based on repentance and God's mercy; teaching of the same by Jesus and authorized by God in raising the killed Messiah from death; the empowering Holy Spirit of God, sent by the ascended Lord.

The Kingdom of God (Acts 1:3)

During the forty days between his resurrection and departure in Acts, Jesus is reported as "speaking [to the apostles] about the kingdom of God."[12] What Luke's audience needs to know of the principles concerning this kingdom — what it is, how to enter it — is recorded in volume one, the gospel, not in volume two, Acts. All of this teaching can be summarized by the term *kingdom of God,* as Luke shows Jesus doing in the opening verses of Acts.

God's kingdom is referred to at eight crucial points in Acts. *Kingdom* is explained thoroughly in Luke's first volume as "the Way of God"[13] and is explicitly referred to thirty-eight times. As Luke's gospel insists, the kingdom is that for which Israel has been waiting.[14] James D. G.

---

10. Paul recognizes the need to "continue in the faith" — as Judas has not — in the face of the expected persecutions (Acts 14:22); the impossibility of this (see Lk 18:26-27); and the possibility of this (see Lk 11:13). Believing is, as we have seen, participating in the same relinquishments taught and practiced by Jesus, including that of life itself (Lk 14:26; see Chapters 12 and 14).

11. That is, serving God's purposes of healing and release for all (Lk 4:18-19). In Acts, going God's Way, being "saved," is customarily linked with the empowering presence of the Holy Spirit (Acts 2:38, for example).

12. Acts 1:3. The author's preface extends either to verse 5 or to verse 11, as we will see.

13. Lk 20:21.

14. Toward the end of the gospel, Joseph of Arimathea — a very godly member of the old-guard leadership in Jerusalem — takes responsibility for the careful entombment of Jesus; he is waiting, not for the consummation of Israel's glory in Jerusalem, but rather "for the coming of God's kingdom" (Lk 23:50-51). Matthew's gospel version has Joseph as a "disciple of Jesus" (Mt 27:57), a detail that helps to highlight the distinctive focus of Luke's insistence on Joseph as "council member" in order to emphasize the coming salvation of Is-

Dunn comments that "the subject of the risen Jesus' teaching during the forty days [beginning of Acts] is given as 'the kingdom of God,' a further striking point of continuity between the Gospel and Acts." Dunn continues:

> If any phrase characterizes Jesus' teaching during his ministry after Jordan, it is "the kingdom of God" (Luke 4:43; 6:20; 7:28; 8:1, 10; 9:2, 11, etc.). And the same phrase recurs sufficiently regularly in Acts as the theme of the expanding mission, not least of the hero of the second half of Acts (Paul), to be more than accidental (8:12; 14:22; 19:8; 20:25; 28:23).[15]

The thirty-eight gospel references to *kingdom* are always in the narrative context of explanation, whereas the eight references in Acts to *kingdom* are always unexplained signal-words, or code-words, depending on the gospel for their meaning.

At the beginning of the gospel, Jesus is "proclaim[ing] *the kingdom of God*"; late in the gospel, Joseph is waiting for the *kingdom* and Jesus is "speaking about *the kingdom of God*"; then, at the very end of the story, in the last verse of Acts, Paul is "proclaiming the *kingdom of God* and teaching about the Lord Jesus Christ."[16]

The first words we hear from the apostles in Acts (1:6) concern the timing of God's kingdom and the status of Israel: "Lord, is this the time when you will restore to kingdom to Israel?" Jesus accepts the premise of the question without answering directly:

> "It is not for you to know the times or periods that the Father has set by his own authority [for fulfillment of the kingdom]. You will receive power when the Holy Spirit has come upon you; and you will be my

---

rael, to be recounted in volume two. Based on Matthew's consistent opposition between "*their* synagogues" (e.g., Mt 9:35) and the "church," it is hard to imagine a second volume of Matthew in which Israel would figure as anything but a people who rejected the Messiah, who called down blood on themselves and their children (Mt 27:25).

15. Further, "Particularly noticeable is its appearance in the very last verse of Acts (28:31): the continuity of gospel theme runs not just through Acts but beyond into the phrase following the closure of Acts. This is all the more striking since the phrase occurs so infrequently elsewhere in the New Testament, and still more rarely as characterizing the evangelistic preaching. Here again, then, we can detect a particularly Lukan emphasis as he attempts to reinforce the closeness of the bond between Jesus' preaching and that of the apostles' mission." James D. G. Dunn, *The Acts of the Apostles* (Valley Forge, Pa.: Trinity Press International, 1996), p. 7.

16. Lk 4:43; Acts 1:3; 28:31.

witnesses in Jerusalem, in all Judea and Samaria, and to the ends of the earth." (Acts 1:8)

What occurs immediately following the departure of Jesus indicates the key role of redeemed Israel in the matter of ushering in the slow-but-sure growth of God's kingdom on earth.[17]

The Kingdom, Israel, and Its *Twelve* Rulers
(Luke 22:28-30; Acts 1:15-22)

The first of nineteen speeches by believers occurs very early in Acts. Delivered by Peter, it concerns finding a twelfth to substitute for the missing Judas. Israel-to-be-redeemed (shown in Acts) requires the twelve rulers for the twelve tribes if God's kingdom is to be ushered in. Jerusalem will be delivered, as will Israel: the mass conversions in Acts are always of Israelites.[18]

At the center point of the journey, in the middle of Luke's gospel, God's kingdom and Jerusalem were held in narrative tension, as we have seen.[19] That tension is resolved in Acts, but in surprising fashion. With their minds open to understanding all that Jesus had been teaching them about the kingdom, Israel's new leadership obediently "returned to Jerusalem"; Jesus had said that "repentance and forgiveness of sins is to be proclaimed in [my] name to all nations, beginning in Jerusalem."[20] After Paul's repentance, he goes to the twelve in Jerusalem; he also goes to the Jerusalem temple for prayers.[21] If we widen the aperture of our viewing lens, we note that the last section of the gospel and the first section of Acts are set in Jerusalem.[22] Jerusalem along with Israel is redeemed, but not as a sacred space and nation. Redeemed Israel, led by the twelve rulers in Jerusalem, is at the heart of the drama: the spread of God's word and the turning of the world upside down.[23]

Israel has been the focus of Jesus' teaching in Luke's first volume. At the heart of Israel is Jerusalem; at the heart of Jerusalem is the temple. In

---

17. See Luke 13:18-21 for a description of kingdom dynamics.
18. 2:41; 4:4; 21:20.
19. Lk 13:18-34; see Chapter 13.
20. Lk 24:53; 24:47.
21. Acts 9:26-28; 22:17.
22. Lk 19:45–24:53; Acts 1:1–8:1.
23. Acts 17:6.

the temple we find the new leadership of faithful Israel, the twelve.[24] But Acts begins with only eleven. As Jesus had said, Israel needs twelve rulers.[25]

In his first speech, just a few verses into Acts, Peter is addressing about 120 individuals within Israel already faithful to the Messiah and his Way:

> "Friends, the scripture had to be fulfilled, which the Holy Spirit through David foretold concerning Judas, who became a guide for those who arrested Jesus — for he was numbered among us and was allotted his share in this ministry." (Now this man acquired a field with the reward of his wickedness; and falling headlong, he burst open in the middle and all his bowels gushed out. This became known to all the residents of Jerusalem, so that the field was called in their language Hakeldama, that is, Field of Blood.) "For it is written in the book of Psalms,
>
> > 'Let his homestead become desolate,
> > and let there be no one to live in it';
> > and 'Let another take his position of overseer.'
>
> So one of the men who have accompanied us during all the time that the Lord Jesus went in and out among us, from the baptism of John until the day when he was taken up from us — one of these must become a witness with us to his resurrection." (Acts 1:15-22)

The gory details of Judas's self-destruction are a reminder that turning back from God's way is nothing less than disaster.[26] Beyond this lesson,

---

24. Acts 2:46; 3:1-10; 5:20, 21, 25; 5:42; 21:26, 27, 28-30; 22:17; 24:6, 12, 18; 26:21. Faithful Israel, in point of historical fact, was still worshiping in synagogues up until the fourth century, the time of Constantine (325). In Acts, Israel worships God in the temple, though as Stephen's speech makes clear, God's presence will not be, and has never been, confined to the temple. But Jerusalem and its temple remain a hub of centrifugal force for all of Acts; God's word, taught by Jesus, spreads from Jerusalem to the ends of the earth.

25. Lk 22:30.

26. "Unlike Matthew (27.3), [Luke] makes no attempt to depict Judas as repenting for his act of betrayal. On the contrary, Judas had been possessed by Satan (Luke 22.3), is shown as unrepentant (he bought a plot of land or small farm with 'the reward of his wickedness'), his death is depicted in classic terms as the death of an evil man (cf. II Sam. 20.10; Wisd. Sol. 4.19; II Macc. 9.9), and he 'went to his own place' (1.25 — presumably hell)." Dunn, *The Acts of the Apostles*, p. 19. To those given much, we recall from the gospel, much is required: to those who have been given teaching about the Way, who have followed that Way, turning back brings horrific judgment (see Chapter 11 and Lk 12:35-48). Luke's Judas will be linked

however, is the main point of Peter's speech: "Let another take [Judas's] place as overseer," Peter says — an "overseer" of Israel, its twelve tribes.[27]

Luke's audience is being prepared for a mass salvation: thousands upon thousands of Israelites among the "devout Jews from every nation under heaven" will soon be turning to their Messiah, with additional numbers of Israelites turning to their Messiah daily.[28] These saved Israelites need a new leadership, the twelve. The importance of this *twelve* is underscored by prior references to the imperfect *eleven:*

- some women return from an empty tomb and "two men in dazzling clothes" speak to *"the eleven* and to all the rest" with news about the risen Son of Man;
- a bit later, two friends who have met the risen Jesus while walking to Emmaus return to Jerusalem and find *"the eleven* and their companions";
- "and they cast lots . . . and the lot fell on Matthias; and he was added to *the eleven* apostles."[29]

These successive emphases on *eleven* prepare Luke's audience for *twelve.* The twelfth who replaces Judas, Matthias, is never again mentioned: what is rhetorically crucial here is an emphasis on the gospel's promise that — with the exception of the "falling" who will be "utterly rooted out of the people" — Israel's redemption, as a people, is at hand, all *twelve* tribes.[30] Up until the very last verses of Acts, Israelites are be-

---

to the deadly end of a husband and wife who also turn away from the rigorous demands of salvation's Way because of money — the clutching of which prompts them to lie to the God they had chosen to serve. On Judas, see Chapter 15; for relinquishment of ownership with regard to possessions and money, see Lk 12:13-34 and 16:1-31 and Chapter 10; for a very rich man made sad at the notion of allowing God's purposes to rule his wealth, see Lk 18:18-27, Chapter 6.

27. "The twelve" are cited in Lk 8:1; 9:1; 9:12; 18:31; 22:3; 22:30; 22:47; Acts 6:2; 7:8.

28. "every nation," 2:5; three thousand Israelites become believers and are "delivered," 2:41; more daily, 2:47; five thousand, 4:4.

29. Lk 24:4, 9, emphasis mine; Lk 24:43; Acts 1:26.

30. Lk 2:34; Acts 3:23. Israel's redemption, in Lk 2:38; later in the gospel we find echoes and questioning of this promise (Lk 21:28; 24:21). For Jesus on the "lost" among Israel, see Lk 13:23-30. Robert Tannehill represents the view of many Lukan scholars that Israel is yet to be redeemed by the end of Acts, that the story's early promise has turned "tragic"; such a view, as I hope to show, does violence both to what is in the text and what is not in the text. Tannehill, "The Story of Israel within the Lukan Narrative," in *Jesus and the Heritage of Israel,*

ing lost even while other Israelites are being saved, adding daily to the thousands of faithful Israel[31] who will bring blessing to all peoples.[32] Acts dramatizes the salvation of Israel within the larger context of Israel's original place in God's purpose. Peter's first speech establishes the expectation that finding a twelfth ruler for Israel is critical for what lies ahead in Acts.

Paralleled Departures (Jesus) and Paralleled Descents (God's Spirit) (Luke 24:49-51; Acts 1:8-11)

With paralleled scenes of departure, the story emphasizes a connection between the ascent of Jesus and the descent of the Holy Spirit:

> *Departure #1* (gospel): "Then he led them out as far as Bethany, and, lifting up his hands, he blessed them. While he was blessing them, he withdrew from them and was carried up into heaven."[33]

> *Departure #2* (Acts): "When he had said this, as they were watching, he was lifted up, and a cloud took him out of their sight. While he was going and they were gazing up toward heaven, suddenly two men in white robes stood by them. They said, 'Men of Galilee, why do you stand looking up toward heaven? This Jesus, who has been taken up from you into heaven, will come in the same way as you saw him go into heaven.'"[34]

The leave-taking of Jesus, offered in both volumes, is monumentally significant: the responsibility for bringing Israel into fulfillment of its covenant now rests with the twelve disciples, empowered by the Spirit.[35] The departure of Jesus is so central to the story in the gospel that Luke lets us overhear the conversation among Jesus, Moses, and Elijah: the

---

ed. David P. Moessner (Harrisburg, Pa.: Trinity Press International, 1999), esp. pp. 332-36; see also Tannehill's *The Narrative Unity of Luke-Acts, Volume 2: The Acts of the Apostles* (Minneapolis: Fortress, 1990), p. 345.

31. 28:24; from the start, numbers grow daily, Acts 2:47.

32. Acts 3:25; Gen 12:3.

33. Lk 24:51; some ancient manuscripts have Jesus withdrawing but not being "carried up into heaven."

34. Lk 24:49-51; Acts 1:8-11.

35. Jesus has taught them, and he has opened their minds fully to this teaching, Lk 24:32, 45.

three "were speaking of [Jesus'] departure," his "exodus."[36] A few verses later, just prior to the "teaching section," Jesus heads for Jerusalem "when *the days drew near for him to be taken up*"; at the beginning of Acts he is once again instructing his disciples "until *the day when he was taken up* to heaven."[37]

The echoing departure scene, #2, provides an expanding of perspective. Two angelic beings put an important question to Israel's future leadership: "Why do you stand looking up toward heaven?"[38] The focus, as in the gospel's transfiguration scene, must be this earth.[39] For the twelve, the coming of God's kingdom begins in Jerusalem, the heart of Israel. There must be a pressing forward with God's purposes on earth, not a "looking up toward heaven." Jesus' departure occasions the great blossoming of Israel into "servant Israel" to the world, as God had originally challenged and promised — a final completion of divine purpose, of salvation history.[40]

To fully grasp the word of God, as the disciples have done by the end of volume one, is one thing; to implement this word in obedience — after Jesus' departure — is quite another. This implementation, a doing of the word, is accomplished in volume two through the empowering Spirit.[41]

Descent of Spirit #1 (gospel): "And see, I am sending upon you what my Father promised; so stay here in the city until you have been clothed with power from on high."[42]

Descent of Spirit #2 (Acts): "But you will receive power when the Holy Spirit has come upon you; and you will be my witnesses in Jerusalem, in all Judea and Samaria, and to the ends of the earth."[43]

36. Lk 9:31. Susan R. Garrett points out, in "The Meaning of Jesus' Death in Luke" (*Word & World* 12, no. 1 [Winter 1992]: 12), that "the Greek word *exodus* used here is the same one used by Jewish writers of Luke's day to refer to the exodus from Egypt, though the allusion to that event is obscured by many modern translations" (for example, RSV, NRSV, NAS, NIV: "departure"; KJV: "decease"; NJB: "passing").

37. Lk 9:51; Acts 1:2.

38. Acts 1:11.

39. Returned "to earth" from their heavenly experience, Peter, James, and John immediately fail Jesus miserably, as do the other disciples. They fail in the ministry of God's kingdom because they fail to pay sufficient attention to a "little one," a forgettable child (Lk 9:28-41; see Chapter 3).

40. Lk 3:21-22; Acts 2:33.

41. Acts 2:33.

42. Lk 24:49.

43. Acts 1:8.

The Paralleled Prefaces (Luke 1:1-4; Acts 1:1-5)

In the preface to Luke's gospel and then again in the preface to volume two, Acts, we hear a *Theophilus* addressed. The name means *lover-of-God.* Luke's ideal audience is anyone who truly seeks to love God.[44]

> *Preface #1* (gospel): I want you to know for certain, "most excellent *Theophilus,*" says Luke at the beginning of volume one, what all of this means about Jesus, about all that in "which you have been *instructed.*"

> *Preface #2* (Acts): "In the first book, *Theophilus,*" Luke begins in Acts, "I wrote about all that Jesus did and taught." (Only "after giving *instructions* through the Holy Spirit to the apostles he had chosen" did Jesus depart.)[45]

Luke thus keeps in the forefront of both volumes the story's main character, God. By now, Luke's audience understands that only those oriented to the love-service of God will recognize "the things that make for peace" lying at the heart of Jesus' teaching, and at the heart of Luke's gospel.[46]

Conclusion

Failure to understand the utter dependence of Acts on Luke's gospel has led otherwise shrewd readers astray.[47]

---

44. Whether Theophilus is a specific individual or patron (he well might have been both/and) is less to the purpose of Luke's story than what his name means in terms of establishing an "ideal" audience — the kind of person who will listen carefully to what Luke has to say — since his story is about listening carefully to what Jesus has to say. A God-lover must always be hearing the teaching of Jesus — "the word of the Lord" — from the likes of Luke's Paul and Silas (Acts 16:32).

45. Lk 1:3-4; Acts 1:2; emphasis mine.

46. Lk 19:42.

47. I cite respected New Testament scholar C. K. Barrett as an example: "The language of imitation [of Jesus, the Way] is not to be found in Acts; nor is the fact to be found without the language. Luke never even points back to his former treatise as supplying a model, or represents the Christian character that he describes as recalling the story of Jesus, the story being presented as an example of Christian behavior. This is part of a larger lacuna in Acts; the book as a whole lays little stress on the ethical component of Christian living." C. K. Barrett, "Imitatio Christi in Acts," in *Jesus of Nazareth: Lord and Christ,* ed. Joel B. Green and Max Turner (Grand Rapids: Eerdmans, 1994), pp. 252-53. Such a view is at odds with much

Take, for example, the theological thinking of Paul about Jesus and his teaching regarding the kingdom, the Way of salvation. Paul is shown at the end of Acts arguing "persuasively about the kingdom of God," "proclaiming the kingdom of God," "testifying to the kingdom of God," and, in the very last verse of Acts, "proclaiming the kingdom of God and teaching about the Lord Jesus."[48] What does Paul argue about this kingdom, and what does he teach about Jesus as Lord? We find answers in his seven speeches — signal-words — that indicate a theology of salvation and the kingdom entirely and exclusively that of Jesus, as recorded in Luke's first volume, the gospel. Acts cannot be understood without this gospel. The hinge-points of early Acts confirm that Luke-Acts is, as commonly accepted, "a single continuous work."[49]

The hazards of not hearing the drama of Acts — its code-words, repeated scenes, and speech clusters — in the light of Luke's gospel can be illustrated in such common misconceptions as these: Acts is a "history of the early church";[50] Acts is a playing out of "divine necessity";[51] Acts is a retrospective and upgraded interpretation — an elaborated theology — of what salvation has been shown to be in the gospels, including Luke's ver-

---

Lukan scholarship and is certainly at odds with what I hope to demonstrate in my chapters on Acts.

48. Acts 19:8; 20:25; 28:23, 31. Luke's Paul unpacks the nature of this kingdom hardly at all, since Luke has already done this, in his gospel. None of the believers in Acts expand on what this kingdom means, so thoroughly and definitively has Jesus taught the Way of God. This kingdom is literally and figuratively at the heart of Luke's gospel (the "bull's-eye," 13:18-20; see Chapter 13). The gospel's entire central section (9:51–19:44) lays out, as we have seen, the leading principles of life according to the Way.

49. Henry J. Cadbury's seminal judgment: regardless of whether, or to what extent, the gospel of Luke and Acts were circulated together in the first centuries of the common era, it is clear to most scholars that the gospel of Luke and Acts constitute a unified story. "In any study of Luke and Acts their unity is a fundamental and illuminating axiom," Cadbury says, a perception that has been increasingly confirmed by most scholarship examining the issue. Luke's gospel and Acts, as Cadbury goes on to say, "are not merely two independent writings from the same pen; they are a single continuous work. Acts is neither an appendix nor an afterthought." *The Making of Luke-Acts* (London: Macmillan, 1927; Peabody, MA: Hendrickson Publishers, 1999), pp. 8-9.

50. Charles Talbert's fine literary studies of Luke-Acts sometimes blur on important summary points like this: "When one recognizes that the narrative of Luke-Acts is a working out of the divine plan," he comments, "one must ask: what aim is the author pursuing against this background? The obvious answer is that in the Third Gospel it is Christology (explicitly stated in Acts 1:1); in the Acts, ecclesiology." *Reading Acts: A Literary and Theological Commentary on the Acts of the Apostles* (New York: Crossroad, 1997), pp. 3-4.

51. Mark Reasoner, "The Theme of Acts: Institutional History or Divine Necessity in History?" *Journal of Biblical Literature* 118, no. 4 (1999): 637.

sion.[52] Rather, the drama of Acts reveals the spread of God's word taught by Jesus as rehearsed by servant Israel.

"Luke shows the apostles as perceiving their main activity as ministering the word of God," as Andrew C. Clark observes.[53] The spread of this word, taught by Jesus defines the main drama of Acts. What we witness is the growth of God's kingdom, described in detail by Jesus and entrusted by him to Israel's new leadership, the twelve. As Israel accepts their Messiah, in Acts, the word of God as illumined by Jesus becomes light to the Gentiles, "for the glory of Israel."[54] The kingdom becomes a blessing for all peoples.

Jesus reinterprets the word of God and notions about the kingdom and salvation. "Listen to him!" says God to the disciples, about Jesus; "Listen to whatever [Jesus-Messiah] tells you," says Peter, quoting the prophetic word of Moses.[55] The reader of Acts is reminded frequently of this word of God: "the word of God continued to spread"; "the word of God continued to advance and gain adherents"; "the word of the Lord spread throughout that region"; "the word of the Lord grew mightily and prevailed."[56] Faithful Israel, those who "belonged to the Way," heal the sick and feed the hungry in the name of Jesus. And in the name of Jesus they proclaim and teach. Those who "accepted the word of God" are taught the Teacher's word.[57] It makes perfect narrative sense, then, that believers like Peter, Stephen, Paul, and Silas "spoke the word of the Lord" in the "name" of that word's teacher — as Jesus himself requested.[58] Not to comprehend that the "word

52. "It is surprising," claims New Testament scholar C. K. Barrett, "that Luke in Acts does not point back to the Third Gospel as depicting the quality of life that members of the young churches should manifest. It is a partial answer that he perhaps felt that he could assume that readers of Acts would have read the earlier work, but this does not explain why (after Acts 1:1) he never refers back to the Gospel." It is Barrett's assumption that is surprising here that Acts is somehow disconnected from "the Way" as taught and demonstrated by Jesus in Luke's gospel. His error is in overlooking the paradigmatic nature of the community shalom in the latter part of Acts 2, where all is held in common for purposes of distributive justice. "In general," says Barrett, "the apostles and their colleagues are witnesses rather than examples, and the Jesus to whom they bear witness is a savior rather than an example." Barrett, "Imitatio Christi in Acts," pp. 253-54, 262.

53. Clark, "The Role of the Apostles," in *Witness to the Gospel: The Theology of Acts,* ed. I. Howard Marshall and David Peterson (Grand Rapids: Eerdmans, 1998), p. 180.

54. Lk 2:32; Acts 2:17.

55. Lk 9:35; Acts 3:21-22.

56. Acts 6:7; 12:24; 13:49; 19:20.

57. Acts 11:1; see Lk 6:40; 7:40; 8:49; 9:38; 10:25; 11:45; 12:13; 18:18; 19:39; 20:21; 20:28; 20:39; 21:7; 22:11; and, for example, Acts 16:32. "Teacher" is a self-referential term used by Jesus — and by others (Lk 22:11).

58. Lk 24:47. To believe is to embrace the word of God taught by Jesus; to participate in

of the Lord" in Acts is the word of the Lord, Jesus, is to miss almost entirely what Acts is about.[59]

Nothing is added by the believers to the teaching of Jesus about salvation. In Acts as in Luke's gospel, for example, the theology of the cross is this: Jesus bears sin's consequence in the same way that followers like James and Stephen will bear others' sins by yielding their own lives to the fury of wrongdoing.[60] There is no further elaboration in Acts from any of the believers, including Paul, concerning this meaning of the cross of Jesus.[61] According to the story told by Luke, the cross's meaning is to be found in the bearing of suffering and even death, but a death overcome by God's raising up of Jesus from this suffering and death.

Writing with the theological thinking of Paul and the other gospel writers in mind, Luke claims to be viewing the big picture: he wants his

---

this Way is to call on the name of the One who taught that Way. "Everyone who calls on the name of the Lord," says the prophet Joel, quoted by Peter, "shall be saved" (Acts 2:21). For the prophet Joel as cited by Luke, this "Lord" is Israel's God. There is, for Luke, *Lord God* (see the first dozen references in Luke's gospel), and *the Lord Jesus.* "God has made [Jesus] both Lord and Messiah" (Acts 2:36), Peter is recorded saying. Calling "on the name of the Lord" for salvation is to put oneself under the teaching of the Lord God's word, the word as taught by God's Messiah called "Lord."

59. Erwin R. Goodenough represents many scholars who either don't emphasize or miss entirely the phenomenon of signal-words in Acts that rely on the gospel, a matter we will be exploring in our eight chapters on Acts. "[Acts] presents many acute problems," claims Goodenough. "For example, the Gospel of Luke, presumably written by the same man, paints an amazingly different picture of the importance of Jesus from Acts. Luke's Gospel gives us our most vivid picture of Jesus the 'rabbi,' as Bultmann called him, the teacher of new law and parables. In Acts not a trace of this Jesus appears. Peter says at Pentecost that the Jews had crucified Jesus although he had been attested before them by his miracles (Acts 2:22), but not a single passage connects the Jesus of whom he says, 'God has made him both Lord and Christ' (Acts 2:36) with the great teacher of parables and ethics in the Gospel. To say the least, here is a new approach. It seems that, like Paul, the author of Acts will know Christ after the flesh no more." "The Perspective of Acts," in *Studies in Luke-Acts,* ed. Leander E. Keck and J. Louis Martyn (Nashville: Abingdon, 1966), p. 51.

60. Luke draws a rather tight parallel, as we will see, between the murders of Jesus and Stephen, and of their respective willingness to relinquish the ultimate thing that Israel and any mortal would clutch after: life itself. Jesus the "innocent-righteous one" (Lk 23:41, 47) is killed for his embrace of God's Way; the shedding of Stephen's blood (Acts 22:20) is likewise the death of an innocent-righteous one (his "face was like the face of an angel," Acts 6:15).

61. That the cross of Jesus might provide in any sense an escape from the consequences of sin is an idea at odds with Luke's story as a whole, a point that becomes clearer as Acts unfolds. Acts 20:28 might seem to be an exception, which I think can only be so with very questionable interpretations of what the ancient manuscripts actually say; see Chapter 21.

instruction to be seen as resting on firm ground.[62] In Luke's perspective, only one murdered word-bearer has ever been raised up from death,[63] and it is by this that the authority of Jesus is established. Therefore, "Listen to him!" — and be saved.[64] That is, be repenting always. The nineteen speeches by believers follow the pattern established by Jesus in his last-words speech, recorded in Luke's gospel and echoed by its parallel at the beginning of Acts: repentance, resurrection, Holy Spirit. Beyond the witness to repentance and resurrection is the empowerment of the Holy Spirit.

As in the beginning of any great narrative, the early part of Acts establishes expectations fulfilled in the drama ahead.

Luke's gospel is more a drama of developing insights regarding the "Way" than of action, whereas Acts is more a drama of action — the spread of this "Way" — than of teaching. The action of Acts, however, is oriented and controlled by clusters of speeches, nineteen in all. These patterned speech-clusters echo the teaching of Jesus, with constant reference to repentance, resurrection, and Holy Spirit. "We cannot keep from speaking," Peter and John say, "about what we have seen and heard."[65] In Acts, that which Peter and the twelve had "seen and heard" from Jesus is presented in highly abbreviated form. The initial action of Acts is oriented around the first three major speeches of Peter, addressed to Israel. Thematically, Peter's three speeches reflect the three emphases of the last-words speech of Jesus in the gospel: repentance leading to forgiveness; resurrection; and the Holy Spirit.[66]

62. Lk 1:1-4; see my Introduction.

63. Lk 13:33-34.

64. Hear the word, and do it, Lk 6:46-49; "Listen!" and listening, Lk 9:35; 16:31; 21:38; listen or be "rooted out" of Israel, lost, Acts 3:22-23.

65. Acts 4:20.

66. Lk 24:46-49.

Chapter 17

Peter: Three Speeches to Fellow-Israelites

Acts 2:14-36; 3:12-26; 4:8-12

Peter gives seven of the nineteen speeches by believers, as does Paul. The action at the beginning of Acts revolves around three major speeches by Peter, all of them addressed to fellow-Israelites (his last three speeches concern Gentiles). Thousands upon thousands of Israelites respond to Peter's consistent call for repentance, and are saved.[1] But Peter's proclamation of the authority of Jesus, attested to by the resurrection, riles the old-guard leadership of Israel. The emphasis repeated in each of the three speeches to Israel is exactly as Jesus had instructed: repentance; resurrection; Holy Spirit.

The people of God emerge in Acts, as Robert Wall nicely observes, as "restored Israel in the last days of salvation's history."[2] Here is the drama of the fulfillment to the ancient covenant established by God with Abraham[3] whereby Israel realizes "its vocation as light to the nations."[4] The Way of God as taught by Messiah Jesus is what Simeon described as a "light for revelation to the Gentiles" brought by "servant Israel"[5] to all peoples, a fulfillment that is "for glory to [God's] people Israel."[6] The godly man's prophetic word about "the falling and the rising of many in Israel"[7] be-

---

1. 2:41; 4:4.
2. *The Acts of the Apostles*, New Interpreter's Bible, vol. 10 (Nashville: Abingdon, 2002), p. 305.
3. Acts 3:25.
4. Wall, *Acts of the Apostles*, p. 305.
5. Lk 1:54.
6. Lk 2:32.
7. Lk 2:34.

comes a key aspect of the plot in Acts, as the multitude that is rising within Israel are harassed by those who are falling. Those select Israelites falling are shown to be the people's old-guard leadership. It is in the first three major speeches of Acts that we find Peter addressing these matters, and the essential gospel, the good news, with his fellow-Jews; many thousands immediately embrace their Messiah, with the old-guard leadership increasingly resistant.

"The plot of Acts," Charles Talbert suggests, is "straightforward: between the ascension and parousia, empowered by the Holy Spirit, the Messianists bear an unstoppable, universal witness to Jesus by word and deed, thereby fulfilling the divine plan."[8] Along with all of Israel's new leadership, Peter speaks and acts in the name of Jesus, who is both "Leader" and "Savior."[9] We find no disconnect whatsoever between the teaching of Jesus and what the believers in Acts rehearse "in the name of Jesus," though discontinuity is a common view among readers of Acts.[10] Repentance, resurrection, and the Holy Spirit are the focal points of Peter's three speeches to fellow Israelites in Jerusalem.

8. *Reading Acts: A Literary and Theological Commentary on the Acts of the Apostles* (New York: Crossroad, 1997), p. 4.

9. Acts 5:31.

10. We have noted some of these views in the Introduction. C. F. Evans adds to this chorus, claiming that "the relation between Luke's two volumes is somewhat puzzling. In the Gospel he reproduces most of Mark's account of Jesus as preacher and teacher in Galilee and Jerusalem, occasionally reinforcing it; and, like Matthew, though in a different way from him, he supplements this with a great deal of ethical instruction, sometimes of a systematic, but more often of an episodic kind. This is especially so in 9.51–19.27, which is largely the journey of an itinerant teacher. In Acts, on the other hand, although Christianity is there called 'the Way,' and apostles are said to teach in the *name of Jesus* and about the *kingdom* of God, there is scarcely any ethics at all." But Evans goes on with some hunches that our exploration will confirm, in part: "Apart from references to community of goods, what conversion entailed in terms of the moral life is not described. The reason for this may be that Luke intended it to be understood that the believers referred to in the second volume lived in accordance with the teaching already set forth in the first volume; though this is not stated, except, perhaps, in Acts 3.22-26, where listening to Jesus as the prophet like Moses is now the condition of belonging under the covenant to the people of God. Or, the reason may be that Luke, unlike Matthew, does not aim to write prescriptively, i.e. to provide a series of moral injunctions, which were to be carried over as applicable to Christians in all circumstances, but descriptively, i.e. to give an account of a particular and unique manifestation of the will of God in the teaching of Jesus, which had brought into being communities of believers, who were then to discover in the light of it, and through the spirit, the true way of life in particular circumstances." *Saint Luke* (Philadelphia: Trinity Press International, 1990), p. 94.

Peter's First Speech to All Israel
(his second speech overall; Acts 2:14-39)

Gathered in Jerusalem "from every nation under heaven"[11] for the Jewish feast of Pentecost,[12] the entire household of Israel is astonished as it hears the new leadership of Israel "speaking in the native language of each [nation]."[13] With no translator, Peter responds to his fellow-Israelites by crediting this phenomenon to the outpouring of God's promised Spirit.[14] He goes on to address the question of authority. Because of God's raising up Jesus — a divine trumping of murder — Israel can know for sure that what Jesus taught is true. "You crucified and killed" him, says Peter, but "God raised him up."[15] After showing from Scripture that this resurrection was anticipated, Luke highlights the point of authority: "*Let the entire house of Israel know with certainty* that God has made him both Lord and Messiah."[16] The only speech in Acts addressed to all of Israel from around the world, Peter's first major speech is a paradigm of the gospel according to Luke. It covers all three thematic emphases of witness in the gospel's last-words speech of Jesus: (1) authority-resurrection; (2) repentance-forgiveness; (3) empowerment for repentance through the Holy Spirit.[17] (A chart is included at the end of this chapter.)

As is often the case in these speeches of Acts, the sections of this programmatic speech by Peter are conveniently marked by a repetition of personal address to the audience:

---

11. "Every nation under heaven" (Acts 2:5) is spelled out in representatively exhaustive detail (2:9-11). Scholars note that some of the nations cited no longer existed when Luke was writing (Parthians, Elamites) but, as Robert W. Wall understands, "the narrative function of the list is theological, defining the inclusive boundaries of the household of Israel" (*Acts of the Apostles*, p. 56).

12. It is the festival of weeks called Pentecost — one of the three great festivals for Israel in which harvest abundance is celebrated. "You shall observe the festival of weeks, the first fruits of wheat harvest, and the festival of ingathering at the turn of the year" (Ex 34:22). "At our festival of Pentecost, which is the sacred festival of weeks, a good dinner was prepared for me and I reclined to eat" (Tobit 2:1).

13. 2:5-6.

14. 2:1-21.

15. 2:23-24.

16. 2:36; emphasis mine.

17. Lk 24:46-49.

Beginning: "Men of Judea and all who live in Jerusalem,
let this be known to you, and listen to what I say."[18]

Middle: "You that are Israelites,
listen to what I have to say."[19]

End: "Therefore let the entire house of Israel
know with certainty."[20]

Peter demands of Israel careful listening; he echoes Luke's own concern as expressed at the beginning of the two-volume narrative, that his audience "know with certainty" what all of this concerning Jesus actually means.[21] The *what* in Peter's "Listen to *what* I say" is echoed by his insistence in his next speech to Israel, that they "listen to *whatever* [Jesus] tells you."[22] What Peter teaches, along with what all other believers in Acts teach, is what Jesus taught.

I. Holy Spirit

"Men of Judea and all who live in Jerusalem, let this be known to you, and listen to what I say. Indeed, these are not drunk, as you suppose, for it is only nine o'clock in the morning. No, this is what was spoken through the prophet Joel:

'In the last days it will be, God declares,
that I will pour out my Spirit upon all flesh . . .'"

(2:14-17; emphasis mine)

The phenomenon of dialects unscrambled, says Peter, is nothing less than an indication that the "Lord's great and glorious day," spoken of by the prophet Joel, is here; "everyone who calls on the name of the Lord shall be saved."[23]

Presumably, the story's audience hears in these words an echo of the alienating confusion of tongues at Babel.[24] This miracle of language breakthrough is nothing less than a reversal of the ancient curse of inter-

18. 2:14.
19. 2:22.
20. 2:36.
21. Lk 1:4.
22. Acts 3:22.
23. 2:16, 21.
24. Gen 11:7.

nation alienation and confusion, a realization of God's promise to "pour out my Spirit upon all flesh"[25] toward a "universal restoration" of global *shalom*.[26] The Holy Spirit is the power of God, and so God's kingdom is being realized, from "near at hand" and "among" the believers to a power with the potential of spreading like wildfire. Of course, at the level of action, this describes the plot of Acts.[27]

II. Resurrection

"You that are Israelites, listen to what I have to say," Peter goes on. "Jesus of Nazareth, a man attested to you by God with deeds of power, wonders, and signs that God did through him among you, as you yourselves know — this man, handed over to you according to the definite plan and foreknowledge of God, you crucified and killed by the hands of those outside the law. But God raised him up, having freed him from death, because it was impossible for him to be held in its power. For David says concerning him . . ." (2:22-25; emphasis mine)

Here is how King David foretold the resurrection, reports Peter: God's Holy One (Jesus) was not abandoned to Hades, but rescued by God from the corruption of death.[28] "This Jesus," Peter concludes, "God raised up, and of that all of us are witnesses." The *us* underscores for Luke's audience the importance of Peter's speaking with and on behalf of the eleven others of the new-guard leadership beside him.[29] Salvation, for Luke, is grounded in this resurrection.

III. What to Do? Repent

The worldwide assembly of the house of Israel asks their new leadership the one crucial question about obtaining salvation. They are "cut to

25. Acts 2:17; it is God's power, this Spirit, a force which the audience of volume one will recognize as able, with merely a divine finger, to cast out demons, announcing "the kingdom of God [that] has come to you" (Lk 11:20).

26. Acts 3:21, 25; the "universal restoration" of Israel, in v. 21, is necessarily coupled with the scope of Israel's fulfilled role in bringing blessing to all peoples of earth, in v. 25.

27. Lk 9:27; 10:9; 11:20; 12:32; 17:21.

28. 2:25-31.

29. 2:32; 2:14.

the heart" and cry out, "what should we do?"[30] The gospel of Luke has prepared us for Peter's answer: "Repent, and be baptized every one of you in the name of Jesus Christ so that your sins may be forgiven; and you will receive the gift of the Holy Spirit."[31] Repentance has been the one-word summary of what the kingdom's Way requires, a turning away from normal ways, self-aggrandizing ways, toward God's purposes of blessing for others — instanced here in an initial turning-around from rejection of Jesus to embracing him as "Lord and Messiah." John had talked about repentance and the baptism offered by Jesus, and had said that such baptism would be associated with "the Holy Spirit."[32] Peter preaches forgiveness of sins based on repentance, as taught by Jesus, and so he can say, "Repent, and be baptized every one of you in the name of Jesus Christ so that your sins may be forgiven."

Therefore (based on the resurrection), "let the entire house of Israel know with certainty that God has made [Jesus] both Lord and Messiah."[33] Knowing "with certainty" echoes Luke's initial explanation, in the gospel, as to why he is retelling the story of these Jesus-events — "so that you may be certain about the meaning of these things about which you have been instructed."[34] The author wants Theophilus to know for sure the meaning of the events being fulfilled in Luke's own time of writing, these "last days" of Messiah some decades after the departure of Jesus. These are days marked, as Peter's speech reveals, by God's pouring out of the divine spirit on all flesh.[35] These are the days of the kingdom come among thousands within the house of Israel who choose to join the Way.[36]

It is the *entire house of Israel* who ask, "What should we do?" The deliverance of Israel starts with three thousand Israelites beginning their journey of salvation by repentance, with many Israelites added daily, and many more thousands to follow, as we will see.[37] "Repent" means what

---

30. 2:37.
31. 2:38.
32. Lk 3:16. The Holy Spirit had been declared by Jesus as the ultimate object of prayer, the best thing a generous God can give (Lk 11:13).
33. Acts 2:36.
34. Lk 1:3-4; my translation.
35. Acts 2:17, 33.
36. Acts 9:2.
37. 2:41, 47.

the gospel teaching has revealed:[38] relinquish the normal and intuitive ways of self-securing in favor of God's Way of paying attention to the other, and especially the outsiders, the "little ones."[39]

To repent means to hear God's truly interpreted word, and do this word — an impossibility without God's empowerment.[40] In this first major speech to the house of Israel, Peter has focused on the three points of the gospel's last-words speech by Jesus, which we have just examined: the resurrection of Jesus, repentance in the name of Jesus that leads to forgiveness, and God's assistance in the rigors of repentance by pouring out the empowering Spirit. The three main emphases of the gospel's last-words speech have intertwined masterfully in this programmatic speech to "the entire house of Israel" by fellow-Israelite Peter — with the other eleven leaders at his side. Israel is being delivered and is under new leadership, a leadership that takes its entire cue from Israel's new "Leader," Jesus.[41]

After Peter's first speech to all Israel, with thousands of Israelites turning to their Messiah, we get to see what God's kingdom of salvation actually looks like. Faithful Israel relinquishes ownership of possessions, as required by repentance.[42] There is *shalom* and communal well-being, sure marks of repentance and salvation expressed with "glad and generous hearts."[43] There are repeated scenes of joyous meals.[44] The kingdom is here, among them; the good news is being taught and done, with the blessing of health administered, just as Jesus described would happen in the "year of the Lord's grace."[45] Specifically, a lame man is given the gift of *standing*, of *walking*, of *jumping*, of *leaping*.[46] The story's narrator seems to be carried away with these verbs of action — a palpable "praising [of] God."[47] This is communal well-being that is inclusive, that brings the outsider in.

---

38. See Lk 13:3, 5; 15:7, 10; 16:30; 17:4; also, the nine chapters of Part II, the journey, or "teaching section."

39. Lk 3:3, 16-17; Lk 17:1-2; see Chapter 9.

40. Lk 18:26-27.

41. Lk 24:46-49; Acts 5:31.

42. Acts 2:44-45; Lk 12:13-34; 16:1-31; see Chapter 10.

43. Lk 2:14; Acts 2:46-47.

44. 2:42, 46.

45. Lk 4:18-19.

46. Acts 3:6-8.

47. 3:8.

Peter's Second Speech to All Israel
(his third speech overall; 3:12-26)

The speech begins in response to Israel's astonishment. The house of Israel is taken aback regarding the healing of a lame man. "You Israelites," Peter responds, "why do you wonder at this, or why do you stare at us, as though by our own power or piety we had made him walk? The God of Abraham, the God of Isaac, and the God of Jacob, the God of our ancestors has glorified his servant Jesus."[48] It is through "faith in his name" that this lame one as been restored to "perfect health."[49] Of such is the kingdom of God; this is the good news brought by Jesus.[50]

The speech continues with a follow-up on the power of God that raised up the lame man. Such power has been overwhelmingly demonstrated in God's raising up Jesus from death. How precisely has Israel's God "glorified" Jesus as God's own "servant"? Peter's speech explains. Though Israel "rejected the Holy and Righteous One" and "killed the Author of life," God "raised [him] from the dead."[51] In this most dramatic of all possible reversals, God has glorified Jesus.

And how has Jesus fulfilled his role as God's servant? The speech proceeds by citing Scripture, specifically the words of Moses. As "Moses said, 'The Lord your God will raise up for you from your own people a prophet like me. You must listen to whatever he tells you. And it will be that everyone who does not listen to that prophet will be utterly rooted out of the people.'"[52] Salvation begins here: *"You must listen to whatever he tells you."* As Peter says here, "the God of Abraham, the God of Isaac, and the God of Jacob, the God of our ancestors has glorified his servant Jesus"[53] by entrusting to Jesus the message of salvation, and assuring its trustworthiness by raising Jesus from suffering and death.

There is salvation in no other name than Jesus. Salvation is a gift from God insofar as God has given the divine word interpreted by Messiah: "Listen [to Jesus], or be rooted out of God's people," Peter says.[54] Salvation is a gift from God insofar as Jesus, through the Holy

48. 3:12-13.
49. Acts 3:16.
50. Lk 4:18-19.
51. 3:14-15.
52. 3:22-23.
53. 3:12-13.
54. 3:23.

Spirit, is able "to bless you by turning each of you from your wicked ways."[55]

Peter is able now to conclude his speech with a powerful punch line:

"And all the prophets, as many as have spoken, from Samuel and those after him, also predicted these days. You are the descendants of the prophets and of the covenant that God gave to your ancestors, saying to Abraham, 'And in your descendants all the families of the earth shall be blessed.' When God raised up his servant, he sent him first to you, to bless you by turning each of you from your wicked ways." (3:24-26)

"Turning each of you from your wicked ways" is the continual act of repentance, the word of God taught by Jesus to Israel and through Israel to the world. "Being saved" for Israel and the world is to be found in a radical and daily reorientation based on God's gift of the illuminating word and empowering Spirit. Saved Israel will bring the good news of God's blessing to "all the families of the earth" — the reason God chose them.

"Repent therefore," Peter has said, "and turn to God so that your sins may be wiped out."[56] God forgives sins, in Luke's story, because God is God, a generous and powerful God; God forgives sins when perfectly ordinary Israelites — and later, Gentiles — turn from their normal and wicked paths to the kingdom's Way. "You must listen to whatever he tells you," Peter insists, citing Moses, because one cannot change directions — especially in such a counterintuitive direction as God's Way — without a clear and compelling word of explanation. This is the Messianic role of Jesus, in Luke's story, which is why volume one is devoted to the teaching of Jesus.

Failure to listen and turn leads to disaster rather than deliverance: you "will be utterly rooted out of the people [Israel]."[57] By the story's conclusion, many within Israel will have been rooted out, but many thousands will have become faithful Israel, "servant Israel."[58]

As in his first speech to all Israel at Pentecost, Peter once again is shown following the gospel script of Jesus' last words, which focused, as we have seen, on *repentance, resurrection,* and *Holy Spirit:*[59]

55. 3:26.
56. 3:19.
57. 3:23.
58. Lk 1:54.
59. Lk 24:46-49.

- *Resurrection:* "God raised [Jesus] from the dead," this "Author of life" whom you killed; "in this way God fulfilled what he had foretold through all the prophets, that his Messiah would suffer" (3:15, 18).
- *Repentance:* "Repent, therefore, and turn to God so that your sins may be wiped out" (3:19).
- *Holy Spirit:* What mortal can obey the rigors of such repentance "*so that* your sins may be wiped out"? The answer is in what God can do, through the Holy Spirit, "by turning each of you from your wicked ways" (3:26). The entire speech is an answer to that which the Holy Spirit has accomplished in raising the lame man through faithful Israelites living out the Way.

As a result of this second speech, "five thousand" more Israelites are saved.[60] Many in Israel will rise, many will fall: the rising or falling is shown to be on the basis of *listening to* what Jesus has taught, repeated by Peter — a repentance which is *turning-away* from wicked ways while *turning-toward* the serving of God's purposes — such as healing this lame man. This is a thing that makes for peace,[61] that to which servant Israel is called as fulfillment of their covenant with God.

The lame man has been restored to health, and Peter has taken the opportunity to speak to astonished Israel of God's power in releasing a lame person from physical debilitation. Implicit within this speech are two questions posed to Israel's old leadership: *What will you do about killing the Author of life? How will you decide about your own need to repent of ways that keep such a lame man outside your attention zone?* Jesus, as Author of life, has given this new leadership God's power to untwist the legs of a lame man and restore him to full life. Such a crippled person would have been marginalized, an outsider to the community. As such, he is a living affront to God's ideal of communal *shalom.* The response of the old-guard leadership addressed by Peter is swift and poisonous. "Much annoyed"[62] by this affront to their authority — both the healing but more so the brazen talk by Peter — the old-guard leadership arrests Peter and his companion John.

---

60. 4:1-4.
61. Lk 19:42.
62. 4:1-3.

Peter's Third Speech to Israel
(his fourth speech overall; 4:8-12)

The old-guard presses the new leadership for credentials, as we saw happen in the case of Jesus.[63] "By what power or by what name did you do this?" they ask, referring to the lame man's healing.[64] Peter's third speech to Israel is to its old-guard leadership. He comes quickly to the point in a speech of only a few lines:

> Then Peter, filled with the Holy Spirit, said to them, "Rulers of the people and elders, if we are questioned today because of a good deed done to someone who was sick and are asked how this man has been healed, let it be known to all of you, and to all the people of Israel, that this man is standing before you in good health by the name of Jesus Christ of Nazareth, whom you crucified, whom God raised from the dead. This Jesus is
>
>> 'the stone that was rejected by you, the builders;
>> it has become the cornerstone.'
>
> There is salvation in no one else, for there is no other name under heaven given among mortals by which we must be saved." (4:8-12)

The answer to the old-guard leadership's question about authority is what we have come to expect: "This man is standing before you in good health by the name of Jesus Christ of Nazareth, whom you crucified, *whom God raised from the dead.*"[65]

"There is salvation in no one else," Peter concludes, "for there is no other name given among mortals by which we must be saved."[66] Only Jesus is authorized, through being raised up from suffering and death, as the ultimate word-bearer from God. Only by embracing Jesus as Israel's cornerstone[67] can there be salvation. There is no other name that can command such allegiance as leads to God's promised deliverance, to the *shalom* of salvation.[68] The speech mentions Jesus as "Leader" and cornerstone; there is no salvation through anyone else. This is Israel's promised Deliv-

---

63. See Chapter 14.

64. 4:7.

65. 4:10.

66. 4:12.

67. Acknowledging Jesus as the cornerstone is to hear the word he teaches and to obey it.

68. Lk 2:14.

erer, and the deliverance is happening now. But what kind of deliverance is this, with the conflict internal to Israel rather than with Rome? What exactly is the redemption of Jerusalem that Anna prophesied would be connected with Jesus?[69]

We heard at the story's beginning, from Zechariah, of fulfillment to the divine promise: that Israel would be freed from its enemies so that they "might serve [God] without fear," that in fact God has now "looked favorably on his people and redeemed them."[70] Now, with Peter's early speeches to Israel, we see thousands and thousands of Israelites turning to their Messiah. The nature of this redemption and this deliverance from enemies is coming true, in Acts — but in counterintuitive and un-normal ways.

"Salvation [is] in no one else" but Messiah Jesus, Peter says to Israel. But is this the salvation envisioned by the Psalmist, the time "when the Lord restores the fortunes of his people" and brings a "deliverance for Israel [that] would come from Zion"?[71] Luke's answer is *yes*. For the godly Zechariah, Jesus is "the dawn from on high" and the One "to give light to those who sit in darkness and in the shadow of death," the One "to guide our feet into the Way of peace."[72] Here is the source of grave confusion both for the old-guard leadership of Israel and for many modern readers: the Way of peace is the path of salvation taught by Jesus, but it is a peace that divides families[73] and fosters family hatred[74] with its radical inclusiveness.[75] This is a counterintuitive peace, just as the salvation and deliverance of Israel represented in Luke-Acts is contrary to most normal expectations of what peace looks like, and what salvation might afford. The ungodly old-guard leadership of Israel refuses this peace, this offered salvation, this long-awaited deliverance. But the thousands upon thousands of those rising in Israel do embrace just this salvation offered by Peter in these first three clustered speeches to Israel. The deliverance of Israel is being dramatized.

And yet: Zechariah had cited the prophets to the effect that Israel

---

69. Lk 2:38.
70. Lk 1:71-73; 1:68.
71. Ps 14:7; 53:6.
72. Lk 1:78-79.
73. Lk 12:51-53; see Chapter 12.
74. Lk 14:26-27; again, see Chapter 12.
75. We have seen this theme throughout Luke; see especially Chapter 5, covering the frame of the journey to Jerusalem with its emphasis on peace, and the inclusiveness of the saying that launches the journey, "Whoever is not against you is for you" (Lk 9:50).

"would be saved from our enemies and from the hands of all who hate us."[76] By the conclusion to the story Luke tells, Israel will not have been freed from Roman rule. But Luke's audience, if closely listening to his story, could not have expected such a constricted view of peace as mere freedom from political tyranny. Consider first of all, that such tyranny is downplayed by Luke: the *enemy* is within Israel itself; "the hand of all who hate us" is internal. The enemy is not so much Rome, for Luke, as the murderous resistance of the old-guard leadership within Israel to the new leadership.[77] The enemy is embodied in the parochially minded religious leaders of Israel who pose a constant threat to faithful Israel and put pressure on Roman authority to do something hateful to the truly faithful Israelites, beginning with Jesus.

But still, there is Rome. Does there remain in Luke-Acts the traditional sense of "Israel" as a nation with a territory and an earthly nationalistic destination? Jesus taught Israel the apparently foreign notion of true Israel as a kingdom of God. Here is a Way, not a Place, a Way of notfearing, of being delivered from enemies even in the face of their killing you.[78] Stephen's experience, in fact, will make it clear that God's "rescue" comes — as it did for Jesus — in spite of physical death. Stephen is *saved from his enemies* though he dies by their murderous hand, a deliverance indicated by his glowing face — "the face of an angel"[79] — as he stands before his murderers and witnesses a Jesus standing, perhaps to welcome him in death.[80] "Do not fear those who kill the body and after that can do nothing more,"[81] Jesus has taught. Furthermore, loving one's enemies — serving them with blessing — is an aspect of being saved from these enemies. This is not the ordinary ideal of personal and clan security that "the wise and the intelligent" of Luke's day could embrace: this peace and freedom from enemies is counterintuitive.[82]

"Rulers of the people and elders," Peter had begun, and then goes on to reveal a new Ruler, a new "cornerstone" — a new "Leader."[83] His will

76. Lk 1:71.

77. Rome is consistently revealed within this story — especially in Acts — as offering more protection than cause for fear.

78. Lk 12:4-12 and 22-32.

79. Acts 6:15.

80. Explored in our following chapter.

81. Lk 12:4.

82. "The wise and the intelligent" do not understand (Lk 10:21); on peace, and enemies, see Lk 2:14; 6:35; 10:5-6; 12:51; 19:42.

83. 4:8; Acts 5:31.

be a new kind of rule, as the angel Gabriel announces to Mary; his will be a "reign over the house of Jacob" characterized by a "kingdom [of which] there will be no end."[84] The kingdom, in Acts, has come to Israel, and scores of faithful Israelites enter the counterintuitive deliverance of this kingdom taught by Jesus. This Teacher and Leader of Israel has been rejected by the accusing old-guard leaders, and as such the falling within Israel stand to "be rooted out of God's people," as Peter has just said.[85]

The old-guard leadership doesn't know how to answer Peter's boldness, recognizing that he and John "were uneducated and ordinary men"; in addition, the old-guard note that "the man who had been cured [was] standing beside them."[86] After conferring, the old leadership simply "ordered them not to speak or teach at all in the name of Jesus."[87] Peter and John do not leave without a rejoinder: "Whether it is right in God's sight to listen to you rather than to God, you must judge; for we cannot keep from speaking about what we have seen and heard."[88]

Peter's Three Major Speeches to Israel: A Summary

As illustrated in the chart at the end of this chapter, Peter's three major speeches to Israel have conformed to a pattern that was briefly detailed in the last-words speech of Jesus, in Luke's gospel.[89] The thematic resolve of each of the three speeches reinforces the centrality of Jesus and his teaching to what unfolds in the action of Acts: "Know with certainty," Peter has said, that God has made Jesus "both Lord and Messiah" (speech #1) — so "listen to whatever he tells you" (speech #2) since there is "salvation in no one else" (speech #3). Know for certain, that is, that the teaching of Jesus regarding repentance is true; know for certain on the basis of God's authorization by raising Jesus from suffering and death. Listen to the authorized word of God as we apostles repeat what Jesus taught: repent; be obedient to the word; be saved. Israel, you can know with certainty (#1), building on your cornerstone (#3), if you begin by hearing the word of God: "You must listen to whatever he tells you"[90] (#2). Do what you hear

---

84. Lk 1:33.
85. 3:23.
86. 4:13-14.
87. 4:18.
88. 4:19-20.
89. Lk 24:46-49.
90. 3:22.

by repenting, through the gift of the Holy Spirit, and join those thousands of Israelites who belong to the Way.[91]

While Israel accepts deliverance from their new "Leader," many within Israel refuse, in particular the old-guard rulers of Israel. As we see next, they meet in their council, and become more and more "annoyed" to the point of murderous jealousy and rage; Stephen is stoned to death after his highly selected rehearsal of Israel's history to the council — the longest speech in Acts.

91. Acts 9:2.

Peter's Three Speeches to Israel

	Peter to All Israel (2:14-39)	Peter to All Israel (3:12-26)	Peter to Israel's Old-Guard (4:8-12)
Resurrection . . .	(a) — You, Israel, had this man crucified and killed	(a) — You, Israel, killed the Author of life	(a) — Jesus Christ of Nazareth whom you, Israel, crucified
	(b) — But God raised him up . . . freed from death	(b) — whom God raised from death	(b) — whom God raised from the dead
	(and again: this Jesus God raised up)	(and again: God raised up his servant)	
is important for . . .			
Authority	Therefore let the entire house of Israel know with certainty	You must listen to whatever he tells you	Salvation in no one else; no other name [for] being saved
Repentance . . .	Repent, be baptized (waters of dying/new life) in name of Messiah, Jesus	Repent, turn to God; you will be turned from wicked ways	(Not to repent is to reject Israel's cornerstone.)
leads to . . .			
Forgiveness	so that your sins may be forgiven	so that your sins may be wiped out	(no repentance, therefore no forgiveness)
Holy Spirit	Drunk? No: "I will pour out my Spirit upon all flesh" (2:15-17)	"Why do you stare at us as though by our own power or piety we had made him to walk?" (3:12)	"'By what power or by what name did you do this?' Then Peter, filled with the Holy Spirit . . ." (4:7-8)
Punch line	Know with certainty; Repent	Listen to him! Repent	(*You will not listen? You are rejecting Israel's cornerstone.*)

Chapter 18

Three Model Speeches:
Stephen, and the Twelve (Two)

Acts 4:23-30; 5:29-32; 6:15–7:60

Twice in Acts the new leadership of Israel speaks in unison, once to God and once to the old-guard leadership of Israel. Together, the two brief speeches provide a perspective of the whole story told by Luke regarding God's unshakable plan for blessing, through "holy servant Jesus" and "servant Israel."[1] Placed as tandem speeches along with Stephen's speech, these are model speeches of three significant thematic emphases: Speech 1, praise to God; Speech 2, proclamation to the old-guard; and Speech 3, a history of Israel involving God's Presence — the Holy Spirit. The three speeches appear between Peter's three speeches to Israel and Peter's three speeches concerning Gentiles. The dramatic backdrop for these three model speeches is four occasions on which the old-guard leadership of Israel, as a council, confront the new-guard leadership — beginning at the end of the gospel with the arrest, trial, and murder of Jesus. The fourth council meeting leads to the arrest, trial, and murder of Stephen, whose blood is shed.[2]

The kingdom's Way has spread astonishingly throughout all of Israel. Initially, three thousand Israelites turn to their Messiah, with more and more added daily.[3] *Shalom* is happening: all possessions are held in common, with distributive justice for all; everyone enjoys intimacy at meals; a lame man is healed. The man healed of lameness seems intent on the possibility of communal intimacy, clinging to Peter and John.[4] "About five thou-

---

1. 4:27, 29-30; Lk 1:54.
2. Acts 22:20; the only other reference to "shed" blood in Luke-Acts is in Lk 11:50: ". . . the blood of all the prophets shed since the foundation of the world."
3. 2:41, 47.
4. 2:41–3:11.

sand" more Israelites have been added to the "three thousand."[5] That the household of Israel is turning to the Way does not please the old-guard. They convene in their ruling council to decide on appropriate reaction.

In the first council scene, in Luke's gospel, the old-guard had its way in the authority struggle: they successfully engineered the murder of Jesus.[6] On the fourth council occasion — the third in Acts — the old-guard leadership of Israel bypasses any appeal to Rome, killing Stephen by their own hand.

Model Speech #1:
The Twelve in One Voice, to God (4:23-30)

Peter and John, rebuffing old-guard orders, are sent away. Overjoyed, the Twelve praise God as one, giving succinct voice to the cosmic and earth-bound purposes of God.

"After they were released, they went to their friends and reported what the chief priests and the elders had said to them. When they heard it, they raised their voices together to God and said,

> Sovereign Lord, who made the heaven and the earth, the sea, and everything in them, it is you who said by the Holy Spirit through our ancestor David, your servant:
>
> > 'Why did the Gentiles rage,
> > and the peoples imagine vain things?
> > The kings of the earth took their stand,
> > and the rulers have gathered together
> > against the Lord and against his Messiah.'
>
> For in this city, in fact, both Herod and Pontius Pilate, with the Gentiles and the peoples of Israel, gathered together against your holy servant Jesus, whom you anointed, to do whatever your hand and your plan had predestined to take place. And now, Lord, look at their threats, and grant to your servants to speak your word with all boldness, while you stretch out your hand to heal, and signs and wonders are performed through the name of your holy servant Jesus." (4:23-30)

The speech begins with God, the story's main character — "sovereign Lord" of the universe — and ends with this God's "holy servant," Jesus.

5. 4:4.
6. Lk 22:66-71; 23:1-6; 13-24.

In the middle, this emphasis on the role of Jesus in relation to God is highlighted by a reference to Scripture. All earthly rulers "have gathered together against the Lord and against his Messiah." Encapsulated within this short speech of praise is the largest possible perspective of what unfolds in Acts, namely, the struggle on earth of God against earthly powers, toward the "universal restoration."[7] Such global *shalom* requires a stretching out of God's "hand to heal" all peoples through the redeemed within Israel, those believing Jews who speak God's word and do kingdom work "through the name of [God's] holy servant Jesus."

This speech to God, a prayer, is actually a lament sandwiched by praise in the beginning and petition at the end. God's sovereignty both in creation and in the implementation of the divine purposes for this created world is praised. But alas, ordinary persons in power have rebelled against these divine purposes and specifically against the Lord's anointed one, Jesus, as was "predestined to take place." From praise through lament we conclude with petition: *let us speak "your word,"* pleads Israel's new leadership with one voice; *continue the healing and restoration*[8] *we are bringing.*

From the universal conflict with which this speech begins we find a narrowing of focus to the specific conflict at hand: "And now, Lord, look at their threats."[9] The twelve are asking for one thing: God, they petition, "while you stretch out your hand to heal" may it be the case that you empower us "to speak your word with all boldness." This is the word, "your word," taught by Jesus.

As a postscript to this prayer-speech we find the crucial note that, "filled with the Holy Spirit," the new leadership "spoke the word of God with boldness."[10]

Model Speech #2:
The Twelve in One Voice, to "the Council" (5:29-32)

Between this model speech by the twelve and the next one, we hear once again of God's kingdom as present, a communal well-being in which

7. Acts 3:21; see the prior chapter, Peter's second speech of three to Israel. "Universal restoration" as applied to Israel only is highly unlikely, given the larger narrative context of the two-volume narrative and the specific narrative context of this second speech, which goes on to speak of Israel's role in bringing universal blessing (3:25).

8. The echo to what Jesus announced as programmatic for his mission and "the day of the Lord" is conspicuous (Lk 4:18-19).

9. Acts 4:29.

10. 4:31.

"no one claimed private ownership," and "there was not a needy person among them."[11] This kingdom Way is demanding beyond any normal expectation of those within the text, as illustrated by an incident about a couple who join the Way and give much of their wealth, but are struck dead for a deceitful holding back of a portion.[12] One can start on salvation's way, but turn back, distracted by money — as was Judas. The lure of normal monetary considerations proves too much for these three members of the Way. Their end appears worse than had they never joined the Way at all. The point of this kingdom reality, this Way of God[13] lived out, is distributive justice ("there was not a needy person among them" because "no one claimed private ownership"). This model of the Way has been anticipated in Luke's first volume, and never changes throughout his second volume: salvation is entry into this kingdom, or it is nothing.[14]

"Yet more than ever," day by day and thousands upon thousands, believing Israelites "were added to the Lord" — to "those who belonged to the Way."[15] These twelve, the new leadership, are held "in high esteem" by Israel. "Filled with jealousy," the old-guard has put all twelve, as we have seen, in jail. Quickly released by an angel of the Lord, the new leadership has returned to Israel's holiest place, the Jerusalem temple. They "went on with their teaching."[16] Brought before the old-guard once more, the new leadership was reprimanded: "We gave you strict orders not to teach in this name [of Jesus]."[17] Once again, as frequently in Acts, the question had turned on authority. "We must obey God rather than any human authority," the twelve respond, in one voice.[18] Then they proceed with their succinct summary of salvation: repentance, resurrection, Holy Spirit. It is, perhaps, the most helpful "model" speech of any in Acts by reason of its clear statement of the gospel.

We must obey God rather than any human authority. The God of our ancestors raised up Jesus, whom you had killed by hanging him on a

11. 4:32, 34; see 2:43-47.
12. 5:1-11.
13. Lk 20:21.
14. Lk 13:23-24.
15. 5:14; 9:2; see 2:41, 47; 4:4.
16. 5:21.
17. 5:28.
18. 5:29; the twelve speak in one voice, though unlike the prior prayer-speech, this time we are told that the prayer in unison is led by Peter.

tree. God exalted him at his right hand as Leader and Savior that he might give repentance to Israel and forgiveness of sins. And we are witnesses to these things, and so is the Holy Spirit whom God has given to those who obey him. (5:29-32)

The communal cohesiveness among the twelve suggests the narrative resolve to the story's main plot, that the word about repentance from God has come to Israel, and there will be, indeed, forgiveness of sins.

We find in this very brief speech the three major elements of all speeches in Acts, the essential gospel content summarized with three signal words:[19]

- *Resurrection:* "God exalted him at his right hand," a grand reversal from the ultimate humiliation, hanging on a tree.
- *Repentance:* Through Jesus, God gives *"repentance* to Israel" through the taught word of God and the empowerment of the Holy Spirit.
- *Holy Spirit,* provided for those who hear the word of God taught by Jesus and do it,[20] a Spirit poured out on "those who obey him"; the obedience that leads to salvation is impossible without such empowerment.[21]

Israel's old-guard is not harangued by Israel's new-guard, but simply put on notice — as is Luke's audience — of what has been preached and taught all along by Jesus, and that this is the entirety of what salvation is, and how God's kingdom is entered.

Model Speech #3:
Stephen and a Selected History of Israel (7:2-53)

Stephen's speech and death, a dramatic pivot-point for Acts, occur at the climax of a progressively hostile triad of old-guard council clashes, moving from mild inquisition to explicit jealousy, rage, and murderous intent — then a grinding of teeth, rage, and actual murder.[22] The murder of Ste-

---

19. Lk 24:46-49.
20. See Lk 6:46-49, for example, and 11:27-28 (Part II, Chapter 4).
21. Lk 18:26-27; 11:13.
22. The first Acts council meeting, 4:5-22; second, 5:17-40 (see 5:17, 33); and third, with Stephen, 6:12–7:60.

phen ironically fuels that for which he was killed: the overwhelming appeal and spread of God's Way among so many within Israel.

Brought before the council on false charges of challenging the Law and threatening the Temple, Stephen enjoys the rapt attention of his interlocutors: "all who sat in the council looked intently at him."[23]

Stephen's speech is the longest of nineteen speeches by believers; it focuses more on Israel's history than any other. The speech, of course, represents a highly abbreviated and highly selective history. Stephen is addressing a hostile council of old-guard leaders who have summoned him on charges that he has been speaking blasphemous words against Moses and God, that he "never stops saying things against this holy place and the law," and that he has been citing Jesus' words about destroying "this place and the customs that Moses handed to us."[24]

Three heroes in Israel's history best support what Luke wishes to emphasize through Stephen's speech. Each hero was rejected by, or left behind, immediate family while exemplifying the Spirit of God: Abraham was called to leave family and ancestors; Joseph was rejected by family and sent away; in Egypt, Moses fled his harassing fellow Israelites only to be forced in his later years to put up with their continuing petulance and dismissiveness. Of the three, Moses receives the greatest attention in Stephen's speech.[25] Israel's leadership "killed those" who were bearers of God's word: the deaths of these prophets and of Jesus himself, "the Righteous One," are costly to God, as Paul points out later, in Acts: this is the precious "blood of God's own."[26]

1. Abraham

The council wants to know if the witness against Stephen is true: has he spoken blasphemously against Moses and God? Has he been "saying things against this holy place and the law" and claiming that "Jesus of Nazareth will destroy this place"?[27]

> And Stephen replied: "Brothers and fathers, listen to me. The God of glory appeared to our ancestor Abraham when he was in Mesopota-

23. 6:15.
24. 6:11, 13-14.
25. Abraham is given 204 words, Joseph 169, and Moses 688.
26. Acts 20:28, explored in Chapter 6 of this Part.
27. 6:11, 13-14.

mia, before he lived in Haran, and said to him, 'Leave your country and your relatives and go to the land that I will show you.' Then he left the country of the Chaldeans and settled in Haran. . . . And God spoke in these terms, that his descendants would be resident aliens in a country belonging to others. . . ." (7:2-6)

The emphasis of the speech is on the presence of God with father Abraham during the journey toward that place — just as God was present with Israel away from their promised land, "resident aliens in a country belonging to others."

The old-guard leadership of Israel assumes Jerusalem and its temple as the prime residence of God, the center and sacred space constituting their identity as a people. Stephen's speech works against this parochial and space-bound bias, building on the foundation of God's presence anywhere the people of God have been located. The Holy Spirit is not limited to this holy city, or to Jerusalem's holy temple. Abraham journeyed. God, the Holy Spirit, was with him. He has become father Abraham while on the road, without a sacred space, a holy "place."

2. Joseph

Jacob, the father of Israel's twelve tribes, is passed over in favor of his son Joseph, who illustrates brilliantly the phenomenon of God's ubiquitous presence regardless of sacred geographical space, a "home." Joseph, as focused on by Stephen, serves Luke's purposes, also, because of the rejection theme as embodied in the hostile response to God's word-bearer Jesus by Stephen's audience, Israel's old-guard leadership.

"The patriarchs, jealous of Joseph, sold him into Egypt; but God was with him, and rescued him from all his afflictions, and enabled him to win favor and to show wisdom when he stood before Pharaoh, king of Egypt, who appointed him ruler over Egypt and over all his household."[28] Like Abraham before him, Joseph has left his homeland, though by force. Nonetheless, like Abraham, "God was with him," a conspicuous refrain from the Genesis story itself.[29] In fact, no one in Scripture rivals Joseph as one with whom the Spirit of God is present, and yet Joseph never returns to his homeland. Neither does his father. Jacob/Israel leaves

---

28. Acts 7:9-10.
29. Beginning with Gen 39:3.

home in his old age, reunited with his entire family, in Egypt. It is a very happy scene; but Jacob never returns home, though his bones make the journey back, for burial.

Stephen's speech emphasizes not only that "God was with [Joseph]," but that his brothers, the patriarchs of Israel, were jealous. The scriptural reference to the "jealous patriarchs" echoes the psychic state of this very same old-guard council addressed by Stephen: they are "filled with jealousy."[30] Stephen will conclude by describing this old-guard leadership as "uncircumcised in heart and ears, . . . forever opposing the Holy Spirit, just as your ancestors used to do." Abraham, we have just heard, experienced with God "the covenant of *circumcision*"[31] — the sign of God's presence — but these offspring of the ancestors are proven to be *uncircumcised* in heart and ears.

Your ancestors, Stephen will conclude, killed those who spoke of "the coming of the Righteous One." Joseph *speaks* of this coming by being, himself, righteous — evidence of God's presence. God "enabled [Joseph] to *win favor* and to *show wisdom* when he stood before Pharaoh, king of Egypt"; Jesus "increased in *wisdom* . . . and in divine and *human favor*."[32] Emphasized by Luke, the Spirit of God who is present with Jesus is the same Spirit of God who is present with Joseph, with the same hallmark wisdom and favor with God and people. Joseph and Jesus are marked, in this narrative, by journey, the accompanying presence of God, and the paradoxical favor and rejection by human associates. Stephen himself is living out a further parallel to the lives of Joseph and Jesus.

3. Moses

Just prior to his address, Stephen had been accused of "blasphemous words against Moses and God" and of championing Jesus, who changed "the customs that Moses handed down to us."[33] Luke shows Stephen taking up the challenge, building his speech toward Moses as the penultimate word-bearer of Israel. Moses shares with Abraham and Joseph the phenomenon of always journeying and always being accompanied by the conspicuous Presence of God. Moses has never had a home: he

---

30. 7:9; 5:17.
31. 7:8.
32. Acts 7:10; Lk 2:52.
33. Acts 6:11, 14.

flees from his birthplace in Egypt, a home that is not home; then he must leave Midian, where he had settled down as an alien; then he wanders in a wilderness as leader of the burgeoning people of Israel by whom he is rejected.

Stephen offers an overview of the life of Moses. Brought up in his father's house in Egypt for just three months, Moses is abandoned and adopted by Pharaoh's daughter. At the age of 40 he sees a fellow Israelite being harassed and goes to help, supposing "that his kinfolk would understand that God through him was rescuing them."[34] Rejected, Moses flees to Midian; another forty years pass (making Moses 80). He fathers two children. God appears and reveals the divine purpose of rescuing Israel, soliciting support from Moses in the rescue plan. In Egypt, Moses is again rejected by his kinfolk. But the deliverance of Israel from Egypt happens anyway, followed by a third forty-year period of time — the wilderness wandering of Moses and the people of Israel. Once again, Moses is rejected by his kinfolk. This time, the refusal to go along with Moses' leadership occurs in spite of God's presence with the people themselves: God is present in an accompanying "tent of testimony."[35]

The speech is focusing, in part, on the rejection of Jesus by the leadership of his own people. In the first forty-year period of his life, Moses is "abandoned" as an infant by his immediate kinfolk and then, as a 40-year-old adult, is "pushed aside"[36] by his countrymen; in the third forty-year period of Moses' life, his kinfolk again "pushed him aside."[37] They have refused to obey his leadership and the living word he brings them from God. The parallel between Moses and Jesus is clear, relative to this old-guard council who are themselves descendants of the ancestors.

Stephen had been accused of countermanding "the customs that Moses handed on to us," and indeed, to the extent that the old-guard council of Israel views the Law of Moses as customs and clan-rules, the charges stand (Israel's new-guard council will adjudicate on the basis of principle and spirit rather than rule and religious scruple).[38] The accusation of flouting religious custom is countered by Stephen's consideration of Moses as a word-bearer from God: Moses is a man beautiful before God, the possessor of godly wisdom; one who has passed along God's "*living* oracles"; a man of "powerful words and deeds." These echoes of Jesus' char-

34. 7:25.
35. 7:44.
36. 7:27.
37. 7:39.
38. Acts 15, explored in the following chapter.

acter, as presented by Luke in his gospel, affirm the emergence of a higher truth, that of God's Way as interpreted by Jesus. Religious customs have indeed given way to the Law interpreted as living principle, "*living* oracles," insights to live by.

The rejection of Moses is about authority: "Who made you a ruler and a judge" over us? With Moses, the rejection theme becomes a litany of abuse: "Our ancestors were unwilling to obey him; instead, they pushed him aside, and in their hearts they turned back to Egypt," just as earlier, in Egypt, they had "pushed him aside."[39] As with Moses and Jesus, Stephen will be pushed aside in as decisive and violent a manner as possible. But the empowerment of God reverses such rejection: echoing what we have heard Peter say in his second major speech to Israel, Stephen continues, "This is the Moses who said to the Israelites, 'God will raise up a prophet for you from your own people as he raised me up.'"[40]

From the rejection of Moses the speech returns to the other thematic focus of God's ubiquitous presence, through the Spirit. Joshua and David are mentioned briefly in respect to this traveling presence of God, along with an acknowledgment that David's son Solomon was the first to build a geographically fixed "place" in which God would dwell.[41] And yet: "the Most High does not dwell in houses made with human hands."[42] The speech clearly highlights the historical fact that, as Gregory Sterling points out, "God's dealings with Israel's heroes [are] away from the Temple and surrounding area."[43]

Returning once again to the theme of rejection, Stephen confronts the old-guard council as allied with all those ancestors who rejected the word-bearers of God. "You are the ones" who "received the law as ordained by angels, and yet you have not kept it"; in fact, "you are forever opposing the Holy Spirit."[44] The old-guard leadership of Israel "became enraged and ground their teeth at Stephen" — and stoned him to death.[45] As was the case for Jesus, Stephen dies *because of* — not *on behalf of* — the sins of these aggressors.[46] Echoing directly the words of Jesus, Stephen cries out, "Lord

---

39. 7:39, 27.

40. 7:37; see 3:22.

41. 7:45-47.

42. 7:48.

43. "Opening the Scriptures," in *Jesus and the Heritage of Israel*, ed. David P. Moessner (Harrisburg, Pa.: Trinity Press International, 1999), p. 213.

44. 7:53, 51.

45. 7:54-60.

46. Luke's point in such parallelism between the deaths of Stephen and Jesus is his in-

Jesus, receive my spirit."[47] And in his very last words, again echoing directly the words of Jesus, Stephen prays to God, "Lord, do not hold this sin against them."[48] Luke's use of the paralleled experience of all word-bearers moves here from Joseph-Jesus to Moses-Jesus to Stephen-Jesus. This continuity with Scripture is maintained in a culmination of Israel's history of word-bearers in the ultimate word-bearer, Jesus. Dying, Stephen asks that Jesus receive his spirit; he has seen "Jesus *standing*" — and again, the "Son of Man *standing* at the right hand of God" — waiting for him?[49] The ignominy of death by stoning or by hanging on a tree is overturned by God's raising and exaltation of Jesus, the essential "paradox" of salvation.[50] Stephen's prayer will be granted, his spirit received into the precincts of God's glory where the Son of Man stands waiting for him.[51]

Stephen's speech brings together the rejection theme with the phenomenon of the Holy Spirit by showing that God was present with precisely those who were reviled. The striving required for entry to God's kingdom, in the face of inevitable rejection, is impossible without God's empowerment through the Holy Spirit. Before his speech, we are told that Stephen was "full of the Spirit and of wisdom."[52] At the end of his speech, "filled with the Holy Spirit, he gazed into heaven and saw the glory of God and Jesus standing at the right hand of God."[53] Focusing on

---

sistence throughout the whole story that the dying of Jesus is a model for the dying and relinquishment to be borne by all true believers. "Luke isolates and pinpoints neither the death of the Lord nor those of his followers," as Eric Franklin points out. "The death of Jesus is significant, not in itself, but for the sufferings and way of life of which it is the climax and for the exaltation to which it leads." Closely connected, "the deaths [of followers] are never isolated, separated out, as the inescapable and vicariously effective means of the extension of salvation. They witness to *a way* followed by the Lord and by every disciple, to a way of constraint, of suffering, of a daily taking up of the cross and of following in the way of him who came into our midst as one who served." Eric Franklin, *Luke: Interpreter of Paul, Critic of Matthew,* Journal for the Study of the New Testament Supplement 92 (Sheffield, U.K.: JSOT Press, 1994), p. 130.

47. Acts 7:59; Lk 23:46.

48. 7:60; Lk 23:34. Other ancient manuscripts lack these words in the gospel, though the consistent paralleling of scenes and words by Luke argues eloquently for the authenticity of the longer manuscript version.

49. 7:59; 7:55-56, emphasis mine.

50. See Peter Doble's fine study, *The Paradox of Salvation* (Cambridge: Cambridge University Press, 1996), esp. pp. 226-44.

51. 7:55.

52. Acts 6:3.

53. 7:55.

three Jewish heroes, Stephen has emphasized the reality of the Holy Spirit as something Israel has always known. "The Most High does not dwell in houses made with human hands," but in the lives of those displaced, like Abraham, Joseph, and Moses — and from those rejected, like Joseph and Moses.[54] Leaving home and family behind is an aspect of repentance insisted upon in volume one, the gospel. Relinquishment for the sake of God's purposes marks the three heroes of Stephen's speech: here is a striving to enter God's kingdom without which salvation is impossible.[55]

Stephen is stoned to death, which accomplishes not just an ironic reversal insofar as Stephen is concerned — he will be received into the realm of God's eternal glory[56] — but leads to the grand irony of further promulgating a Way the old-guard had intended to squash.[57] Abraham, Joseph, and Moses represent just such a moveable feast of the kingdom provided by God, a divine willingness to locate anywhere God's people are — to be present with them, though they are far from the sacred space of a specially privileged holy site.[58] Rooted in Jerusalem with the twelve who reside there, God's Way nevertheless moves outward from Jerusalem to Israelites scattered "to the ends of the earth," and, through saved Israel, to all peoples.[59] Such were God's purposes in choosing a special people, a people who would become faithful and serve as priests to the world.[60]

Stephen's speech reminds Luke's audience that this two-volume narrative is a story of God. The speech is framed by an initial reference to "the God of glory" who "appeared to our ancestors" and "the glory of God" seen by Stephen at the end.[61] The glory of God is given flesh and blood, in Acts, by believers who are serving God's purposes, entering God's kingdom themselves and making it possible for other Israelites to do so as well — all in the name of God's "holy servant," Jesus.[62]

54. 7:48.

55. Lk 13:23-30; see Chapter 13.

56. Acts 7:59.

57. The Way begins to spread beyond Jerusalem, as a result of persecution like that of Stephen's (chapter 8 of Acts).

58. Lk 13:23-30.

59. Acts 1:8; 3:25.

60. Gen 12:3; Acts 3:25; the covenantal idea is spoken of in Exodus in terms of Israel becoming for all nations "a priestly kingdom and a holy nation" (Ex 19:6).

61. 7:2, 55.

62. 4:27, 30.

Three Model Speeches: A Summary

Three model speeches are presented in narrative succession. The new leadership speaks in the name of Jesus, and they do so in unison only twice, both times in response to confrontations with the council of Israel's old-guard leadership. In the first, they praise the cosmic rule of God; in the follow-up speech, the new leadership expresses its utter fidelity to God and a succinct rehearsal of the gospel's good news.

The hostile council of old-guard leadership precipitates the first speech and hears the second. The new leadership of Israel comports itself as Jesus did in his confrontation with the same council. These three council confrontations are followed by a fourth, with Stephen. The old leadership hears a model history of Israel in which two interrelated themes are emphasized: journeying word-bearers from Scripture who were rejected by many within Israel, but were nonetheless sustained by God's ever-present and empowering Spirit. Jesus is in the line of Israel's faithful: he journeyed as an alien with no home to call his own,[63] was filled with the Holy Spirit,[64] and was rejected by the traditional leadership of Israel. In their experience of God's empowering Spirit, according to this model speech, alien residents Abraham, Joseph, and Moses prepare the way for Jesus, while Stephen echoes even more closely the experience of Israel's "Leader and Savior."[65] For speaking these words from God, Stephen is rejected by this old-guard council and stoned to death. Dying, Stephen is granted sight of the welcoming Son of Man standing "at the right hand of God," the "Lord Jesus" who will receive Stephen's spirit into the precincts of God's glory.[66]

- "Listen to whatever [Jesus] tells you," Moses has said about Jesus, as understood by Peter.[67]
- *Let Moses be your guide about God's truth revealed in Jesus,* Stephen says.

Stephen's speech is a pivot point in the action of Acts, an action that turns now to the spread of the Way taught by Jesus, illustrated by the repentance of Peter. This new-guard leader repents once again, discovering the true nature of the original covenant made by God with Israel in bringing God's blessing to all peoples of the earth.

63. Lk 9:58.
64. Lk 3:22; 4:1, 14, 18.
65. Acts 5:31.
66. 7:55, 59.
67. Acts 3:22.

Chapter 19

Peter: Three Speeches about
Non-Jews Joining Faithful Israel

Acts 10:34-43; 11:4-17; 15:7-11

The confrontation between one of the new leaders of Israel and Israel's old-guard leadership has ended with Stephen's murder. Peter, for his part, is faced with the call to relinquish clan and religious loyalties. As a faithful Israelite, he must allow an outsider in. The outsider, a godly non-Jew, is part of a dramatic scenario that reveals the repentance not only of Peter but of all twelve of Israel's new leadership regarding the "outsider." The action unfolds around three speeches of Peter concerning this matter of including within faithful Israel, and God's blessing, all peoples on earth. We come to a great moment in the story Luke is telling about God's ancient desire for the world, through Israel.

Israel's Salvation Completed

Peter breaks ground on the most spectacular aspect of repentance for Israel, the final flowering of its salvation: Israel fulfills its ancient covenant by bringing God's blessing of peace to all peoples.[1] Peter leads the way, but Paul takes over. So critical is this aspect of Israel's salvation that Luke has both Peter and Paul in somewhat parallel roles:

- **Peter**: "My brothers," Peter says to his fellow leaders in Jerusalem, "you know that in the early days God made a choice among you, that I should be the one through whom the Gentiles would hear the message of the good news and become believers."[2]

1. Acts 3:25; Gen 12:3.
2. 15:7.

- **Paul**: "[Paul] is an instrument whom I have chosen," says God to Ananias, "to bring my name before Gentiles and kings and before the people of Israel."[3]

These two heroes of Acts, the two most prominent leaders within Israel, are each assigned a role in Israel's inclusion of the Gentiles among those Israelites "who belonged to the Way."[4] Though many Gentiles are reported as coming to the Way, their mention is always a minor though critical narrative note: the main dramatic focus of the two-volume story is Israel's salvation, a salvation marked by that which ensures "*universal* restoration," the inclusion of believing non-Jews into the *ekklēsia* of Israel.

The inclusion of non-Jews within saved Israel and God's family proves, for Peter, a fulfillment of the ancient vision of God, expressed to Abraham, that through his nation God would provide blessing to "all the families of the earth."[5]

From Acts 7 on, the text indicates the outward thrust of the gospel, through Israel to all peoples. We hear of Stephen's stoning in chapter 7, a murder that led to the spread of the Way beyond the parochial boundaries of Jerusalem to scattered Jews, and for the first time to the hated "half-Jews," the Samaritans. "Philip went down [north] to the city of Samaria and proclaimed the Messiah to them," and later the Holy Spirit is given to these new Samaritan believers.[6] These were neighbors sharing with Jerusalem Jews the same scripture (i.e., the Torah, the five books of Moses) but with differing interpretations, messianic expectations, and designated "holy space" — Mount Gerizim rather than Jerusalem. Neighbors who are not neighborly are not true neighbors: Luke's gospel uses the judgmentalism of traditional Israel toward Samaritans to great effect, accentuating the significance here to illustrate the Way's spread beyond Jerusalem to the despised Samaritans.[7] As suggested by Luke's story, true inclusivity is most difficult with neighbors — a blind beggar, a

---

3. 9:15.

4. Acts 9:2, referring at this point exclusively to Israelite believers.

5. Acts 3:25.

6. Acts 8:5, 17.

7. Lk 9:52-55; 10:33-35; 17:11-19; "Luke's narrative presupposes an awareness of the Samaritans' status as foreigners . . . who are not as peripheral to conventional understandings of God's purposes as Gentiles would be, but who are nonetheless not expected to exemplify the graciousness of God." Joel B. Green, *The Gospel of Luke*, New International Commentary on the New Testament (Grand Rapids: Eerdmans, 1997), p. 405.

Jewish tax-collector — or nearby clan-groups: Samaritans, just over the border.

In Acts 8 we hear of Philip's being sent from Samaria in the opposite direction, south toward Gaza. On the road from Jerusalem to Gaza, he finds a godly Ethiopian official (whether Jewish or not we are not told) who is returning from Jerusalem. This eunuch would have been kept from temple worship because he is castrated. Here is another instance, along with Samaritans, of conspicuous outsider status.[8] The Ethiopian eunuch is illumined and baptized by Philip.

The inclusion of Samaritans and of an African eunuch into the people of God is a surprise that pales in comparison to what happens next — the repentance of Saul, the most avid of the persecutors of fellow Israelites "who belonged to the Way."[9] In repenting of his zeal for a rules-bound purity of Israel, Saul — his name changed to Paul — receives a challenge from God to reach out as a faithful Israelite toward the grossly impure, those beyond Israel or any of its sects. Once an old-guard Israelite, Paul will remain a Pharisee who now worships God "according to the Way."[10]

Immediately after hearing of Paul's repentance, we are given Peter's repentance — a turning-around that parallels Paul's transformation.[11] Like Paul, Peter is reoriented radically toward a kingdom reality that allows non-Jews into the worship and practice of God's delivered people — and without the clan-markings of circumcision. In Peter's case as in Paul's, God's empowering Spirit makes such repentance possible. For Peter, as we see next, the all-inclusive nature of the Holy Spirit becomes the main focus of his three speeches concerning Gentiles. (A chart at the end of this chapter highlights the pattern of message and audience in these three speeches concerning Gentiles.) We recall that Peter's first speech to Israel made a great deal of Joel's prophecy that in the last days God's Spirit would be poured out on *all* flesh.[12]

---

8. 8:38.

9. 9:2. The shock is expressed, representatively, by the disciple Ananias, who balks at being involved with Saul's healing. "Lord," he remonstrates, "I have heard from many about this man, how much evil he has done to your saints in Jerusalem; and here he has authority from the chief priests to bind all who invoke your name" (9:13-14).

10. 9:2, 15, 18; 24:14.

11. Paul, 9:1-30; Peter, 10:1-48.

12. 2:17-21; 2:33, 38.

Peter's First Speech Concerning the Gentiles
(Peter's fifth speech overall; 10:34-43)

Just prior to his experience with Cornelius, a Roman centurion, Peter had raised the dead, an event captured in a very brief passage (seven verses).[13] But with the Cornelius story Luke's narrative moves on to something of even greater dramatic interest, indicated both by narrative length (68 verses)[14] and by Luke's prior narrative concern with Israel's status.

Cornelius, a Gentile servant of Rome, had received a vision from God through an angel. The centurion seems not to need the message of repentance (and we do not hear it), since he is already doing "deeds consistent with repentance": he is "a devout man who feared God with all his household; he gave alms generously to the people and prayed constantly."[15] The angel announces God's favor: "Your prayers and your alms have ascended as a memorial before God" — *send for Peter.*[16] God favors Cornelius because Cornelius favors God, a principle that volume one made clear in its twelve preparatory poems.[17]

As the company of "devout soldiers" and slaves from Cornelius make their way to Joppa, Peter goes up on a roof for noon prayers. Hungry, he falls into a trance and sees animals whose flesh was forbidden by religious rule as food for Israelites. But a heavenly voice tells Peter to kill and eat.[18] "By no means, Lord," says Peter.[19] "What God has made clean," says the voice, "you must not call profane or unclean."[20] Again the voice says, kill and eat. Again Peter remonstrates. And again the heavenly voice says, kill and eat. And once again Peter balks: "By no means, Lord!" he says, and apparently persists in arguing.[21] Here we have a serious impasse, it would appear, between God and one of Israel's prominent new leaders. Meanwhile, of course, the men of Cornelius are on their way to find Peter and deliver him back to the unclean-eating Roman centurion.

13. 9:36-42.
14. Extending from 10:1 through 11:18.
15. 10:31; 26:20; 10:2.
16. 10:4-5.
17. See Chapters 2 and 3.
18. 10:9-13.
19. 10:14.
20. 10:15.
21. 10:15-16.

Peter is still puzzling over what this vision from God could mean — a vision that concludes with a standoff between Peter and God — when "suddenly the men sent by Cornelius appeared."[22] Peter's repenting comes in stages. First, Peter provides lodging for the men of Cornelius.[23] Next, he agrees to travel to Caesarea the very next day, and to meet with the Gentile centurion, servant of Rome.[24] Finally, Peter grasps the significance of the vision, and the standoff with God is resolved: "You yourselves know," Peter confesses to Cornelius and friends, "that it is unlawful for a Jew to associate with or to visit a Gentile; but God has shown me that I should not call anyone profane or unclean."[25] For his part, Cornelius relates the vision God gave him. Peter hears that "a man in dazzling clothes" had appeared to Cornelius with these words: "Cornelius, your prayer has been heard and your alms have been remembered before God."[26]

Peter's Speech

"Then Peter began to speak to them."[27] What will he say? What possible gospel can be rehearsed for this man favored by God, this non-Jew servant of Rome who fears the living God?

> "I truly understand [says Peter] that God shows no partiality, but in every nation anyone who fears him and does what is right is acceptable to him. You know the message he sent to the people of Israel, preaching peace by Jesus Christ — he is Lord of all. That message spread throughout Judea, beginning in Galilee after the baptism that John announced: how God anointed Jesus of Nazareth with the Holy Spirit and with power; how he went about doing good and healing all who were oppressed by the devil, for God was with him. We are witnesses to all that he did both in Judea and in Jerusalem. They put him to death by hanging him on a tree; but God raised him on the third day and al-

22. 10:17.

23. 10:23.

24. Compounding the "otherness" of this Gentile is his service on behalf of the presumably evil empire of Rome. As we have noted, however, Roman justice is portrayed by Luke as consistently more even-handed toward Israel than Israel's leadership's justice to its own.

25. 10:28.

26. 10:30-31.

27. 10:34.

lowed him to appear, not to all the people but to us who were chosen by God as witnesses, and who ate and drank with him after he rose from the dead. He commanded us to preach to the people and to testify that he is the one ordained by God as judge of the living and the dead. All the prophets testify about him that everyone who believes in him receives forgiveness of sins through his name." (10:34-43)

The nature of God's blessing for the world is given in the single summary word *peace*. Luke's audience will not be surprised at this echoing of the angel's one-word message to the shepherds.[28] This is the evidence of salvation, a "message of the good news" that promises peace.[29]

In this gospel message to non-Jews, delivered by believing Israel as represented by Peter, Luke's audience hears rehearsed two of the three major emphases of the salvation message, as determined by Jesus in his last-words speech:[30]

- the question of authority resolved in the *resurrection* of Jesus, Messiah;[31]
- the outpouring of God's empowering *Holy Spirit*.[32]

Repentance is the missing theme — but of course Cornelius is already "doing deeds consistent with repentance."[33]

The dramatic fact of repentance is best illustrated here in the turnaround of Peter himself. For what reason, then, does Cornelius need to hear the gospel news, since he has proven himself "acceptable to [God]" and anyone who is acceptable to God surely is experiencing God's salvation?[34] The narrative context suggests that Cornelius needs

---

28. Lk 2:14.

29. Speech #2, 11:14; Speech #3, 15:7.

30. Lk 24:46-49.

31. "judge of the living and the dead," 10:42; "God raised him on the third day," 10:40.

32. 10:44.

33. 10:2, 31, 34-35; Cornelius "does what is right"; he is "a devout man who feared God with all his household; he gave alms generously to the people and prayed constantly" (10:35 & 2). "All the [Jewish] prophets testify," Peter says to Cornelius, "that everyone who believes in him receives forgiveness of sins through his name" (10:43). Everyone? For Peter, this is a breakthrough from the clutches of parochialism. Repentance turns out to be more vividly illustrated here by Peter than by Cornelius: it is Peter who must do an about-face. Peter is beginning to understand, as Cornelius surely is hearing in this speech, that God, through Jesus, wants to be "Lord of all," of "*everyone* who believes," non-Jew and Jew alike.

34. One might argue that divine acceptance is not enough for salvation, that such fa-

empowerment from the Holy Spirit toward an embrace of Jesus and the full disclosure of a Way that leads to communal well-being and the in-breaking of God's kingdom. Becoming a believer in Jesus and experiencing the "forgiveness of sins through his name"[35] is for Cornelius a reality that must play out in a new sort of community, a kingdom community. The Roman military man "had called together his relatives and close friends"[36] as communal participants whose ultimate allegiance is no longer to Lord Emperor but to Lord Jesus, the Messiah of their now-friends, the Jews. Jewish believers witnessing the events surrounding Cornelius "were astounded that the gift of the Holy Spirit had been poured out even on the Gentiles," not just on Cornelius, the godly one.[37] The Cornelius clan, servants to Rome, will join the *ekklēsia* within Israel, people of the Way.

"Everyone who believes in [Jesus]," Peter has said, "receives forgiveness of sins through his name." Believing in Jesus, as we have seen, means an engagement with a community whose Lord is Jesus. To his fellow Israelites, Peter will recall the vision Cornelius had received: the centurion was to expect a message from Peter "'by which you and *your entire household* will be saved,' and as I began to speak," Peter adds, "the Holy Spirit fell *upon them.*"[38] The salvation of Cornelius is a corporate affair, an identification from henceforth with those Israelites who belonged to the Way.

Cornelius needs to know that this Jesus has been appointed "Lord of all, and Judge of the living and the dead." The basis for what the Judge judges is all that Jesus taught, while the basis for the status of Jesus as Judge is the authority vested in Messiah by God's raising him from death. "Everyone who believes in him," then, will obey that teaching and "receive forgiveness of sins through his name."[39]

---

voring as experienced by Cornelius must lead to confession of Jesus as Lord for salvation to be effected; this is tortuous thinking, I think, since God's "forgiveness of sin" is invariably linked in this story to repentance, about which Cornelius does not need to hear since he is living a repentance-life. The narrative point in this story points to God's desire to include Cornelius and friends with the furthering of God's kingdom reality through the empowering Spirit and the power of a community of believers.

35. 10:43.
36. 10:24.
37. 10:45.
38. 11:14-15.
39. We have rehearsed this idea of "believe" in the Introduction and in my first chapter

For the community assembled by Cornelius, this resurrection-basis for the status of Jesus as Judge of all the world is especially poignant. "We are witnesses," Peter says to Cornelius, that "they[40] put him to death by hanging him on a tree, but *God raised him* on the third day."[41] Peter repeats here the phrase "hanging him on a tree" that was used by the Twelve in their accusation of the old-guard leadership of Israel.[42] But of course it was the Roman practice to crucify criminals, and Roman authority that finally capitulated to pressure from Israel's old-guard in considering Jesus a criminal worthy of crucifixion. Cornelius serves a Roman emperor he takes as "the lord of the whole world";[43] now Cornelius hears of a Lord who trumps all lords by leading a kingdom unlike any other. As does Paul in his only speech to Gentiles (explored in a later chapter), Peter underscores to the non-Jew the role of Jesus as Judge.

The pious members of Luke's Jewish audience might associate the horror of Rome's torturous practice of murder by "hanging on a tree" with the curse of God for any corpse left unburied.[44] If this is an intentional echoing of Scripture, the irony of reversal so prevalent in the larger story is made all the more clear: the judgment incited by old-guard Israel to "crucify him"[45] is undercut by God's raising Jesus from death. That is, the one whom Israel's old-guard leadership presumed to put under God's judgment by having him hung on a tree is in reality exalted by God as Judge and "Lord of all."[46] The reversal from ridicule — and death, Roman style

---

on Acts, Part IV; we will offer one last summary look at this idea in the Conclusion in terms of a Gentile jailer who is told to believe in Jesus as Lord in order to be saved.

40. *They* — Romans? Old-guard leadership? Presumably, "they" means what we have seen in the case of Jesus: Israel's old-guard leadership drumming up charges to the Roman authorities, and whipping Israel into mob frenzy and condemnation, however momentary (see Chapter 16).

41. 10:36-40.

42. 5:30.

43. *"Lord* of all" (10:36) is possibly an echo used by Luke of an inscription for Nero, "lord [emperor] of all the world." Nero, emperor of Rome two or three decades before Luke wrote, liked the title *kurios* ("lord," "ruler"), and in fact was known by an inscription "lord of all the world." *The NIV Theological Dictionary of New Testament Words,* ed. Verlyn D. Verbrugge (Grand Rapids: Zondervan, 2000), p. 725.

44. Deut 21:23.

45. Lk 23:13-24.

46. As I have suggested in the prior chapter, especially in reference to Peter Doble's *The Paradox of Salvation* (Cambridge: Cambridge University Press, 1996), esp. pp. 226-44. Neither here nor anywhere else in the two-volume story is there any suggestion of the death of Jesus as a sacrifice for sins — a bearing of sins by being under the curse of God. The point

— to life and exaltation as "judge of the living *and the dead*" could not be greater. Such reversal-of-the-normal has been anticipated by Mary in the story's very first poem and illustrated repeatedly — nowhere in more startling fashion than by Jesus himself.[47] In a prior speech by all twelve to the old-guard council of Israel, reference to the one "whom you had killed by hanging him on a tree" is followed immediately and triumphantly with "God exalted him at his right hand as Leader and Savior . . ."[48] And here, in Peter's speech to the Roman military man, the "hanging him on a tree" is overcome by God's raising Jesus.

Though the emphasis for Cornelius and his community is on this sense of Jesus as Lord — as "judge of the living and the dead" — they are "baptized in the name of Jesus *Christ*."[49] That is, through the dying of baptism they are raised into a new life in the people of God, the *ekklēsia* of Israel; their new life, then, is lived "in the name" of Israel's Messiah.[50]

Peter's Second Speech Concerning the Gentiles
(Peter's sixth speech overall; 11:4-17)

Peter's first speech to Gentiles resulted from a vision from God about extending blessing to a Gentile, expressed in table intimacy and articulation of the good news. This second speech follows up by recounting that vision to the other eleven new leaders of Israel.

> "I was in the city of Joppa praying, and in a trance I saw a vision. There was something like a large sheet coming down from heaven, being lowered by its four corners; and it came close to me. As I looked at it closely I saw four-footed animals, beasts of prey, reptiles, and birds of the air. I also heard a voice saying to me, 'Get up, Peter; kill and eat.'

---

here about hanging on a tree seems rather to implicate Rome (and Cornelius indirectly) for its widespread cruelty of death by hanging victims on a tree. As this speech by Peter goes on to emphasize, it is the resurrection of Jesus that provides a basis for salvation and judgment. "He is the one," goes the thinking here, raised up and exalted — "ordained by God as judge of the living and the dead" (10:42). Just as Peter has one speech to Gentiles and emphasizes Jesus as world judge by virtue of being raised from death, so too Paul has one speech to Gentiles and emphasizes precisely the same point, as we will see.

47. Lk 1:51-53.

48. 5:31.

49. 10:48.

50. 10:48. The incorporation of Gentiles into the called-out ones *(ekklēsia)* of Israel will become especially clear in Peter's third speech, Acts 15.

But I replied, 'By no means, Lord; for nothing profane or unclean has ever entered my mouth.' But a second time the voice answered from heaven, 'What God has made clean, you must not call profane.' This happened three times; then everything was pulled up again to heaven." (11:5-10)

Peter continues in his speech by recalling what God had told him before he met the party from Cornelius in Joppa. It is crucial information: "The Spirit told me to go with them and not to make a distinction between them and us."[51]

Peter recounts his response of surprise about the Gentiles receiving the Holy Spirit: "I remembered the word of the Lord, how he had said, 'John baptized with water, but you will be baptized with the Holy Spirit.' If then God gave them the same gift that he gave us when we believed in the Lord Jesus Christ, who was I that I could hinder God?"[52] Having resisted God at first,[53] Peter has embraced what was previously unsavory and unthinkable, reoriented now toward God's purposes of *peace*, a reconciliation between *them* and *us* in the sharing of God's empowering Spirit.

The new leadership in Jerusalem has listened well to Peter, and "they praised God, saying, 'Then God has given even to the Gentiles repentance that leads to life.'"[54] It is a repentance so humanly impossible to achieve that the gift of God's empowering Spirit is required. When Peter had been speaking to Cornelius and his family, we recall, "the Holy Spirit fell upon them."[55] This gift is proof positive for the Twelve that God, indeed, has given to Gentiles a "repentance that leads to life."

Peter's Third Speech Concerning the Gentiles
(Peter's seventh and last speech; 15:7-11)

Before this third speech concerning Gentiles, Peter's last of seven speeches, Paul will have delivered his first of seven speeches, a major address to his fellow Israelites "and others who fear God."[56] The eight-

---

51. 11:12.
52. 11:15-17.
53. "By no means, Lord," 10:14.
54. 11:18.
55. 11:14-15.
56. 13:16; see Chapter 20.

chapter narrative overlap between Peter and Paul[57] helps to emphasize the thematic overlap and paralleled experiences between these two major heroes of Acts. Peter's speech concerning Gentiles here in chapter 15 involves serious issues that Paul's proclamation and teaching have raised.

Some time after Paul's repentance on the road to Damascus, a number of "Jews" come into Lystra (Asia Minor) and stir up the crowds against Paul; "they stoned Paul and dragged him out of the city, supposing that he was dead."[58] But Paul recovers the next day, and he and Barnabas travel from here to there, in rapid narrative fashion.[59]

Paul and Barnabas run into controversy about the salvation status of uncircumcised Gentile believers and are sent to Jerusalem for a conference with the Twelve and the elders.[60] And so it is that Peter with the eleven others and the elders meet with Paul and Barnabas. Some Pharisee believers thought it "necessary for [Gentiles] to be circumcised and ordered to keep the law of Moses."[61] Who could be among those who belonged to the Way, the believers within faithful Israel?[62] What does it mean to be faithful Israel, and to be joined by Gentiles who come to share in that faithfulness to God? This is the matter before Israel's new leadership in Jerusalem. "After there had been much debate, Peter stood up and said to them,

> 'My brothers, you know that in the early days God made a choice among you, that I should be the one through whom the Gentiles would hear the message of the good news and become believers. And God, who knows the human heart, testified to them by giving them the Holy

---

57. "Peter and the apostles" respond to the old-guard in 5:29-42; Stephen takes up chapters 6 and 7. Paul ("Saul") is mentioned at the beginning of chapter 8, which follows with mention of Peter and John along with Philip. Paul takes up the first part of chapter 9 (1-31), Peter, the second part (9:32-43). Peter and Cornelius, chapters 10 and 11:1-18; Paul, 11:25-26; then Peter again, 12:3-19. Paul again, 13:1-52 — including Paul's first and quite major speech, to Israel (primarily). Paul, chapter 14; Peter, chapter 15 — at which point Peter fades from the dramatic scene in favor of Paul, up through the end of Acts in the 28th chapter.

58. 14:19.

59. 14:21-28.

60. 15:1-2.

61. 15:5.

62. 9:2; to persist with "church" as a translation for *ekklēsia* is, I think, a distortion of fact within the story Luke tells. Any contemporary idea or definition of "church" (Jews leaving Israel to join a "church" that believing Gentiles also join) is a concept completely foreign to this narrative. *Ekklēsia* is used as a term for pagan assemblies also (Acts 19:32)!

Spirit, just as he did to us; and in cleansing their hearts by faith he has made no distinction between them and us. Now therefore why are you putting God to the test by placing on the neck of the disciples a yoke that neither our ancestors nor we have been able to bear? On the contrary, we believe that we will be saved through the favor of the Lord Jesus, just as they will.'" (15:7-11)

Israel's new leadership, the twelve, listen next to Paul and Barnabas. Then James affirms what Peter has said, citing Scripture and declaring that "we should not trouble those Gentiles who are turning to God" with circumcision.[63] There is the Torah taught by Jesus as a Way that brings God's blessing to others, and there is the Torah as Peter has just pointed out, placed "on the neck of the disciples . . . that neither our ancestors nor we have been able to bear."[64]

The outcome of James's confirmation of Peter's speech among the new-guard leadership in Jerusalem is their corporate repenting — in this case, of clan-rules for religious identification. Such continuing transformation is central to the fulfillment of the ancient covenant, and is indicated by a letter to be sent up north to Antioch, for the non-Jewish believers: "it has seemed good to the Holy Spirit and to us to impose on you no further burden [rules] than these essentials: that you abstain from [grossly defiled food: idol sacrifices, blood-food, food resulting from strangulation] and fornication."[65]

If the rule-aspect of the Law is a burdensome yoke,[66] then what from the newly understood Law is liberating, for Peter and Paul as presented by Luke? The answer is encoded within Peter's last speech, above: salvation comes to those who "would hear the message of the good news and become believers."[67] Such code language, used throughout Acts, refers the alert audience back to volume one, Luke's gospel. There, as we have

---

63. 15:12-21; James does add, however, that certain dietary rules — not eating food offered to idols or "strangled and from blood" — should be followed if Gentiles are to join in with faithful Israel (15:20). See James D. G. Dunn's helpful discussion on the food matters; clearly not all the Jewish dietary code is included here, given Peter's vision that we have just looked at, preceding the Cornelius visit. James D. G. Dunn, *The Acts of the Apostles* (Valley Forge, Pa.: Trinity Press International, 1996), pp. 205-6.

64. 15:10.

65. 15:28-29.

66. Except for the minimal rules of no-fornication and no-eating of idol and blood food.

67. 15:7.

seen, the Way is unfolded as principles that are the opposite of rules — a dynamic for living that is best understood by the metaphor Luke uses of a journey. This journey, the Way taught by Jesus, is the teaching believers in Acts offer on behalf of Jesus, in the name of Jesus. Earlier, Luke had given a bird's-eye view of that upon which Paul and Barnabas base all their preaching and teaching, the Way as taught by their Messiah: "The whole city gathered to hear the word of the Lord."[68]

"We believe," says Peter in the conclusion to his last recorded speech, "that we will be saved through the favor [grace] of the Lord Jesus, just as they [non-Jews] will."[69] To those hearing "the words of the Lord" and doing the turn-around that characterizes repentance, grace is extended in the form of forgiveness and the empowering Spirit.

Peter's Three Speeches Concerning Non-Jews: A Summary

- "I will pour out my Spirit upon all flesh" (Acts 2:17).
- "Glory to God in the highest heaven, and on earth peace among those whom he favors" (Lk 2:14).

Peter's first speech to unbelievers at the Pentecost festival placed great emphasis on the Holy Spirit.[70] The dramatic focus on the Holy Spirit in Peter's last three speeches underscores Luke's perspective on God's desire to be fully present with all peoples everywhere. Peter articulates this inclusivity explicitly in his last three speeches; this openness of God has proven to Peter both revelatory and transforming. Israel will be saved insofar as the covenant is fulfilled, as redeemed Israel becomes servant to the world.[71] Peter's very first major speech to Israel and these last three speeches concerning non-Israel emphasize the importance of the Holy Spirit as empowerment to *all* flesh willing to hear and do the word taught by Jesus.[72]

In the last-words speech of Luke's gospel, as noted, we find highlighted the twin gospel themes of resurrection and repentance, along with the promise of God's empowering Spirit.[73] This same Spirit is ech-

68. 13:44.
69. 15:11.
70. 2:14-36.
71. 10:34-43; 11:4-17; 15:7-11.
72. Acts 3:25; Gen 12:3; Acts 2:17.
73. Lk 24:46-49.

oed in the second last-words speech of Jesus, in Acts.[74] Bearing witness to the resurrection, which has been central in Peter's prior speeches, becomes a moot point in the last two speeches to the Jerusalem leadership who already accept this resurrection. Repentance turns out to be more a matter for Peter and the Twelve than for Cornelius, who nonetheless experiences "forgiveness of sins through his name" in coming to embrace Jesus as Lord. What looms dramatically in all three of these last speeches by Peter is the key role of the Holy Spirit.[75]

Peter's speeches, then, have come full circle, from the pouring out of God's Spirit on Israel to this pouring-out on the "all flesh" of even non-Jews.[76] Here is the one undeniable mark of salvation for everyone, namely, the presence of God through the gift of the Holy Spirit. Empowering those who choose the Way, God's gift makes possible the worldwide *shalom* envisioned from the very start: a blessing for all peoples characterized by recovery, release, and restoration.[77] This is "the message," as Peter has said to Cornelius, that God "sent to the people of Israel, preaching peace by Jesus Christ."[78] This preaching of peace has been laid out brilliantly and thoroughly by Luke in his gospel, through the teachings by Jesus of principles based on the Law.

"Anyone who fears [God] and does what is right is acceptable to him"; believers are "not to make a distinction between them and us."[79] Here we see the fruits of "the message of peace." The normal world of "them and us" is being turned on its head; the kingdom Way is working its yeast-and-seed reality.[80] "These [Way] people . . . have been turning the world upside down," we hear a non-believer saying.[81]

Faithful Israel has been witnessing exclusively to unfaithful Israel up until the time of Stephen. Israel will continue to be the main focus of the salvation message — for Paul as well as Peter — but the ultimate goal of "servant Israel" is clear by the time we finish Peter's seven speeches. Peace comes through Jesus: he *casts* light on the Jewish scripture through teaching, and he *is* light in his enactment of that scripture.

Up to this point of his experience on the journey of repentance, Peter

74. 1:5, 8.
75. 10:44-47; 11:15-17; 15:8.
76. The Pentecost speech is addressed to Israel, 2:17; 15:8.
77. Lk 2:14; 4:18-19; Acts 10:36; Gen 12:3; Acts 3:25.
78. 10:36.
79. 10:35; 11:12.
80. Lk 13:18.
81. Acts 17:6.

Peter's Three Speeches concerning Gentiles

	Peter, to Gentiles (10:34-43)	Peter, about Gentiles (11:4-17)	Peter, about Gentiles (15:7-11)
Message of Peace and Inclusivity	"the message [God] sent to the people of Israel, *preaching peace* by Jesus Christ" (10:36)	". . . 'a message by which you and your entire household will be saved'" (11:14)	". . . the message [to non-Jews] of the good news . . ." (15:7)
	Peace, through an impartial God: "anyone who fears [God] and does what is right is acceptable to [God]" (10:35)	*Peace* looks like this: ". . . not to make a distinction between them [non-Jews] and us" (11:12)	*Peace* looks like this: ". . . [God] has made no distinction between them [non-Jews] and us" (15:9)
Repentance	— More for Peter than for Cornelius	— More for the twelve	— More for the twelve
	— Cornelius and companions baptized	"God has given even to the Gentiles the repentance that leads to life" (11:18)	"Cleansing their hearts by faith" — suggesting baptism, repentance? (15:9)
Resurrection	"God raised [Jesus]" (10:40)	(moot point, since the new leadership and not Gentiles are the audience)	(moot point, since the new leadership and not Gentiles are the audience)
Holy Spirit	"While Peter was still speaking, the Holy Spirit fell on all who heard the word" (10:44)	"If then God gave them the same gift [Spirit] that [God] gave us . . . who was I to hinder God?" (11:17)	"God . . . testified to them by giving them the Holy Spirit, just as he did for us" (15:8)
Jesus, Judge	Jesus is "ordained by God as judge of [all] living and the dead" (10:42)	(moot point, since the new leadership and not Gentiles are the audience)	(moot point, since the new leadership and not Gentiles are the audience)

had apparently thought the message of this Way, its peculiar peace, was exclusively for Israel, in spite of his mouthing of the ancient and most basic of challenges/promises to father Abraham regarding Israel: that through them the peoples of the world would be blessed.[82] Luke's patterning of repetitious elements in Peter's last three speeches, indicated by the chart above, highlights the global direction in which the preaching of Israel's Christ was headed all along. As we saw in Luke's gospel, Jesus had been focused on Israel in order to transform Israel into Mary's "servant Israel." Jesus' "preaching of peace" referred to by Peter becomes a preaching that Peter himself must hear, take to heart, and obey.

As faithful Israelite Peter repents, so too does zealous Israelite Paul. Peter's first speech addresses all of Israel, and so do Paul's first and last speeches. For Paul as for Peter, there is witness to the gospel truth of volume one: repentance and resurrection. What Paul adds is invitation and warning to those within Israel who have not joined the thousands of Israelites who are following the Way.

82. Acts 3:25; Gen 3:25.

Chapter 20

Paul in Acts: His Two Framing Speeches to Israel

Acts 13:16-41; 28:25-28

Just as Peter has seven major speeches, so too does Paul.[1] Paul's first speech, intended primarily for Israel, ends with a warning to those Israelites who are refusing Jesus as Messiah, while his last speech is aimed primarily at the resistant within Israel, and is all warning. Even here, however, there are Israelites still responding well to their Messiah. What Luke covers of Paul's journeying and mission has to do primarily with Israel and its salvation. With Paul leading the narrative way, thousands within Israel are still being added to the thousands within Israel who have already decided to go the Way of God, as taught by Jesus.[2] Only one of Paul's speeches is directed exclusively to those outside Israel, a fact that underscores the narrative focus in Luke's two-part story on the unfolding drama of Israel's redemption.

Paul in Acts: An Introduction

Paul has a greater portion of Acts devoted to him than any other figure. Like Peter, he has seven speeches that fall into set narrative patterns, depending on audience. His adventures are marked most significantly by a momentous journey to Jerusalem, a setting out that parallels Jesus' journey to Jerusalem.[3] And Paul shines in the two-volume story as a whole

---

1. Acts 13:16-41; 17:22-31; 20:18-35; 22:1-21; 24:10-21; 26:1-23; 28:25-28. I exclude what might be considered a speech, though it lacks some of the formal elements of the seven listed, 14:15-17.

2. Acts 21:20 (2:41; 4:4); 9:2.

3. See Lk 9:51 and Acts 19:21.

because he is the sterling example of an old-guard's transformation to Israel's true Way. Paul remains a Pharisee who follows Jesus as Israel's Christ. (Paul does not call himself, and is never called by the narrator, a "Christian." In Luke's narrative perspective, such terminology would connote a breakaway from Israel.[4]) Paul counts himself a faithful Israelite "who belonged to the Way."[5] He is one of the Pharisees, as portrayed in Luke's gospel, to whom much has been given and from whom much is expected. Paul delivers.

Three times we find the scene of Paul's repentance from old-guard mentality to the Way taught by Jesus. No such turn-around happened among old-guard leaders with whom Jesus was involved in the gospel, unless we consider council member Joseph, "a good and righteous man" who cared for the corpse of Jesus.[6] Paul becomes, for Luke, an important addition to the twelve new rulers of Israel; he is an exceptional "thirteenth" by virtue of encountering the risen Jesus.[7] Through all the adventures of Paul, including shipwrecks and jail escapes, the story focuses most on Paul's "theological" thinking — his view of what the death and resurrection of Jesus really mean, and where Israel fits in the Big Picture of God's will for the world. Writing at least a decade after Paul's epistles were in circulation, Luke insists on his familiarity with Paul's theological thinking not only by including seven speeches by Paul, but also by placing himself, as author, into the story as one of Paul's traveling companions.[8]

4. "Christian" is used only twice in Acts, once derogatorily by the Jewish king of the Jews to Paul, as a quip that flies in the face of that upon which Paul has been insisting, his own identity as a zealous follower of Israel's Law and Messiah (26:28). The other appearance of the term is when the narrator reports on the fact that these Way people were being referred to as "Christians" for the first time in Antioch (11:26) — a possibly negative put-down of believers as Jews breaking away from Israel's true religion (which of course Luke insists is not the case). "Those who belonged to the Way" (9:2) never referred to themselves as Christians. In any case, the story certainly shies away from the term in favor of its overriding concern to promote the earliest believers as saved Israel — and Gentile believers as joining saved Israel as the *ekklēsia* within Israel.

5. Acts 9:2; 24:14.

6. Lk 23:50-53.

7. "I saw Jesus saying to me," Luke records Paul saying in the second of three co-missioning/transformation accounts (22:18). *Seeing the risen Jesus:* this criterion of being witness becomes for Paul the focus of almost everything he says in his seven speeches (Acts 1:22).

8. Luke takes the nearly unprecedented step of putting himself in the narrative, alongside Paul, with a shift in point of view from third-person objective to first-person (the so-called "we" passages, starting at 20:6-8). This awkward shift in point-of-view is a powerful

Paul is a special "Thirteenth." Unlike the Twelve, he cannot bear witness to the resurrection on the basis of having been with Jesus,[9] but he emerges nonetheless in the last two-thirds of Acts as a major witness to this same resurrection through a special visitation from the resurrected Messiah. This witness includes speeches. Paul's seven speeches — as well as Peter's seven speeches — insist on the light that Jesus has brought to God's word about the kingdom and its Way, and on the authority of Jesus as word-bringer, established by God's raising him from death. Paul and Barnabas, "with many others," were busy in this: "they taught and proclaimed the word of the Lord."[10]

Paul's vision of salvation's core is expressed in five of seven speeches as a repentance marked by an about-face "from darkness to light."[11] *Repent,* says John; *repent,* says Jesus; *repent,* says Peter; *repent,* says Paul.[12] When Luke's Paul testifies to an entering of God's kingdom based on repentance as taught by Jesus, there is no substantial difference from Peter's testifying.[13] What Luke highlights in Paul's thinking even more than in Peter's speeches is a salvation grounded in the resurrection of Jesus.

While Paul and Peter agree on this matter of Jesus proclaiming the light of God's word (the Way)[14] and the resurrection as God's divine im-

---

reminder that Paul's is one account of Jesus with which Luke is familiar, first-hand: he has rubbed elbows with Paul, and at a late date in Paul's career. What has puzzled scholars about these "we" passages seems quite clear in respect to this, at the very least: Luke wants his audience to be assured that the accounts he claims to have investigated so carefully include the thinking of Paul (Lk 1:1-4).

9. Acts 1:21-22.

10. Acts 15:35; see also, 4:31; 6:2; 6:7; 8:14; 8:25; 11:1; 12:24; 13:5; 13:7; 13:44; 13:46; 13:49; 15:36; 16:32; 17:13; 18:11; 19:10; 19:20.

11. "Through [Jesus] forgiveness of sins is proclaimed" (13:38; Speech #1:), which we have seen always follows repentance; "[God] commands all people everywhere to repent" (because judgment is coming; 17:30-31; Speech #2); "I testified to both Jews and Greeks about repentance toward God and faith toward our Lord Jesus" (20:21; Speech #3); "Be baptized," Ananias says to Paul, "and have your sins washed away, calling on [Jesus'] name" (22:16; Speech #4); repentance spelled out as turning "from darkness to light" (26:18; Speech #6).

12. Lk 3:3; Lk 13:3; 13:5; 16:30; 17:4; Acts 2:38; 3:19; Acts 17:30; 26:20.

13. What Luke captures so dramatically in the spread of the Way by Paul is the bedrock from which springs Paul's liberating vision of the gospel, as recorded in his letters or in letters ascribed to him. One common thread between Luke's Paul and the Pauline epistles' Paul is this, that through repentance and forgiveness in Christ, all humankind is freed from clan parochialism and a status-clinging based on superior performance of the Law.

14. Peter, 3:22-23; Paul, 26:22-23.

primatur on that teaching for salvation, the tone of Paul's speeches is different from Peter's.[15] It is a tone of warning and of judgment. For Paul in Acts, Jesus is "the Righteous One," a phrase that echoes usage by Isaiah and Luke's Peter and Stephen.[16] This "Righteous One" is the One by whom Israel and all peoples must be judged, on the basis of righteousness as taught from Scripture by Jesus. Just as the momentous journey to Jerusalem recorded in Luke's gospel ends in the weeping of Jesus over the sad fate of Jerusalem, so too the dramatically prominent journey of Paul to Jerusalem and on to Rome ends with a reluctant but certain judgment on the unfaithful of Israel.[17]

For Paul as for Peter, God is the story's main character, and God's deliverance of Israel is paramount. Not until Paul's house arrest in Rome at the end of the story does the spread of God's Way promise to move in a concerted manner from its primary growth within Israel to all peoples of earth: at the conclusion of volume two, the mission to Israel has been completed, successfully, even though many are counted among those "falling" — "utterly rooted out of the people."[18] For Luke, God's story is a story of God's dealing with Israel, that through one chosen people the blessing of *shalom* would come to all peoples.[19] For failing to bring all peoples God's blessing through Messiah, those Israelites thwarting God's purposes will be most certainly judged. Paul is shown bearing this message.

Three of Paul's speeches constitute a self-defense (or apologia) that focuses on Israel and Paul's experience as an Israelite (#4, before Israel but in earshot of Roman authority; #5, before an equal mix of Israel and Roman authority; #6, before Roman authority which is Jewish). The second and third speeches cover a range of audiences that allows the full spectrum of the salvation message to be stated: to Gentiles on one hand and to believers on the other. The first and last speeches function as a frame for all seven; they are addressed to Israel and so reflect the main drama of Acts. Together, these seven speeches confirm what has come before, in both Luke's gospel and Acts: God's concern has been with Israel and its salvation toward the end of serving all nations. (A chart at the end of this chapter makes visually clear the audiences and patterns of Paul's seven speeches.)

15. Lk 24:46-49.
16. 22:14; Is 24:16; 53:11; Acts 3:14; 7:52.
17. Lk 19:42-44; Acts 28:25-28.
18. Acts 28:28; see Acts 3:23.
19. Gen 12:3; Acts 3:25.

Paul has gone from approval of Stephen's stoning to being almost killed for joining those who "belonged to the Way."[20] His first and programmatic speech, to a predominantly Jewish audience, is sandwiched between Peter's sixth and seventh speeches (both of which concerned the Gentiles). Preceding this impassioned address to Israel by Paul, we hear of how God's Way is being spread beyond Jerusalem by faithful Israelites: "A great many people" are being "brought to the Lord"; again, there is the teaching of "a great many people"; "the word of God" is continuing "to advance and gain adherents."[21] On the other hand, recalcitrant Israel — its old-guard leadership — increases its attacks, and it is to the hostile ones within Israel that Paul will first speak. "During the festival of Unleavened Bread," the Rome-appointed King Herod[22] pleases the Jewish old-guard leadership by killing James, brother of John, and then imprisoning Peter.[23] Rescued by an angel in such a miraculous manner as to seem more dream than reality, Peter has to pinch himself — he finally "came to himself" — as he walks "along a lane" outside the city, alone.[24] The Herod mini-drama comes to an end with Herod's demise. Angry and proud, he addresses the people of Tyre and Sidon, who keep shouting, "The voice of a god, and not of a mortal!"[25] "Because he had not given the glory to God, an angel of the Lord struck him down, and he was eaten by worms and died."[26] But Herod has been set up, in a sense, by the bloodthirsty reactionaries among Israel's old-guard whom he seeks to please, the same resistant ones who had sought to kill Paul.[27]

Paul's first speech is anticipated immediately, deftly, by a textual echo of the powerful (and murderous) resistance within Israel to the embrace of their Christ. After completing their year-long teaching mission in Antioch,[28] Barnabas and Saul return to Jerusalem. Thereafter on Cyprus Paul confronts a "Jewish false prophet," a magician.[29] Along with the resistant old-guard leadership in Israel, then, Paul finds a false prophet like

20. 9:2, 23.

21. 11:19, 24, 26; 12:24.

22. This Herod is the grandson of Herod the Great (referred to in Lk 1:5, reigning during the time that Zechariah is visited by an angel); a Jew, he is Rome's ruler of areas that include Samaria and Galilee.

23. 12:1-3.

24. 12:6-11.

25. 12:20-22.

26. 12:23.

27. 9:23.

28. 11:25-26.

29. 13:6.

this Bar-Jesus — a "son-of-Jesus" who is no child of God at all. Bar-Jesus is thwarting a civic official from hearing the Way taught by Paul; the administrator had "wanted to hear the word of God" even as the magician tries "to turn the proconsul away from the faith."[30] Filled with the Holy Spirit, Paul looked "intently at him and said, 'You son of the devil, you enemy of all righteousness, full of all deceit and villainy, will you not stop making crooked the straight paths of the Lord?'"[31] Early in volume one, John the Baptizer had spoken of repentance, quoting from Scripture: "prepare the way of the Lord, make his paths straight."[32] Paul is as stern with this magician as Peter was with a magician earlier.[33] "Listen," Paul says, "the hand of the Lord is against you," and Bar-Jesus, the worker of evil power, is struck blind.[34] The observing proconsul is astonished, not with the display of God's power against evil, but with "the teaching about the Lord."[35] It is after this encounter that Paul is asked one sabbath day by synagogue officials "for a word of exhortation."[36] Paul obliges. The text has prepared its audience well for this great first and paradigmatic speech by Paul to all those within Israel who refuse the deliverance brought by Jesus the Messiah.

Paul's First Speech: Intended Primarily for Israel (first speech overall; 13:16-41)

In rehearsing the gospel presented in volume one, Paul focuses in this first speech on the two gospel truths insisted upon by Jesus in his last recorded words of the gospel: repentance leading to forgiveness and resurrection as the answer to authority. Jesus accomplished something regarding repentance and forgiveness that was more than what Moses and the Law could provide, argues Paul, and on this basis Paul is shown warning the resistant within Israel.

---

30. 13:6-8.

31. 13:9-10.

32. Lk 3:3-4. Anyone with the power of evil like this magician — who defies "the Way of the Lord" by "making crooked the straight paths of the Lord" — is an "enemy of all righteousness."

33. 8:9-24.

34. 13:11.

35. 13:12.

36. 13:15.

The speech is partitioned into three major sections, each of which begins with a personal appeal:

- Section I: "You Israelites, and others who fear God, listen" (13:16)
- Section II: "My brothers, you descendants of Abraham's family, and others who fear God" (13:26)
- Section III: "Let it be known to you therefore, my brothers" (13:38)

Section I. A Short History of Israel's Leadership, Up Through John and Jesus (13:16-25)

"You Israelites, and others who fear God, listen. The God of this people Israel chose our ancestors and made the people great during their stay in the land of Egypt, and with uplifted arm he led them out of it. For about forty years he put up with them in the wilderness. After he had destroyed seven nations in the land of Canaan, he gave them their land as an inheritance for about four hundred fifty years. After that he gave them judges until the time of the prophet Samuel. Then they asked for a king; and God gave them Saul son of Kish, a man of the tribe of Benjamin, who reigned for forty years. When he had removed him, he made David their king. In his testimony about him he said, 'I have found David, son of Jesse, to be a man after my heart, who will carry out all my wishes.' Of this man's posterity God has brought to Israel a Savior, Jesus, as he promised; before his coming John had already proclaimed a baptism of repentance to all the people of Israel. And as John was finishing his work, he said, 'What do you suppose that I am? I am not he. No, but one is coming after me; I am not worthy to untie the thong of the sandals on his feet.'" (13:16-25)

The progression of leadership begins with God: God alone led Israel out of Egypt, says Paul, but then God assigned leadership of Israel to judges, then to the prophet Samuel, then to a king, David, and finally, through that king's line, a Savior, Jesus.

Closely linked with Jesus is John, who "*already* proclaimed a baptism of repentance." That is, the baptism of repentance proclaimed by Jesus has *already* been proclaimed by John. But Jesus is far greater, according to Paul's understanding of John's ministry. Even within this first of three sections, then, at least one distinctive aspect about the role of Jesus emerges: his offering of forgiveness through repentance. This is the Way prepared by John but made clearer by Jesus, with the implicit suggestion of what John could not provide — the enabling Spirit.

It is God's story, for Luke. God delivered the people from Egypt, with no mention in the speech of the crucial role played by Moses.[37] The progression from judges to prophet, to king, to Savior, suggests, possibly, how Jesus fits all the roles. Where there were judges, Jesus is now Judge; where there were prophets, Jesus is the last;[38] where there were kings, Jesus is *the* king, Lord (title of emperors); where there are saviors/deliverers (Caesar Augustus was called such), Jesus is *the* Savior, Deliverer.[39] The short history of this first section has come full circle: Jesus as Deliverer echoes the speech's beginning, God as deliverer.[40] But Paul has not yet spelled out how it is that Israel can be assured that this Jesus is, indeed, the Messiah and Savior.

Section II. Jesus Raised Up (13:26-37)

"My brothers, you descendants of Abraham's family, and others who fear God, to us the message of this salvation has been sent. Because the residents of Jerusalem and their leaders did not recognize him or understand the words of the prophets that are read every sabbath, they fulfilled those words by condemning him. Even though they found no cause for a sentence of death, they asked Pilate to have him killed. When they had carried out everything that was written about him, they took him down from the tree and laid him in a tomb. But God raised him from the dead; and for many days he appeared to those who came up with him from Galilee to Jerusalem, and they are now his witnesses to the people. And we bring you the good news that what God promised to our ancestors he has fulfilled for us, their children, by raising Jesus; as also it is written in the second psalm,

'You are my Son;
today I have begotten you.'

37. That Moses is left out is perplexing. Perhaps Luke wants to emphasize God's role in leading Israel out of Egypt, in giving Israel judges — then prophets, then kings, and finally, Jesus.

38. Lk 13:33.

39. Acts 5:31.

40. Acts 13:17.

As to his raising him from the dead, no more to return to corruption, he has spoken in this way,

'I will give you the holy promises made to David.'

Therefore he has also said in another psalm,

'You will not let your Holy One experience corruption.'

For David, after he had served the purpose of God in his own generation, died, was laid beside his ancestors, and experienced corruption; but he whom God raised up experienced no corruption." (13:26-37)

What is distinctive about Jesus, here, is his status as "Son" who was raised up. "Today I have begotten you," says God; you are the "Holy One" who exists beyond the "corruption" of death. King David died; Jesus was raised up. So Jesus is superior to David. But what is this resurrection to mean for Israel, and what, for Luke, is the significance of Jesus being God's "Son"?

Section III. Jesus Superior to Moses' Law (13:38-41)

"Let it be known to you therefore, my brothers, that through this man forgiveness of sins is proclaimed to you; by this Jesus everyone who believes is set free from all those sins from which you could not be freed by the law of Moses. Beware, therefore, that what the prophets said does not happen to you:

'Look, you scoffers!
Be amazed and perish,
for in your days I am doing a work,
a work that you will never believe, even if someone tells you.'"

(13:38-41)

In Paul's last major speech (sixth overall), we will find an echo of *proclamation*, and the relationship between what is proclaimed and "forgiveness of sins":

"To this day I have had help from God, and so I stand here, testifying to both small and great, saying nothing but what the prophets and Moses said would take place: that the Messiah must suffer, and that, by being the first to rise from the dead, he would *proclaim light* both to our people and to the Gentiles." (Acts 26:22-23)

317

The distinction of Jesus in setting Israel "free from all those sins from which [they] could not be freed by the law of Moses" consists not in any covering of sins accomplished by death on the cross, an absence clear to Luke's audience by this point in the two-volume story; rather, this unique freeing from sin lies in what Jesus proclaimed — the light he brought to Scripture — and the Spirit that was poured out upon all flesh upon his departure.

- "John had already **proclaimed** a baptism of repentance to all the people of Israel."[41]
- "Through this man forgiveness of sins is **proclaimed** to you."[42]
- "He would **proclaim** light both to our people and to the Gentiles."[43]

That which John proclaimed and taught is a precursor of what Jesus proclaimed and taught at much greater length; what John could not do is done by Jesus, in rising from death, departing earth to sit with God, and sending God's Spirit upon all flesh.[44] Paul's gospel appears to be a succinct summary of Luke's gospel. His later speeches confirm the impression.

Jesus does better than Moses, but without negating Moses (according to Paul as represented in Luke's second volume). As we might have expected from Jesus' teaching based on the Law, Paul (in Acts) holds to the essential Mosaic Law as taught and refined by Jesus. Later in the story, Luke places Paul's commitment to the Law at a dramatically strategic point in the narrative. "When we arrived in Jerusalem," Luke says (he is now a character in his own story!), "they welcomed us warmly"; after hearing about God's action among Gentiles, "they praised God."[45] Paul's arrival in Jerusalem echoes the arrival of Jesus in Jerusalem.[46] What comes next, for Paul as earlier for Jesus, will be momentous. Paul's Jewish brothers want to emphasize something: "You see, brother [Paul], how many thousands of believers there are among the Jews, and they are all zealous for the Law."[47] Here is the worry, these Jerusalem broth-

41. 13:24.
42. 13:38.
43. 26:23.
44. What John begins to do is bring "light" to Scripture, which is to be the "light" proclaimed and taught by Jesus to "both our people and to the Gentiles" (Acts 26:23).
45. 21:17-20.
46. Lk 19:45.
47. 21:20.

ers go on: it has been told us "that you teach all the Jews living among the Gentiles to forsake Moses" — and you instruct them "not to circumcise their children or observe the customs."[48] The brothers have a solution for Paul: "go through the [Law's] rite of purification" so that "all will know that there is nothing in what they have been told about you, but that you yourself observe and guard the Law."[49] Paul agrees, and does so — because, indeed, he himself does *observe and guard the Law.*"[50] In no manner, Paul says on another occasion, have I "committed an offense against the Law of the Jews."[51] He worships "the God of our ancestors," but "according to the Way" — the Jesus-taught Law.[52] In good conscience, Luke's Paul can assert that he subscribes to "everything laid down according to the Law or written in the prophets" and interpreted by Jesus.[53] Jesus is "Savior" for Luke's Paul in providing proclamation of — shedding light on — God's word; with the risen and departed Jesus there comes a Spirit who enables a continual turning-around that leads to God's merciful forgiveness of sins.

While Paul observes and guards the Law (in Acts), he clearly distinguishes between the interpretation of the Law offered by his former old-guard peers and the interpretation of the Law taught by Jesus. Neither the Law's distillation as principle nor the unleashing of the Spirit has been accomplished by Moses or the Mosaic Law as interpreted by Israel's old leadership. It is in Jesus and through believers who proclaim the good news in his name that Israel finds its salvation.

Luke is consistent from the beginning of his story to the end: those who hear and do the word of God as taught and done by Jesus are those being transformed. These believers are entering the kingdom of God; it is they who are being "saved."[54] The drama of Acts is filled with witness to the word taught and done by Jesus. Believers teach the word — and do it, as Paul is to say later, "with deeds consistent with repentance."[55]

---

48. 21:21.
49. 21:24.
50. 21:24.
51. 25:8.
52. Lk 20:21.
53. Acts 24:14.
54. Lk 6:46-49; 13:23-30.
55. 26:20.

Section IV. Conclusion, Warning

Paul concludes his first speech with a warning that serves as invitation to the otherwise "falling" within Israel:

> "Beware, therefore, that what the prophets said does not happen
> to you:
> 'Look, you scoffers!
> Be amazed and perish,
> for in your days I am doing a work,
> a work that you will never believe, even if someone tells you.'"
>
> (13:40-41)

That "work" has been done through the teaching and healing of Jesus, as Luke records it in his gospel, and through the sending of the Holy Spirit by Jesus, as Luke records it in Acts. "In your days I am doing a work" echoes Luke's reference at the story's very beginning to "the events that have been fulfilled among us" these decades after the departure of Jesus [56]

Paul's "beware" and his skeptical view toward the recalcitrant portion of Israel ("you will never believe, even if someone tells you") echo precisely the gospel words of "father Abraham," that "if they do not listen to Moses and the prophets, neither will they be convinced even if someone rises from the dead."[57] There, too, the issue was repentance.[58]

"Beware," warns Paul; "be amazed and perish." The authority for such judgment is sure; Paul's thinking (in Acts) parallels Peter's precisely — and echoes the witness demanded by Jesus in the last-words speech of Luke's gospel:

- Set free from sins (forgiven by God, depending on repentance as taught by Jesus)
- "God raised [Jesus] from the dead"[59] and "he whom God raised up experienced no corruption."[60]

"Let it be known to you *therefore*," says Paul.[61] *Therefore* connects resurrection with believing in Jesus and his teaching: know *therefore* "that

56. Lk 1:1.
57. Lk 16:31.
58. Lk 16:30.
59. 13:30.
60. 13:37.
61. 13:38.

through this man forgiveness of sins is proclaimed to you."[62] For any within Israel who refuse Jesus, however, there is the warning with which Paul concludes his speech: "be amazed and perish."[63] Paul's first speech builds toward this warning for Israelites refusing their Messiah; his last speech to Israel's rulers, in Rome, is all warning.

Paul's Last Speech: Intended for Israel
(seventh speech overall; 28:25-28)

Borrowing from their mutually shared scripture, Paul warns his fellow Jews in the very last speech of Acts, Paul's seventh. It is a lament and final challenge. Immediately preceding this speech, Paul has been "testifying to the kingdom of God [to Israelites] and trying to convince them about Jesus both from the law of Moses and from the prophets."[64] This word about what it is that constitutes Paul's primary message, "the kingdom of God" and "Jesus," is critical, of course, in its placement just before the last warning to those who are falling in Israel. Some in Israel are still being convinced, right up to the end of Luke's story; others are not.[65]

Paul's last words, with which the entire two-volume story ends, signal the end of faithful Israel's proclamation of the Way to unfaithful Israel. "The Holy Spirit," says Paul, "was right in saying to your ancestors through the prophet Isaiah,

'Go to this people and say,
You will indeed listen, but never understand,
and you will indeed look, but never perceive.
For this people's heart has grown dull,
and their ears are hard of hearing,
and they have shut their eyes;
so that they might not look with their eyes,
and listen with their ears,
and understand with their heart and turn —
    and I would heal them.'" (28:25-27; Is 6:9-10)

---

62. 13:38.
63. 13:41.
64. 28:23.
65. 28:24.

Israel, as Simeon foresaw, is split: those who were rising have risen; those who were falling have fallen.[66] It is the Gentiles' turn now. Servant Israel — faithful Israel, delivered Israel — will serve the non-Jews, even "to the ends of the earth."[67]

The unfaithful within Israel have shut their eyes. They have not looked, or listened. They have not understood, and they have not *turned*, Paul has said.[68] That is, they have willed not to heed God's word as taught and demonstrated by Jesus. *Repent and be forgiven,* says Paul — or "be amazed and perish," you "scoffers."[69]

"Listen with [your] ears," Paul says — but to what, exactly? What is the basis of judgment that either permits or prohibits the healing referred to here? First, of course, listen to Paul. But what is Paul proclaiming? His "teaching *about* the Lord Jesus" centers on the teaching *of* the Lord Jesus, as attested in all of his speeches and action. What Paul proclaims is the light proclaimed by Jesus "to our people and to the Gentiles."[70]

Just as this last speech is prefaced with "testifying to the kingdom of God" and convincing Jews "about Jesus," it is followed with an echo of Paul "proclaiming the kingdom of God and teaching about the Lord Jesus" — the two-volume story's very last words.[71] At the beginning of Acts, in his last meeting before departing, Jesus is found "speaking about the kingdom of God."[72] At the beginning of his recorded ministry, Jesus speaks of needing to "proclaim the kingdom of God."[73]

With a final verdict of "guilty" for those Israelites refusing their Messiah, faithful Israel's mission will now turn to non-Jews with the good news of God's kingdom blessing.[74] In the story's very last verses, however, awaiting trial under house arrest in Rome, Paul is testifying to "all," including fellow Israelites: he is "proclaiming the kingdom of God and teaching about the Lord Jesus Christ to all peoples, Jew and non-Jew."[75]

---

66. Lk 2:34.
67. Lk 1:54; Acts 28:28; 3:25.
68. 28:27.
69. 13:41.
70. 26:23.
71. 28:23; 28:31.
72. 1:3.
73. 4:43.
74. 28:28.
75. 28:31.

The ending of Luke's story is as powerfully bittersweet as anything in world literature. It is thoroughly sweet because of the thousands rising within faithful Israel and because the mission of redeemed and covenantly fulfilled Israel is under way, but it is thoroughly bitter because of the falling ones within Israel who are lost.

The First and Seventh Speeches by Paul: A Summary

In Luke's second volume, Paul, like Peter before him, neither adds to nor subtracts from what Jesus was shown teaching about salvation in Luke's first volume. Throughout Luke's two-volume story, but especially in Acts and the last part of the gospel, the question of authority and judgment — to whom shall Israel listen? — has been at the heart of the divide between rising and falling Israel.

For the Paul of Acts, Jesus is Judge. His judgment is based on how Israel and others "listen to him."[76] This is a judgment authorized by God's raising Jesus from death and based on righteousness. The Law as taught by Jesus and demonstrated perfectly by Jesus is the standard by which one will be judged as part of God's kingdom, or not. Failure to listen and obey will bring judgment from within the precincts of salvation: "go away from me all you evildoers!" the Judge will say to those knocking too late on the kingdom's door.[77] Warning concerning such judgment is the conclusion of Paul's first speech and the entire content of his seventh speech.

The purpose of Luke's motif of warning is a form of pleading: be forewarned, you who are falling within Israel. Join in with those "rising." After Paul has given the warning to scoffers in the first frame speech ("be amazed and perish"), we find a narrative postscript. "*The Jews*[78] saw the crowds" and "were filled with jealousy"; they "contradicted what was spoken by Paul." Paul and Barnabas suggest, as Paul does again in his very last speech, that they "are now turning to the Gentiles" since "you [Jewish leadership] reject it and judge yourselves to be unworthy of eternal life."[79]

---

76. Acts 10:42.

77. Lk 13:27.

78. 13:45; *the Jews,* throughout Acts, almost always refers to the old-guard leadership — not all the Jews of Israel.

79. 13:46.

"For so the Lord has commanded us, saying,
    'I have set you to be a light for the Gentiles,
    so that you [Israel] may bring salvation to the ends of the earth.'"

(13:47)

The continuity of vision shared by Luke's gospel and Acts centers on God's purpose for global *shalom* through Israel. Simeon's claim to seeing salvation is being echoed:

"a light for revelation to the Gentiles
and for glory to your people Israel." (Lk 2:32)

Israel's glory will consist in bearing "a light for revelation to the Gentiles," which Peter has initiated and Paul will begin to put into full motion; not until the very end of Acts will the primary mission of delivered Israel be directed to the non-Jews of the world.[80]

Paul's next speech in Luke's narrative chronology is the only one out of seven that is addressed exclusively to Gentiles. That ratio suggests the degree of narrative focus in Acts on Israel versus Gentiles, even in the ministry of Paul. For Luke, Israel must complete its salvation (by the thousands and thousands and thousands) before it comes into its "glory" in bearing the Way's "light for revelation to the Gentiles."

80. Acts 28:23-31.

Paul's Seven Speeches: Patterns

Speeches	The Pattern	Audience	Motifs
Speeches #1 & #7 13:16-41; 28:25-28	*Framing Speeches*	Israel	— Repent; resurrection; be warned, Israel: Gentiles next #1
			— be warned, Israel: Gentiles next #7
Speeches #2 & #3 17:22-31; 20:18-35	*Salvation's Full Demands*	Gentile Skeptics #2	— Repent; — Man appointed by God will judge, on the basis of righteousness; — Resurrection; assurance of this truth #2
		Believers #3	— Repentance; — "Faith toward our Lord Jesus" which entails: — striving ("be alert," as I have been), readiness to have your blood shed (as all of God's "own" have had to be) #3
Speeches #4, #5, #6 22:1-21; 24:10-21; 26:1-23	*Self-Defense*	Before Israel; Roman authority also #4	— My authority based on encounter with *risen Jesus* #4
		Before Israel and Roman authority #5	— All authority (also the basis of charges against me) based on *resurrection* #5
		Before Roman authority; Israel also #6	— My authority based on encounter with *risen Jesus* #6

Chapter 21

The Gospel according to Paul:
Back-to-Back Speeches

Acts 17:22-31; 20:18-35

In his second speech, before an all-Gentile audience, Paul points to a God who "will have the world judged in righteousness by a man whom [God] has appointed"; this man has been authorized by God's "raising him from death."[1] *Judgment is based on turning around from wickedness to righteousness — on hearing and doing the word of God made clear by Jesus. Next in narrative order is what can be seen as a companion speech, delivered not to non-Jews but to Jewish (and presumably non-Jewish) believers from Ephesus. Here, repentance is expanded in its challenge to cover the difficulties of going God's Way that Jesus taught. These two speeches by Paul cover salvation's spectrum, the gospel according to Paul in Acts.*

As we recall, Paul was in the audience for Peter's last recorded speech of Acts to his fellow leaders concerning the Gentile believers and the issue of being circumcised. "Why are you putting on the neck of the disciples," Peter had asked, referring to circumcision and other Torah rules, "a yoke that neither our ancestors nor we have been able to bear?"[2] The Jerusalem leadership decided that circumcision was not, in fact, necessary, and Paul and Barnabas traveled north again, up through Syria and Asia Minor. Almost always beginning in the synagogue in whatever city they visited, they "taught and proclaimed the word of the Lord."[3] The two have a seri-

---

1. 17:29-31.
2. 15:10.
3. 15:35.

ous disagreement, however, and Silas replaces Barnabas as a traveling companion to Paul.[4]

Immediately preceding Paul's second speech, his only address to an exclusively Gentile audience,[5] we find a major action vignette involving the healing of a slave girl with a spirit of divination, and imprisonment for Paul and Silas followed by miraculous escape (we have here another parallel between the experiences of Paul and Peter). While in the jail, Paul and Silas have borne faithful and fruitful witness about Jesus to a Gentile jailer and his family. Paul continues his journeying, concentrating as usual on fellow Jews and visiting the synagogues.[6]

The Gospel According to Paul:
To Non-Jews (Paul's second speech overall; 17:22-31)

Paul and Silas have passed through Asia Minor and Macedonia over into Greece. Some Athenians are curious about the novel religious view being expressed by the itinerant Paul. They ask him to speak out, taking him to the hill of Athens called Areopagus. In this place of public debate and oratory, Paul begins his brief address by complimenting his Athenian audience for their religious seriousness, and then announces an answer regarding the identity of their "unknown god," as one of their altar inscriptions reads.[7] Paul alludes to the Jewish scripture when asserting that "from one ancestor [God] made all nations to inhabit the whole earth."[8] Idols are a foolish counter to this living God, Paul continues, and then he reaches his gospel statement involving Jesus:

> "While God has overlooked the times of human ignorance, now he commands all people everywhere to repent, because he has fixed a day on which he will have the world judged in righteousness by a man whom he has appointed, and of this he has given assurance to all by raising him from the dead." (17:30-31)

The basis of judgment upon which the "appointed" One will judge is the word taught by Jesus as it is heard and obeyed; Jesus will judge, as

---

4. 15:37-41.
5. Implied: there is no mention of Jews in this Athenian audience.
6. 17:10-15.
7. 17:23.
8. 17:26.

Paul puts it, "in righteousness." Even in this one speech before an exclusively Gentile audience, Paul's gospel as viewed by Luke remains essentially the same as for fellow Israelites. He concludes with the twin-themes stressed by Jesus: repentance and resurrection.[9]

- *Repentance:* God "will have the world judged in righteousness by a man whom [God] has appointed" in response to God's Law; God "commands all people everywhere to repent," which Jesus has shown to be the essence of the Law.[10]
- *Resurrection:* All of this is certified Truth, says Paul, since God "has given assurance to all by raising [Jesus] from the dead."[11]

The third term of the last-words speech of Jesus in Luke's gospel, echoed in the last-words speech of Acts 1, the Holy Spirit, is absent.[12] Such righteousness is impossible for mortals, Luke's audience will know, without the empowerment offered through the gift of God's Spirit. Paul does not progress that far in this speech, however: "When they heard of the resurrection of the dead, some scoffed," while others were still curious and wanted to hear more.[13] News of the Holy Spirit would be central in the "more." Paul's gospel for these Greek Gentiles is the same essential gospel delivered to all Israel. The God of Israel is faithful not only in creating all nations out of one (part of Israel's story in Torah) but also in responding with favor toward all those who favor God, who "grope for him"; those who strive toward God, without prior access to God's Way, will "find him."[14] With this early brief speech to Gentiles, Paul is poised, in terms of the narrative drama, to implement the great shift toward the Gentiles that takes place only at the very end of the two-volume story.

9. Lk 24:46-48.

10. Acts 17:30. The core term of what salvation requires is once again front and center, a summary term that requires Luke's gospel to be understood. Judgment will be rendered on the basis of how one hears and obeys the word of God taught by Jesus, that is, as Paul says here, on the basis of one's righteousness.

11. Acts 17:31.

12. Lk 24:46-49.

13. 17:32.

14. 17:26; 17:27.

The Gospel According to Paul:
To Believers (Paul's third speech overall; 20:18-35)

From Athens Paul moves into other areas of Greece, then back to Turkey and Ephesus, where a summary statement indicates the conclusion of a significant narrative sequence: "the word of the Lord grew mightily and prevailed."[15] The narrative stops, in a sense, or pauses. We are reminded of what the action of Acts is all about: the teaching of Jesus, "the word of the Lord."

Then come the dramatically highlighted lines announcing Paul's intent to undertake a journey to Jerusalem, and on to Rome: "Now after these things had been accomplished, Paul resolved in the Spirit to go through Macedonia and Achaia, and then to go on to Jerusalem. He said, 'After I have gone there, I must also see Rome.'"[16] It is on this journey that Paul offers some last teaching to believers from Ephesus. Echoes back to Jesus abound. The speech to Ephesian believers is a last bit of teaching that parallels much of what Jesus taught the disciples in his final days.[17] Paul has been determined to journey toward Jerusalem, and certain persecution. Just as Jesus "had set his face to go to Jerusalem," so too "Paul resolved in the Spirit to go . . . on to Jerusalem," and finally to Rome.[18]

Pausing on his journey to Jerusalem and bypassing Ephesus, Paul calls for the believers in Ephesus to meet him in Miletus, a short distance south on Paul's route toward Jerusalem. It appears that he wants an undistracted and very focused word with them. The speech is divided into two halves: (1) Paul's insistence on his utter commitment to the gospel message; (2) a plea for the same from his Ephesian friends, for their alertness and readiness in the face of dark possibilities.

With the unbelieving Greeks, Paul offered a bare-bones account of how salvation begins: repentance based on righteousness as taught and demonstrated by Jesus and authenticated by his resurrection. But with believers, Paul can complete a picture of what "faith toward our Lord, Jesus" entails and what striving to enter the kingdom requires.

---

15. 19:20.
16. 19:21.
17. See Chapter 15.
18. Lk 9:51; Acts 19:21; 20:22-23.

Section I. Paul's Insistence on the Gospel Message

"You yourselves know," Paul begins, "how I lived among you the entire time from the first day that I set foot in Asia, serving the Lord with all humility and with tears, enduring the trials that came to me through the plots of the Jews."[19] He goes on to summarize his message among them, with key references to "repentance," "faith toward our Lord Jesus," and "kingdom":

> "I did not shrink from doing anything helpful, proclaiming the message to you and teaching you publicly and from house to house, as I testified to both Jews and Greeks about repentance toward God and faith toward our Lord Jesus. And now, as a captive to the Spirit, I am on my way to Jerusalem, not knowing what will happen to me there, except that the Holy Spirit testifies to me in every city that imprisonment and persecutions are waiting for me. But I do not count my life of any value to myself, if only I may finish my course and the ministry that I received from the Lord Jesus, to testify to the good news of God's grace. And now I know that none of you, among whom I have gone about proclaiming the kingdom, will ever see my face again." (20:20-25)

Paul's statement at the beginning of this sequence, "Proclaiming the message to you and teaching you," is paralleled by his phrase "proclaiming the kingdom" at the end. Sandwiched between insistence on *proclamation* and *proclamation* is the "meat" of this proclaiming: "repentance toward God and faith toward our Lord Jesus."

Message, teaching, and *kingdom* are signal words that take the audience back to Luke's gospel. Paul is addressing, remember, believers. They would have recognized, as surely the text's audience would have, that the kingdom is at the heart of Paul's gospel, is what Jesus taught. As we saw in the prior chapter, word of Paul's "testifying to the kingdom of God" and convincing Jews "about Jesus" before his last speech is echoed just after the speech, in the story's very last words: Paul was "proclaiming the kingdom of God and teaching about the Lord Jesus."[20] As readers of the text, we ourselves must always be reminded of what for the original hearers is conjured up with the signal-words, or code-words, *message, teaching,* and *kingdom.*

Paul is under the Ruler, Lord Jesus. These Ephesian believers are be-

19. 20:18-19.
20. 28:23, 31.

ing reminded that Paul's "humility" consists, among other things, of his utter deference to, "faith toward," the Jesus whose teaching of God's kingdom Paul proclaims and teaches. "Faith toward our *Lord* Jesus" indicates trust in and commitment to Jesus as *Lord*, Ruler and Leader.[21] Faith, *pistis*, is "the trust that someone may place in other people or in the gods [God]"; the term suggests the "credibility" of someone or something in which trust is placed toward action.[22] The credibility of Jesus is of utmost importance in this text, as we saw in the last third of the gospel: such authority is central as well for Paul's gospel in Acts, established by God's raising of Jesus from death. *Faith-toward* is an embrace of the word taught by Jesus, a word whose credibility has been established by God's raising Jesus from suffering and death. For both Paul and Peter, faith hinges on repentance, an embrace of God's word that is both a hearing and a doing; faith is a turning-from and a turning-toward, for both of the main protagonists of Acts.

Luke shows Peter, in his first and programmatic speech, suggesting that God's blessing to Israel lies in "turning each of you from your wicked ways"; before Jewish and Roman authorities Paul will claim that he has been sent by God "to open [Jewish and non-Jewish] eyes so that they may turn from darkness to light and from the power of Satan to God" (3:26; 26:18). "Faith toward our Lord Jesus," as Paul puts it to his Ephesian audience here, is repeatedly linked to "repentance toward God," a turn-around.[23]

Section II. Entering God's Kingdom Requires Striving

Such faith toward Jesus, for Luke's Paul, is accompanied by striving: "It is through many persecutions that we must enter the kingdom of God," he has said, echoing the words of Jesus.[24] Paul repeats the challenge here, to his Ephesian audience — just as Jesus had repeatedly admonished his followers on his own journey to Jerusalem.[25]

At the heart of this striving is the need to "keep watch over your-

21. Acts 5:31.
22. The same Greek root, *pistis,* serves for both "believe" and "have-faith-in" or "faith-toward." *The NIV Theological Dictionary of New Testament Words,* ed. Verlyn D. Verbrugge (Grand Rapids: Zondervan, 2000), p. 1027.
23. 20:21.
24. Lk 13:23-24; Acts 14:22.
25. Acts 20:19; Lk 12:37; Part II, Chapter 7; also, Lk 21:36.

selves and over all the flock."[26] In shepherding people of the Way, this "flock," leaders may well become part of a long line of "God's own" whose blood has been shed as bearers of God's word.[27] With the certainty of his own death as backdrop, Paul's two citations of "blood" indicate the costly nature of striving:

> "And now I know that none of you, among whom I have gone about proclaiming the kingdom, will ever see my face again. Therefore I declare to you this day that I am not responsible for *the blood of any of you,* for I did not shrink from declaring to you the whole purpose of God. Keep watch over yourselves and over all the flock, of which the Holy Spirit has made you overseers, to shepherd the [called-out people] of God that he obtained with *the blood of his own.*" (20:25-28; emphasis mine)

The word "blood" appears first as a warning, and then as an indication of what these believers themselves must anticipate as "God's own."[28]

Paul is not responsible for the waste of life ("the blood of any of you") should any turn back from the Way. The echoing reference to "blood" in the very next sentence ("God obtained [a called-out people, *ekklēsia*][29] with the blood of his own") is in the context of a challenge rather than warning: God's gathering of a people has cost God the shedding of blood, from the prophets on up through John, Jesus, Stephen, and James — "the blood of his own." That is, these Ephesian believers are being challenged to follow in the line of these who have shed their blood on God's behalf: "I know that after I have gone, savage wolves will come in among you, not sparing the flock." Luke's audience has seen that such wolves are both literally and figuratively bloodthirsty. Stephen's murder is referred to by Paul as the shedding of

26. 20:28a.

27. 20:28b.

28. This translation, "blood of God's own," reflects the literal rendering of the Greek, which the RSV uses (the NRSV has added "Son," as in "God's own *Son*"). See n. 32 for elaboration.

29. *Ekklēsia* (*ek,* out of; *kaleō,* call) is the Greek translation (the Septuagint) of *qahal,* assembly/congregation. It should be noted that "church" is a peculiar and inconsistent translation of *ekklēsia* in Acts (in Acts 19:32, for example, the *ekklēsia* included worshipers of the goddess Artemis and no believers — certainly not a "church"). Here, the text indicates *ekklēsia* as that assembly marked as God's called-out ones, God's people. This is an important point in Luke-Acts, since the text stresses continuity with God's people in the Jewish scripture, not the discontinuity suggested by the translation "church."

blood.[30] Here, he is pleading for recognition of, and willingness for, the ultimate relinquishment of one's own life-blood, in the light of Israel's history in which the people of God have always been "obtained" — called out — by the blood of God's word-bearers.[31] The people of God, the *ekklēsia* or called-out ones, have become the people of God at the cost of the prophets' blood — "God's own."[32]

Paul concludes the challenge in this his final farewell to these Ephesian believers with a warning that parallels exhortations from Jesus to his disciples, including some concluding words, about being alert in the face of everyday and mortal danger: "Some even from your own group," warns Paul, "will come distorting the truth in order to entice the disciples to follow them. Therefore be alert, remembering that for three years I did not cease night or day to warn everyone with tears" (20:29-31).[33]

Paul indicates in this last-words speech to believers in Ephesus that his own journey toward Jerusalem and Rome will be a journey toward relinquishment and possible shedding of blood. You "will never see my face again," he says, words echoed ominously by a concluding reminder "that they would not see him again."[34]

Undoubtedly these Ephesian believers have been taught by now that "whoever comes to [Jesus] and does not hate father and mother, wife and children, brothers and sisters, yes, and *even life itself,* cannot be my disci-

---

30. Acts 22:20.

31. Lk 13:32-34.

32. It is a temptation to read into this ancient text the view that "God's own" is Jesus, a view that not only does violence to the lexical evidence but to Luke's narrative context as well. Luke never refers to the blood of Jesus shed for a covering of sins as a "cost" to God.

On "God's own": the singular form of *own* — *tou idiou* — as F. F. Bruce points out, is "used . . . as a term of endearment to near relations." *The Acts of the Apostles: Greek Text with Introduction and Commentary* (London: The Tyndale Press, 1951), p. 381. While many scholars see very little evidence in this passage of blood as "covering of sins," F. F. Bruce — who acknowledges the conspicuous absence of substitutionary atonement in Luke's story — believes that this passage may qualify. "Even when the Ethiopian is reading of the Servant's suffering," Bruce notes, "the words which bring out the vicarious efficacy of that suffering are not reproduced. Whether such words are deliberately not reproduced — cf. the absence of 'to give his life a ransom for many' (Mk. 10:45) from Lk. 22:25-27 — or the words actually reproduced carry their vicarious context with them by implication, cannot be affirmed with certainty" (*The Acts of the Apostles,* p. 65). Bruce is alert to what I have been emphasizing especially in the journey narrative: "The conditions necessary for obtaining salvation are repentance and faith — a forsaking of old attitudes and an embracing of new attitudes" (p. 54).

33. Lk 21:36; see also 12:37.

34. 20:25; 20:38.

ple" and inherit eternal life.[35] At the heart of going God's Way, these believers would know, is the challenge of taking up one's cross, daily.[36] The good news is also a dark and disruptive news, as Luke's nine preparatory chapters to his gospel had established.[37] It is this bittersweet quality of the Way about which Paul wants to instruct and encourage believers from Ephesus, because this too is part of what is required for those who belong to the Way, those who would enter the kingdom of God.

The Gospel according to Paul: Summary and Conclusion

Whether or not the narrative structure of Acts warrants viewing the speech to Gentile unbelievers and Ephesian believers as a pair is a point that may be argued; taken in tandem, however, the two speeches suggest the full range of the gospel preached by Paul. What becomes clear from hearing these narratively consecutive speeches is the full picture of salvation that Luke has been pursuing, beginning with the succinct essentials of repentance and resurrection to the Greek Gentiles and proceeding, to Ephesian believers, with that which repentance requires — a turning-around that requires the willingness to relinquish "life itself" even as a shepherd risks life for the flock. By now Luke's audience knows that one cannot proceed on the kingdom Way without the Spirit, to whom Paul claims, in this last-words speech to fellow-believers, he is captive.[38] The full gospel spectrum, then, has been covered in tandem speeches representing the widest possible audience among Paul's listeners.

Paul's full gospel, as viewed in these two speeches — and in relevant aspects of his other five speeches or the rest of Luke-Acts — omits any reference to an atoning sacrifice for sins through the Cross of Christ. This omission helps to highlight the salvation Luke is dramatizing.

To the non-Jews of Athens, Paul has made it clear that the essential gospel includes a worship of the God of "all nations," a God who "commands all people to repent." We have seen that only such repentance brings forgiveness of sins, from a generous God who can forgive because, for Luke, God is God. That which has been sufficient in John's forgiveness of sins and Jesus' forgiveness of sins, in the gospel, remains the same

---

35. Lk 14:26.
36. Lk 9:23; 14:27.
37. See Chapter 4.
38. Acts 20:22.

for Peter and Paul, in Acts.[39] Paul tells the Athenians that, with the advent of Jesus, any failure to turn around from normal ways to God's Way (repentance) will be judged by one appointed by God. Jesus judges "in righteousness," that is, on the basis of a right-doing as defined by the principles of the Way unfolded in volume one. The implicit assumption that emerges from Luke's unrelenting focus on salvation is that the basis of forgiveness cannot be within the old rule-bound structure and requirement of blood-sacrifice as covering of sins, through scapegoat animals or through one last sacrifice of God's own Son. From the perspective of Luke's narrative interpretation of the events surrounding Jesus, the entire vicarious sacrificial system has been abolished once and for all and replaced with an opposing impetus: that every follower of the Way bear the consequences of others' wrong-doing while doing the right thing on behalf of others. Salvation, for Luke, is not other than the dynamic of serving God's purposes in bringing the blessing of true peace to outsiders while turning away from normal self-aggrandizement and clan-protection. As Paul tells the Athenians, God forgives on the basis of a clear understanding of God's righteousness and the appropriate action of repentance. Jesus has been appointed Judge in this matter of salvation since it is he who has redefined righteousness, on the basis of God's word.[40] The "knowledge of God" has been the focus of what Jesus has come to do as Messiah, as we have seen in Luke's gospel, and as Paul has proclaimed to the Athenians.

Hosea is among the prophetic voices echoed by Luke's view of salvation:

> For I desire steadfast love and not sacrifice [says God],
> the knowledge of God rather than burnt offerings. (Hosea 6:6)

In former times, says Paul, the peoples of the earth "would search for God and perhaps grope for him and find him," but now, through Jesus, "the knowledge of God" — as Hosea puts it — is known definitively through Jesus:

> "While God has overlooked the times of human ignorance, now he commands all people everywhere to repent, because he has fixed a day on which he will have the world judged in righteousness by a man

---

39. John, Lk 3:3, 7-18; Jesus, Lk 5:20, 23; 7:48.
40. Acts 17:31.

whom he has appointed, and of this he has given assurance to all by raising him from the dead." (Acts 17:30-31)

Luke's perspective insists on Jesus' distillation of the Law, and a simple and repetitive insistence on doing that reinterpreted Law. Such a view is anticipated by the writer of Deuteronomy: "So now, O Israel, what does the LORD your God require of you? Only to fear the LORD your God, to walk in all his ways, to love him, to serve the LORD your God with all your heart and with all your soul.[41] Such difficult simplicity combined with such complex psychological overhaul is intimated also by still another prophet, Micah:

> He has told you, O mortal, what is good;
> and what does the LORD require of you
> but to do justice, and to love kindness,
> and to walk humbly with your God? (Mic 6:8)

Those within Israel who are falling, the old-guard leadership, have been shown in volume one to be disastrously vulnerable at precisely this point. They "neglect justice and the love of God" and so fail to recognize "the things that make for peace."[42] Believers enter the kingdom of God, as intimated in Paul's speech to the believers from Ephesus, if they strive to "do justice" and "love kindness"; such salvation is gained only if persons "walk humbly" with God.[43] The problem with Israel's old-guard leadership, according to Luke's Jesus, is their fetish with systems of sacrifice and ritual perfection while "neglecting justice and the love of God."[44] This is the "righteousness" on the basis of which the world will be judged by Jesus, referred to by Paul in his gospel speech to the non-Jews of Athens.

Salvation, as Paul informs the Athenians, is grounded in the resurrection insofar as God "has given assurance to all by raising him from the dead"; therefore obey God's command and "repent, because he has fixed a day on which he will have the world judged in righteousness."[45] The ground of salvation is the solid authorization and glorification of Jesus. The reversal from death to exaltation, anticipated by Jesus in the gospel[46]

---

41. Deut 10:12.

42. Lk 11:42; 19:42.

43. Mic 6:8; see Lk 18:9-14 for a vignette illustrating the truth that "all who exalt themselves will be humbled, but all who humble themselves [before God] will be exalted."

44. Lk 11:42; see Chapter 9.

45. Acts 17:30-31.

46. Lk 9:21-22, for example.

is thought of by Paul as *the hope of Israel*.[47] "Jesus is the rejected man, hung on the cross, and the Son of God," as James Dawsey points out; he is "simultaneously humiliated and exalted."[48] The gospel has prepared the narrative way for what Peter Doble calls the great paradox: "for Luke, cross and resurrection were a paradox of salvation that laid claim on Jesus' followers."[49] As the gospel put it, *the last will become first; the first, last*.[50] Paul's seven speeches — along with all speeches by believers in Acts — are conspicuous, as Joel B. Green understands, in emphasizing the Cross as the uttermost point of relinquishment; conspicuous in Paul's thinking, as rehearsed in Acts, is "absence of any straightforward atonement theology — that is, of any Pauline [epistles]-type interpretation of the cross."[51] For Paul and all believers in Acts, as we are seeing, the cross is the dark side of the good news; such was the case in the gospel presentation of the cross. For Jesus and all followers of the Way, the daily picking up of one's cross indicates an orientation of being *last*. The endpoint of being *last* comes with the most horrific of "persecutions," death by murder, the assumption of Paul's plea to the Ephesians, "therefore be alert."[52]

We have seen that to the Greek Gentiles, Paul proclaimed God's kingdom, a call for "all people everywhere to repent" in the light of a righteousness that was taught "by a man whom [God] has appointed."[53] The trustworthiness of Jesus as Teacher and Judge is assured "by [God's] raising him from the dead."[54] Paul is shown reminding Ephesian believers, in his next speech, about his teaching of this kingdom.[55] The significant difference in these two speeches of Paul to the most dissimilar of audi-

---

47. Acts 23:6; 28:20.

48. *The Lukan Voice: Confusion and Irony in the Gospel of Luke* (Macon, Ga.: Mercer University Press, 1986), p. 156.

49. *The Paradox of Salvation* (Cambridge: Cambridge University Press, 1996), p. 226. The ridicule and shame of this ultimate stage of relinquishment, Doble goes on, are accentuated by Luke in "speaking of Jesus' *hanging on a tree*" — an aspect of Luke's "strategy to make sense of Jesus' death and to counter protest that so shameful a death could only be of one cursed by God (Deuteronomy 21:22-3; Acts 13:29)" (p. 229). We note (in Chapter 18) this matter of those "hanging on a tree" being under God's curse, and how this idea is countermanded by Luke, suggested here by Doble.

50. Lk 13:30.

51. Joel B. Green, "The Message of Salvation in Luke-Acts," in *Ex Auditu: An International Journal of Theological Interpretation of Scripture*, vol. 5 (Allison Park, Pa.: Pickwick Publications, 1989), p. 22.

52. 20:31.

53. 17:30-31.

54. 17:31.

55. 20:20-21.

ences is not in the essential kingdom proclamation, but in the call for committed believers, in the Ephesians speech, to keep on journeying the Way, to strive, to be alert, to shepherd the flock in the face of bloodthirsty wolves who might yet succeed in shedding their blood. That is, as we heard in the gospel, they must participate in the sufferings and death of Jesus, literally. Together with the Athenian speech, this speech to believers underscores the often-dark news connected with the kingdom, an "instruction" Luke is so concerned about giving his audience as to how one is to be saved — to be forgiven on the basis of right-doing rather than face judgment by the one appointed as Judge.[56] Only through such striving and the Spirit's empowerment is one forgiven and permitted entrance to God's kingdom and its joyous feasting.[57]

In the remaining speeches, numbers 4, 5, and 6, Paul is shown homing in on the question of authority, his own and that of Jesus. After all, this is a word of God that is being contested; it must be trusted and obeyed if there is to be salvation. In two of the speeches Paul highlights his own encounter with the risen Jesus, recounting details of his own repentance and embrace of Jesus as Israel's Messiah. In the third defense speech, Paul briefly assures hostile authorities that all the trouble drummed up by the old-guard about himself — as a "pestilent fellow" and "agitator" — boils down simply to Paul's insistence to Israel that God has raised Jesus from death.[58] Once again, Luke's audience is able to hear what has been true throughout the story, that the resurrection is God's authorization for Jesus as Israel's Messiah: he is the one appointed to reinterpret God's word such that one must "listen to whatever he tells you" if salvation is to be realized.[59]

56. Lk 1:4; Acts 1:2; see Chapter 3.
57. Lk 13:23-30.
58. 24:5.
59. Acts 3:22.

From Gentile Skeptics to Believers:
The Full Gospel of Paul

	Speech #2 (of 7) Acts 17:22-31	**Speech #3** (of 7) Acts 20:18-35
Audience	*Gentiles* (Paul's only speech exclusively to non-Jews): Athenian skeptics	*Believers* (Paul's only speech exclusively to believers): Ephesian leaders
The Full Gospel, Paul	— *repent* ("all people everywhere," 17:30)	— *repentance* ("toward God," [rehearsal] 20:21)
	— *faith* implicit in the call to repentance based on the "assurance" of the resurrection	— *faith* explicitly, "toward our Lord Jesus," 20:21; *repentance* paralleled with — echoed by — *faith*
	— *resurrection* ("assurance to all by raising [appointed man] from the dead," 17:31)	(*resurrection* a moot point for believers addressed)
	— *judgment* universal, "judged in righteousness," 17:31	— *judgment* implicit: "some even from your own group will come distorting the truth in order to entice" . . . with the result of depriving the tempted from "the inheritance among all who are sanctified" (20:30-32)
	— *striving* implicit in the call for repentance, as gospel and the action of Acts make clear	— *striving* explicit here: to enter the kingdom — "the inheritance" — "Keep watch"; God's "own" have shed blood; "Be alert"; give rather than receive, 20:28, 31-32, 35

Chapter 22

Paul: Three Defense Speeches
before Israel and Rome

Acts 22:1-21; 24:10-21; 26:1-23

With the frame speeches (#'s 1 and 7) and the speeches to non-Jewish believers and then believers (#'s 2 and 3), the full and elaborated gospel is proclaimed by Paul. The remaining three speeches offer Paul's defense before hostile authorities including and instigated by Israel's old-guard leadership (#'s 4, 5, 6). Having repented of his approval for the murder of Jewish Way-people, Paul will himself face death for living and worshiping "according to the Way."[1] In these three speeches of defense, Paul establishes what he takes as the heart of the charges against him, a hope in the resurrection. Paul also makes clear that repentance leads to forgiveness and brings salvation, a repentance requiring the "light" that Jesus brings to the Law and prophets. Paul's stress on his credentials as a religious Jew, past and present, is an indicator of salvation's continuity in spite of what appears to the old-guard Israelites as a breakaway sect. From within the ranks of the old-guard leadership comes one who has seen the light, grasping the nature of the ancient covenant between God and Israel and its intended blessing of all peoples.

Paul's need to defend himself occurs almost immediately after his repentance and transformation. Stephen has been stoned to death, with Paul looking on approvingly, but the Way has now spread beyond Israel and Jerusalem, a fact accentuated by the baptism of an African state official (head of the Treasury) who joins the Jews belonging to the Way.[2] "Meanwhile," we hear, "Saul — still breathing threats and murder against the disciples of the Lord — went to the high priest and asked him for letters

---

1. 24:14.
2. 8:1; 8:26-40.

to the synagogues at Damascus, so that if he found any who belonged to the Way, men or women, he might bring them bound to Jerusalem."[3] There he would turn them over for proper punishment. But the risen Jesus interrupts these plans, appearing to Paul in a vision. Paul repents.

After his repentance, Paul begins testifying in synagogues; just as quickly, the old-guard "plotted to kill him"; shortly after, some Hellenist Jews in Jerusalem were "attempting to kill him."[4] Precisely the same plots were directed at Jesus, with his own townspeople trying to murder him by throwing him off a cliff.[5]

The narrator's account of Paul's repentance is followed up in the narrative by Peter's own repentance, regarding the Gentiles; for six chapters in Acts, the two leaders share overlapping narrative time.[6] Within this narrative mix we find references to Paul's teaching and to his testifying in synagogues; Paul's first speech, as we have seen, occurs in a synagogue.[7] "Unbelieving Jews" constantly stir up the crowds.[8] As Peter had, Paul confronts a magician, heals a lame man, and, with Barnabas, fends off adoring praise: Peter and Paul are shown on parallel paths in their experience of God's Way, but the two heroes of Acts also parallel the experiences of Jesus, as dramatized by Luke in his gospel.[9]

The dramatic ascendancy of Paul in the story begins to eclipse Peter's narrative presence through Peter's seventh and last speech, after which Peter disappears altogether.[10] From this point on, Paul is shown journeying constantly, visiting synagogue after synagogue of scattered Israel; finally, he "resolved in the Spirit to go through Macedonia and Achaia [Greece], and then to go on to Jerusalem," where he expects trouble, as did Jesus.[11] On his way back to Jerusalem, as we have just seen,

---

3. 9:1-2.

4. 9:23, 29.

5. Lk 4:29.

6. Acts 9:1 to 15:21.

7. Acts 11:22-30; 13:5, 14; 14:1; 13:16-41.

8. 14:1-2.

9. Parallels between Peter and Paul, 13:6-12; 14:8-20; Charles Talbert notes at least seven explicit parallels. He also traces more than a dozen parallels between Jesus and the two heroes of Acts. "The succession of a way of life [the "Way," Lk 20:21] is reflected in the correspondences between Jesus' career in Luke and the disciples' mission in Acts." Talbert's examples, he claims, "are illustrative, not exhaustive." *Reading Acts: A Literary and Theological Commentary on the Acts of the Apostles* (New York: Crossroad, 1997), pp. 9-15.

10. 15:7-11.

11. 17:1, 10, 17; 18:4, 7, 19, 26; 19:8; Jerusalem journey begins at 19:21; certainty of trouble, 20:22-24.

Paul calls together Ephesian believers to meet him for a hurried last-words address.[12] Paul expects very hard times ahead, he tells these believers, and it turns out as he predicted. Once back in Jerusalem, Israel's old-guard leaders "were trying to kill him," just as they tried to kill Israel's true "Leader."[13]

As Jesus undertakes a momentous journey to Jerusalem, so too does Paul; as Jesus faces great trouble in Jerusalem, so too does Paul; as Jesus faces legal charges before Roman authority brought upon him by his own people, so too does Paul. Upon his arrival in Jerusalem, Paul is welcomed warmly, as was Jesus, but after completing Jewish purification rites in the Temple, Paul is dragged out by a crowd roused to murderous intent by Jewish leaders.[14] As with Jesus, the old-guard leaders' antagonism results from what they perceive as a usurpation of authority; they are jealous.[15] And so it is that Paul's three defense speeches go to the heart of the authority question; the common denominator of all three is the resurrection of Jesus.

The first and third speeches focus on accounts of Paul's own experience with the risen Jesus. The first speech is a public hearing before a hostile crowd, primarily Israelites; the second is before authorities from both Rome and Israel; the third is a semi-private hearing before an interested Jew appointed by Rome as king of the Jews, plus "tribunes" and "prominent men."[16] Paul moves in each speech from insistence on his own faithfulness as an Israelite toward what in his third speech he insists on as the Messiah's clarity about repentance: "that [Israel] should repent and turn to God and do deeds consistent with repentance."[17] And what is the authority for such interpretation of the Law and prophets as offered by Jesus and by Paul's own teaching of the same? The answer in these speeches lies in God's raising Jesus from death, a resurrection which Paul himself has been privileged to experience in visitations from the risen Jesus.

The repeated thematic emphases of these three speeches, along with their respective audiences, are charted at the end of this chapter. Paul focuses on three themes:

12. 20:18-35; see Chapter 21.
13. Acts 20:23-24; 21:17, 27-31; Jesus is Israel's "Leader" and "Savior," 5:31.
14. 21:27-31.
15. 5:17; 13:45; 17:5.
16. First, 22:1-21; second, 24:10-21; third, 26:1-23.
17. 26:20.

- I am and have been a zealous Jew, upholding, then and now, the Law.
- Repentance, my own and yours, requires doing deeds consistent with repentance.
- Resurrection: I have heard and seen the risen Jesus; Israel's hope (second speech).

Paul's First Speech in Self-Defense, Before Jews (his fourth speech overall; 22:1-21)

The first of the three consecutive defense speeches is before a crowd whipped into a frenzy by Israel's old-guard leadership, some "Jews from Asia" who have made a point of coming down to Jerusalem to foment hostility against Paul. They all were "trying to kill him," and, as with Jesus, they shout, "Away with him!"[18] Paul's impromptu public protest establishes (1) impeccable Jewish credentials along with (2) a reference to the Gentiles, who figure so prominently in the ancient Jewish covenant with God.

(1) Jewish Credentials

Yanked from the hostile Jewish crowd by Roman protectors, Paul asks for a moment to speak to his fellow-Israelites, and is given permission to do so. He speaks from the steps before a Roman barracks:

> "Brothers and fathers, listen to the defense that I now make before you." When they heard him addressing them in Hebrew, they became even more quiet. Then he said: "I am a Jew, born in Tarsus in Cilicia, but brought up in this city at the feet of Gamaliel, educated strictly according to our ancestral law, being zealous for God, just as all of you are today. I persecuted this Way up to the point of death by binding both men and women and putting them in prison, as the high priest and the whole council of elders can testify about me. From them I also received letters to the brothers in Damascus, and I went there in order to bind those who were there and to bring them back to Jerusalem for punishment." (22:1-5)

Paul goes on to speak of his own repentance through an encounter with the risen Jesus and, by way of servant Ananias, a word from Jesus

18. Acts 21:31, 36; Lk 23:18.

that he is to be baptized and have his sins washed away, "calling on [Jesus'] name."

(2) Gentiles and Old-Guard Uproar

"After I had returned to Jerusalem and while I was praying in the temple," Paul says, the very voice of Jesus told him of his being sent to Gentiles:

> "I fell into a trance and *saw Jesus saying*[19] to me, 'Hurry and get out of Jerusalem quickly, because they will not accept your testimony about me.' And I said, 'Lord, they themselves know that in every synagogue I imprisoned and beat those who believed in you. And while the blood of your witness Stephen was shed, I myself was standing by, approving and keeping the coats of those who killed him.' Then he said to me, 'Go, for I will send you far away to the Gentiles.'" (22:17-21; emphasis mine)

At Paul's mention of Gentiles, the Israelites gathered before the barrack steps shouted, "Away with such a fellow from the earth!"[20] When Jesus opened his public speaking, fellow-Jews and neighbors sought to do away with him at the mention of his own and the prophets' ministry to non-Israelites.[21] Continually we are being reminded that while thousands of Israelites have come to accept their mission to non-Jews, as "servant Israel," others within Israel reject this Messiah and his message, as well as messengers like Paul who speak and do all "in his name."

"I am a Jew," Paul points out, "brought up in this city at the feet of Gamaliel, educated strictly according to our ancestral law, being zealous for God, just as all of you are today." The fact that upon his repentance Paul returns to the temple in Jerusalem for prayers is an important narrative reminder that Paul remains an Israelite in religion, belonging to the same Way-community within Israel that he had once been persecuting.

---

19. The unusual business of "seeing" someone speaking, when only the voice is actually mentioned, is a narrative clue that Paul is being added as an "eyewitness" to the resurrection, and is therefore highly qualified — though not completely qualified — to join the twelve new leaders of Israel. See Acts 1:21-22 for criteria, which include being an eyewitness not only to the resurrection but also to the entire earthly life of Jesus.

20. 22:22.

21. Lk 4:23-29.

Luke takes every possible opportunity to emphasize Paul's seriousness as a faithful though reconstructed Israelite, "zealous for Israel's God" in the past, in the present, and extending into the future.

Paul's appeal to his fellow-Israelites creates a murderous ruckus at the end of his speech. The thought that Paul, an Israelite, would be told by God to reach out toward Gentiles has proven intolerable to this Jewish crowd, presumably under the influence of its troublemaking old-guard leaders.[22] The old-guard has overlooked the very heart of their covenant with God, to bring blessing to Gentiles.[23]

Paul will either be protected by Rome — as Jesus had been, initially — or maimed by the frenzied crowd. Roman authority initially protects Paul, coming to his rescue and ensuring at least the start of a fair legal proceeding. This Roman protection leads to the proposal for a meeting between Paul and his old-guard antagonists in order to clear up the problem.[24] As with Jesus, the council meeting does not go very well for Paul: "the dissension became [so] violent" that the Roman tribune orders protection; "fearing that they would tear Paul to pieces, [he] ordered the soldiers to go down, take him by force, and bring him into the barracks" for protection.[25] Rome helps to arrange a clandestine escape for Paul from certain death at the hands of Jewish leadership in Jerusalem.[26] Ambush avoided, Paul is taken by Roman soldiers to Caesarea, where Lysias, the Roman tribune, has arranged for Paul to meet with Felix the Roman governor in order to review Paul's case; the session is attended by old-guard Jewish leaders. Asked to speak by the Roman governor, Paul is then summoned before a full house of Roman and Jewish authority and speaks once again in his own defense.

Paul's Second Speech in Self-Defense, Before Israelite and Roman Authority (his fifth speech overall; 24:10-21)

The audience for Paul's second defense speech is a mixture of representative authority from both Israel and Rome. In this middle defense

22. 22:21-22.

23. Acts 3:25; Gen 12:3.

24. We have explored the narrative pattern of council confrontation, beginning with Jesus and culminating with Stephen, in Chapter 18.

25. 23:10.

26. 23:12-35.

speech, Paul focuses on the resurrection of Jesus, since authority is the issue (in the first and third defense speeches, the resurrection is implicit, since Paul has encountered the risen Jesus, an important feature of his personal witness). Here, Paul locates his defense (1) in his credentials as a Law-following Jew and (2) in the resurrection of the dead, with implicit appeal to the God-given authority over Israel of Jesus, whom God raised from death. This matter of the resurrection, Paul claims, is the whole problem.

(1) Credentials: "believing everything laid down according to the Law . . ."

As in his prior defense, Paul begins with his Jewish credentials, and with his non-contentious ways.

Paul is represented as quite upbeat at the opportunity given him to speak in his own defense before both Jewish and Roman authority:

> "I cheerfully make my defense, knowing that for many years you have been a judge over this nation. As you can find out, it is not more than twelve days since I went up to worship in Jerusalem. They did not find me disputing with anyone in the temple or stirring up a crowd either in the synagogues or throughout the city. Neither can they prove to you the charge that they now bring against me. But this I admit to you, that according to the Way, which they call a sect, I worship the God of our ancestors, believing everything laid down according to the law or written in the prophets." (24:10-14)

Paul will return in this defense to his past and continuing faithfulness as a religious Jew, but he jumps here to something in the Law and prophets that is of special interest to Israel while pointing implicitly and cleverly to Jesus as Messiah. After all, it has been reported that Jesus was raised from death by God.

(2) Resurrection of the Dead: The Implicit Authority of Jesus

> "I have a hope in God — a hope that they themselves also accept — that there will be a resurrection of both the righteous and the unrighteous." (24:15)

In fact, as the story makes clear, certain old-guard leaders within Israel did accept this resurrection, while others did not.[27] This hope in God, for Paul, begins with the resurrection of Jesus, which the book-end defense speeches suggest. He concludes by vindicating himself further as a faithfully religious Jew:

> "Therefore I do my best always to have a clear conscience toward God and all people. Now after some years I came to bring alms to my nation and to offer sacrifices. While I was doing this, they found me in the temple, completing the rite of purification, without any crowd or disturbance. But there were some Jews from Asia — they ought to be here before you to make an accusation, if they have anything against me. Or let these men here tell what crime they had found when I stood before the council, unless it was this one sentence that I called out while standing before them, *'It is about the resurrection of the dead that I am on trial before you today.'*" (24:16-21; emphasis mine)

With "this one sentence" Paul concludes his defense. "It is about *the resurrection of the dead* that I am on trial before you today" echoes the prior confession, "I have a hope in God — a hope that they themselves [Israel] also accept — that there will be *a resurrection of both the righteous and the unrighteous.*"

This second defense speech has revealed the crucial status of the resurrection as the ground of Israel's salvation, a resurrection powerfully implied by the first and third speeches insofar as Paul "saw Jesus speaking" in the first defense speech and engages in intimate conversation with the risen Jesus, in the third. Winding down the action of Luke's two-volume story, these three major speeches bring to the narrative foreground that upon which salvation rests. Paul stresses a Messiah raised from suffering and death by God, a living Messiah whose "light" on Jewish scripture is authoritative in its presentation of God's Way. As a representative of "the Way," Paul's claim to authority rests on his encounter with the risen Jesus and on the risen one's authoritative teaching about salvation.

The hearing before Jewish and Roman authorities adjourns with no verdict. But Felix wants to hear more from Paul, since the Roman tribune "was rather well informed about the Way."[28] Hearing more about the Way and its demands for "justice, self-control, and the [threat of] coming

27. 23:6-10.
28. 24:22-24.

judgment," Felix "became frightened."[29] He wants to extract money — an obsession explored in Luke's gospel[30] — and pursues conversation but with no apparent intent to repent and go God's Way. Felix is warned of "the coming judgment" for his lack of justice and self-control — and wants to hear no more of it.

Nothing has come of Paul's defense one way or another. He is kept in prison two additional years, since Felix "wanted to grant the Jews a favor."[31] As is almost always the case in Acts, "the Jews" here refers to the old-guard leadership within Israel. Felix retires, and Festus takes over as the Roman tribune.

Paul's Third Speech in Self-Defense, Before Israelite and Roman Authority (his sixth speech overall; 26:1-23)

Traveling to Jerusalem, Festus is given a report against Paul by "the chief priests and the leaders of the Jews,"[32] who ask that Festus transfer Paul from the prison in Caesarea to Jerusalem. "In fact," we are told, the old-guard leadership was "planning an ambush to kill him along the way."[33] Come along with me, responds Festus: "if there is anything wrong about the man, let them accuse him."[34] Back in Caesarea, Paul answers "many serious charges against him, which they could not prove." Paul makes claims we have heard before: "I have in no way committed an offense against the Law of the Jews, or against the temple, or against the emperor."[35]

Festus, "wishing to do the Jews a favor," asks Paul if he desires to be tried in Jerusalem. Paul says *no*, appealing rather to the "emperor's tribunal" in Rome.[36] As always, Luke portrays the Roman authority as good and the old-guard Jewish authority as bad. Paul chooses the more favorable authority. Festus agrees and proceeds to make arrangements with King Agrippa and his wife Bernice, together with Paul, in order to figure out exactly what charges will be levied against their prisoner before they send him off to Rome.

29. 24:25.
30. 24:26.
31. 24:27.
32. 25:2.
33. 25:3.
34. 25:5.
35. 25:7-8.
36. 25:10.

Paul's audience for this last major speech in Acts[37] is both Jewish and Roman. He addresses the prominent local authorities, most significantly the Rome-appointed Jewish Agrippa and Agrippa's Jewish wife Bernice. Also present are the Roman tribune Festus and an august group of "tribunes" and "prominent men of the city."[38] Paul is given a chance to explain what he himself understands regarding the charges raised against him by the council of old-guard Israelite leadership. He responds by offering a speech in four parts: (1) Credentials as an Israelite; (2) My "Problem": Holding to Israel's Hope of the Resurrection; (3) The Risen Jesus Spoke with Me, and I Repented; (4) Here Is the Gospel Essence, for Israel and the World.

(1) Credentials as an Israelite

After crediting the king with knowledge about all things Jewish, Paul begins as he has in his other two defense speeches, by pointing to his credentials as a religiously observant Jew.

> "I consider myself fortunate that it is before you, King Agrippa, I am to make my defense today against all the accusations of the Jews, because you are especially familiar with all the customs and controversies of the Jews; therefore I beg of you to listen to me patiently. All the Jews know my way of life from my youth, a life spent from the beginning among my own people and in Jerusalem. They have known for a long time, if they are willing to testify, that I have belonged to the strictest sect of our religion and lived as a Pharisee." (26:2-5)

As in the prior defense speech, Paul moves from his impeccable record as an observant Jew to the centrality of the resurrection both in the charges against him and in the salvation message being offered.

(2) My "Problem": Holding to Israel's Hope of the Resurrection

> "And now I stand here on trial on account of my hope in the promise made by God to our ancestors, a promise that our twelve tribes hope to

37. The next and last speech, Paul's seventh, concludes Acts with a brief warning to Israel (see Chapter 20).
38. 25:23.

attain, as they earnestly worship day and night. It is for this hope, your Excellency, that I am accused by Jews! Why is it thought incredible by any of you that God raises the dead?" (26:6-8)

Having established the resurrection as both central to Israel's hope and the main point of contention between himself and the Jewish leadership, Paul elaborates on the matter of his own authority and religious pedigree with which he began his defense. He has been a zealous Jew concerned with clan purity.

(3) The Risen Jesus Spoke with Me, and I Repented

"Indeed, I myself was convinced that I ought to do many things against the name of Jesus of Nazareth. And that is what I did in Jerusalem; with authority received from the chief priests, I not only locked up many of the saints in prison, but I also cast my vote against them when they were being condemned to death. By punishing them often in all the synagogues I tried to force them to blaspheme; and since I was so furiously enraged at them, I pursued them even to foreign cities. With this in mind, I was traveling to Damascus with the authority and commission of the chief priests, when at midday along the road, your Excellency, I saw a light from heaven, brighter than the sun, shining around me and my companions. When we had all fallen to the ground, I heard a voice saying to me in the Hebrew language, 'Saul, Saul, why are you persecuting me?'" (26:9-14)

That the voice spoke to him "in the Hebrew language" is a powerful reminder for this Jewish king of the Jews, as we see in the next chapter, that of course the Risen One knows the preferred religious dialect of Israel.[39] As in the first defense speech, Paul goes on to recount his own repentance, but here this account leads to an explicit reference at the heart of his mission, the proclamation of such repentance to "both small and great."

---

39. We explore in our next and concluding chapter this interesting phenomenon of the narrator's note regarding the Hebrew dialect of Jesus.

(4) Here Is the Gospel Essence, O King, for Israel and the World

> "After that, King Agrippa, I was not disobedient to the heavenly vision, but declared first to those in Damascus, then in Jerusalem and throughout the countryside of Judea, and also to the Gentiles, that they should repent and turn to God and do deeds consistent with repentance. For this reason the Jews seized me in the temple and tried to kill me. To this day I have had help from God, and so I stand here, testifying to both small and great, saying nothing but what the prophets and Moses said would take place. . . ." (26:19-22)

Precisely as in the prior defense speech, Paul once again returns to — and concludes with — the common theme of all three defense speeches, which proves to be the gospel's essence.

> "I stand here, testifying to both small and great, saying nothing but what the prophets and Moses said would take place: that the Messiah must suffer, and that, by being the first to rise from the dead, he would proclaim light both to our people and to the Gentiles." (26:22-23)

The proclamation of "light" by Jesus is affirmed as authoritative by the fulfillment of Scripture in the Messiah's resurrection — "the first to rise from the dead." Israel's hopes in this Messiah and in the resurrection turn out to be the essential charges against me, says Paul. With one rhetorical thrust Paul is shown establishing two things: (1) his understanding of what most rankles the old-guard of Israel in their charges against him, namely, the hope of Israel that there is resurrection of the dead; (2) the fact that this very resurrection is fundamental to Israel's scripture and its witness to Israel's Messiah as Israel's authoritative teacher.

Paul's Three Defense Speeches: A Summary

Luke reserves for the last major speech of Paul a summary of God's divine will for Israel that echoes the vision of Peter, as we have seen: *all people*, says Paul, *must "repent and turn to God and do deeds consistent with repentance. . . . I stand here, testifying to both small and great, saying nothing but what the prophets and Moses said would take place: that the Messiah must suffer, and that, by being the first to rise from the dead, he would proclaim light both to our people and to the Gentiles."* Holding the infant Jesus, Simeon claimed to have seen God's salvation, "prepared in the presence of all peoples" — "*a light* for revelation to the Gentiles and [a light] for glory to [God's] people Israel," a citation of the prophet Isaiah.[40] Simeon's words are echoed in Paul's third defense speech. It outlines the big picture of Luke's story.

As attested by his "being the first to rise from the dead," Paul's argument goes, Jesus is in a position to "proclaim light both to our people and to the Gentiles."[41] As we will see in the following chapter, this "light" is the teaching of Jesus, an illumination that demands obedience if salvation is to become a reality. To participate in this Way of salvation, one must "do deeds consistent with repentance," as Paul is recorded as saying.

Paul now lives and worships "according to the Way," as he has said in his second defense speech;[42] the Way is authorized by God's raising the Way's teacher from death. Right up through the end of the two-volume story, the question remains: Who in Israel has the authority to interpret Scripture, and toward what end? Paul's three speeches in self-defense include implicit or explicit reference to what Jesus taught: repentance and resurrection, as we might have expected from the last-words speech of Jesus in Luke's gospel.[43]

Paul's mission, focused primarily toward Israel, is always the same: "trying to convince [Jews] about Jesus both from the Law and from the prophets" while "testifying to the kingdom of God" as taught by Jesus.[44] Only when Israel is fully on board as "servant Israel" is its mission in bringing the blessings of peace to all peoples fully under way. That is the promise with which the story ends, as indicated by Paul's last words with which Acts concludes.[45] Saved Israel is on board, and the covenant with God has been fulfilled, and now Israel — the thousands upon thousands who belong to the Way — will turn their full attention to the Gentiles.[46] Luke's perspective on the continuity of the Jewish religion up through

---

40. Lk 2:32; Is 49:6.

41. 26:23; perhaps, in view of a scriptural resurrection like that performed by way of Elijah (1 Kings 17:18-24), Luke is pointing to the idea that Jesus is the first of God's word-bearers, the prophets, to be raised from suffering and death (see Lk 13:33). It is unlikely Luke did not know of Elijah's use of God's power to raise the little boy from death.

42. Acts 24:14.

43. Lk 24:46-49.

44. 28:23.

45. 28:28.

46. Acts 3:25; 28:28; Gen 12:3.

Self-Defense: Three Speeches by Paul

	Acts 22:1-21, #4	Acts 24:10-21, #5	Acts 26:1-23, #6
Trial or Hearing?	Public hearing	A trial, or trial-like	Semi-private hearing
Audience	Israelites in Jerusalem (Lysias, Roman tribune, soldiers "in the wings")	Tribune Lysias sends Paul to Governor Felix: Roman authority, Israel old-guard authority	Festus succeeds Felix; brings Paul before King (Herod) Agrippa, who with his wife is Jewish; "tribunes and the prominent men of the city" (25:23)
Accusations and/or Examinations	*By old-guard Israel:* Paul teaches against Israel & Law & Temple; defiles Temple	*By old-guard Israel:* Paul is agitator; leader of political sedition; Jewish sect ringleader	*From Roman authority:* Paul given opportunity to explain charges against him
Paul's Self-Defense: (The Speech)	— had been "zealous for [Israel's] God"	— am zealous in worship and rites, and for temple and synagogues	— have been strict Pharisee, from my youth; with authority of priests, I persecuted
1. Faithful Israelite	— ancestral Law (education)	— ancestors' God, I worship; I believe in all of the Law and prophets	— ancestors' God promised: resurrection; our twelve tribes' hope
	— had persecuted this Way as anti-Israel; Israel's council can vouch for me	— I now worship according to Israel's Way	— My "way of life" from youth up until now, as a Pharisee
2. Repentance leads to forgiveness of sins	— repentance: Paul's own	— repentance yields to resurrection emphasis — though after the speech, Felix refuses repentance	— repentance, Paul's own; need of turning from darkness to light, to deeds worthy of repentance
3. Resurrection	— I "saw Jesus saying to me" (vision of *risen* Jesus, in Temple)	— Israel's hope: *resurrection* of both the righteous and unrighteous	— my hope and Israel's: "that God raises the dead"
	— hears voice from heaven: it's the risen Jesus, alive!	— "It is about the resurrection of the dead that I am on trial before you today" (last words)	— hears voice from heaven: it's Jesus (speaking Hebrew!)
			— Messiah, first to rise from death (as Moses said)
			— "heavenly vision" (*risen* Jesus)

these decades after the departure of Jesus is reinforced powerfully by Paul's consecutive speeches of defense in which he argues his own present and past commitment to Israel's God and Israel's religion. Paul has been "converted," not to Christianity or into the church (in any possible modern conception of those terms), but into the Jewish sect known in Paul's own words as "the Way."[47]

In defending himself, Paul is shown by Luke as taking the offense, citing his own adherence to the Law and Scripture's foretelling of the Messiah and his resurrection, the hope of Israel. What Paul points to is the authority of Jesus, based on the resurrection, to teach the Way of God, Israel's salvation. So it is that we find Paul, in the story's very last verse, "proclaiming the kingdom of God" as taught by Jesus and "teaching about the Lord Jesus."[48]

"Resurrection" and "repentance" are the two most important signal words of Acts; with repentance especially, Luke's audience needs to be always keeping in mind the masterful presentation of teaching about repentance in Luke's gospel. We conclude now with a closer look at the three accounts of Paul's repentance. We will discover in the apparently glaring inconsistencies among the three accounts of this repentance a coherent development of focus that helps to establish Paul's last major speech — his third defense speech — as a wonderful overview of Paul's theology presented by Luke.

47. 24:14.
48. 28:31.

Chapter 23

Paul: Three Repentance Accounts

Acts 9:1-19; 22:1-21; 26:1-23

That we find three accounts of Paul's repentance indicates its importance to the story Luke is telling. Luke's narrator offers the first version, while Paul himself recounts the experience twice, in the first and third defense speeches we have just explored.[1] Paul's authority and the authority of Jesus are mutually reinforced through a narrative strategy that includes differing and apparently contradictory detail among the three accounts.

In the three successive accounts of Paul's repentance, a voice from heaven is heard by Paul's companions, then not heard, and finally not mentioned at all with regard to the companions. Meanwhile, the voice becomes more focused on Paul himself, intimately.

Heaven's light shines brighter and brighter as we move through the three occurrences, until finally, at its brightest, the light becomes crucially metaphorical as well as literal, the "light" for the Gentiles prophesied by Simeon.[2]

An intermediary, Ananias, goes from being "a disciple" in the first account to "a devout man according to the Law" in the second, and is finally not mentioned at all in the third. Luke's message about his hero Paul becomes clear in this intricate pattern of repentance accounts.

The thrice-repeated account of Paul's repentance provides an emphasis on the story's prize example of repentance, an old-guard leader who turns from parochial clan-promotion to God's purposes of healing and

---

1. Acts 9:1-19; 22:4-16; 26:9-18.
2. Lk 2:32.

restoration for all peoples. But the repetition does much more than merely add emphasis. In addition, we find a striking development of a dramatic theme within the larger story, namely, the role of Jesus in bringing light to Scripture so that Israel might listen, obey, and be saved — turning around from religious rules and clan protection toward bringing God's blessings of communal peace to all peoples.

Similarities and Conspicuous Differences in the Three Accounts

In each of the three repentance accounts, the risen Jesus interrupts Paul's plans to continue persecuting "those who belonged to the Way"[3] with the words, "Saul, Saul, why do you persecute me?"[4] In each account there are important but differing references to heavenly light and apparently contradictory details about who hears the heavenly voice, and what exactly is heard by Paul himself. By tracing these differences we readers will be able to "hear again" what Luke's audience would have heard in this artful repetition.

In the narrator's account, the first, the voice is heard by Paul and by his companions. In Paul's first recounting of the same experience, his companions explicitly *do not* hear the voice. In the third instance of this same scene, whether the companions hear or do not hear is not mentioned, and the voice speaks at much greater length to Paul alone.

In the first account, Paul apparently has heard nothing directly about the plans God has for him, since the voice has explained everything to an intermediary, Ananias. In the second account, Paul's first recounting, Ananias tells Paul of these purposes. Finally, in the third and last account, Paul's second recounting, Ananias disappears from the text and Paul is able to hear of God's plans from Jesus himself. Confusion? Are these jumbled details of no great concern to our author? Quite the opposite appears to be the case, as we will see.

The light is another source of inconsistency. In terms of sheer volume, there is a steady increase in story space devoted to this heavenly light. More significant are the increasing intensity of the light and its spreading breadth of illumination. In #1, a light from heaven flashes around Paul, while in #2 it is "a *great* light" that "suddenly shone about me"; for #3,

---

3. Acts 9:2.
4. 9:4; 22:7; 26:14.

however, the intensity is greatest, "a light from heaven, *brighter than the sun*, shining around me and my companions."[5] Most strikingly, this brighter-than-the-sun light of the third version complements what is crucial in Luke's perspective of salvation: Israel is to bring *light* to all peoples.

What appears to be contradictory in these three versions of Paul's great repentance experience turns out to be a coherent development of focus that is congruent with the underlying motif of the three defense speeches, a narrative insistence on Paul as a witness to the "light to the Gentiles" which is "for the glory of Israel."[6] Paul's fundamental testimony is to repentance, and to resurrection, "the hope of Israel"; Paul is a thirteenth to the twelve apostles in his faithfulness of witness concerning that which Jesus offered as a last instruction.[7]

First Repentance Account, from the Narrator (9:1-19)

Paul is interrupted by Jesus on the road to Damascus. He is challenged to an about-face from his religious zeal - - protecting the faith of Israel and its privileged relationship with God — in favor of journeying God's counterintuitive Way of blessing for others, for outsiders, at great personal cost.

> Now as he was going along and approaching Damascus, suddenly a light from heaven flashed around him. He fell to the ground and heard a voice saying to him, "Saul, Saul, why do you persecute me?" He asked, "Who are you, Lord?" The reply came, "I am Jesus, whom you are persecuting. But get up and enter the city, and you will be told what you are to do." The men who were traveling with him stood speechless because they heard the voice but saw no one. (9:3-7)

Paul is blinded and told to go to Damascus. Meanwhile, a "disciple" in Damascus is approached by the Lord:

> "Ananias." He answered, "Here I am, Lord."[8] The Lord said to him, "Get up and go to the street called Straight, and at the house of Judas

5. 9:3, 8; 22:6, 9, 11; 26:13.
6. Lk 2:32.
7. Acts 28:20; 23:6; Lk 24:46-49.
8. This is a resounding echo to Scripture's accounts of godly persons responding to the voice of God with "here I am," an indication of willing presence and service: Abraham (Gen 22:1); Jacob (Gen 31:11); Moses (Ex 3:4); the boy Samuel, who mistakes God's voice for Eli's,

look for a man of Tarsus named Saul. At this moment he is praying, and he has seen in a vision a man named Ananias come in and lay his hands on him so that he might regain his sight." But Ananias answered, "Lord, I have heard from many about this man, how much evil he has done to your saints in Jerusalem; and here he has authority from the chief priests to bind all who invoke your name." But the Lord said to him, "Go, for he is an instrument whom I have chosen to bring my name before Gentiles and kings and before the people of Israel; I myself will show him how much he must suffer for the sake of my name." (9:10-16)

Presented here as an Israelite faithful to Israel's Messiah, Ananias obeys God's strange request by laying hands on the one who had been persecuting Israelites who "belonged to the Way."[9] Paul regains his sight, receives the baptism of repentance, and is filled with the Holy Spirit.[10] "Immediately [Paul] began to proclaim Jesus in the synagogues, saying, 'He is the Son of God.'"[11] Almost as quickly, some "Jews plotted to kill him"; Paul's repentance is authentic, as attested to by the sure fruits of suffering at the hands of the old-guard leadership, the very ones among whom Saul/Paul had moved with such approval.[12]

Second Repentance Account
(Paul's first speech in self-defense; 22:1-21)

The first time we hear from Paul himself about his repentance is during his first defense speech. After calling on his "brothers and fathers" to

---

responding "here I am"; Eli advises young Samuel that next time he say to God, "Speak, for your servant is listening" — an apt interpretation of what the words "here I am" actually mean (1 Sam 3:4-10). The author of Luke's story would have cherished this story of Samuel, if not actually referring to it; we find a precise echo of young Samuel's experience in moving from "here I am" to "speak, for your servant is listening" in Mary's "here am I, servant of the Lord; let it be with me according to your word" (Lk 1:38). A further clue as to the meaning of "here I am" is found in Psalm 40:6-8, where the narrator responds with "here I am" to God's desire for an "open ear," then goes on to detail precisely how the *open ear* of "here I am" plays out: "I delight to do your will, O my God."

9. 9:2.

10. The mention of the Holy Spirit here in conjunction with repentance signifies the baptism of Jesus versus the baptism of repentance alone offered by John (9:17-18; Lk 3:16).

11. 9:20.

12. Acts 9:23.

hear him — "addressing them in Hebrew" — Paul puts forth his credentials as an Israelite in good standing, including his work of harassing those Jews who had joined the Way sect within Israel.[13] The reversal wrought by repentance could not be more dramatic. Paul goes on to tell of his encounter with Jesus:

> "I persecuted this Way up to the point of death by binding both men and women and putting them in prison, as the high priest and the whole council of elders can testify about me. From them I also received letters to the brothers in Damascus, and I went there in order to bind those who were there and to bring them back to Jerusalem for punishment. While I was on my way and approaching Damascus, about noon a great light from heaven suddenly shone about me. I fell to the ground and heard a voice saying to me, 'Saul, Saul, why are you persecuting me?' I answered, 'Who are you, Lord?' Then he said to me, 'I am Jesus of Nazareth whom you are persecuting.' Now those who were with me saw the light but did not hear the voice of the one who was speaking to me." (22:4-9)

A basic story line from the narrator's account is repeated: Paul has litigious intentions against members of the Jewish Way. On his way to Damascus, he encounters the risen Jesus. However, there are small and seemingly insignificant changes in details: (1) the light becomes "great," (2) the companions now "did *not* hear the voice of the one speaking to me," and (3) there is a place of origin that Jesus adds regarding himself, "I am Jesus *of Nazareth*, whom you are persecuting." Paul's speech continues:

> "I asked, 'What am I to do, Lord?' The Lord said to me, 'Get up and go to Damascus; there you will be told everything that has been assigned to you to do.' Since I could not see because of the brightness of that light, those who were with me took my hand and led me to Damascus. A certain Ananias, who was a devout man according to the law and well spoken of by all the Jews living there, came to me; and standing beside me, he said, 'Brother Saul, regain your sight!' In that very hour I regained my sight and saw him. Then he said, 'The God of our ancestors has chosen you to know his will, to see the Righteous One and to hear his own voice; for you will be his witness to all the world of what you have seen and heard. And now why do you delay? Get up, be baptized, and have your sins washed away, calling on his name.'" (22:10-16)

---

13. Acts 22:1-3.

Repentance leads to baptism and sins being "washed away." "Calling on his name," for Paul, as for all believers, is to embrace all that Jesus has taught about repentance as Messiah. "Repent," Peter had said to Israelites; "be baptized every one of you *in the name of Jesus Christ* so that your sins may be forgiven; and you will receive the gift of the Holy Spirit."[14] "In the name of Jesus Christ" is an invocation of the authority God has invested in Jesus, through the resurrection, as interpreter of Scripture for Israel and through Israel to the world.

The Twists

How is it that in the narrator's account of Paul's speech, this repentance, companions hear the voice, but in this second account, they do not?

And why does the flashing "light" seen by Paul in the narrator's account become, in Paul's account here, a "great light" that shines so brightly that Paul is explicitly "blinded"?

Furthermore, why does the description of Ananias change from "disciple" to "a devout man"?[15] We could assume that Luke had differing and confused sources and blindly followed these, or, as I will try to show, that Luke worked these confusing details toward an integrated and compelling point he wishes the narrative to make about Paul's authority in relation to the authority of Jesus.

A final twist of difference in this second telling is what Jesus adds in identifying himself to Paul: "I am Jesus *of Nazareth* whom you are persecuting."[16] The added town of origin signifies for the primarily Jewish crowd listening to Paul (and for Luke's audience as well) an ironic tragedy shared by both Jesus and Paul with regard to their reception among their own. Jesus is rejected in his hometown of Nazareth ("no prophet is accepted in the prophet's hometown"),[17] while Paul, too, is being vilified by his fellow-Israelites, right here in their shared religious home, Jerusalem. Immediately after the speech, while praying in the temple, Paul is advised by Jesus to "hurry and get out of Jerusalem quickly, because they will not accept your testimony about me."[18] With apparent surprise, Paul responds, "Lord, they themselves know that in every synagogue I impris-

14. Acts 2:38.
15. 9:10; 22:12.
16. 22:8.
17. Lk 4:16, 24.
18. 22:17-18.

oned and beat those who believed in you. And while the blood of your witness Stephen was shed, I myself was standing by, approving. . . ."[19] Such expectation of resistance from the old-guard, however, is in perfect harmony with what Jesus has said privately to Paul just prior, that "I am Jesus *of Nazareth* . . .": those with whom you are most closely associated are those who will resist most.[20]

Difference in Description of Ananias

As a "disciple," Ananias is linked directly with Jesus and to those "who belonged to the Way."[21] It was at this narrative point that the Way had just begun to spread beyond Jerusalem and, in token fashion, beyond Israel itself (Samaritans, the African state official).[22] In the action between the narrator's account in chapter 9 and this version by Paul in chapter 22 there has been escalating hostility within Israel between the rising and the falling. At this point, then, there is perfect narrative logic in Paul's insistence before old-guard "purists" on the excellence of this Israelite Ananias not so much as a Jesus-disciple but as "a devout man according to the law and well spoken of by all the Jews living there." And of course the story continues to insist on the fact that disciples of Israel's Christ — Paul above everyone — are all "devout [persons] according to the law."[23]

Another twist on the Ananias appearance in this second account is the devout man's volubility. He speaks more in this second account. In the narrator's version, the voice tells Ananias of God's purposes for Paul: "Go, for he is an instrument whom I have chosen to bring my name before Gentiles and kings and before the people of Israel; I myself will show him how much he must suffer for the sake of my name."[24] There is no record of Ananias telling Paul of these purposes. But in Paul's account, Ananias speaks of God's purposes directly to Paul. "Then [Ananias] said, 'The God of our ancestors has chosen you to know his will, to see the Righteous One and to hear his own voice; for you will be his witness to

---

19. Acts 22:19-20.
20. Acts 22:8.
21. 9:2, 10.
22. 8:5, 26-39.
23. As we have seen, one's becoming a follower of Messiah — in Luke's story — in no way cancels out one's devotion to the law, since the role of Messiah was precisely to clarify this law in order that Israel would be freed to hear it rightly and obey it daily.
24. 9:15-16.

all the world of what you have seen and heard.'"[25] As a defense measure, this would work well: a devout man according to Israel's Law acts as word-bearer and intermediary between God and Israelite Paul. So it was with the prophets who brought God's word to the leaders. What Ananias is shown declaring from the mouth of the Lord to Paul is the divine purpose from ancient times, the covenant involving Israel and Israel's mission "to all the world."[26]

Discrepancy with the Voice and Difference of Light

Paul's account adds the information that after Damascus he had returned to Jerusalem. In the temple he was praying, a sign that Paul, like mentor/mediator Ananias, remains "a devout man according to the law." In the temple, Jesus visits Paul again. This time Paul "*saw* Jesus *saying*"; he *sees* the risen Messiah and *hears* a divine word that echoes the message of Ananias, that Paul will go "to the Gentiles" (that is, "to all the world").[27]

The heavenly voice has come progressively "closer" to Paul, with increased intimacy of detail. Here in the second account of repentance, Paul's companions do not hear the voice at all; it is for Paul alone. And Paul now is able to hear from Ananias what God intends for him.

In this second account the voice has become more focused on Paul, and the light has gotten brighter, explicitly linked to Paul's becoming blind. The increase of light and the greater intimacy of voice are accentuated by apparent contradiction: the voice is heard by companions in the first account, not in the second; this development culminates in the third repentance account with resolve and rhetorical brilliance.

Third Repentance Account
(Paul's third speech in self-defense; 26:1-23)

The third account of Paul's repentance is Paul's second telling, this time before the Jewish Agrippa, Roman-appointed king of the Jews, Bernice his wife, the Roman tribune Festus, and town dignitaries. This is Paul's last major speech. Here we find further change and also contradiction in

25. 22:14-15.
26. 3:25.
27. 22:18; 22:15, 21.

the pattern of details about light, voice, and Ananias. The "disciple" who is also "a devout man according to the Law" disappears entirely.

Paul begins with an insistence on his credentials as an old-guard leader with a special zeal for keeping the religious clan pure and its rules infallible doctrine. Those Israelites who "belonged to the Way" clearly deviated from the one true religion. "With this in mind," he says,

"I was traveling to Damascus with the authority and commission of the chief priests, when at midday along the road, your Excellency, I saw a *light* from heaven, brighter than the sun, shining around me and my companions. When we had all fallen to the ground, I heard a voice saying to me in the Hebrew language, 'Saul, Saul, why are you persecuting me? It hurts you to kick against the goads.' I asked, 'Who are you, Lord?' The Lord answered, 'I am Jesus whom you are persecuting. But get up and stand on your feet; for I have appeared to you for this purpose, to appoint you to serve and testify to the things in which you have seen me and to those in which I will appear to you. I will rescue you from your people and from the Gentiles — to whom I am sending you to open their eyes so that they may turn from darkness to *light* and from the power of Satan to God, so that they may receive forgiveness of sins and a place among those who are sanctified by faith in me.'" (26:12-18; emphasis mine)

The shift in repeated details from the first account of Paul's repentance by the narrator to the second, Paul's first telling of the experience, finds its narrative purpose completed here in the third account, Paul's final major speech.

The Light

The physical "light" that shines brighter and with greater scope as the accounts progress becomes associated finally, in this last account, with the metaphoric light that has been a motif throughout the two-volume story. Paul himself turns from darkness to "light," and Paul will bring the "light" of Jesus to Israel and to all peoples, echoing Simeon's "*light* to the Gentiles and for glory to [God's] people Israel."[28]

28. Lk 2:30-32.

The Voice

Light and voice lie at the heart of the authority question: *to whom will Israel listen?*[29] In account #1, the narrator's, the voice is heard by Paul and his companions; later, the voice tells Ananias of God's purposes for Paul. We do not hear what Ananias tells Paul. In account #2 (Paul's first recounting) the voice is heard by Paul but *not* by his companions. This time, Paul hears from Ananias of God's purposes for him. In account #3 (Paul's second recounting) the voice is heard by Paul, with no mention of companions hearing anything. Furthermore, Paul hears the voice directly, in Hebrew, explaining God's purposes for him. The focus of the voice increasingly narrows in these three accounts to Paul as its sole audience; other auditors fade completely out of the picture.

Only in the third and last account do we discover that Jesus spoke directly to Paul of God's purposes; only then do we discover that Jesus used Hebrew with Paul. Perhaps the narrative is suggesting that Paul's companions heard a voice in the first account that amounted to gibberish since it was (as we find out later) in Hebrew, not the more commonly spoken Aramaic.[30] That is, they heard a voice, but it was undecipherable noise, which the second version interprets as hearing, in effect, no voice at all. Luke's audience would know that educated Jews like Paul would know Hebrew, the true language of Israel.[31]

29. Lk 9:35; Acts 3:22.

30. Or perhaps, as many scholars say, this reference to the Hebrew language in 26:14 is too complex an issue to resolve by the translation "Hebrew" or "Aramaic." It is suggested that *tē Hebraidi dialektō,* with its clear reference to "Hebrew," should actually be translated "Aramaic," since Aramaic, some scholars believe, was the common dialect for Jews and non-Jews at that time and place. Aramaic would be the most common dialect with learned Jews also conversant in Hebrew (see the following footnote).

31. The textual progression on this matter of "voice," which emphasizes an increasingly intimate focus on the conversation between Jesus and Paul, is very possibly strengthened in its effect by the saved information that the voice spoke in Israel's true language, the less well-known and less-spoken Hebrew language. The dramatic effect of hearing that the heavenly voice speaks in Hebrew parallels the stated effect on the audience of Paul's first defense speech (the second account of his transformation). When Israel realizes that Paul is addressing them in Hebrew, not the common Aramaic of the day, there is a noted response. "When they heard him addressing them in Hebrew, they became even more quiet" (22:2). This is Jerusalem, where it is probable that learned Jews, along with their facility with the more common dialect (Aramaic), also would have been conversant in Hebrew, language of the tribe. Paul's Damascus-road companions, not necessarily from Jerusalem and perhaps not even Jews, could have been ignorant of Hebrew, while the Jerusalem Jews of 21:40, specified as Paul's audience, would have known both

For Luke's audience, it would be a striking scene, this Jewish king of the Jews and his Jewish wife hearing that Hebrew was the language spoken by Jesus to the learned Jew Paul. Paul's companions were of a less select crowd, less well trained, not privileged perhaps to sit as Paul had at the feet of the famous Jewish rabbi Gamaliel;[32] they heard a voice, yes (account #1), but it amounted to mere noise, in effect no real voice at all (account #2). By the third repeated account, whether the companions either hear or do not hear the voice, becomes irrelevant. And now, Ananias is not present at all: only Jesus is mentioned, speaking everything to Paul for the first time, and telling Paul directly of God's purposes for him.

The rhetorical effect of an increasingly focused and intimate voice over the three accounts is reinforced by what happens to the voice of Ananias in regard to Paul.

- **Voice, via Ananias, #1:** The voice of *Jesus* . . . . . *to Ananias*
- **Voice, via Ananias, #2:** The voice of *Ananias* . . . . . *to Paul*
- **Voice, no Ananias, #3:** The voice of *Jesus* . . . . . *to Paul*[33]

In the final account, the intimate voice of Jesus speaking of God's purposes to Paul without the intermediary Ananias parallels the intimacy of Jesus in using the specialized liturgical language — Hebrew — of Israel.

The full-flowering of intimacy in voice over the three accounts can be indicated, also, by the small detail added by Jesus in the initial challenge, "Saul, Saul, why do you persecute me? *It hurts to kick against the goads.*"[34] We hadn't heard this before, this understanding of Jesus that for Paul to wrestle against "the goads" is hurtful, to himself of course but also possibly to Jesus. "The sayings of the wise are like goads," remarks an ancient seer from Scripture, possibly echoed here.[35] In the scene of this last account, the royal Jewish couple appointed as rulers by Rome are being drawn into what for Luke's audience is a compelling focus on the intimacy between Israel's Messiah and Paul. And now, for both the Jewish king of the Jews and Luke's audience, the story can explain the emphasis on physical light, linking it with the story's repeated emphasis on spiritual light.

Hebrew and Aramaic and would have been impressed with Paul's fluency in the tribal/ religious language.

32. 22:3.

33. 9:15-16; 22:14-16; 26:16-18.

34. 26:14.

35. Eccl 12:11. Or, this could be a proverbial saying meaning, as C. K. Barrett thinks (borrowing from Bultmann), that "man cannot withstand the divine." *A Critical and Exegetical Commentary on The Acts of the Apostles*, vol. 2 (Edinburgh: T. & T. Clark, 1998), p. 1158.

Light and the Turning "from Darkness to Light"

In account #1 (narrator's), Paul "was going along and approaching Damascus" when "suddenly *a light from heaven* flashed around him."[36] That Paul's blindness is caused by this light is implied but not stated. In account #2 (Paul's first defense speech), Paul provides a slight elaboration suggesting greater light: "While I was on my way and approaching Damascus, about noon *a great light from heaven* suddenly shone about me"; in fact, this time we hear explicitly that Paul was blinded by the light. "I could not see because of *the brightness of that light,* [so] those who were with me took my hand and led me to Damascus."[37] In account #3 (Paul's third defense speech), it was "at midday along the road, your Excellency," says Paul to Agrippa, that "I saw *a light from heaven, brighter than the sun,* shining around me and my companions." Here in the third telling, voice and light coalesce with powerful impact. Paul reports *words of Jesus spoken directly to him,* that Jesus will rescue Paul from Jew and non-Jew alike, sending him to both Jew and non-Jew *"to open their eyes so that they may turn from darkness to light* and from the power of Satan to God, so that they may receive forgiveness of sins and a place among those who are sanctified by faith in me." Paul concludes this third account of his repentance with the assertion that none less than Moses predicted "that the Messiah must suffer, and that, by being the first to rise from the dead, he would *proclaim light* both to our people and to the Gentiles."

Proclamation comes by voice; light is accessible by eye. Voice has become more intimate and detailed in the development from the first to third accounts, just as the light has become brighter and is finally associated with the light brought by Jesus through his teaching.

The increasing intensity of light[38] underscores the authority question that dominates the end of Luke's gospel,[39] a thematic focus of the two-volume narrative that increases with dramatic interest throughout Acts. It is important to remember that this authority issue and the matter of *light* have been present from the start and run throughout the story Luke tells, from Simeon's citation of Isaiah that the Messiah would be *"a light* for revelation to the Gentiles and [a light] for glory to [God's] people Israel,"[40] to

36. 9:3.

37. 22:6; 22:11.

38. That is, the dramatically described intensity: the actual intensity, presumably, was a single fact common to the three accounts.

39. 19:45–24:53.

40. Lk 2:32; Is 49:6.

Paul's reaffirmation that Jesus, being "the first to rise from the dead," would "proclaim light both to our people and to the Gentiles."[41]

"Proclaim light both to our people and to the Gentiles": In this third retelling of his repentance, Paul states a core truth of the whole story, that the role of Jesus is to proclaim, and in so doing to bring light. "Light" is seen, while "proclamation" is heard. By tracing a development of the literal light that at one point is able to blind Paul, the text moves compellingly to the metaphoric use of light as insight, as a seeing with the heart. To see is to embrace. As Zechariah had alerted us at the story's beginning, Jesus has come "to give light to those who live in darkness and in the shadow of death, to guide our feet into the way of peace."[42] "Listen to him!" we heard God say to Peter, James, and John.[43] "Listen to whatever he tells you," Peter has said regarding Jesus, by way of Moses.[44] For Luke, Jesus is primarily teacher of God's Way, the kingdom, and sender of God's empowering Spirit. Light equals illumination, the "revelation" that Jesus himself brought in his teaching.[45]

The Three Accounts of Paul's Repentance:
A Summary and Conclusion

What constitutes "the light" of revelation for Gentiles? Luke's first volume, his gospel, has answered that. For Paul, as portrayed by Luke, the chief offering of God's Christ, who is the entire world's "Lord," is "to *open their eyes* so that they may *turn from darkness to light* and from the power of Satan to God, *so that* they may receive forgiveness of sins and a place among those who are sanctified by faith in [Jesus]."[46] Repentance begins with listening to Jesus, "opening eyes" to this definitively interpreted word in order to *see* the truth and obey, turning "from darkness to

41. 26:23.

42. Lk 1:79.

43. Lk 9:35.

44. Acts 3:22.

45. Lk 2:32; we need to recall that "Teacher" occurs as a title for Jesus fifteen times in Luke's gospel, while the teaching of Jesus (verb and noun forms) is mentioned sixteen times. No other title or activity of Jesus is cited nearly as often in Luke's story, as we have noted, except "Son of Man," which occurs twenty-five times in Luke's gospel and once in Acts. This latter disproportion indicates the extent to which Acts rests on Luke's gospel, since it is Jesus, risen, that the believers bear witness to. What "Son of Man" means has been unpacked in volume one.

46. Acts 26:18.

light." The *turning* referred to by Paul is from a psychological, emotional, and spiritual *darkness* described by Jesus in the gospel at great length, toward a *light* lived out and taught by Jesus and summarized as "the things that make for peace."[47]

Such turning from darkness to light leads to forgiveness, which is conditional: do *this* and then *that* will happen. Do what it takes to turn from darkness to light, "so that," as Paul says, you "may receive forgiveness of sins."[48] From John the Baptist through Jesus to Paul, the whole story's thematic emphasis has remained unchanged.

Paul himself must respond to the voice and its proclamation of Light. When Paul repents, he turns toward God's Way, which is — as for all believers in Luke's story — to embrace "mission." The turning-around of repentance is a turning toward "mission." One is not "saved" in order to go on "mission"; rather, one is "saved" by striving to enter God's kingdom, which striving *is* "mission."[49] For Luke, then, the light of salvation is not an illumination of propositions but of a path. To find oneself among those being "sanctified by faith," as Paul puts it in his third defense speech, is to be journeying God's "Way of salvation."[50] This is the Way according to which Paul worships God, a "faith" based on God's word to which "priests became obedient."[51] This is a Way of peace; there are specific "things" that need to be recognized and embraced if such peace — an unusual and mostly unwanted peace — is to be "made."[52]

Luke uses the image of illumination and light to bolster his dramatic case for what it is that Jesus primarily accomplishes.[53] Illumination is not an esoteric knowledge or belief-system, as Luke presents the matter; rather, Jesus brings to light a Way, a journey-to-take, a light-to-follow. "The word of the Lord" taught by Paul[54] is a rehearsal of the light of Jesus regarding salvation and the need for striving and shrewd-

47. Lk 19:42.
48. Acts 26:18.
49. Lk 13:23-24.
50. 26:18; 16:17.
51. 24:14; 6:7.
52. Lk 19:42.
53. "Whatever you have said in the dark," Jesus has said, "will be heard in *the light,* and what you have whispered behind closed doors will be proclaimed from the housetops" (Lk 12:3). And Jesus is shown referring to "children of light," albeit in a lament: a dishonest manager is commended by his master "because he had acted shrewdly; for the children of this age are more shrewd in dealing with their own generation than are the *children of light*" (Lk 16:8).
54. Acts 16:32; see my Conclusion for a spelling-out of this narrative fact.

ness.[55] As Luke's story has it, the Law as rule binds and chokes — a yoke around one's neck; such systems of belief and registry of rules partake of the darkness from which believers must turn, just as Paul has been shown doing in these repeated accounts of his repentance. The Law as principle is a "good news" that brings "release";[56] it partakes of the light toward which believers turn in their ongoing and daily repentance.[57]

Just after the first of his seven speeches, Paul reminds Israel from Scripture of its covenantal responsibilities, its salvation: "For so the Lord has commanded us, saying, 'I have set you [Israel] to be a *light* for the Gentiles, so that you may bring salvation to the ends of the earth.'" From Luke's perspective, this fulfillment of the ancient covenant happens, though not for all within Israel.[58] Jesus has accomplished his mission, as described by Simeon, to be "a light of revelation to the Gentiles" through "servant Israel," a bringing of blessing that will be "for glory to your people Israel."[59] And Jesus has accomplished his mission, as described by Zechariah, to give light to those who live in darkness and in the shadow of death, to guide our feet into the way of peace.[60] In Paul's last major speech, the last major speech of Acts and the third retelling of Paul's own repentance, some of the story's major motifs come to a perfect integrity: *the voice* of Jesus that must be listened to, described throughout as proclamation, preaching, instruction, teaching, and *the light* that must be followed, referred to from the very start of the story as revelation, a guide for feet seeking a Way of peace.

From Luke's perspective there is a "divine necessity" to all this: redeemed Israel accepts its covenantal role as "servant Israel," bringing the blessing of Jesus-as-light to all peoples.[61] And so Israel is delivered, as the early poems of Luke's gospel intimated. But not only in the fulfillment of

---

55. Lk 13:23-24; 16:8; as discussed, always "the word of the Lord" taught by Paul and other believers in Acts refers to the word of God taught by Jesus (Acts 16:32; Lk 24:44-49).

56. Acts 15:10; Lk 4:18-19.

57. "Repent" in Acts 2:38 is the verb *metanoēsate*, an imperative that implies a decisive turning-around. Indeed, Peter's challenge is for his fellow-Jews to turn-around from their rejection of Jesus as Messiah, and to join the Way — which requires ongoing repenting, as he himself demonstrates both at the end of the gospel and dramatically in the case of turning-around regarding the inclusion of Gentiles. The call to take up one's cross daily, as we have seen, is a striving that is part of repentance and not a luxury option *after* repentance, but part of the repentance journey itself (Lk 9:23; 14:27; see Part I, Chapter 3).

58. 13:47; Gen 12:3; Acts 3:25.

59. Lk 1:54; 2:32.

60. Lk 1:79.

61. Acts 3:22; Lk 1:54; Acts 3:25.

the ancient Abrahamic covenant does the salvation of Israel lie. As well, in perfect synch with the upside-down world of the good news taught by Jesus and the coming of the Holy Spirit, deliverance and salvation are redefined, and perfectly exemplified in the experience of Paul. Israel as a national entity, as a state with a holy city, has evolved into the kingdom reality of a true people of God whose defense against enemies is a love that defies ordinary logic but ordinary captivity as well. Stephen is murdered by enemies whom Stephen nonetheless loves and forgives, and moves his bloodied face upward to see the living Messiah at God's right hand, standing as if waiting for Stephen's arrival. Paul faces certain imprisonment and death, as he lets his Ephesian friends know, but what we see in the last half of Acts is a Paul-as-Israel delivered — but in a kingdom sort of way. On trial, it's as if Paul presides as judge; imprisoned at the end, Paul holds forth as if with words of life and freedom; shipwrecked, prisoner Paul acts in the role of captain and brings his guards and everyone else safely to shore, submitting once again to being a prisoner. Or is he ever really a prisoner in this new Way of living? Freed from jail by the apparent quirk of an earthquake, Paul ministers to his jailer and in turn has his wounds bathed and his hunger appeased — and returns to jail, much to the jailer's astonishment. Who is prisoner, who is free? Who is captain, who is crew and prisoner? Who is on trial, the titular judges or the one supposedly judged? Paul is the epitome of Israel, a stand-in for the thousands upon thousands upon thousands of Israelites who have been delivered as Paul has been. Israel is saved.

As we have seen, Paul's primary mission is an unrelenting rehearsal of what Jesus taught both to his fellow-Israelites and, simultaneously and necessarily, all peoples of the earth. Never does Paul stop "trying to convince [Jews] about Jesus both from the Law and the prophets" and "testifying to the kingdom of God" as taught by Jesus. Always, right up through the very last verses of the story, Paul is successful in bringing more and more Israelites into covenant relationship with God, while with other fellow-Jews, he fails.[62] Only at the story's conclusion, at the very end of Acts, will he and all of servant Israel turn their full attention to the Gentiles, though still others within Israel continue to listen.[63] In Luke's perspective of God and the history of God's salvation purposes, Israel is poised at last to serve God's original intent for choosing a special people. When the world listens to Jesus, and obeys, peace will be made and bless-

62. Acts 28:23-24.
63. 28:28-31.

Three Accounts of Paul's Transformation

	Acts 9:1-19 (narrator)	**Acts 22:4-16** (Paul's 4th speech)	Acts 26:9-18 (Paul's 6th speech)
Light	"light from heaven flashed around him" (vv. 3, 8)	"a *great* light" shined; companions also see the light, which explicitly blinds Saul (vv. 6, 9, 11)	light "brighter than the sun" on Saul and on companions (v. 13)
The Voice	"Saul, Saul, why do you persecute me?" (v. 4)	"Saul, Saul, why do you persecute me?" (v. 7)	"Saul, Saul, why do you persecute me? It hurts to kick against the goads." (v. 14)
	[Paul, "Who are you, Lord?" (v. 5)]	[Paul, "Who are you, Lord?" (v. 8)]	[Paul, "Who are you, Lord?" (v. 15)]
	— "I am Jesus, whom you are persecuting." (v. 5)	— "I am Jesus *of Nazareth*, whom you are persecuting." (v. 8)	— "I am Jesus, whom you are persecuting." (v. 15)
	Saul hears voice; companions hear voice. (vv. 4, 7)	*Saul hears voice; companions "did not hear the voice of the one speaking to me."* (vv. 7, 9)	"I heard a voice" ("in the Hebrew"); no mention of others hearing (v. 14)
	God to Ananias: "I have chosen Saul to bring my name before Gentiles." (v. 15)	(just) Ananias to Saul: "The God of our ancestors has chosen you [as] witness to all the world" (vv. 14-15)	(just) Jesus to Saul: "testify to the things you have seen . . .; I send you to Jew and Gentile" (vv. 16-17)
Ananias	. . . is *"a disciple"* (v. 10)	. . . is *"a devout man according to the Law"* (v. 12)	. . . no Ananias

ing brought. The kingdom is being realized on earth, and there will be "the universal restoration" of what God intended by creating the earth and all it holds.[64] The voice of Jesus will have been listened to and obeyed; the light of revelation will shine within individuals whose community of *shalom* makes real the promise of God's kingdom.

To summarize and conclude our exploration of Luke-Acts, I offer what only a great literary masterpiece can yield: the whole story by way of one small vignette. A Macedonian jailer's question in Acts regarding "being saved" illustrates everything we need to know about Luke's perspective, if we discipline ourselves to hear well what the signal words signal.

64. 3:21.

Conclusion

"Believe on the Lord Jesus, and You Will Be Saved"
The Whole Story in One Scene

Peter has yielded the dramatic spotlight to Paul by the middle of Acts. In a very brief scene that suggests the whole two-part story Luke is telling, Paul and his companion Silas are set free from imprisonment by an earthquake. Prisoners' chains fall off and cell doors fly open. A Gentile jailer, fearing execution for dereliction of duty, is about to kill himself. Paul and Silas stop him. "Sirs," asks the distraught jailer, "what must I do to be saved?" The two Jewish prisoners respond, cryptically, "Believe on the Lord Jesus, and you will be saved, you and your household."[1]

Believe on the Lord Jesus, and you will be saved, you and your household. The jailer would be at a dangerous loss with these words only: they make no sense until he hears from Paul and Silas the teachings of Jesus, "the word of the Lord."[2] The less that is known by the jailer about what "saved" means, the more he can interpret and twist these strange words into the magic solution for which he is pleading. Audience of Luke-Acts, beware.

We look more closely at this jailer scene, both in its immediate context and in the larger context of the whole two-volume story. I highlight the frequently used terms we will be exploring in this Conclusion:

> Paul shouted in a loud voice, "Do not harm yourself, for we are all here." The jailer called for lights, and rushing in, he fell down trembling before Paul and Silas. "Sirs, what must I do to be saved?" They

1. Acts 16:30-31.
2. Acts 16:32.

373

answered, "*Believe* on the *Lord* Jesus, and you will be *saved*, you and your household." They spoke *the word of the Lord* to him and to all that were in the house. At the same hour of the night he took them and *washed their wounds;* then he and his entire family *were baptized* without delay. He brought them up into the house and *set food before them;* and he and his entire household *rejoiced* that he had become a *believer in God.* (Acts 16:28-34)

By viewing these key "notes" within a symphonic whole, we will see how essential aspects of Luke's two-volume story interconnect and how impossible it would be to understand any one of the code-words or actions without the whole story. I begin with a count of important word-forms:

1. Believe (and "believer")   (9, Lk; 65, Acts)
2. Lord   (77, Lk; 96, Acts)
3. saved (and "Savior")   (17, Lk; 14, Acts)
4. The word (Scripture)   (13, Lk; 31, Acts)
5. washed their wounds   (Lk 10:34)
6. baptized   (11, Lk; 25, Acts)
7. set food before them   (frequent meal scenes, both)
8. rejoiced   (21, Lk; 9, Acts)
9. God (believer in)   (120, Lk; 159, Acts)

1. "Believe" (9 occurrences in Luke; 65 in Acts)

"Believe on the Lord Jesus," say Paul and Silas to the jailer. Of the seventy-four references translated "believe" or "believing" in Luke's two-volume story, there are very few instances of *belief* or *beliefs*. For Luke, believe is, as with the imperative offered by Paul and Silas, a verb, not a noun. *Believing* means "trusting obedience," as illustrated at the very beginning of the story with Mary, who responds to the word brought to her by the angel with a willingness to obey as "servant of the Lord." Zechariah was not able to express the trusting obedience of Mary's believing, her response of "Let it be with me according to your word."[3] The religious professional failed in this matter of believing, *pisteuō*, and is therefore stripped of his priestly responsibilities as mediator of God's word to the people.[4] Mary's

3. Lk 1:38; see 1:20.
4. "He kept motioning to them and remained unable to speak" (Lk 1:22).

believing is her willingness to be "servant of the Lord."[5] The jailer and his household can be "saved" only by submitting, like Mary, to the "word of the Lord" that Paul and Silas go on to teach.[6]

"I testified to both Jews and Greeks about repentance toward God," says Paul at a later time, "and faith [or 'belief,' *pistis*] toward our Lord Jesus."[7] Repentance and *pistis* are two faces of one coin. The jailer's believing will mean repenting, turning around from normal ways that are self-protecting to God's Way of serving others. Only this is "faith toward our Lord Jesus," which is why Paul is shown linking it in parallel fashion to "repentance toward God." The scriptural perspective embraced by Luke's Jesus is a believing whose dynamic is a listening-doing integrity. "Why do you call me 'Lord, Lord,'" asks Jesus, "and do not do what I tell you?"[8] In believing that Jesus is "Lord," the jailer must be like someone "who comes to [Jesus], hears [his] words, and acts on them."[9]

Even in Luke's rare reference to *"the* faith"[10] we find something participated in, rather than possessed. "The word of God continued to spread; the number of the disciples increased greatly in Jerusalem, and a great many of the priests *became obedient to the faith.*"[11] "Obedient to the faith" is believing, doing what they had heard of the word of God as rehearsed by believers faithful to the teaching of Jesus. As evidenced within Luke's two-volume narrative, it is possible to *believe* for a while, and then quit. Some belong to salvation's Way but turn back from the journey, lasting "only for a while."[12] The jailer might receive this word of God, and with great joy, but — like Judas or Ananias and Sapphira — can turn back and be lost. "These have no root," as Jesus points out; "they *believe* only for a while and in a time of testing fall away."[13] In such "a time of testing," Ananias and Sapphira, along with Judas, fell away from belief, from obedience to the faith.[14]

---

5. Lk 13:23-24 is the heart of this perspective, as explored in Chapter 13; all of Part II covers the teaching of Jesus regarding the Way and its demands and purpose.

6. Acts 16:32; we explore this matter in a moment.

7. Acts 20:21, emphasis mine.

8. Lk 6:46.

9. Lk 6:47.

10. Acts 6:7; 13:8; 14:22; 16:5.

11. Acts 6:7, emphasis mine.

12. Lk 8:12-13.

13. Lk 8:13, emphasis mine.

14. Acts 4:32–5:11; this couple, who had joined the Way, lied against the indwelling Holy Spirit and were struck dead — lost.

Believing is journeying "the Way of God."[15] That is why Paul can testify before a Roman governor that, "according to the Way, which they call a [Jewish] sect, I worship the God of our ancestors, *believing* everything laid down according to the law or written in the prophets."[16] *Believing* is grounded in this Scripture, as taught by Jesus and rehearsed by Paul;[17] Jesus has taught followers of his own presence within that Scripture, to which Paul attests.[18] For the jailer and his family, believing will be a participatory action within a new kind of community of Way-people, of "those who belonged to the Way."[19] To do so is to believe, accepting Jesus as "Lord."

2. "Lord" (77 occurrences in Luke; 96 in Acts)

Believe in the *Lord* Jesus?[20] (There is no *Christ* here, of course, since the audience is non-Jewish.[21]) The jailer would have to be thinking of a switch in ultimate allegiance, from the lord — *kyrios* — of Rome to this Jesus as *kyrios*. In the years of Jesus' childhood, the emperor Augustus was referred to as *theos kai kyrios*, "god and lord." By midpoint of the common era's first century, the emperors were using the title *Kyrios* for themselves, signifying an elevated status of "Emperor." For this Roman employee, choosing Jesus as *Kyrios* is to choose Jesus as God's ultimate earthly authority, "Leader" of God's Way and "Savior."[22] The Roman emperors were thought of in similar terms — Leader, Lord, Savior — and as such, there was at least the hint of divine status in their titles. The jailer has

15. Lk 20:21.

16. Acts 24:14.

17. Lk 16:16-17.

18. Paul rehearses for Jews in Rome the presence of Jesus in Scripture (Acts 28:23), a rehearsal of what the risen Jesus has done in Luke's gospel in opening the mind of his followers to references regarding himself in Scripture (Lk 24:44-45).

19. Acts 9:2.

20. For his Jewish peers, Paul will use the longer "Lord Jesus *Christ*." Christ, or Messiah, would be appropriate only for Israel, of course. For this non-Jewish jailer, Paul highlights "Lord."

21. Throughout Acts, Israel must embrace its Christ (Messiah); a godly non-Jew like Cornelius is already familiar with the background of his new believing — "the message [God] sent to the people of Israel, the preaching of peace [to Israel] by Jesus Christ" (Acts 10:36). Unlike the jailer, Cornelius and his household are "baptized in the name of Jesus Christ" (10:48).

22. Acts 5:31.

been serving the Lord — believing in the Emperor, that is — but is now being asked to choose between competing Lords, to offer ultimate allegiance to Jesus as *Kyrios.*

The jailer needs to be taught what "Lord" means, which is why Paul and Silas go on into the night teaching him "the word of the Lord,"[23] as recorded in Luke's gospel. In the opening sentences of Luke's gospel we find eighteen references to the God of Israel as "Lord."[24] Field hands hear messengers' word from God about the birth of one who is to be a "Savior," the "Messiah, the *Lord.*"[25] As *Lord,* Jesus is shown to be God's "holy servant,"[26] or in God's own recorded words, "my Son, my Chosen" to whom all must listen.[27] Chosen for what? Luke's story makes it clear that Jesus is chosen by God as ultimate word-bearer and demonstrator of that word. His interpretation of Scripture is "the word of the Lord." Within this interpretation, recorded in Luke's gospel, we hear this about *Lord,* from the lips of Jesus himself: "Why do you call me 'Lord, Lord,' and do not do *what I tell you?*"[28] Do what? *What I tell you.*

As we just saw in regard to believing, being "saved" requires a *pistis* or trusting submission to Jesus as *Lord:* the jailer must be like someone "who comes to [Jesus], hears [his] words, and acts on them."[29] This is why Paul and Silas "spoke the word of the Lord" to the jailer. "Listen to him!" says God to three disciples.[30] To accept Jesus as Lord, for the jailer or anyone else in this story, is to act upon the light given by Jesus to the word of God, and daily[31] to "turn from darkness to light and from the power of Satan to God."[32] Paul and Silas have begun with words that for someone unfamiliar with anything else Luke has written — the jailer himself, for example, — would be highly enigmatic and impenetrable: "Believe in the Lord Jesus and you will be saved." From its narrative context, however, we know what the jailer will come to know about what it means to be "saved."

23. Acts 16:32.
24. Lk 1:1–2:9.
25. Lk 2:11.
26. Acts 4:27, 30.
27. Lk 9:35.
28. Lk 6:46.
29. Lk 6:47.
30. Lk 9:35.
31. Lk 9:23; 14:27; as we have shown (Chapter 4), the daily bearing of one's cross is God's Way for believers in the world, the only "Way of salvation" (Acts 16:17).
32. Acts 26:18, the words of Paul before the lord emperor's appointed king of the Jews, the Jewish Agrippa.

3. "Saved" (17 occurrences in Luke; 14 in Acts)

Jesus has been portrayed by Luke in the gospel explaining the good news of salvation, a matter of entering God's kingdom.[33] That kingdom is shown being lived out in Acts, an action oriented by nineteen speeches that refer to being "saved," but without the explanation we find in volume one. Here are three important gospel passages (of the 17) that happen to have the actual word "saved" in them:

— "The ones on the path are those who have heard; then the devil comes and takes away the word from their hearts, so that they may not believe and be *saved*."[34]

— "Someone asked him, 'Lord, will only a few be *saved*?' He said to them, 'Strive to enter through the narrow door; for many, I tell you, will try to enter and will not be able.'"[35]

— Entering God's kingdom takes un-normal relinquishment (at this point he is teaching about money). "Those who heard it said, 'Then who can be *saved*?'[36] He replied, 'What is impossible for mortals is possible for God.'"[37]

In the first reference, God's word is heard, and has sunk into the person's heart. But the devil snatches it away. This sad scenario could happen to the jailer, just as it has for Judas and for Ananias and his wife Sapphira.[38] Hearing the word and acting upon it will be the beginning of salvation for the jailer and his household. As suggested by the second gospel reference above, the jailer will have to strive in entering God's kingdom of salvation. Such striving and salvation will be impossible, as the third reference suggests, without a divine empowering documented throughout in the fast-paced action of Acts.[39] The Holy Spirit will make possible the impossible, for the jailer and his household. One needs to always be crying

33. Lk 13:23-24. Note the question about how many will be "saved" that precipitates the response of Jesus about striving to enter the kingdom of God (Chapter 13).

34. Lk 8:12.

35. Lk 13:23-24.

36. Lk 13:23; 18:26.

37. Lk 18:25-27.

38. Satan's activity in taking away the word works, for Judas, in conjunction with his own culpability, his "turning-back." See Chapters 15 and 16 for Judas; Chapter 20, for Ananias and Sapphira.

39. See Acts 2:17, for example.

out for mercy in the journey of salvation. Only in persistent prayer for the Holy Spirit — the best of all "good gifts" given by a generous "heavenly Father" — will the jailer and his friends be empowered to hear "the word of the Lord," do this word, and be saved.[40]

"There is salvation in no one else," as Peter is recorded saying; there is "no other name under heaven given among mortals by which we must be saved."[41] When the jailer comes under "the name of Jesus," he comes under the rule of Jesus as Lord; this is life in God's kingdom, a daily hearing and doing of God's word taught by Jesus and repeated by Paul and Silas.

4. "The word of the Lord" (13 occurrences in Luke; 31 in Acts)

The scene with the jailer has moved so quickly. "The word of the Lord" comes moments after earthquake damage and the jailer's despair:

> "Sirs, what must I do to be saved?" They answered, "Believe on the Lord Jesus, and you will be saved, you and your household." They spoke *the word of the Lord* to him and to all that were in the house. (16:30-32)

We never find Paul or anyone else in Acts adding any explanation to what Jesus has already taught about this "word of the Lord." Spoken by Paul and Silas to the jailer on into the night, what the jailer hears is what Luke's audience has already heard, in the story's first volume.

This signal phrase is fundamental to Acts. Of course the jailer must be taught. All of the apostles "did not cease to teach and [to] proclaim Jesus as the Messiah"; for example, we hear elsewhere that "Paul and Barnabas . . . with many others taught and proclaimed the word of the Lord."[42] To *teach* and to *proclaim* Jesus as the risen Messiah is to teach and proclaim what Jesus taught and proclaimed.[43] Luke has shown Jesus as Teacher fifteen times in his gospel, with the activity of "teaching" referred to an additional sixteen times. The narrative bulk of Luke's gospel

---

40. Lk 18:9-14; 11:13.

41. Acts 4:12.

42. Acts 5:42; 15:35.

43. The emphasis of the speeches in Acts underscores the reliability of Jesus as Messiah, appointed by God as Teacher, as the revelatory "light" and power that was foreseen by Simeon (Lk 2:32; 20:21).

is the teaching of Jesus, an illumination of God's word that will be the "light for revelation to the Gentiles" (like this jailer) "and for glory to your people Israel" (represented here by Silas and Paul).[44] The action of Acts is punctuated by references to the teaching and spread of this "word of the Lord" and oriented by nineteen speeches that rest on the gospel teaching of this word of God.

One of the most significant of these counterintuitive kingdom principles, based on "the word of the Lord" taught by Jesus, is the highly unnormal notion of loving your enemy.[45] The Macedonian jailer washes his prisoners' wounds. These are prisoners who, in turn, could have run off, leaving their jailer in the lurch. The Way turns things upside down. The jailer is being "saved," and we see this journey beginning with a reversal of his role as overlord: he honors and heals his prisoners by washing their wounds.

5. "He washed their wounds" (a motif)

In Luke's gospel, a Samaritan becomes the exemplar of one who did the word of God, who was journeying God's Way. Being "saved," the text implies, means doing what Jesus considers the right thing — in this case, acts that include washing a stranger's wounds.[46] The gospel's Samaritan and this jailer have "recognized the things that made for peace" by going out of their normal way, on behalf of persons in need.

In the tale Jesus tells, the Samaritan was third in line, after two religious professionals who went on their self-important and ritually clean way. The Samaritan, though, pays attention. On the road he finds someone stripped of clothing, beaten, robbed, half dead. The Samaritan "went to him and bandaged his wounds, having poured oil and wine on them."[47] The jailer demonstrates the same salvation with strangers who are still his prisoners — who let themselves remain in the jailer's custody. "At the same hour of the night, [the jailer] took them and washed their wounds."[48] The gospel's paradigmatic tale about how to inherit eternal life, illustrated by the outsider Samaritan who obeys the word of God regarding the wounded stranger, is echoed here in Acts by the outsider

44. Lk 2:32.
45. Lk 6:35.
46. Lk 10:25-37; see Chapter 6.
47. Lk 10:34.
48. Acts 16:33.

jailer, whose inheritance of eternal life is being enacted in obedience to the word of God by bringing the blessing of health to wounded strangers, prisoners. "Servant Israel"[49] is represented here by two prisoners offering God's blessing of salvation to one outside their Jewish sect;[50] in serving, they are served, in turn, by one to whom they bring the blessing of God.

The jailer might have thought that being "saved" meant a stay of execution. The opposite, of course, is true, as Stephen has already illustrated in being stoned to death. But an audience that is alert to Luke's hearing clues will recognize in this very short scene a significant perspective on salvation, explored in the gospel. Things, all things, are caught in a dynamic of reversal. A jailer normally ensures his prisoners' imprisonment, but the "good news" reveals salvation as release from captivity.[51] Rather than worry about a new set of chains, the jailer serves the prisoners, freeing them from the pain and infection of their wounds. Being "saved," for Luke, is "the leader [becoming] like one who serves."[52] Such extreme reversal, or repentance, is a moving from the death and wickedness of normal ways to the life and righteousness of God — the essence of baptism as viewed by Luke.

6. "Then he and his entire household were baptized" (11 occurrences in Luke; 25 in Acts)

Salvation is always communal, for Luke, or it is nothing. The jailer will join those who belonged to the Way, as Acts makes clear must be the case, since it is "servant Israel" fulfilling God's covenant, not isolated individuals.[53] That the jailer is joined by "his entire household" — family and servants — makes this occasion particularly joyous. But there is the rather sobering reality of baptism.

What do Paul and Silas explain to the jailer about this "baptism"? Beginning with John, early in Luke's gospel, baptism has signified as it does throughout the two-volume narrative a repentance from the old way of life, with a complete reversal to God's Way of life — a dying to one and an embrace of the other. Such a repentance, as we have seen,

---

49. Lk 1:54.
50. Acts 24:14, where Paul cites the opinion of others who regard "the Way" as a Jewish sect.
51. Lk 4:18-19.
52. Lk 22:26.
53. Lk 1:54; Acts 3:25.

brings a cleansing — a forgiveness — of sins through the generosity of God.[54] Baptism signifies the beginning of one's salvation journey, of life "according to the Way."[55] For Luke, baptism is movement, an ongoing reversal of everything a society (or at least the society represented in this story) considers normal. In the symbolic down-and-up motion of baptism is the counterintuitive, un-normal quality of the Way — losing one's ordinary life only to find an extraordinary way of being in the world.[56]

Acts dramatizes what John himself foretold would distinguish his baptism from the baptism of Jesus, the addition of Holy Spirit and fire. Both baptisms signify repentance and forgiveness of sins, but with the baptism of Jesus comes empowerment to continue striving in this Way of turning around and turning toward. Baptism is entering into salvation through a repentance that brings forgiveness of wicked ways, as we have seen from Peter: "turning . . . from your wicked ways"[57] and "turn[ing] to God" by "listen[ing] to whatever he tells you."[58] Only with such a "baptism of repentance for the forgiveness of sins"[59] will the jailer be saved. "Repent therefore," as Peter has put it earlier in Acts, "and turn to God so that your sins may be wiped out."[60] The jailer and his entire household are "saved" by a fundamental turning from normal but wicked ways toward the un-normal but righteous Way of God. And so the jailer and his family, having been taught the word of the Lord, are baptized. The turning of repentance is immediately in process, with an unusual meal.

---

54. "Within the Lukan narrative," Joel B. Green points out, "'baptism' takes its meaning in part from the ministry of John (Luke 3:1-20), with the result that it expresses a desire to embrace God's purposes anew and to be embraced into the community of those similarly oriented around the way of God. . . . Repentance (or 'turning to God') is often mentioned explicitly as an appropriate response to God's salvific work (cf., [Acts] 2:38; 3:19; 5:31; 11:18; 17:30; 20:21; 26:20). Again, Luke's portrayal of this response is rooted in his account of the ministry of John (esp. Luke 3:1-14), where repentance is marked by behaviour that grows out of and demonstrates that one has indeed committed oneself to service in God's purpose (cf., Luke 3:10-14; Acts 26:20)." "'Salvation to the End of the Earth' (Acts 13:47): God as Savior in the Acts of the Apostles," in Witness to the Gospel: The Theology of Acts, ed. I. Howard Marshall and David Peterson (Grand Rapids: Eerdmans, 1998), p. 104.

55. Acts 24:14; Lk 9:23.

56. Lk 9:24.

57. Acts 3:26.

58. Acts 3:19; 26:20; 3:22.

59. Lk 3:3.

60. Acts 3:19.

7. "He brought them up into the house and set food before them" (motif of meals)

It has already been a long evening, with no mention of eating. But Jews do not eat with Gentiles, or jailers with their prisoners. The Way, though, is very different. And so the jailer "brought them up into the house and set food before them."[61] As suggested by the gospel, salvation's Way has to do with the jailer serving his prisoners by washing their wounds, then bringing them home and setting food before them.[62] The gospel's crucial highlighting of meals is being echoed.[63] Here is a new community, and by conventional standards, an unlikely community. No corporate action in Luke's world was more intimate and more an expression of communal solidarity — and exclusivity, normally — than eating together at a table. And so, in Luke's perspective, the Way insists on a different kind of eating together: this is where salvation is to be found.[64]

For the attentive reader of the whole story, this sharing of a meal is no mere eat-and-run exigency. Rather, it echoes a meal motif from the gospel that signals a new community. Such table sharing is a sign, if not the full presence, of the kingdom, a community whose membership does not "neglect justice and the love of God."[65] These new principles of living together in kingdom *shalom,* based on God's word, will be recognized and implemented, indeed, as "the things that make for peace."[66] Sharing table together, especially under such potentially strained circumstances, is an indication of *shalom.* Here is a Gentile household hosting two itinerant Jews who are still prisoners of the jailer. We witness the falling away — the turning from — normal societal boundaries between high-ranking and low, between social outcasts and in-group, between family and friends — or even between friend and enemy.[67] "When you give a luncheon or a dinner," Jesus teaches, "do not invite your friends or your brothers or your relatives or rich neighbors"; and *do not invite status-helping associates or wealthy neighbors* "in case they may invite you in return, and you will be repaid." Rather, invite "the poor, the crippled, the

---

61. Acts 16:34.
62. See Lk 10:34 and Lk 9:13.
63. See especially Chapter 12, and the capstone banquets of Lk 13:24-30; 15:1-2; 15:22-24.
64. Lk 19:5; Acts 2:46; 5:42.
65. Lk 11:42.
66. Lk 11:42; 19:42.
67. Lk 6:35.

lame, and the blind" because "they cannot repay you."[68] Surely the jailer and his household know that Paul and Silas can never repay them with a dinner visit.

What can the jailer gain by bringing home these two Jews? Being "saved," Luke's story insists to the audience of his day, involves loving God by bringing into one's life those most likely never to benefit you in any normal way, precisely those who most often need a good meal and the camaraderie of kinship-like intimacy. This is a picture of God's salvation, a participatory gift. "Things that make for peace" are difficult to "recognize" precisely because they are so counterintuitive.[69]

Repentance is reciprocal here. The jailer turns around from a normal jailer-prisoner hierarchy to the jailer serving his prisoners, but there is also the reversal chosen by Paul and Silas, who are willing to experience a reversal of everything they had grown up to believe honorable and proper according to the Law and their religious clan. They sit at this meal served by a Gentile jailer who, furthermore, is beholden to Rome, the presumed enemy of Israel. A whole new Way of thinking and acting emerges — as Jesus envisioned the kingdom — in a community not defined by national boundaries and holy capitals.[70]

This reversal on the part of Paul and Silas plays out in a wonderful "touch" at the end of the episode. Bandaged and fed and presumably well rested, these two representatives of "servant Israel" submit to being the prisoners they still are, rather than insisting on their deliverance, their salvation. Here in microcosm is Israel's unexpected deliverance. Their salvation is not a matter of national security, after all. Here is a "way of salvation"[71] that frees Israel to eat at table with employees of the enemy, a Way that delivers Israel from the sword by the power to heal an enemy's sword-wrecked ear as Jesus did. This is God's Way for Israel, bringing salvation and fulfillment of its glorious destiny as light-bearer to the world.[72]

Here is cause for something beyond mere happiness. Here is rejoicing. And the joy is real, even though not the whole of what the follower of the Way experiences.

---

68. Lk 14:12-13.

69. Lk 19:42.

70. Acts 24:14; Paul's worship "according to the Way" has been demonstrated throughout Acts as a life "according to the Way," as here with this table scene.

71. Acts 16:17.

72. Lk 22:50-51; Acts 16:17; 3:25.

8. "And he and his entire household rejoiced"
("joy," 21 occurrences in Luke; 9 in Acts)

All is quite wonderful as the curtain falls on this brief but illustrative scene. The jailer "and his entire household rejoiced." Very early in volume one, an angel host appears to the shepherds with "good news of great joy," a joy that translates shortly into their song of "peace on earth among those whom God favors."[73] Being "saved," for Luke, is about the joy of *shalom,* true communal well-being. The spread of God's word that has "been turning the world upside down" is a dynamic of reversal, the upside-down quality of life foreseen by Mary.[74] "Love your enemies," for example: prisoner, love your jailer; jailer, love your prisoner. This, indeed, is cause for "rejoicing."

But it does not take the story's audience long to understand that this is a difficult joy, and a strange peace. As we have seen in Luke's gospel[75] and in the lives of believers in Acts, there is a dark side to the good news, an inevitable disruption. Beyond the disturbing counterintuitive matter of recognizing "the things that make for peace"[76] (rather than merely "keeping peace") is the certainty of disruptiveness. "You will have joy," the angel tells Zechariah, "and many will rejoice at [your son's] birth."[77] But Zechariah and his wife Elizabeth have to bear their son's departure into the wilderness, hear of his being thrown into prison, and hear of his beheading. Surely this is a strange "joy and gladness" for the parents, as it must prove to the jailer and his household if they continue salvation's journey. Paul has talked to believers about the inevitability of their having to suffer.[78] The references in Acts to salvation's joy and rejoicing, rather rare, echo the fuller picture offered in Luke's gospel.

The complex interplay of suffering and joy is captured in the immediate narrative context of this jailer scene. Before being thrown into this jailer's prison, Paul and Silas were "stripped of their clothing" and "beaten with rods," and "flogged" (precise echoes of the ordeal suffered by Jesus in Jerusalem, Lk 22:63; 23:16, 22). They had deprived the handlers of a diviner of their income by liberating the woman from her demon. To this one who is freed from her imprisonment and restored to

---

73. Lk 2:10, 14.
74. Acts 17:6; Lk 1:51-53.
75. Chapter 4.
76. Lk 19:42.
77. Lk 1:14.
78. Acts 20:18-35; see Chapter 21.

community, surely there is peace, and joy — but what of Paul and Silas? Strangely, perhaps, the spirit of rejoicing remains for Paul and Silas, who sing hymns in the prison-house after their flogging, with the bleeding wounds the jailer later washed.[79] Earlier, after his first speech in Antioch of Pisidia and subsequent persecution, Paul and Barnabas shake the dust off their feet, as Jesus had commanded; retaining an obvious peace in spite of harassment, they "were filled with joy and with the Holy Spirit" in the company of other disciples.[80]

What is the peace promised by angels to the shepherds? What is the joy promised to John the Baptist's parents? "The Spirit of the Lord is upon me," Jesus had announced, borrowing from Isaiah, "to bring good news to the poor," *to free a slave girl from her imprisonment, to release prisoners from jail and a jailer from himself and his fear.*[81] Luke is telling a story of God and the divinely determined plan for a "restoration of all things"[82] as they were in Eden. Such blessing to all families on earth is reflected in the simple statement here, that the jailer "and his entire household rejoiced."[83]

The scene began with a plea to the jailer from servant Israel to "believe in the Lord Jesus" to be "saved," and now the scene moves full circle with the jailer believing in God, whose purposes "holy servant" Jesus has perfectly upheld.[84] The joy of the jailer and his family reflects God's generous will "to guide our feet into the Way of peace."[85] Luke's story is a story of God and God's steadfastly loving purposes of blessing for all peoples.

9. "A Believer in God"

The scene's curtain falls on the household's rejoicing "that he had become a believer in God."[86] This climactic note can easily be missed, its significance lost, unless we have been hearing the symphonic whole of Luke's narrative. Paul's initial recommendation to "believe in the *Lord Jesus*" shifts to the narrator's closing comment "that he had become a be-

---

79. Acts 16:25.

80. Acts 13:50-52, echoing the instructions of Jesus to disciples about spreading their message of peace (Lk 10:5, 9-12).

81. Lk 4:18.

82. Acts 3:21; explored especially in Chapter 15.

83. Acts 16:34.

84. Acts 4:27, 30; Lk 4:18.

85. Lk 1:79.

86. Acts 16:34.

liever in *God.*"[87] Does the narrative suggest that to believe *in the Lord Jesus* is synonymous with *believing in God*? On the other hand, does the text suggest that *believing in the Lord Jesus* leads and points to *believing in God*? Perhaps a combination of the two? Such intelligent query by Luke's audience will lead to a recollection of the frequent associations made by Luke between Jesus and God: ideas such as Jesus being chosen and anointed by God,[88] or Jesus as God's "holy servant" and "my Son, my Chosen," to whom all must listen.[89] Jesus is appointed by God and publicly authorized through God's raising him from the dead to serve God's purposes of making clear God's word and the good news of the kingdom. The purpose of Jesus, as explained by Luke in his gospel, is to point toward God and God's word. Jesus proclaims and demonstrates the Way of God, bringing to Israel — and through Israel to the world — an illumination of God's word, the "light for revelation."[90] The narrative role of *the Lord Jesus* underscores God as the story's main character, just as the jailer in this scene comes to *believing in God,* in the end, through an initial *believing in the Lord Jesus.*

Summary

Believe on the Lord Jesus, and you will be saved, you and your household. Luke's audience knows what the jailer could not have known; we are in possession of the story's first part, Luke's gospel, in which is recorded a full account of the imperative offered to the jailer by Paul and Silas. That is why the passage goes on immediately to point out that Paul and Silas go on into the evening teaching the jailer "the word of the Lord."[91] That is, they rehearse for the jailer the contents of Luke's first volume, the gospel, since it is only there that a record of God's word interpreted by Jesus — "the word of the Lord" — can be found. And so the jailer will come to understand what Luke's audience already knows from the gospel about signal words like *saved, Lord,* and *believe.* That is, the jailer hears words and phrases that Luke's audience hears throughout Acts; these words signal the interpretation of God's word by Jesus, principles of the Way that the jailer must embrace as "the word of the Lord" if he is to enter the journey of salvation.

87. 16:31, 34.
88. For example, Lk 4:18; 9:35.
89. Acts 4:27, 30; Lk 9:35.
90. Lk 2:32.
91. Acts 16:31-32.

"My mother and my brothers," Jesus has said in the gospel, "are those who hear the word of God and do it."[92] Those are blessed with salvation "who hear the word of God and obey it!" Jesus exclaims to a woman gushing over the prospect of having a son like him.[93] "The one who hears and does not act," warns Jesus, "is like a man who built a house on ground without a foundation. When the river burst against it, immediately it fell, and great was the ruin of that house."[94] Nothing in Acts changes these bedrock statements. What Acts offers in addition to God's gift of the teaching by Jesus of God's word, recorded in Luke's gospel, is the completion of God's grace in the offer of the Holy Spirit as empowerment for those choosing to "hear the word of God and do it."

Nothing in Luke's two-volume story ever changes regarding the centering vision regarding God's message, summarized by Peter as "preaching peace by Jesus Christ."[95] There is a great deal of scholarly uncertainty on this crucial point.[96]

This message of peace, of how Jesus serves as Israel's Messiah, is vital for Luke. Only "after investigating everything" that others have written about the events surrounding Jesus has Luke decided that his own account is necessary.[97] "Everything" would have included the gospels by Mark and Matthew (or a source common to Matthew and Luke), and Paul's thinking, if not his letters. Luke would have "investigated" much of what came to constitute the New Testament, about a quarter of which he himself is accountable for. His story's implicit moral vision — its "theology" — can be summarized briefly:

92. Lk 8:21.
93. Lk 11:27-28.
94. Lk 6:49.
95. Acts 10:36.
96. As respected and excellent a New Testament scholar as C. K. Barrett suggests a disconnect between volumes one and two. As already mentioned, he puts the matter in terms of "imitation" — that somehow the "ethics" of Jesus, his teaching, mostly disappear in Acts. "The language of imitation [obeying principles of the Way as Jesus did] is not to be found in Acts; nor is the fact to be found without the language. Luke never even points back to his former treatise as supplying a model, or represents the Christian character that he describes as recalling the story of Jesus, the story being presented as an example of Christian behavior. This is part of a larger lacuna in Acts; the book as a whole lays little stress on the ethical component of Christian living." "*Imitatio Christi* in Acts," in *Jesus of Nazareth, Lord and Christ: Essays on the Historical Jesus and New Testament Christology* (Grand Rapids: Eerdmans, 1994), pp. 252-53. In *Theologia Crucis — Signum Crucis: Festschrift für Erich Dinkler zum 70. Geburtstag*, ed. C. Andresen and G. Klein (Tübingen: J. C. Mohr [Paul Siebeck], 1979), pp. 73-84.
97. "I too," Luke declares, "decided to write an orderly narrative" (Lk 1:1-3). See Introduction.

- God's gracious salvation for Israel, its long-awaited deliverance, is to be found in hearing the word of God as interpreted by their long-awaited Messiah, Jesus, and obeying it. Through Israel, such salvation is made available for all peoples.
- Obeying this word involves a daily repentance that is counterintuitive, reversing the normal priorities of self-securing interests and status; one must strive to enter the kingdom of God.[98]
- Such striving is humanly impossible, so "who can be saved?"[99] Empowerment is provided by God through Jesus who sends God's empowering Spirit to those who pray for the best of all possible gifts.[100]
- Jesus saves, then, by interpreting Scripture and demonstrating it for others to follow, but Jesus also saves by sending the Holy Spirit for empowerment to recognize and implement "those things that make for peace."[101]
- Israel's salvation depends on God's grace toward the purpose of bringing God's blessing of peace[102] to all peoples[103] — a fulfillment of the original blessing and challenge to Abraham, and a "universal restoration" of the creation harmonies.[104]

The whole story comes full circle. At the beginning we find Mary, "servant of the Lord," proclaiming the fulfillment of Israel's redemption as "servant Israel" to the world.[105] At the story's conclusion we find "servant Israel" poised to serve all non-Jewish peoples of the earth. Thousands of Israelites,[106] and still more thousands[107] and, much later in the story, yet more thousands[108] will turn to the Gentiles; the people chosen by God to bring blessing to all peoples are doing so. The story of

---

98. Lk 13:23-24; salvation is going "the Way of God" (Lk 20:21), a Way of counterintuitive peace for all people, not merely a security for "me" or "mine" (Lk 11:21-23; 19:42); it is to pay radical attention to others — "release to the captives and recovery of sight to the blind," as Jesus puts it (Lk 4:18-19).

99. Lk 18:26-27.

100. Lk 11:13; 24:49; Acts 2:33.

101. Lk 2:14; 19:42.

102. Lk 2:14.

103. Acts 3:25.

104. Gen 12:3; Acts 3:25; 3:21. A *New Jerusalem Bible* note accurately identifies this restoration as "the renewal of all creation."

105. Lk 1:38, 48, 54.

106. Acts 2:41.

107. 4:4.

108. 21:20.

God and God's necessary will is being accomplished in these "last days" toward the "universal restoration" of peace.[109] Luke never lets us forget that God, who has emerged by the end of Acts as the story's central character, is concerned primarily about sending one key message to Israel, "preaching peace by Jesus Christ."[110] Such peace marks God's "Way,"[111] as it is called both in Luke's gospel and especially in Acts. What such un-normal peace looks like is demonstrated concretely in early Acts, after the empowering Spirit has been given to the thousands[112] of believing Israelites. Here is a model for what will characterize God's peaceable kingdom come-to-earth: individual ownership gives way to stewardship on behalf of all.[113] Here is salvation, which is based on the deliverance of Israel, another frequently missed feature of Luke's account. By the end of Acts, and not until then, believing Jews are so numerous as to constitute "servant Israel"[114] on behalf of a *shalom* for all peoples on earth.[115] Those resisting their Messiah are to be "rooted out of the people."[116]

"Listen to him," God is quoted as saying to three disciples.[117] What must be listened to obediently is a teaching centered on God's overriding concern, expressed through Jesus, for implementing "the things that make for peace."[118] Luke never lets us forget that the story's main character is God,[119] and that God has a message that needs to be taught by "holy servant Jesus."[120] Thousands of Jews come to obey "the message [God] sent to the people of Israel preaching *peace* by Jesus

---

109. Acts 28:28; 2:17; 3:21.

110. Acts 10:36.

111. Believers are referred to in Acts as "those who belonged to the Way" (Acts 9:2).

112. Acts 2:41; a bit later, we read of still more "thousands" within Israel turning to their Messiah (4:4).

113. Acts 2:41-47.

114. Lk 1:54.

115. Acts 3:25; 15:13-21.

116. Acts 3:23.

117. Lk 9:35.

118. Lk 19:42.

119. Observed by most scholars: Jacob Jervell, for example, notes that "Luke intends to write about how God has fulfilled and is fulfilling his promises." "The Future of the Past: Luke's Vision of Salvation History and Its Bearing on His Writing of History," in Ben Witherington III, ed., *History, Literature, and Society in the Book of Acts* (New York: Cambridge University Press, 1996), p. 116. Robert Brawley captures this central truth in the title of his study, *Centering on God: Method and Message in Luke-Acts* (Louisville: Westminster/John Knox, 1990).

120. Acts 4:27, 30.

Christ."[121] *Peace* is the one-word summary of salvation in this story, first announced by the angel's one-word promise to the shepherds.[122] Zechariah concluded his brilliant poem by referring to the coming Jesus as the one who will "guide our feet into the way of peace."[123] Regarding Jerusalem and its traditional leadership, Jesus is overcome with weeping. "If you, even you, had only recognized on this day the things that make for peace!"[124] What is uttered as profound lament regarding Zechariah's "Way of peace" in Luke's gospel becomes joyous resolve in Acts.

In the very last verses of Acts, Israelites in Rome are listening to Paul as he recounts what Jesus had taught about God's kingdom; some Jews are still coming to claim Jesus as Lord by embracing Paul's teaching of Jesus, while others within Israel are still refusing to listen.[125] For Luke, redeemed Israel[126] is fulfilling, at last, its ancient covenant with God; repenting of self-promoting and clan-protecting ways, they are becoming "servant Israel"[127] to the world, bringing Jesus' "preaching of peace" and its kingdom reality to "all the families of the earth."[128] Delivered Israel is ushering in the "universal restoration" of creation harmonies, the ancient biblical dream of *shalom*.[129]

121. Acts 10:36; emphasis mine.
122. Lk 2:14; see Chapter 2.
123. Lk 1:79.
124. Lk 19:42.
125. Acts 28:23-24, 30-31.
126. Lk 1:68.
127. Lk 1:54.
128. Acts 3:25.
129. 3:22.

Selected Bibliography

Achtemeier, Paul J. *Introducing the New Testament: Its Literature and Theology,* edited by Joel B. Green and Marianne Meye Thompson. Grand Rapids: Eerdmans, 2001.

Albright, W. F. "Appendix I," in *Acts.* Anchor Bible Series. Garden City, N.Y.: Doubleday, 1967.

Arlandson, James Malcolm. *Women, Class, and Society in Early Christianity: Models from Luke-Acts.* Peabody, Mass.: Hendrickson Publishers, 1997.

Bailey, Kenneth E. *Poet and Peasant.* Grand Rapids: Eerdmans, 1976.

Barrett, C. K. "*Imitatio Christi* in Acts," in *Jesus of Nazareth, Lord and Christ: Essays on the Historical Jesus and New Testament Christology,* edited by Joel B. Green and Max Turner. Grand Rapids: Eerdmans, 1994.

Bauckham, Richard. "Kerygmatic Summaries in the Speeches of Acts," in *History, Literature, and Society in the Book of Acts.* New York: Cambridge University Press, 1996.

Bock, Darrell L. *Luke: 9:51–24:53.* Grand Rapids: Baker, 1996.

———. *Proclamation from Prophecy and Pattern: Lucan Old Testament Christology.* Sheffield, U.K.: Sheffield Academic Press, 1987.

———. "The Son of Man and the Debate over Jesus' 'Blasphemy,'" in *Jesus of Nazareth, Lord and Christ: Essays on the Historical Jesus and New Testament Christology,* edited by Joel B. Green and Max Turner. Grand Rapids: Eerdmans, 1994.

Bolt, Peter G. "Mission and Witness," in *Witness to the Gospel: The Theology of Acts,* edited by I. Howard Marshall and David Peterson. Grand Rapids: Eerdmans, 1998.

Bonz, Marianne Palmer. *The Past as Legacy: Luke-Acts and Ancient Epic.* Minneapolis: Fortress Press, 2000.

Brawley, Robert L. *Centering on God: Method and Message in Luke-Acts.* Louisville: Westminster/John Knox, 1990.

————. *Luke-Acts and the Jews: Conflict, Apology, and Conciliation.* Atlanta: Scholars Press, 1987.

Bruce, F. F. *The Acts of the Apostles: Greek Text with Introduction and Commentary.* London: Tyndale Press, 1951.

————. *The Hard Sayings of Jesus.* Downers Grove, Ill.: InterVarsity Press, 1983.

Cadbury, Henry J. *The Making of Luke-Acts.* Peabody, Mass.: Hendrickson Publishers, 1999.

Cameron, Ron, ed. *The Other Gospels: Non-Canonical Gospel Texts.* Philadelphia: Westminster Press, 1982.

Childs, Brevard S. *The New Testament as Canon.* Philadelphia: Fortress Press, 1984.

Clark, Andrew C. "The Role of the Apostles," in *Witness to the Gospel: The Theology of Acts,* edited by I. Howard Marshall and David Peterson. Grand Rapids: Eerdmans, 1998.

Craddock, Fred. *Luke.* Interpretation, A Bible Commentary for Teaching and Preaching. Louisville: John Knox Press, 1990.

Culpepper, R. Alan. *The Gospel of Luke.* Nashville: Abingdon Press, 1995.

————. "The Plot of John's Story of Jesus," in *Gospel Interpretation,* edited by Jack Dean Kingsbury. Harrisburg, Pa.: Trinity Press International, 1997.

Cunningham, Scott, *'Through Many Tribulations': The Theology of Persecution in Luke-Acts.* Sheffield, U.K.: Sheffield Academic Press, 1997.

Dahl, Nils A. "The Story of Abraham in Luke-Acts," in *Studies in Luke-Acts,* edited by Leander E. Keck and J. Louis Martin. Nashville: Abingdon Press, 1966.

Dain, Ronald, and Joe van Diepen. *Luke's Gospel for Africa Today.* Nairobi: Oxford University Press, 1972.

Danker, Frederick W. *Luke: Proclamation Commentaries.* Philadelphia: Fortress Press, 1976.

Darr, John A. *Herod the Fox: Audience Criticism and Lukan Characterization.* Sheffield, U.K.: Sheffield Academic Press, 1998.

————. *On Character Building: The Reader and the Rhetoric of Characterization in Luke-Acts.* Louisville: Westminster/John Knox Press, 1992.

Dawsey, James M. *The Lukan Voice: Confusion and Irony in the Gospel of Luke.* Macon, Ga.: Mercer University Press, 1986.

Denova, Rebecca I. *The Things Accomplished among Us: Prophetic Tradition in the Structural Pattern of Luke-Acts.* Sheffield, U.K.: Sheffield Academic Press, 1997.

Doble, Peter. *The Paradox of Salvation.* Cambridge: Cambridge University Press, 1996.

Drury, John. *Tradition and Design in Luke's Gospel: A Study in Early Christian Historiography.* London: Darton, Longman and Todd, 1976.

————. *The Literary Guide to the Bible,* edited by Robert Alter and Frank Kermode. Cambridge, Mass.: Belknap Press of Harvard University Press, 1987.

Dunn, James D. G. *The Acts of the Apostles.* Valley Forge, Va.: Trinity Press International, 1996.

Edwards, O. C., Jr. *Luke's Story of Jesus.* Philadelphia: Fortress Press, 1981.

Esler, Philip F. *Community and Gospel in Luke-Acts.* Cambridge: Cambridge University Press, 1987.

Evans, C. F. "The Central Section of Luke's Gospel," in *Studies in the Gospels,* edited by D. E. Nineham. Oxford: Basil Blackwell, 1955.

———. *Saint Luke.* Harrisburg, Pa.: Trinity Press International, 1990.

Evans, Craig A. *Luke.* New International Biblical Commentary. Peabody, Mass.: Hendrickson Publishers, 1990.

Farrer, A. M. "On Dispensing with Q," in *Studies in the Gospels,* edited by D. E. Nineham. Oxford: Basil Blackwell, 1955.

Farris, Stephen. *The Hymns of Luke's Infancy Narratives: Their Origin, Meaning, and Significance.* Sheffield, U.K.: JSOT Press, 1985.

Fitzmyer, Joseph A. *The Gospel According to Luke.* The Anchor Bible series, volumes 28 and 28a. New York: Doubleday & Company, 1981, 1985.

France, R. T. "Jesus the Baptist?" in *Jesus of Nazareth, Lord and Christ: Essays on the Historical Jesus and New Testament Christology,* edited by Joel B. Green and Max Turner. Grand Rapids: Eerdmans, 1994.

Franklin, Eric. *Christ the Lord: A Study in the Purpose and Theology of Luke-Acts.* Philadelphia: Westminster Press, 1975.

———. *Luke: Interpreter of Paul, Critic of Matthew.* Journal for the Study of the New Testament Supplement 92. Sheffield, U.K.: JSOT Press, 1994.

Garrett, Susan R. "The Meaning of Jesus' Death in Luke." *Word & World* 12, no. 1 (Winter 1992).

Gaventa, Beverly Roberts. *From Darkness to Light: Aspects of Conversion in the New Testament.* Philadelphia: Fortress Press, 1986.

Geldenhuys, Norval. *Commentary on the Gospel of Luke.* New International Commentary on the New Testament. Grand Rapids: Eerdmans, 1988.

Gerhardsson, Birger. *Memory and Manuscript: Oral Tradition and Written Transmission in Rabbinic Judaism and Early Christianity.* Denmark: Villadsen og Christensen Kobenhavin, 1964.

Gill, David. "Observations on the Lukan Travel Narrative and Some Related Passages." *Harvard Theological Review* (1970): 199-221.

Goodenough, Erwin R. "The Perspective of Acts," in *Studies in Luke-Acts,* edited by Leander E. Keck and J. Louis Martyn. Nashville: Abingdon Press, 1966.

Goulder, Michael D. *Luke: A New Paradigm.* 2 volumes. Sheffield, U.K.: Sheffield Academic Press, 1989.

Green, Joel B. "Good News to Whom? Jesus and the 'Poor' in the Gospel of Luke," in *Jesus of Nazareth, Lord and Christ: Essays on the Historical Jesus and New Testament Christology,* edited by Joel B. Green and Max Turner. Grand Rapids: Eerdmans, 1994.

———. *The Gospel of Luke.* New International Commentary on the New Testament. Grand Rapids: Eerdmans, 1997.

———. "Internal Repetition in Luke-Acts: Contemporary Narratology and Lucan

Historiography," in *History, Literature, and Society in the Book of Acts*, edited by Ben Witherington III. New York: Cambridge University Press, 1996.

―――. "'The Message of Salvation' in Luke-Acts." *Ex Auditu* 5 (1989): 21-34,

―――. *New Testament Theology: The Theology of the Gospel of Luke*. Cambridge: Cambridge University Press, 1995.

―――. "'Salvation to the End of the Earth' (Acts 13:47): God as Savior in the Acts of the Apostles," in *Witness to the Gospel: The Theology of Acts*, edited by I. Howard Marshall and David Peterson. Grand Rapids: Eerdmans, 1998.

Haenchen, Ernst. *The Acts of the Apostles: A Commentary*. Philadelphia: Westminster Press, 1971.

Hill, Craig C. "Acts 6:1-8:4: Division or Diversity?" in *History, Literature, and Society in the Book of Acts*, edited by Ben Witherington III. New York: Cambridge University Press, 1996.

Jervell, Jacob. "The Future of the Past: Luke's Vision of Salvation History and Its Bearing on His Writing of History," in *History, Literature, and Society in the Book of Acts*, edited by Ben Witherington III. New York: Cambridge University Press, 1996.

Johnson, Luke Timothy. *The Gospel of Luke*. Collegeville: Liturgical Press, 1991.

―――. *The Literary Function of Possessions in Luke-Acts*. Missoula, Mont.: Scholars Press, 1977.

Juel, Donald. *Luke-Acts: The Promise of History*. Atlanta: John Knox Press, 1983.

Karris, Robert J. *Invitation to Luke: A Commentary on the Gospel of Luke with Complete Text from the Jerusalem Bible*. New York: Image Books, 1977.

Kim, Kyoung-Jin. *Stewardship and Almsgiving in Luke's Theology*. Sheffield, U.K.: Sheffield Academic Press, 1998.

Kimball, Charles A. *Jesus' Exposition of the Old Testament in Luke's Gospel*. Sheffield, U.K.: Sheffield Academic Press, 1994.

Kingsbury, Jack Dean. "The Plot of Luke's Story of Jesus," in *Gospel Interpretation*, edited by Jack Dean Kingsbury. Harrisburg, Pa.: Trinity Press International, 1997.

Krodel, Gerhard A. *Acts*. Minneapolis: Augsburg Publishing House, 1986.

Kurz, William S., S.J. *Reading Luke-Acts: Dynamics of Biblical Narrative*. Louisville: Westminster/John Knox Press, 1993.

Larson, Bruce. *Luke*. The Communicator's Commentary. Waco, Tex.: Word, 1983.

Lee, David. *Luke's Stories of Jesus*. Sheffield, U.K.: Sheffield Academic Press, 1999.

Lenski, R. C. H. "The Third Part: When Jesus Faced Jerusalem," in *The Interpretation of St. Luke's Gospel*. Columbus: Wartburg Press, 1946.

Lewis, C. S. *An Experiment in Criticism*. Cambridge: Cambridge University Press, 1961.

Lieu, Judith. *The Gospel of Luke*. Peterborough, U.K.: Epworth Press, 1997.

Maddox, Robert. *The Purpose of Luke-Acts*. Edinburgh: T&T Clark, 1982.

Marguerat, Daniel. "The Enigma of the Silent Closing of Acts (28:16-31)," in *Jesus and the Heritage of Israel,* edited by David P. Moessner. Harrisburg, Pa.: Trinity Press International, 1999.

Marshall, I. Howard. *The Acts of the Apostles.* Tyndale New Testament Commentaries. Grand Rapids: Eerdmans, 1980.

―――. *Commentary on Luke.* New International Greek Testament Commentary. Grand Rapids: Eerdmans, 1979.

―――. "How Does One Write on the Theology of Acts?" in *Witness to the Gospel: The Theology of Acts,* edited by I. Howard Marshall and David Peterson. Grand Rapids: Eerdmans, 1998.

―――. *Luke: Historian and Theologian.* Grand Rapids: Zondervan, 1976.

―――. *Witness to the Gospel: The Theology of Acts,* edited by I. Howard Marshall and David Peterson. Grand Rapids: Eerdmans, 1998.

Mattill, J., Jr. "Chapter VI: The Purpose of Acts: Schneckenburger Reconsidered," in *Apostolic History and the Gospel: Biblical and Historical Essays,* edited by W. Ward Gasque and Ralph P. Martin. Grand Rapids: Eerdmans, 1970.

Matson, Mark A. *In Dialogue with Another Gospel? The Influence of the Fourth Gospel on the Passion Narrative of the Gospel of Luke.* Atlanta: Society of Biblical Literature, 2001.

Menzies, Robert P. *The Development of Early Christian Pneumatology with Special Reference to Luke-Acts.* Sheffield, U.K.: Sheffield Academic Press, 1991.

Miesner, Donald R. "The Missionary Journeys Narrative: Patterns and Implications," in *Perspectives on Luke-Acts,* edited by Charles H. Talbert. Danville, Va.: Association of Baptist Professors of Religion, 1978.

Minear, Paul S. "Luke's Use of the Birth Stories," in *Studies in Luke–Acts,* edited by Leander E. Keck and J. Louis Martin. Nashville: Abingdon Press, 1966.

Moessner, David. "The Appeal and Power of Poetics (Luke 1:1-4): Luke's 'Superior Credentials,' 'Narrative Sequence' and 'Firmness of Understanding for the Reader,'" in *Jesus and the Heritage of Israel,* edited by David P. Moessner. Harrisburg, Pa.: Trinity Press International, 1999.

―――. *Lord of the Banquet: The Literary and Theological Significance of the Lukan Travel Narrative.* Minneapolis: Fortress, 1989.

―――. "The 'Script of the Scriptures' in Acts: Suffering as God's 'Plan' for the World for the 'Release of Sins,'" in *History, Literature, and Society in the Book of Acts,* edited by Ben Witherington III. New York: Cambridge University Press, 1996.

Moore, Stephen. *Literary Criticism and the Gospels: The Theoretical Challenge.* New Haven: Yale University Press, 1989.

Morris, Leon. *Luke.* Tyndale New Testament Commentaries. Grand Rapids: Eerdmans, 1988.

―――. *The Gospel According to St. Luke: An Introduction and Commentary.* Downers Grove, Ill.: InterVarsity Press, 1974.

Moule, C. F. D. "The Christology of Acts," in *Studies in Luke-Acts,* edited by Leander E. Keck and J. Louis Martyn. Nashville: Abingdon Press, 1966.

Moxnes, Halvor. *The Economy of the Kingdom: Social Conflict and Economic Relations in Luke's Gospel.* Philadelphia: Fortress Press, 1988.

Neale, David A. *None but the Sinners.* Sheffield, U.K.: Sheffield Academic Press, 1991.

Nelson, Richard D. "David: A Model for Mary in Luke." *Biblical Theology Bulletin* (October 1988): 138-42.

Nolland, John. *Luke 1–9:20.* Word Biblical Commentary, Volume 35A. Dallas: Word Books, 1989.

Ong, Walter J. *Orality and Literacy.* New York: Methuen & Co., 1988.

O'Toole, Robert F. *The Unity of Luke's Theology: An Analysis of Luke-Acts.* Wilmington, Del.: Michael Glazier, 1984.

Packer, J. W. *The Acts of the Apostles.* London: Cambridge University Press, 1966.

Paffenroth, Kim. *The Story of Jesus according to L.* Sheffield, U.K.: Sheffield Academic Press, 1997.

Parsons, Mikeal C. *The Departure of Jesus in Luke-Acts: The Ascension Narratives in Context.* Sheffield, U.K.: Sheffield Academic Press, 1997.

Peabody, David B. "Luke's Sequential Use of the Saying of Jesus from Matthew's Great Discourses: A Chapter in the Source-Critical Analysis of Luke on the Two-Gospel (Neo-Griesbach) Hypothesis," in *Literary Studies in Luke-Acts,* edited by Richard P. Thompson and Thomas E. Phillips. Macon, Ga.: Mercer University Press, 1998.

Pervo, Richard. "Israel's Heritage and Claims upon the Genre(s) of Luke and Acts: The Problems of a History," in *Jesus and the Heritage of Israel,* edited by David P. Moessner. Harrisburg, Pa.: Trinity Press International, 1999.

Pilgrim, Walter E. *Good News to the Poor.* Minneapolis: Augsburg Publishing House, 1981.

Porter, Stanley E. *Paul in Acts.* Peabody, Mass.: Hendrickson Publishers, 2001.

Powell, Mark Allan. "Salvation in Luke-Acts." *Word & World* 12, no. 1 (Winter 1992).

———. "Toward a Narrative-Critical Understanding of Mark," in *Gospel Interpretation,* edited by Jack Dean Kingsbury. Harrisburg, Pa.: Trinity Press International, 1997.

Rapske, Brian. "Opposition to the Plan of God and Persecution," in *Witness to the Gospel: The Theology of Acts,* edited by I. Howard Marshall and David Peterson. Grand Rapids: Eerdmans, 1998.

Reasoner, Mark. "The Theme of Acts: Institutional History or Divine Necessity in History?" *Journal of Biblical Literature* (1999): 635-59.

Reicke, Bo. *The Gospel of Luke.* Richmond: John Knox Press, 1962.

Reid, Robert Stephen. "On Preaching 'Fictive Argument': A Reader-Response Look at a Lukan Parable and 3 Sayings on Discipleship." *Restoration Quarterly* 43, no. 1 (2001).

Riesner, Rainer. "James's Speech, Simeon's Hymn, and Luke's Sources," in *Jesus of Nazareth, Lord and Christ: Essays on the Historical Jesus and New Testament*

Christology, edited by Joel B. Green and Max Turner. Grand Rapids: Eerdmans, 1994.

Ringe, Sharon H. *Luke.* Louisville: Westminster/John Knox Press, 1995.

Robbins, Vernon K. "From Enthymeme to Theology," in *Literary Studies in Luke-Acts: Essays in Honor of Joseph B. Tyson,* edited by Richard P. Thompson and Thomas E. Philips. Macon, Ga.: Mercer University Press, 1998.

Robinson, William C., Jr. "The Theological Context for Interpreting Luke's Travel Narrative (9:51ff.)." *Journal of Biblical Literature* 79 (1960): 20-31.

Rosner, Brian S. "The Progress of the Word," in *Witness to the Gospel: The Theology of Acts,* edited by I. Howard Marshall and David Peterson. Grand Rapids: Eerdmans, 1998.

Schnackenburg, Rudolph. *Jesus in the Gospels: A Biblical Christology.* Louisville: Westminster/John Knox Press, 1995.

Schweizer, Eduard. "Concerning the Speeches in Acts," in *Studies in Luke-Acts,* edited by Leander E. Keck and J. Louis Martyn. Nashville: Abingdon Press, 1966.

————. *The Good News According to Luke.* Atlanta: John Knox Press, 1984.

Soards, Marion L. *The Passion According to Luke.* Sheffield, U.K.: Sheffield Academic Press, 1987.

————. *The Passion According to Luke: The Special Material of Luke 22.* Sheffield, U.K.: JSOT Press, 1987.

Sterling, Gregory E. "Opening the Scriptures," in *Jesus and the Heritage of Israel,* edited by David P. Moessner. Harrisburg, Pa.: Trinity Press International, 1999.

Talbert, Charles. "The Acts of the Apostles: Monograph of 'bios'?" in *History, Literature, and Society in the Book of Acts,* edited by Ben Witherington III. New York: Cambridge University Press, 1996.

————. *Literary Patterns, Theological Themes, and the Genre of Luke-Acts.* Missoula, Mont.: Scholars Press, 1974.

————. *Reading Acts: A Literary and Theological Commentary on the Acts of the Apostles.* New York: Crossroad, 1997.

————. *Reading Luke: A Literary and Theological Commentary on the Third Gospel.* New York: Crossroad, 1982.

Tannehill, Robert C. *Luke.* Abingdon New Testament Commentaries. Nashville: Abingdon Press, 1996.

————. *The Narrative Unity of Luke-Acts: A Literary Interpretation,* Vol. 1: *The Gospel According to Luke.* Philadelphia: Fortress Press, 1986.

————. "The Story of Israel within the Lukan Narrative," in *Jesus and the Heritage of Israel,* edited by David P. Moessner. Harrisburg, Pa.: Trinity Press International, 1999.

————. "What Kind of King? What Kind of Kingdom? A Study of Luke." *Word & World* 12, no. 1 (Winter 1992).

Thiselton, Anthony C. "Christology in Luke, Speech-Act Theory, and the Problem of Dualism in Christology after Kant," in *Jesus of Nazareth, Lord and Christ: Essays on the Historical Jesus and New Testament Christology*. Grand Rapids: Eerdmans, 1994.

Thompson, Richard P., and Thomas E. Phillips, eds. *Literary Studies in Luke-Acts*. Macon, Ga.: Mercer University Press, 1998.

Tiede, David L. "The Kings of the Gentiles and the Leader Who Serves: Luke 22:24-30." *Word & World* 12, no. 1 (Winter 1992).

————. *Luke*. Augsburg Commentary on the New Testament. Minneapolis: Augsburg, 1988.

Trites, Allison A. "The Prayer Motif in Luke-Acts," in *Perspectives on Luke-Acts*. Edinburgh: T&T Clark, 1978.

Tyson, Joseph B. *The Death of Jesus in Luke-Acts*. Columbia: University of South Carolina Press, 1986.

Verbrugge, Verlyn D. *The NIV Theological Dictionary of New Testament Words*. Grand Rapids: Zondervan, 2000.

Walaskay, Paul W. *'And So We Came to Rome': The Political Perspective of St. Luke*. Cambridge: Cambridge University Press, 1983.

Wall, Robert W. *The Acts of the Apostles*. The New Interpreter's Bible, Volume 10. Nashville: Abingdon Press, 2002.

Wenham, David. "The Story of Jesus Known to Paul," in *Jesus of Nazareth, Lord and Christ: Essays on the Historical Jesus and New Testament Christology*, edited by Joel B. Green and Max Turner. Grand Rapids: Eerdmans, 1994.

Wenham, David, and Steve Walton. *Exploring the New Testament*. Downers Grove, Ill.: InterVarsity Press, 2001.

Wenham, John. *Redating Matthew, Mark and Luke: A Fresh Assault on the Synoptic Problem*. London: Hodder & Stoughton, 1991.

Willimon, William H. *Acts*. Interpretation, A Bible Commentary for Teaching and Preaching. Atlanta: John Knox Press, 1988.

Witherington, Ben, III. "Editing the Good News: Some Synoptic Lessons for the Study of Acts," in *History, Literature, and Society in the Book of Acts*. New York: Cambridge University Press, 1996.

————. *History, Literature, and Society in the Book of Acts*. New York: Cambridge University Press, 1996.

————. "Salvation and Health in Christian Antiquity: The Soteriology of Luke-Acts in Its First-Century Setting," in *Witness to the Gospel: The Theology of Acts*, edited by I. Howard Marshall and David Peterson. Grand Rapids: Eerdmans, 1998.

Wolter, Michael. "Israel's Future and the Delay of the Parousia, according to Luke," in *Jesus and the Heritage of Israel*, edited by David P. Moessner. Harrisburg, Pa.: Trinity Press International, 1999.

York, John O., *The Last Shall Be First*. Sheffield, U.K.: JSOT Press, 1991.

Index of Authors

Index of Subjects